TECHNOLOGY INTEGRATION AND TRANSFORMATION OF ELECTIONS IN AFRICA

An Evolving Modality

Edited by
Cosmas Uchenna Nwokeafor

Foreword by Ike S. Ndolo

Hamilton Books
An Imprint of
Rowman & Littlefield
Lanham • Boulder • New York • Toronto • Plymouth, UK

Library of Congress Control Number: 2016958684
ISBN: 978-0-7618-6879-8 (pbk : alk. paper)
eISBN: 978-0-7618-6880-4

⊖™ The paper used in this publication meets the minimum
requirements of American National Standard for Information
Sciences—Permanence of Paper for Printed Library Materials,
ANSI Z39.48-1992

DEDICATION

This book is dedicated in the honor of my grandson,
Ogemdi Ahanna Nwokeafor.
I thank God Almighty for his birth, which brings
a glow of joy and excitement to our family.

TABLE OF CONTENTS

FOREWORD

The integration of technology into the electoral process is generating considerable interest and concern among voters, scholars of political science, historians, and practitioners across continental Africa. This has resulted in electoral management bodies using new technologies for publication, with the aim of improving the electoral process. These technologies range from the use of basic office automation tools, such as word processing and spreadsheets, to more sophisticated data processing tools, such as database management systems, optical scanning, and geographic information systems. Some of these tools and resources, which have been available in the world market for some time, have no doubt resulted in a reasonable interest among buyers who need them to solve various human challenges, including elections. These technological tools have also resulted in changes in several of the voting systems used to automate the recording and/or counting of votes cast in elections in most African countries. Other systems verify voter eligibility and voter authentication. Some countries are also experimenting with Internet voting as a way to facilitate the voting process, as well as increase voter participation in elections. All of these efforts are primarily to ensure the credibility of the democratic process and the reliability of election results.

While these technologies open up new frontiers and offer new possibilities for the electoral process in Africa—especially for voting operations—there may be unforeseen risks involved, such as an increase in vote selling or difficulty in auditing election results. The various chapters in this book will show the impact technology has had just in the recent past since its integration to elections in Africa; however, careful consideration needs to be given to the risks of inappropriate or untimely introduction of technology, especially if it has the potential to compromise transparency, local ownership, or the sustainability of the electoral process. These technological innovations may have changed people's lifestyles and introduced new ways of addressing societal challenges, including those associated with election malpractice; however, among all the new technologies being introduced, public attention is focused mainly on those that support electronic voting (e-voting), which is currently being integrated into the electoral process in Africa.

The motive behind the writing of this textbook lies in the efforts of the contributing authors to present resounding arguments regarding how the integration of technological paraphernalia has contributed tremendously in reducing corrupt practices that have doomed election processes in Africa in the past. The book also reviews, critiques, and recommends various activities related to the administration, integration, and transformation of elections and their necessary impact in Africa's changing electoral processes.

The argument as to whether the evolving modality of technology integration and transformation in Africa's changing electoral landscape will impact the outcome of election results, thereby minimizing electoral corrupt practices as obtained in the industrialized nations, has stirred discussion among this book's chapters, with detailed literature on the existing technology, its integration to the election process, and how this has resulted to the transformation of elections in various African countries. The editor of this book, in collaboration with the various chapter authors, utilized elaborate and detailed empirical research with data extrapolation to test the extent and validity of how technological-driven electoral practices could enhance future election results and delivery modalities in Africa's electoral environment.

This book also provides an overview of technology's role and its various transformation agendas in the revolution currently taking place in the election process in Africa. In addition, it shows how the integration of technological innovations and transformation structure has impacted both the present and future elections in Africa.

In reality, Africa's experience with electoral democracy has been mixed. While progress has been made so far, challenges still remain. In the past several years, elections have been held in various Africa countries such as Nigeria, Kenya, Zimbabwe, Cameroon to Ghana, Uganda, Democratic Republic of Congo (DRC), and Sierra Leone. However, as rightly opined by this book, the integration of technology into the campaign and voting processes has become a historical landmark for different reasons, as documented in the African countries where technology has played a key role in bridging all sorts of election malpractices. This mix of electoral experiences has generated considerable debate and passion on the subject of transparent, free, and fair electoral processes among election stakeholders, including international observers and Western leaders, especially as democratic progress itself can come with further challenges. As more elections are held, and as these elections become increasingly competitive, one-party and military regimes face potentially destabilizing challenges that could increase the risk of fraud and violence.

Pertinent topical areas which constitute the chapters of this book are presented by the various authors, such as: technology/quality assurance and financing elections in Africa; technology usage in training and support during elections; technology-enhancing party/voter registration; voter identification methods using technology; the use of technology to reach a wide spectrum of voters; the use of social media/audio-visual applications in African electoral processes; Internet and computer-assisted programs for the grassroots sensitization of voters; technology/electronic voting operations and capabilities; card readers as facilitators in the voters' accreditation process during elections in Africa; technology enhancement of voting operations and voting abroad; technology interface with media and elections in Africa; technology integration in elections; a review of the parties, candidates, as well as civic/voter education; technology and elections: a look at electoral integrity, results, and management democracy, technology integration in elections; the transformation of politics in Nigeria; transformation of elections in Africa; content analysis of election misconduct in selected African countries; technology integration in Morocco's political systems; technology integration in the long-run growth and economic policy in Cameroon: a co-integration analysis; electronic voting operations and capabilities in sub-Saharan Africa; and a cost-benefit analysis.

The empirical findings of the various studies legitimize the significance of this book, which is very timely and shows how the integration of technology has recently transformed elections on the continent of Africa. Technological applications have gone a very long way toward bridging the gap between the level and extent of knowledge the electorate gleans from media messages, most importantly as social media has gained a much stronger ground in various African countries. The use of card readers in the March/April elections in Nigeria, for instance, evolves within the emergence of technology considered the most significant invention of our time, which has so far had a tremendous impact on the electoral system, as well as the election outcome in the democratic process in Africa's changing election modalities.

Ike S. Ndolo, Ph.D.
Professor of Mass Communication
Enugu State University of Science & Technology
Enugu, Nigeria

PREFACE

Everything changes but change itself.
Greek philosopher, Heraclitus of Ephesus

Election is defined as the act or process of electing someone to fill an office or position (American Heritage Dictionary). By this process, *officers are chosen by election and not by appointment.* An instance of this predicates the fact that election assists a community, an organization, or entity in the sense of a common cause. A nation makes a choice of benefit, a predestined salvation from a common cause, especially as conceived by a Calvinist predisposition. Borrowing from the origin of election, which dates back to the Middle English "eleccioun," from Old French "election" from classical Latin "electio," all point toward the common meaning of a choice. In Ecclesiastical Late Latin terms, the word *election* connotes a similar meaning as the election of believers.

Webster's New World Legal Dictionary defines *election* as the process by which an individual is chosen to occupy a public office, or in some cases, a private one (such as a director serving on a corporate board); in litigation, the making of a choice among remedies, whereby the selection of one may preclude the use of others; in estate law, a choice between inheriting under a will, and pursuing a legal remedy other than as provided in the will. In this era of technological intervention, in all facets of modern human dynamics in Africa, it becomes imperative to take a closer overview of Africa's history with elections, and how democracy fits into the continent's overall growth and political development. It is also necessary to look into the recent outcomes of elections in African nations to highlight what has worked in the past, and how the continent can improve its democratic efforts. This includes the integration of access and valuable resources from the international community, to help foster legitimate and valid elections in Africa so that the habit of transferring power peacefully through the ballot is not only cemented into the political culture of the continent, but also woven into their political development structure.

Almami Cyllah, the Regional Director for Africa and Global Health on the African continent (2010), in his testimony to the United States House Committee on Foreign Affairs, Africa and Global Health Subcommittee, highlighted crucial indices on how democracy fits into Africa's overall economic, social, and political advancement. He gave a number of important recommendations for how the United States and the international community can help Africa prosper by strengthening its democratic institutions. Looking at democracy and elections in Africa, and the most recent trends in democratic dispensations as witnessed in a considerable number of African nations that have strongly embraced democracy and the roles the international community could play in fostering sustainable democratic culture, the following conditions should be in place: (1) good governance, where a ruling democratic government and its officials manage public institutions and budgets efficiently and transparently so as to address citizens' concerns and aspirations; (2) set up an atmosphere that encourages and fosters a rule of law that must establish judicial independence and enforcement; (3) create an atmosphere that harnesses a transparent, accountable, and open government; (4) establish an independent agency that regulates government programs that would fight fraudulent activities and freedom from corrupt practices by elected government officials and the entire citizenry; (5) establish a representative democracy that should respect and recognize the voices of all citizens, particularly through the engagement of civil society organizations and the media, and be populated by citizens who know their rights and responsibilities; and most importantly, (6) lay a strong foundation that must respect basic human rights, such as freedom of speech and assembly (Cyllah, 2010).

These conditions are not an end in themselves; rather, they are a necessary means to a sustainable democratic system, without which democracy in the African region cannot thrive. It goes well also to support President Barack Obama's remark in Ghana about democracy, when he rightly opined that democracy "is about more than just holding elections...to be a genuine representative democracy, a country must go beyond holding free and fair elections. Democracy requires good governance, which prevails when government officials efficiently and transparently manage public institutions so as to address citizens' concerns."

While these conditions are nominally independent of elections, elections in any country around the world, including the continent of Africa, represent an essential piece of the democratic process and serve as means to these ends. While elections do not guarantee democratic progress, they tend to advance the overall goals of democracy. For example, elections discourage mismanagement and corruption by holding leaders accountable for their actions, and democratically elected governments are far more likely to uphold human rights and serve the basic needs of their people (ACE, 2010). Moreover, elections—oftentimes even if flawed—help to motivate citizens to engage with their government and become more involved in the democratic process, as well as to increase citizens' understanding of democratic principles and processes. The 2015 election process and its possible outcome in Nigeria shows considerable understanding of the underlying democratic principles and practices among the citizens, and is completely devoid of the regular flaws and corrupt practices that have continued to plague the nation's electoral engagements in the past.

Elections are not only integral to all the identified areas of democratic governance, but are also the most visible representations of democracy in action. They are also, in most cases, the most complicated and expensive single event a country (such as Nigeria) will undertake. The list of African elections in 2010 through 2015 reveals how many of these complicated and expensive events are scheduled to take place in a five-year span alone. Thus, while support to all aspects of democratic governance is crucial—in particular, fostering good governance, upholding rule of law, and supporting civil society—this testimony examines all of these areas in the context of elections.

Indeed, if the very purpose of elections is to achieve participatory governance without violence through political rather than physical competition, African nations and their leaders must work much harder and cohesively in the integration of technology to enhance and maintain a level playing field that will harness the evolving political atmosphere, which would, of course, change the electoral process. In recent times, a considerable number of African nations have been successful not only in conducting free and fair elections, but in transferring from one elected government to another without violence.

TECHNOLOGY INTEGRATION IN ELECTIONS IN AFRICA

"Technology" can be defined holistically as anything involving the application of science and engineering. This broad definition can cover any manufactured item, so a more limited definition is adopted to consider items directly relevant to election administration (IDEA, 2010). "New technology" can mean new in one place, and old in another, in addition to being an evolving concept. The Gutenberg printing press, wristwatches, manual typewriters, and ballpoint pens were once considered new technology when they were developed, but in the 21st century they are hardly thought of as technology (IDEA, 2010). "Elections and technology" often refers to software programs and electronic equipment, such as computers, printers, scanners, bar code readers, and the Internet. However, there are other technologies used in elections that do not directly involve computers, but rather new materials, such as cardboard, fiberglass, and plastic used in polling equipment. As contextualized in this book, "technology" may refer to existing or so-called old technology, as well as emerging or developing technology. It may include computer hardware and software, other electronic equipment, mechanical devices, and certain materials. References might also be made to non-electronic innovations and techniques with specific electoral applications integrated into elections on the continent of Africa to harness the election process. The main focus of this book is on practical issues relevant to the type of technologies that are currently in use globally and which have permeated the electoral process in Africa, as well as the guidelines for the implementation, maintenance, and sustenance of these technologies over time.

The introduction of technology into the electoral process is generating both interest and concern among voters, as well as practitioners across the globe, most essentially the nations of Africa (ACE Projects, 1998-2015). According to ACE Projects publications (1998-2015), most electoral management bodies (EMBs) around the world today use new technologies with the aim of improving the electoral process. These technologies range from the use of basic office automation tools, such as word processing and spreadsheets, to more sophisticated data processing tools, such as database management systems, optical scanning, and geographic information systems. Some of these tools have been available for some time, and their strengths and weaknesses are well known (ACE Project, 1998-2015).

Every year, new technologies and tools that are not as well known are introduced to the market. Presently, for instance, there are several voting systems in use that automate the recording and/or counting of votes cast (ACE Project, 1998-2015). Other systems verify voter eligibility and voter authentication. Some countries are also experimenting with Internet voting as a way to facilitate voting and to increase voter participation in elections. ACE Projects (1998-2015) indicate that all of these efforts aim to ensure the credibility of the democratic process and the reliability of elections results.

While these technologies open up new frontiers and offer new possibilities for the electoral process in Africa, especially for voting operations, there may be unforeseen risks involved, such as an increase in vote selling or difficulty in auditing election results. ACE Projects (1998-2015) report that careful consideration needs to be given to the risks of inappropriate or untimely introduction of technology, especially if it has the potential to compromise transparency, local ownership, or sustainability of the electoral process. Among all of the new technologies being introduced, public attention is focused mainly on those that support electronic voting (e-voting), which is still being considered for integration in the electoral process in Africa.

The aim of this book is to review, critique, and recommend various activities related to the administration, integration, and transformation of elections and their necessary impact in the African changing electoral processes.

The argument as to whether the evolving modality of technology integration and transformation in the changing electoral environment of Africa will impact the outcome of election results, thereby minimizing electoral corrupt practices as obtained in the industrial nations, will constitute discussions of detailed magnitude as literature of existing technology integration and transformation of elections in various African countries will be explored. Detailed research and data extrapolation will be gathered to test the extent and validity of how technological-driven electoral practices could enhance the future election results and delivery modalities in Africa's electoral environment.

There is very little research done in the area of technology integration and transformation of elections on the continent of Africa, hence this book will be timely and highly recommended as a masterpiece to provide required references for students, researchers, and various government agencies. The International Institute for Democracy and Electoral Assistance (IDEA), an intergovernmental organization with member states that supports sustainable democracy worldwide, has considerable amounts of data and information that reflect how the global electoral process functions. The Administration—a portal to the world of elections that promotes credible and transparent electoral processes with emphasis on sustainability, professionalism, and trust in the electoral process—has an online knowledge repository that provides comprehensive information and customized advice on electoral processes. This repository contains in-depth articles, global statistics and data, an Encyclopedia of Elections, information on electoral assistance, observation and professional development, region- and country-specific resources, daily electoral news, an election, quizzes, and expert networks (ACE, 1998-2015). There may be other outlets that may have conducted research on elections that do not deal specifically with technology, such as Nwokeafor and Langmia (2014) in their book, *Media Role in African Changing Electoral Process,* which provides a strong source for information in the area of the role of media in political communication on the continent of Africa. The book has built a strong foundation that delivers the contentious critical perspectives in media studies in Africa's changing electoral process.

This book will contribute to the growing body of knowledge, and extrapolates from existing literature about recent trends and the role technology plays in transforming elections in Africa's 54 individual countries—the planet's second largest continent, the second most populous continent (after Asia)—along with numerous other issues that have resulted in fraudulent election practices in the past. It will address many questions, among which are:

- To what extent will technology integration and transformation of elections in Africa promote credible and transparent electoral processes?
- To what extent will technology integration and transformation of elections in Africa significantly improve the outcome of election results?
- How does the voter identification card and card-reading technology facilitate free and fair elections in Africa?
- To what extent will the integration of technology and transformation of elections in Africa enhance party/voter registration/identification methods?
- How does the use of technology facilitate reaching a wide spectrum of voters in both the city and at the grassroots level during elections in Africa?

List of Countries, Capital and Population in Africa

Countries in Africa	Capital	Population
Algeria	Algiers	34.1 million
Angola	Luanda	12.8 million
Benin	Benin	8.8 million
Botswana	Gaborone	2 million
Burkina Faso	Ouagadougou	15.7 million
Burundi	Bujumbura	8.9 million
Cameroon	Yaoundé'	18.9 million
Cape Verde	Praia	429,000
Central African Republic	Bangui	4.5 Million
Chad	N'Djamena	10.3 Million
Comoros	Moroni	752,000

Democratic Republic of the Congo	Kinshasa	69.5 Million
Djibouti	Djibouti	623,000
Djibouti	Cairo	82.9 million
Equatorial Guinea	Malabo	633,000
Eritrea	Asmara	5.6 million
Ethiopia	Addis Ababa	84.3 Million
Gabon	Libreville	1.5 Million
Gambia	Banjul	1.7 Million
Ghana	Accra	23.8 million
Guinea	Conakry	10 million
Guinea-Bissau	Bissau	1.5 million
Ivory Coast	Abidjan, Yamoussoukro	20.6 million
Kenya	Nairobi	39 million
Lesotho	Maseru	2.1 million
Liberia	Monrovia	3.4 million
Libya	Tripoli	6.3 million
Madagascar	Antananarivo	20.6 million
Malawi	Lilongwe	14.2 million
Mali	Bamako	12.6 million
Mauritania	Nouakchott	3.1 million
Mauritius	Port Louis	1.2 million
Morocco	Rabat	34.8 million
Mozambique	Maputo	21.6 million
Namibia	Windhoek	2.1 million
Niger	Niamey	15.3 million
Nigeria	Abuja	170 million
Republic of the Congo	Brazzaville	4 million
Rwanda	Kigali	10.4 million
São Tomé and Príncipe	São Tomé	212,000
Senegal	Dakar	13.7 million
Seychelles	Victoria	87,000
Sierra Leone	Free Town	6.4 million
Somalia	Mogadishu	9.8 million
South Africa	Bloemfontein, Cape Town, Pretoria	51.7 million

South Sudan	Juba	8.2 million
Sudan	Khartoum	30.8 million
Swaziland	Mbabane	1.1 million
Tanzania	Dodoma	44.9 million
Togo	Lomé	6 million
Tunisia	Tunis	10.4 million
Uganda	Kampala	32.3 million
Zambia	Lusaka	11.8 million
Zimbabwe	Harare	11.3 million

The rationale in publishing this textbook far outweighs its timeliness, but speaks highly of its significance because it deals with technology integration and transformation of elections on the continent of Africa, a region whose elections have been continuously marred by corruption and incessant, fraudulent activities perpetrated by citizens, various political parties, and the umpires whose responsibilities were to present a credible election. It has been so indicated from various foreign observers that when an election in Africa draws international attention, the news is seldom good. For instance, the elections in Kenya fueled violence that left 1,500 dead and 300,000 displaced, while elections in Zimbabwe suffered from massive fraud and brutal suppression. In Nigeria in 1999 and 2011, the result of the elections was a shambles, and some of the parties that lost the election took to the streets, resulting in the death of significant percentage of innocent people. Accordingly, Colonel Muammar Gaddafi, former Chairman of the African Union, suggested in recent times that multiparty democracy in Africa can only lead to bloodshed. Even some supporters of democracy in general agree that most African countries are not ready for elections (The International Institute for Democracy and Electoral Assistance [IDEA], 2015).

Recent headline-grabbing electoral failures, however, do not justify abandoning efforts at developing electoral democracy in Africa. Although elections are often fraught with fraud or incompetence, and do sometimes result in violence, no other means have brought about nonviolent transitions of power with the same consistency. Most Africans agree. According to a 2005 Afro barometer survey, 60 percent of Africans believe democracy is preferable to all other forms of government (ACE 1998-2015). Even in some of the mentioned countries in Africa that have suffered most from failed or flawed elections, and in most of the countries where elections have failed entirely, the people have responded not by abandoning democracy, but by increasing their demands for accountability and reform. A typical example could be drawn from the March 28 and April 11, 2015 peaceful and transparent election in Nigeria, which has implications to the advancement of democracy in Africa. As the most populous country and largest economy in Africa, Nigeria is the most important country on the continent and has the potential to influence development not only in West Africa, but indeed, the entire continent. Transparent elections will strengthen the country's leadership role on the continent, both as an example of successfully resolving conflicts and as a stalwart against undemocratic transitions. In addition, entrenchment of democracy in Nigeria is bound to translate into better economic performance with positive spillover effects to other African countries.

The significance of this book shows how the integration of technology has recently transformed elections in Africa. There are several guiding principles that resulted in the choices associated with the strength in editing this book. Among these principles were the crucial strength a reader would derive from this book from the detailed chapters that concentrate on the specific, technology-driven approach taken by the unique African nations in bringing about the integration of technology and the transformation of elections in Africa. Very few publications and textbooks have been written and published in the area of technology integration and transformation of elections in Africa, regardless of the preponderance of scholarly work done, and a few published articles by African scholars. The International Institute for Democracy and Electoral Assistance (IDEA), an intergovernmental organization with member states that supports sustainable democracy worldwide, the International Foundation for Electoral Systems, and Administration and Cost of Elections (ACE) electoral knowledge network have published considerable articles on the issue of elections and technology. Furthermore, the significance of this book and the quality of the research done to abstract chapter information to shed light on diverse aspects of technology integration and transformation of elections in Africa differentiates this book from other research publications.

The clarity of presentation and the ease of reading are among the level of attractiveness that defines a major strength criterion for this textbook. The author's most crucial intent has been to include the most recent and thought-provoking scholarly work done in the area of technology and elections from the perspective of his experience and the most recent election outcomes from various African countries. These include Ghana, Kenya, Zimbabwe, Mali, Benin, Sierra Leone, Liberia, and most of all, the highly acclaimed May 28 and April 11, 2015 general elections in Nigeria. This information contributes monumentally in bringing validity to the textbook. To stimulate critical thinking about the processes of knowledge acquisition, along with thinking about substantive technology integration and transformation of elections and other related issues in Africa, several of the readings confirm that there is a paradigm shift as technology has introduced a new election modality that has not only enhanced the voting system, but has also changed the electoral process in Africa.

To ensure that readers' interest is captivated at the beginning of the chapters, a brief introduction that serves as an introductory excerpt to the entire chapter is documented. The structure of the book gives the chapter contributors ample research data to analyze, so they can present their findings regarding how the integration of technology has overwhelmingly impacted the tenets of elections in continental Africa, thereby introducing a dynamic modality in voting and reporting election results to the electorates.

The introductory chapter captures a glimpse of technology integration and transformation of elections and the electoral process in Africa from a historical vantage point. This introductory discourse posits that the use of technology in elections in Africa has minimized the historical trajectory of election violence in Africa. It also argues that technology infusion into elections has the capacity of capturing a significant population of eligible voters and presenting them with election outcomes very different from what was the norm in the past. The introductory chapter finally argues that the integration of technology goes a long way to allowing election agencies to maintain full and adequate control of the voting and electoral processes, thereby preventing all measures of potential illegal manipulation of the voting polls.

Chapter 1 looks at the resistance to election technology with the view of assessing communication, democracy, and vicissitudes of electoral outcomes. The chapter further posits that elections in Africa, most importantly in Nigeria, have moved to a reliance on technology as a way to restore public confidence in elections and to seek the achievement of true public democratic voice. Chapters 2 and 3 discuss technology integration into elections from the perspective of the lessons learned from the experience in Ghana. The contributing authors argue that the advancement in technology has created a welcome modality, which includes electronic voting, which has resulted in minimizing the election malpractices that used to be very popular in previous elections in Ghana. The authors of Chapters 4 and 5 raise the issue and importance of social media in elections. As Chapter 4 presents social media communication using Internet radio to transmit and transform elections' outcomes, thereby contributing in the building of interacting communication, Chapter 5 deals primarily with social media and politics in Burkina Faso, where traditional forms of communication are being outpaced by mobile telephony and Internet-driven Smartphones and tablets.

The authors of Chapter 6, 7, 8, and 9 focus on the impact the integration of technology would have, or is having, in elections in Nigeria. Whereas Chapter 6 presents technology as proffering a far-reaching solution to the growing wave of corruption practices during elections in Nigeria, Chapter 7 takes an evaluator discourse approach on the role of technology in the conduct of the 2015 general elections in Nigeria. In the process of evaluating selected presidential elections in Nigeria, Chapter 8 appraises the influence of technology in covering those selected elections, while Chapter 9 looks at how the integration of technology has impacted the electoral integrity, results, and management of electoral issues. Chapter 10 provides a historical perspective of elections and the integration of technology in the electoral process in Uganda, with specific attention directed at the need and importance of the 2016 election outcome. The contributing authors of Chapters 11, 12, and 13 point us to the need to look closer to the corrupt practices associated with elections in Africa prior to the use of technological mechanisms and what direct influence technology integration to the system is welding into politics, the conduct of elections, and governance in Africa with specific reference to the Nigerian experience.

The authors of Chapters 14 and 15 concentrate on democracy and technology as a yardstick to measure transformational political agendas, and a content analysis of election misconduct in five selected African nations. They argue that the importance of democracy and fair elections is imperative in the growth and development of a nation, while the issues of election malpractice could be reduced to a bare minimum by integrating technology and the six recommendations outlined at the end of the book.

The final phase of the book examines the phases of technology integration to elections in Cameroon, Great Maghreb, and the voting capability and operations in sub-Saharan Africa with emphasis on the drawbacks of corrupt election practices. The tenet of this final phase hinges on three broad perspectives, which are: (1) to clarify the reader with the understanding of how the Cameroon electoral system functions under the tutelage of a hegemonic system that tends to favor the Francophone zone of the nation, as opposed to the Anglophone-speaking Cameroonians; (2) to showcase Great Maghreb and the endemic corrupt practices that have hindered development in the country; and (3) to demonstrate the usage of electronic voting capability and how it should be operating on a continent marred by incessant election malpractices.

The evolving modality that has considerably infused technology as the gateway to effective and corrupt-free elections in Africa has opened up an pathway to the electoral process on a continent bedeviled with election atrocities of the past. Although Africa may be gaining some insight as to how the new technology is gradually shaping the dynamics of how elections are conducted in a new dawn of the region, such directions speak highly of other regions and even developed nations of the world. Scott Entwistle (2012), in his article titled "How Social Media and Technology Have Changed the Election Process," clearly stated:

> Technology has changed our lives in more ways than can possibly be written about in one article. It has probably changed more things than we can even realize, and the fact that it is all around us is starting to be taken for granted. Recently, while reading various news articles about the latest debate and how people perceived the candidates, I finally realized just how much tech and social media have impacted something as important and life changing as the presidential election. This is very evident in most of the elections conducted in various African countries such as Nigeria, Cameroon, Sierra Leone, Kenya, Uganda, South Africa, and Zimbabwe where the lines of elections, handling of the voters' boxes, counting and the announcement of results are handled quite differently. In the case of the Nigerian experience, at Otueke, the country home of the former president, Goodluck Jonathan, he was seen among his people during the 2015 presidential election accreditation with members of his family. The technology seems to have failed in getting him accredited, however, he spent inordinate time waiting for the technology to resolve the challenges, before he leaves the accreditation arena. The patience for an incumbent president to stand the line and wait for his turn regardless of the his high-profiled position defines a new dimension that would not have happened in the past.

The fast pace by which information is spread among the electorates has had the biggest impact that technology has had in elections. In the past, things had to be looked up in an encyclopedia, or you had to find someone who was knowledgeable in the subject so that you could ask them questions. Today, virtually every piece of information known to man is available literally *at our fingertips* (Entwistle, 2012).

Technological innovation and the interplay of its parts seems to have drastically changed the *speed* of everything we do today, including the spread of information, and this is most evident in the various elections conducted in various African nations. In the past, elections could be completely decided by how strong the physical campaign was for the candidate, his ability to drop off big bags of money through his thugs, and the numerous empty promises and conspicuous shenanigans associated with elections in Africa. The incessant intimidation and lies, coupled with election box stuffing in their private homes, and inordinate corrupt practices and inhuman atrocities were the order of the day. It was relatively simple, really: if you visit more places and speak convincingly, more people will be willing to vote for you.

Today, the dynamics of the political landscape are completely changed by the advent of new technology integration into elections and the easy access we have to all sorts of information. All of a sudden, the information asymmetry that candidates were counting on simply is gone. This has had a huge impact on how we perceive the candidates, and I believe how we vote (Entwistle, 2012).

Election debates among contesting candidates have now been considered during elections in Africa. This is a new dimension that was borrowed from most of the developed countries, like the United Kingdom, the United States of America, and France. One of the biggest examples of the effects of technology during elections in Africa is in the presidential debates. In the past, debates were never a part of the scheduled election events, and people from various African nations thought that it ultimately could not sway the results of an election, nor factor into its impact in the overall analysis of how the knowledge and promises of their candidates would be brought to the doorsteps of the electorates. According to Entwistle (2012), many thought that while opinion may change slightly, it wouldn't affect the outcome of the election unless one candidate flat-out humiliated or dominated the other one. Then, of course, word would spread. However, spreading the word in the age of the Internet is infinitely easier than it was 10 years ago. This means that people can Tweet, post status updates, or send friends messages instantly to say what they feel about a particular presidential debate. Instead of being alone or with a group of friends/family watching the debates, the electorates are now in groups of thousands and millions, where tons of opinions are being thrown around. This is a unique way of sharing information and making quick election decisions made possible by the use of the advanced technological infrastructure.

The opportunity for the electorates to verify what the candidates present during their campaigns has made the technology a great gem in the process of proving facts to be real. The idea of "fact-checking" websites that have popped up all over the Internet has made the technology a favorite encyclopedia of knowledge. The idea that they're out there has a very positive effect on the elections, and on politics in general (Entwistle, 2012). In the past, candidates could spread lies and make bogus claims that positioned them on a much better pedestal than their opponent in the view of the general public, and if they were convincing, that was all that mattered. While this is still true in some situations, the fact that you can jump on your Smartphone or laptop and check to see if what you were told was actually true really shifts the power away from crafty words and convincing personalities (Entwistle, 2012).

Social media, one of the off-shoots of technology, seems to have created numerous avenues and opportunities for voters to reason differently during elections, most importantly as African nations accept its usage. Social media chapters in this book discuss in detail the opportunities and benefits it brings to elections; however, one of the most interesting impacts social media has had on elections is its usage in discussing the candidates. For example, during political campaigns, debates, and party conventions, live Tweets were displayed in real time on the screen so that viewers could get an idea of what others were thinking about the campaign, debate, or convention. This is very obvious in such political events in the developed society. While this may seem harmless, and even collaborative as Entwistle (2012) opined, it can change the impact and perception of the discussion. Tweets that are discussing what is currently happening effectively decide where the attention is being focused during the discussion. These can be something as harmless as, "Why was Rubio pausing to get a sip of water during a debate?" Or in the 1980 presidential debate between Reagan and Carter, Reagan's statement, "There you go again"; 1988 vice presidential debate between Bentsen and Quayle, "You are no Jack Kennedy, Mr. Vice President"; the 1992 presidential debate, where Bush consistently looked at his watch, and in the 2011 presidential election in Nigeria, Jonathan's "shoe story." All have the potential to lead to millions of people ignoring the words and only looking at facial expressions.

While I strongly believe that technology and the way it has been used to disseminate election information has drastically changed the public perception of candidates, it hasn't altered the process enough to completely change politicians themselves. They still lie, they still speak in half truths, and they still do their best to manipulate the public. The smart ones are jumping on the technology wagon and using it efficiently to continue to perpetuate the lies and propaganda by taking to social networks or posting viral videos (Entwistle, 2012).

As technology continues to be more pervasive in our lives, more people will get their information from channels on the Internet. Be it Tumblr, Twitter, Facebook, or even a blog that you regularly read, these places are quickly and effectively changing the minds of many citizens who regularly access them. I would like to believe that in the future, the impact of technology in elections will lead to more truthful election campaigns, debates, and conventions, which will no doubt minimize the blatant lies and corrupt practices that have for years been associated with the process of elections in Africa, and elsewhere in the world, everything being equal (*ceteris paribus*).

The importance of the issues raised in the various chapters of this exciting book, and the fascinating examples that lead to critical research perspectives in exploring this new area of study regarding how technology integration in elections has introduced a new modality in African elections, should be attractive to inquisitive readers and scholars. It will engender a new beginning and a pattern of discourse among African political scholars, communications professionals, media experts, undergraduate and graduate students, government agencies, diplomats, educational policy makers, intercontinental agencies, and corporations all over the world who are all contributing specifically in the transformation of African elections and the electoral system. These parties endeavor to depart from the old, crude, and corrupt election practices through the use of the new technology systems in achieving a common goal that will present a dignified means of election, as is very unique with the developed practices.

Cosmas Uchenna Nwokeafor, Ph.D.
Professor & Dean
Graduate School, Bowie State University
Center for Business and Graduate Studies
Suite 1312
14000 Jericho Park Road
Bowie MD 20715
cnwokeafor@bowiestate.edu

REFERENCES

Ace Projects (1998-2015 Report)

American Heritage Dictionary

Cyllah, A. (2010) Testimony to the United States House Committee on Foreign Affairs

Entwistle, S. (2012). "How social media and technology have changed the election process." News, social network web techerator. October.

Nwokeafor, C. U. and Langmia K., (2014). *Media Role in African Changing Electoral Process.* University Press of America, Inc., Lanham MD.

The International Institute for Democracy and Electoral Assistance (IDEA), 2015.

Webster New World Legal Dictionary

ACKNOWLEDGMENTS

I have found it quite necessary and most valuable to be linked and indebted to the chapter contributors to this book, who gave of themselves so fully in conducting such a rigorously driven, empirical research and data abstraction to support their various claims. I have learned much from their respective theoretical and conceptual frameworks, and it has given me great pleasure to work with them. In view of their thought-provoking discourse on the necessary integration of technology to elections in Africa, I have come to understand a lot more of other dimensions relative to how technology has come to make significant changes in the way elections are held today in the fast-growing democracy in Africa. I am privileged to be able to call these chapter contributors my colleagues, and most of all, good friends.

My special appreciation goes to my friend and colleague, Prof. Ike. S. Ndolo, former Head of Department of Mass Communication at Enugu State University of Science and Technology and currently the Pro-Chancellor of Saint Christopher University, Mowe, in Ogun State of Nigeria, who, despite his busy professional schedule, found time to write the foreword of this book.

I have, in fact, debts too numerous to list in this textbook. As I work on the structure of this book, I tend to run into people whose encouragement has fortified me and motivated me even further to wake up in the early hours of the morning to put in a few hours before my exercise regimen, and before going to work. Among these individuals are my editor at Manuscripts To Go Book & Manuscript Services, Mrs. Cris Wanzer, who has continuously worked with me, sometimes on a tight deadline, and still presents a quality and professional final product; the publishing staff at the University Press of America, who has worked with me on three other textbooks that I have previously published; and most of all, my family, who allowed me to invest our family time on working on this project. Thanks to my research assistant, Ugochi Ijoma, an MBA graduate student at Bowie State University, who provided administrative support.

As I take full responsibility for errors or omissions that my readers may find in this book, I rejoice in the completion of yet another thought-provoking, timely, academic and professional compendium that will not only contribute to scholarship and provide the necessary repository for references, but will also stand the test of time as a required resource by scholars of today and researchers of the future. I remain very much indebted to all the scholars, agencies, organizations, and private individuals whose works were cited to support the claims in this project.

INTRODUCTION
A Glimpse at Technology Integration and Transformation of Elections and the Electoral Process in Africa: A Historical Perspective

Cosmas Uchenna Nwokeafor
Bowie State University

Technology has changed the world and the lives of its inhabitants in more ways than can possibly be written about in a book. It has most likely changed more things than we can even realize, and the fact that it is all around us is starting to be taken for granted. The integration of modern technology in elections and the electoral process in Africa, the second largest continent in the world, has begun to interest both African scholars and foreign experts who are watching with rapt interest as the changes in the electoral process gain ground. Technology integration into elections is permeating the fabric of elections in Africa, thereby making room for innovative election protocols, which includes the manual registration of voters.

It is no longer news that the 2015 elections in Nigeria were, so far, the most peaceful. There were instances of slight misunderstandings and violence here and there, but foreign and national observers recorded the election as a huge success in the country's political history. Election violence has been a major enemy of Africa's democratic consolidation since the post-colonial era. Taking a historical trajectory of election violence in Africa, one would recall that the 1964 elections in Nigeria were characterized by severe violence, especially in some parts of the western protectorate where 22 school children were killed (Olubodun, 2015). Elections that were conducted since the birth of the fourth republic in Nigeria were plagued by an unprecedented magnitude of violence. The 2011 post-election violence, which resulted in the killing, displacement, and destruction of innocent lives and property, was one that cannot be easily forgotten. However, the 2015 election took a different turn—a peaceful one—and was considered an election that not only elevated Nigeria in the comity of nations, but also elated the citizens because it disassociated the country from the era of voting vandalism, thuggery, corrupt practices such as the rigging and snatching of voter boxes, and political and election apathy. One could feel under one's skin the palpable joy that engulfed the nation, and almost embrace the utmost glee that radiated from the eyes of Nigerian youths and children (Olubodun, 2015).

Recently, election processes have included debates among candidates. While reading various news articles about the latest debate and how people perceived the candidates in the 2015 general elections in Nigeria, it becomes quite obvious just how much technology and social media has impacted something as important and life changing as the presidential election. The use of the modern technology, which includes information and communication technology (ICT) during elections is gradually gaining solid ground in Kenya, Ghana, South Africa, Mozambique, Zambia, and most recently in Nigeria. These technologies range from social and mobile media systems, to the most recent M2SYS biometric solution technology, which was able to capture millions of Nigerian eligible voters and present election outcomes differently from times past, and has significantly revolutionized the election and voting processes. It was also able to allow election agencies to maintain full and adequate control of the voting and electoral processes, thereby preventing all measures of potential illegal manipulation of the voting polls by incumbent leaders and political parties.

The years 2011 through 2015 have so far witnessed many significant elections in Africa. With powerhouses like Nigeria and South Africa holding national and local elections respectively, an independent referendum in South Sudan, plus a presidential election in fast-growing Uganda, these years have been full of vote casting on the continent (Laverty, 2011). To finish off 2011, an anticipated presidential election by a Mubarak-less Egypt, held in the fall, provided windows into the development of democracy and freedom on the continent. The year span of 2011-2015 was also the start of a new decade on the African continent; one that follows significant economic development fueled by the high prices of natural resources. While the continent has almost widely consolidated economic reforms in the first decade of the 21st century, democratic reform still lags in comparison. Crises in Zimbabwe, Democratic Republic of Congo, Cote d'Ivoire, and Sudan, among others, highlight the ongoing struggles that the continent faces in terms of democratic consolidation (Laverty, 2011).

In the most recent elections in various African nations, such as Kenya, Ghana, South Africa, and Nigeria, the usage of social and mobile technology seems to have played a crucial role in the process of monitoring elections from the central offices to the various voting centers. Technology usage has also helped in the solicitation of feedback from citizens on various election issues, providing the capability to manage crises that occur following election result disputes, and tracking and keeping result data after they have been retrieved.

The history of the use of modern technology during the election periods in Africa can be traced back to the Kenyan 2007 election, which had a disputed outcome that resulted in election violence that led to the cancellation of the results. The Kenyan technology usage in the election, though not successful as a result of the violent outcome, marked the beginning of what has later been described as the birth of the integration of technology in elections in Africa. Ghana, which seems to be considered the African model of democracy, though very volatile, conducted a national election in the most recent past, and is about to participate in a presidential election this year using technology as a key driving force to accomplish positive election results. In South Africa and various other countries, technology integration seems to be gaining stronger ground, thereby yielding to very different and immediate outcomes than in the past.

In Nigeria, for instance, the 2015 general elections—where the election governing body Independent National Electoral Commission (INEC) integrated technology to the entire electoral process—resulted in the creation of a revived political atmosphere among the two most popular political parties who contested in the election. The use of a biometric card reader and the personal voter card— all products of the Atlanta Georgia Technology company that provided human-recognition technology that allows computers to identify fingerprints—has not only redefined the election and voting processes in Nigeria, but has also set a standard for many other African nations to follow. The 2015 elections in Nigeria, which were organized in a much more controlled and peaceful atmosphere, were categorized as being a game changer, which has established a new electoral system and a voting platform that will stand the test of time in a nation previously overwhelmed with numerous election malpractices, vices, and high rates of corruption.

Today, as technology commands a significant influence in all facets of life, including elections in certain African countries, voters have a right to blog, twig, call, and text their observations, results, and other pertinent election outcomes to their friends and family members. They now use a medium made possible by the new technology to convey their observations to the election staff, as well as utilizing the same technology-driven means to retrieve information as it pertains to the elections from the comfort of their respective homes or offices.

In Western societies such as the United States, Britain, Germany, Japan, China, and Russia, the use of technology in elections, which has sustained itself over time, generates obvious discussion. There are several ways that technology integration in elections in these countries has significantly impacted the outcome of the election results. In the United States, for instance, technology has impacted presidential elections in four different ways:

(1) Social Influence: According to Cutler (2015), Twitter and Facebook have transformed the way candidates interact with their constituencies. Ten years ago, presidential campaigns in the United States were drastically different from what they are today because social media has been able to give candidates a direct line of communication to the American people. That's a positive change. But on the flip side, social media is an uncontrolled, democratized soap box where individuals can spread opinions that are not substantiated, which can change the public's view of a candidate overnight (Cutler, 2015).

(2) Threat of Virality: During an election, candidates are always under the microscope, but new technology allows the media to watch them more closely. Social media runs in real time, and with a variety of channels, from Twitter to YouTube, candidates' words are replayed, dissected, and played again. Once something hits the web, it stays there forever (Cutler, 2015). The presence of social media and its impact on election and election processes has made candi-dates live under the assumption that there is always someone with a Smart-phone, camera, microphone, or other recording device capturing their actions to

share with the world. While this constant monitoring of candidate activity has brought more transparency to elections, it has also brought more sensationalism and often reduced political coverage to paparazzi-style reporting. Nothing is off limits. For the same reason of creating sensationalism among the candidates, their family members are also targeted on social media, and their words and actions are turned into memes to live on in infamy (Cutler, 2015). A typical example of what impact Smartphones have had on candidates was the recent Republican candidate for the presidency, Sen. Marco Rubio, who, during the presidential primary debate, had his own meme created when he took a pause in a televised speech to take a drink of water. His short water break from the televised speech went viral on the Internet (Cutler, 2015).

(3) Smarter Campaigns: Candidates always relied on polls to give them insight on where they stand with the public and what they should change about their campaigns. With the rise of big data and analysis, candidates can now understand much more deeply what's working and what's not in their campaigns. With this information, campaigns become more effective and can be tailored to garner the votes, funds, or public opinion needed from a particular region or constituency.

(4) New Issues: Technology itself brings new issues to the debate floor that candidates must know about, speak about, and take a position on (Cutler, 2015). Crucial constituent topical issues such as the state of the economy, security, abortion, job market, and cybersecurity need to be addressed, and candidates should be versed on them in order to speak about them and answer questions when asked.

These new issues, and other related impacts technology has had on elections, have drastically changed the public's perception of candidates. It hasn't altered the process enough to completely change politicians themselves, because they still lie, make half-true statements, and do their best to manipulate the public. The smart politicians are using the existence of the technology to continue to perpetuate the lies and propaganda by taking to social networks or posting viral videos. They create funny and decisive links about their opponents to trap them and/or build a negative impression about them. They also attempt to link their opposition with humiliating and negative advertisements, which are pointedly political and calculated attempts to tear down the image of the other candidate. These images are shown on national television programs or consistently run through social media.

As technology continues to be more pervasive in our lives, more people will get their information from television channels, the Internet, LinkedIn, Tumblr, Twitter, Facebook, via text, or even a blog that you regularly read. These places are quickly and effectively changing the minds of many citizens who regularly access them. In the future, this will lead to more truths being told, and fewer lies being allowed.

The Internet has long been a place where facts are overruled by opinions, where stories that have no real basis are picked up, and entertainment trumps anything related to sense and responsibility. There are many tools available to greatly improve things in the election process, but it remains to be seen whether these tools are used more by people who make positive changes, or people who take advantage and use them negatively. In addition, candidates need to keep up-to-date with technology, otherwise they will be viewed as outdated and irrelevant. Candidates who don't use the Internet, LinkedIn, Tumblr, Facebook, and Twitter, for example, won't be taken seriously. The more in touch candidates are with technology, the more people they will reach. Understanding new technologies and trends is now a key part of connecting with voters and running a successful campaign.

The integration of technology in elections in Africa has become a real game changer, particularly given the viral nature of information on social media channels and how hard it can be to monitor such information flow. The case is especially so for Africa, given the fact that it is only in recent or upcoming elections that the full extent of the impact of the Internet via social media is being felt. Social media across Africa has grown significantly in recent times.

The impact technology has had on elections in Africa has become so pronounced for two key reasons: (1) Accessibility: These channels are being made accessible and usable from non-traditional interfaces (i.e., web browsers). Twitter and Facebook can be accessed from basic (dumb) phones via mobile browsers and even SMS; (2) Cost: The cost of using social media has significantly diminished to near zero, which makes it possible for users to make use of Facebook without paying the data fee. In any case, the cost of data in sending a tweet is considerably minimized compared to sending an SMS.

There is no doubt that electoral credibility should be considered an indispensable condition, element, or factor that is essential to peaceful elections. Sadly, over the years electoral credibility has been one major area in which elections in Africa, most importantly in Nigeria, are deficient. Nigeria, as well as other nations in Africa, has lacked the structure and moral standards to organize and present a decent and violence-free election until very recently. The introduction of electronic registration and the use of the biometric card readers for the 2015 election in Nigeria gave hope for credible elections—an outcome that is presently reshaping the practice of credible elections in other countries of the continent. The 2015 election in Nigeria was the first time that technology was integrated into the electoral process, compared to the manual process in previous elections, which was subject to election fraud and lacked credibility. The introduction of electronic voting is an improvement on manual voting used in the past. For instance, the electoral umpire, Independent National Electoral Commission (INEC), was able to give Nigerians the exact figures of registered voters and number of Permanent Voter's Cards collected because records were captured electronically. This, to an extent, made election malpractice difficult.

The use of manual methods in previous elections made the election exercise difficult due to human error and inadequacies, providing opportunities for reckless rigging (Olubodun, 2015). There are several arguments, discussions, and statements from political pundits who felt that the results of the 2015 elections in Nigeria were not credible. Their reason for such an observation was due to the failure of the biometric card readers, challenges associated with the INEC staff arriving on time, difficulty in locating the polling stations, and necessary logistics. Some of these challenges were so insignificant that their occurrences may be blown out of proportion by either of the two major political parties or pundits, who had already developed apathy based on unfriendly experiences of the past. The elections were not all perfect, but political experts, as well as the international observers that represented their countries, clearly stated that the election was free and fair, and was considered to be the most fair, free, and credible election in the history of Nigeria.

According to some Nigerian observers, the 2015 election made history and indeed set the pace for politics and elections in Africa (Olubodun, 2015). The elections, though not perfect, resulted in an outcome that seems to have presented a lot of ideas, knowledge, and technology-driven skills to Nigerians, to the degree that they have come to realize that transparency and credibility can be possible and the spirit of sportsmanship should be maintained at all levels, both during and after the election campaigns.

The African elections database, created on October 2004 with the purpose of providing a comprehensive archive of past and present election results for the 49 countries of Africa, supports the historical perspective of the introductory chapter of this book and validates the claim that the advent of the new technology has not only revolutionized the global work force, but also has led to various changes in the way elections are conducted across the globe, including the continent of Africa. This is according to election data obtained from a variety of Internet sources from many African countries, including the national electoral authorities, official government documents such as government gazettes, court rulings, and electoral observer mission reports, online newspapers and periodicals, as well as research papers (Nohlen et al. 1999).

REFERENCES

Cutler, Z. (2015). "Four ways technology has impacted presidential elections." Entrepreneur –Business Accelerated.

Laverty, A. (2011). ICT, Social Media, and Elections in Africa: A Prospective Study.

Nohlen, D. et al., (1999). Elections in Africa: A Data Handbook. Oxford University Press

Olubodun, O. (2015). "Nigeria's 2015 elections – history made, lessons learnt." Voices of Youth.

CHAPTER 1
Resistance to Election Technology: Communication, Democracy and Vicissitudes of Electoral Outcomes

Chuka Onwumechili
Howard University, Washington, D.C.

INTRODUCTION

Political elections in African states have often been fraught with malpractice and violence, which combine to encourage electorate apathy. Collier and Vicente (2011) studied elections in Sub-Saharan Africa and reached the conclusion that weak challengers resort to violence, a weak incumbent uses repression, and a strong incumbent prefers bribery and ballot fraud. None of the three strategies are positive in nature, but they indeed reflect how political stakeholders fight over elections.

In reaction to these problems, some states, including Nigeria, have moved to a reliance on technology as a way to restore public confidence in elections and to seek the achievement of a true public democratic voice. Diamond and Plattner (2010) identified digital and cellular technologies as critical to fairer elections in several African states. Those technologies are indirectly linked to the election process, but additionally the directly-linked technologies, such as biometrics used for voter accreditation, have also contributed to opportunities for fairness. The 2015 Nigerian presidential election, which used several of those measures, may have provided numerous positives for the country, particularly for the future of the electoral process.

For years, elections were plagued with rigging, which led to declining confidence in the accuracy of electoral results. Previous attempts to introduce technology to curb rigging had failed. However, the Independent National Electoral Commission (INEC) made critical changes to the electoral process for the 2015 presidential elections. The Commission introduced, among other things, an electronic voter card as well as a card reader. These introductions were not easily adopted or accepted. Instead, the political class vigorously resisted reform through a series of attempts to persuasively communicate to both the Electoral Commission and voters. Nevertheless, many have attributed the success of the 2015 presidential elections to reform and the ability to push back on resistance from the political class. While it is difficult to claim that electoral reforms were solely responsible for the success of the electoral process, it is safe to state that they were significant contributors.

Invariably, the purpose of this chapter is to analyze the resistance among the political class to the introduction of measures improving elections. Therefore, this chapter focuses attention on analyzing Nigerian newspaper narratives to discover themes used by the political class to resist measures that prevent election fraud. To study this phenomenon effectively, we organize the chapter in the following ways: background to electoral problems in Nigeria, the impact of those electoral problems, what happened in 2015, method for our research, our findings, and conclusions and discussions.

BACKGROUND TO ELECTORAL PROBLEMS

To fully understand the problems associated with electioneering in Nigeria requires a deep study of its background. Elections have been understood as a zero-sum game in Nigeria, as the winner often has access to state funds. As Richard Joseph pointed out, this also means the ability to practice *prebendal* politics in a patron-client relationship. Joseph (1987) describes prebendal politics as situations where elected officials believe that they are personally entitled to share state funds. He noted that this entitlement was widely believed in Nigeria, where even members of political constituencies describe the phenomenon by talking about "our share of the national cake"; or, to use an Igbo saying, *Onye ube roo elu, nya ra chaa* (whoever has access to the pear should eat it). In essence, it was expected that an elected official should dip into the state funds for his/her personal use. On the other hand, the loser of an election is left to face the vicissitudes of life, with nothing but financial debt. While many candidates participate in fundraising from well-wishers, they have to spend a significant amount of their own finances, particularly during the early period of campaigns. In certain cases, candidates spend most of their fortunes, and may have to dispose of property to raise campaign funds. Thus, losing an election can be devastating for most candidates as there are no state funds to draw from.

Unfortunately, without financial protection for those who may lose an election, elections become very stressful for the participants and a high-stakes game. Ultimately, this encourages fraud and corruption as each candidate attempts to increase his or her odds of winning and recovering expenditures via prebendal practices.

Furthermore, elections in Nigeria are not simply won by access to funds, and the willingness to use such funds for campaign purposes and to win elections. It is far more complicated than that. Olarinmoye (2008) wrote insightfully on the importance of *Godfatherism* in Nigerian politics and elections. Godfathers are "king makers." The godfathers often do not contest elections, but use their funds, and specifically their know-how, to manipulate election results in favor of their candidates with a huge return of favors as soon as the candidates occupy elected positions. Ibrahim (2006) captured the essence of godfatherism in the following statement:

> Whether you like it or not, as a godfather you will not be a governor, you will not be a president, but you can make a governor, you can make a president. I am the greatest godfather in Nigeria because this is the first time an individual single-handedly put in position every politician in the state.

Ibrahim was referring to Reverend Jolly Nyame, a former governor of Taraba State in Nigeria who was being interviewed by *The Sun* newspaper in Nigeria. The statement by Jolly Nyame was about his control of electoral positions in one of the northern states in Nigeria. The same scenario is prevalent in other states, both in the north and south states of the country. These godfathers are essentially political or electioneering brokers whose experience and willingness to employ extralegal means to ensure the enthronement of a political candidate is their calling card. Olarinmoye (2008) argues that the godfather uses several fraudulent maneuvers to accomplish his goals, including manipulating the voter list, illegal printing of voter cards, illegal possession of ballot boxes, bribing election officials, falsification of election results, and multiple voting, among other measures. Olarinmoye went on to explain how some godfathers have gone to extremes to secure control of their candidate/client. He cited the cases of Chris Uba in Anambra State, and Chief Olusola Saraki in Kwara State. In the case of Uba, Olarinmoye noted as follows: "... he had his clients sign legal agreements which explicitly identified him, Uba, as the 'patron' ... having his clients swear to abide by their agreement with him before priests of a dreaded local traditional shrine based in Okija..." (p. 71). Olarinmoye argued that in Saraki's case, "it is his son who is securing his access to state resources through his occupying the seat of governor" (p. 72).

Many of these infamous activities did not begin recently. Since the first elections in the early 1960s, the election process has been inundated with rigging and other problems as each candidate attempts to increase the odds of winning. Abubakar (2015) and Ajayi (2007) have claimed that Nigeria has been defined by political instability derived from continuing electoral crises. Though Ajayi (2007) focused on preparations for elections in 2007, he listed issues of fraud that plagued previous elections. Abubakar (2015) affirmed this by chronicling a litany of electoral crises, beginning with the national elections of 1964 and the Western region election of 1965, which led to the first military putsch in the country. The 1964 and 1965 elections were marred by the massive rigging of votes and subsequent violence. These incidences repeated during the 1979 and 1983 elections, and also in the 1999, 2003, and 2007 elections, according to Abubakar. *The Economist* highlighted these incidences by noting that Nigerian elections feature "... gun men beating up opponents, intimidating voters, snatching ballot boxes and stuffing them with pre-marked ballots. Winning candidates piled up huge victories on high turnouts in places where the ballot papers had never even arrived. The rewards for such rigging can be impressive. In 2006, for instance, the Governor of Rivers State, Peter Odili, had a budget of $1.33 billion to spend, considerably more than the budgets of some (other) West African countries..." ("Big men, big fraud..." 2007). Rivers State is just one example of access to funds that accrue to those who manage to win a Nigerian election, and thus, the motivation to win at all costs.

But election rigging is not only verifiable through incidences such as the one reported by *The Economist*. There are also tests using psycho-mathematical probability. Beber and Scacco (2012) studied results from Nigeria's 2003 presidential election and compared it to the known probability for occurrence of certain digits in results from fair election procedures, and also against election results in Sweden (2002) and Senegal (2000 and 2007). For instance, similar last digits occur with equal frequency in fair elections. Beber and Scacco's calculations show that Nigeria's results deviated significantly from the norm, and thus increased the chances that the results were manipulated.

The 1993 election was excluded from those marred by electoral crises. Why is this so? It was widely acknowledged as the most successful, until the 2015 election. The 1993 election used an open ballot system, known as Option A, that was devised by the then Chairman of the National Electoral Commission (NEC) of Nigeria, Professor Humphrey Nwosu. The system required voters to line up behind their choice candidate prior to voting so that they could be counted in view of everyone, including party representatives (Kew, 2010; Campbell, 1994; Nwokedi, 1994). Thereafter, voters proceeded to cast their votes in privacy. Statistically, the headcounts and total votes, when tallied, should not significantly deviate. This is a way to prevent and discourage result alterations and ballot box snatching. It proved successful even though it was tedious. However, it remained an election considered to be free and fair.

IMPACT OF ELECTORAL PROBLEMS

The electoral problems that we have described contribute to several other troubling outcomes, which we address in this section. These outcomes include "capture" of democracy by a few "rogue elites," a diversion of focus away from development of the state, and increasing disenchantment of the constituencies.

We previously pointed to Olarinmoye's (2008) work on godfatherism in Nigerian politics. These proclaimed "godfathers" are best described as "rogue elites" who capture the electioneering system. Their activities, which we described in the previous section, subvert the democratic process in various ways. First, they use their political influence and funds to autocratically select political candidates within the political parties. Secondly, they prevent the general public from participating in democratic voting for candidates by using violence, bribery, and massive rigging to install their anointed candidates. Thirdly, "elected" officials become beholden to these "rogue elites," instead of the public or constituencies that they ostensibly represent. It is not surprising that Lewis and Alemika (2005) noted as follows: "Only one in 10 Nigerians believed that elected leaders commonly listen to them or look out for their interests..." (p. viii).

Furthermore, the state's inability to assure and secure the public's participation in political elections has increasingly disenchanted the public. Afrobarometer's survey results of 2,428 Nigerians amply demonstrates public disillusionment with politicians and politics (Lewis and Alemika, 2005). The survey, taken since civilian rule of 1999, shows an increasing decline in public confidence in the system. For instance, in 2003 only 35 percent of Nigerians were fairly/very satisfied with how democracy works in Nigeria compared to 84 percent in 2000. Assessment of the effectiveness of the electioneering process in Nigeria fell from 86 percent to 60 percent from 2000 to 2003. The percentage of Nigerians who felt that elections were conducted fairly/very honestly fell by as much as 25 percent from 2000 to 2003 in all six geopolitical zones. Though participation in electoral voting remained strong at 73 percent of those interviewed, fewer Nigerians believed their political engagement made a difference.

The disconnect between "elected" leaders and those who they are supposedly there to serve has also meant that the focus of government service shifts away from development activities. Instead of the State focusing on building basic infrastructure, providing basic human needs, and ultimately improving personal living conditions, the State has failed in several of those areas. The reason for such failures is not far-fetched. Those who are elected have pursued prebendal activities and have paid more attention to the demands of rogue elites instead of the demands of the general public. Lewis and Alimeka (2005) found that among Nigerians who reported their personal living conditions as bad, the disenchantment with democracy increased. In essence, this group of people believes that their condition is linked to the nation's democratic practice.

Ultimately, the litany of electoral problems forced several interest groups, particularly civil society organizations, to mount pressure toward reform. Oromareghake (2013) cites the Electoral Reform Network (ERN) and Centre for Democracy and Development as examples of civil society organizations that submitted reform ideas to the Uwais Electoral Reform Committee (ERC).[1] Additionally, the Save Nigeria Group (SNG), which is a coalition of civil society organizations, also voiced its recommendations for change, focusing on securing autonomy for the Election Commission.

THE 2015 ELECTIONS

In an address at Chatham House in London on July 4 of 2012, the INEC Chairman Attahiru Jega outlined new changes to Nigeria's electoral process (Jega, 2012). He noted that most of the measures were designed to prevent multiple voting, snatching and switching of ballot boxes, as well as several other types of electoral fraud.

The changes were indeed monumental when compared to processes in place prior to the appointment of Jega in 2010. They are listed as follows:

- Unique numbering of ballot boxes to correspond to polling stations.
- Color-coded ballot papers and serial-numbered ballots.
- Introduction of accreditation periods to limit movement of persons from one polling unit to another.
- Divorced INEC staff participation from collection and announcement of results. Instead, these tasks were to be completed by academic leaders and members of the National Youth Corps.
- Allowed for polling station recording and live media coverage to speed up declaration of results.
- Employed direct data capture of biometrics during voter registration, which generated a database of registered voters. This was then used to produce chip-based voter cards that could not be easily duplicated.
- Employed use of card readers, which were used along with the biometric data during accreditation to validate registered voters.

Importantly, Mr. Jega was a member of the Electoral Reform Committee (ERC) under Justice Muhammadu Uwais, which submitted far-reaching recommendations back on December 2008. Some of ERC's recommendations included a requirement that the judiciary, instead of the president, appoint the INEC chairman. Thus, it is not surprising that many of those recommendations were not implemented. Though the president nominated Jega, several interest groups supported the nomination because it first received approval by the National Council of State, which includes former heads of state.

The appointment of Jega represented a positive move. Jega was invested in reforming the electoral process in the country. One of the key reforms he introduced for the 2015 general elections was the use of a digital card reader and a digital Permanent Voter Card (PVC). The PVC had an inserted chip, which allowed for verification of its authenticity, and it was to be used in the voter accreditation process. Additionally, the card's handheld reader had the ability to tally and transmit voter information to a central INEC server via the GSM data service. This tally can then be compared to actual number of votes to ensure that vote counts were not altered.

However, changes from the ERC and those enumerated by Jega at Chatham House meant that political stakeholders in the elections could be adversely affected. The affected stakeholders were clearly desperate politicians, rogue elites, and political parties who invested in the process of election rigging and fraud. INEC's scheme was indeed a problem for this group of stakeholders, and as would be expected, they resisted these changes in several ways. In this study, we have indicated our interest in identifying how this group of stakeholders employed their resistance to changes in the electoral process.

METHOD FOR OUR STUDY

We employed a thematic analysis of Nigerian newspapers in order to identify types of resistance put forward by Nigerian politicians to electoral reforms. We selected the period from Mr. Jega's appointment on June 8, 2010, to the last date of the 2015 Nigerian election, which was April 11, for our study. We searched the LexisNexis research database, which keeps record of global newspaper reports, as the pool from which we selected newspapers for study. The newspapers were then selected based on two keyword searches for "Nigeria" and "elections." These led to 739 newspaper articles in the pool. However, we wanted to focus on the top four Nigerian newspapers that had the most stories on the topic for the stated period. The top four newspapers — *This Day* (102), *The Vanguard* (95), *Daily Independent* (83), and *Daily Trust* (76) — were responsible for 356, or nearly 50 percent of the total stories. We then browsed through the stories to identify those that involved reform and comments on the reform by politicians. These stories were then read several times in order to extract the most important themes.

Boyatzis (1998) recommends the use of thematic analysis to discover patterns in order to gain insight and knowledge from narrative data. Our unit of analysis was the entire newspaper story, which we read and reread. Significant themes reoccur across stories and newspapers. These themes are not preimposed or predetermined by the research. Instead, the researcher allows the data to lead him/her to significant themes. In this way, thematic analysis is an inductive process.

With the mass of data within the newspaper narratives that we selected, we applied Corbin and Strauss's (2008) suggestion on constant comparison analysis (CCA) in order to break down the data. Though the CCA has been used mostly with and is closely associated with the method of grounded theory, Boeije (2002) and Fram (2013) have argued for its application beyond grounded theory. This suggestion is what we took to heart in this study. In the CCA process, preliminary themes are identified from the initial reading of the narratives. This is called the "stage of open coding." Thereafter, we moved to comparing initial themes, constantly, with the data in order to confirm themes or further reduce, expand, or collapse the themes in the subsequent process of axial coding. This constant comparison is used over several iterations until a moment of exhaustion is reached. It is a moment where no new themes are unearthed and the existing themes are affirmed.

FINDINGS

The outcome of the thematic analysis points to six significant themes that occurred repeatedly over the period of research. It should be noted that not all politicians complained about the introduction of technological reform in the election process as one may think. The criticism of the reform depended upon which political party one belonged. Resistance largely came from members of the ruling party—the People's Democratic Party (PDP). *The Vanguard* of March 8, 2015 concluded as follows:

> Making the wrong arguments—and worse still, suggesting that they do not want the device (Card Reader Technology) to be used for the forthcoming general elections—members and leaders of the ruling PDP are expressing fears about the use to which the devices would be put. ... conversely, the opposition All Progressives Congress (APC) appears confident in the belief that only the card reader can deliver free, fair, and credible elections.

This was surprising, because election rigging was not the intent or mainstay of the ruling party, although rigging had been practiced by politicians from both the ruling and opposition parties in the past. So why did resistance come significantly from the PDP? There may be multiple reasons for this. First, parties in Nigeria have come to believe that incumbency provides advantages in effective election rigging and fraud in the country, particularly at the national level where the federal government controlled both the army and the police, which had been used to intimidate opponents during electioneering periods. In the past, they could be used to limit the movement of opponents during electioneering and they could be used to provide security for ballot-box-snatching thugs, among other nefarious activities. However, with the introduction of reform in the electioneering process, the use of these forces appeared to be limited. Ballot box snatching was no longer gainful, among other things. The advantages of incumbency were greatly minimized by the reform, and thus, resistance was a way to push for the limit in implementing the reform program. Second, there may have been a sense that the opposition had gained momentum during the electioneering campaign, and thus, the only option of victory for the PDP was through rigging—but that option was being blocked by the reforms. Again, the only way out appeared to be to protest reform implementation.

In any case, it is clear that the PDP's concerns could be traced back to 2010, five years before the general elections. *The Daily Trust* of June 25, 2010 made a startling report just after President Jonathan had nominated Attahiru Jega for the INEC Chairman. This is what the president told Nigerians, resident overseas, during a visit to Toronto, Canada:

> When we nominated Professor Attahiru Jega as the Independent National Election Commission Chairman, some members of our party came to me asking "Jonathan do you really want PDP to win these elections?" ... They said the nominee is a radical who will not succumb to any pressure. I told them, "We must work hard and as well present the best candidates because there will be no room for manipulations."

The passage clearly shows that the president could use his position to appoint a compromised INEC chairman who becomes beholden the president and his party. However, in this case, President Jonathan chose not to do this. In addition, the passage also confirmed that votes and results could be and were previously manipulated by ruling parties during elections.

THE THEMES

We examined communications from politicians that appeared in the newspapers about reform. These narratives or communications were largely intended to persuade the Commission and voters that democratic principles were violated with the introduction of election reforms.

The six themes that we found in examining the media narratives were as follows: (1) The use of the PVC readers contravened the Electoral Act; (2) the distribution of digitized permanent voters cards (PVCs) were unevenly distributed; (3) introduction of PVCs was designed to disenfranchise majority of voters; (4) PVCs were distributed to both minors and illegal immigrants; (5) the use of card readers and PVCs was not properly tested; and (6) the INEC chairman should be replaced as he was bribed by the opposition. We address each theme in the subsequent paragraphs.

Early during our research period, politicians from various parties had repeatedly urged the National Assembly to amend Section 52(2) of the Electoral Act, which banned the use of technology in voting during Nigerian elections. This was the issue from news reports from 2010 to 2014. Four parties—the United Democratic Party, Alliance for Democracy, Action Alliance, and the Allied Congress Party of Nigeria—also filed a suit, claiming the plan to use the card reader contravened the Electoral Act. The judge refused to grant a ruling against the INEC. However, a few months prior to the elections it appeared that the section was reinterpreted to affirm that the use of PVC readers was not a violation. The INEC argued that card readers are not electronic voting machines, as they are not to be used in voting, but only for *accrediting* voters. Moreover, the INEC argued that card readers add value to the election process, match international best practices, and assist in meeting the yearning of Nigerians for credible elections. However, this did not stop top PDP officials from calling on the INEC to discontinue plans to use card readers by citing the "contravention of the Electoral Act."

Another theme was the criticism of reported distribution of PVCs to voters in various states of the country. The data showed that large numbers of such cards were distributed in the northern part of the country compared to the south. The PDP took advantage of this statistic to call for the abandonment of the cards, noting that it was suspicious that more cards were distributed in the north, which was a stronghold of the opposition party. In one example of this resistance, the head of the Oodua Peoples Congress (OPC), Mr. Gani Adams, led a protest and was cited as stating the following:

> Over 5 million people are yet to collect their PVCs in the South West; over 2.5 million in the South South and 2 million in the South East, while Jega claimed to have recorded 90 percent distribution in the North, despite the high level of insecurity there. (*The Daily Independent*, March 21, 2015)

Adams's complaint was just one of the protests. It must be noted that another faction of the OPC condemned Adams's protest and described Adams as a stooge of the ruling party (the PDP). There were similar narratives from leaders of the PDP and other organizations that cater to ethnic interests, particularly in the south.

Adams, as well as others, who called for the discontinuation of a plan to use PVCs, also argued that the PVC technology was unnecessary for Nigeria because many voters would be unable to understand how to use it, and therefore it would end up confusing voters and preventing a majority of voters from participating in the elections. This argument was strange when one considers that a large number of Nigerians were already using telephones and texting. The PVC card readers were to be operated by trained election personnel and voters were only required to arrive at polling units with a card, which the election personnel would verify as to its authenticity. There was not much to confuse the Nigerian voter!

Further, the anti-reform group also argued that PVCs had been issued to underaged persons in the northern part of the country, and to illegal immigrants in the northern part of the country. This claim cannot be dismissed because there were indeed reports of illegal immigrants in possession of PVCs before the start of the elections. However, a reported crackdown on illegal immigrants by Nigerian authorities occurred in the border towns, which both the opposition as well as the ruling parties considered a stronghold.

An additional theme focused on a claim that the card readers should not be used because they had not been tested. The chairman of the PDP, Mr. Adamu Mu'azu, was one of the key complainants on this issue. The claim was that without the testing, the cards could not be considered reliable and therefore should not be used. The Attorney General and Minister of Justice, Mohammed Bello Adoke, filed a suit in an Abuja Federal Court against the INEC's plan to use the card reader, claiming that there was danger that many voters would be disenfranchised. However, several reports quoted the INEC as responding that the political parties were the first to participate in tests of the PVCs involving card integrity, quality assurance, and functionality. In several stress tests across the country, numerous problems of card failure occurred in Ebonyi State, which the INEC then proceeded to correct in subsequent weeks. Moreover, the INEC agreed to substitute incident report forms in cases where a voter's name was in the register, but the voter had a PVC that was not readable by the card reader.

Finally, a theme surrounded the call for removal of the INEC Chairman, Attahiru Jega. This, of course, was a last-ditch effort by the ruling party and ethnic organizations to change leadership and perhaps open an opportunity for change in the electoral process. This call, by top PDP official Edwin Clark, was reported across newspapers. Mr. Clark claimed that the Northern Elders Forum (NEF) had met with Jega and bribed him to rig the elections in favor of the opposition party (the APC). Then there were reported street protests by ethnic organizations such as the OPC (Gani Adams's group) in the South West and the Movement for the Actualization of the Sovereign State of Biafra (MASSOB) in the South East. In each of the protests, the main call was for the removal of Mr. Jega.

CONCLUSIONS AND DISCUSSIONS

The six themes that we identified affirm resistance by politicians. In this case, the politicians were primarily from the ruling party. This was an attempt to stop reform of the electoral system. The resistance failed as the elections went on, with reforms in place and used for the elections. The ruling party lost the election and it became the first time a ruling party had lost the general elections to the opposition in Nigeria. In the end, several observer groups, including those from the European Union and the United Nations, commended the Nigerian elections. Morrison (2015) reported that the U.N. Secretary General Ban Ki-Moon "praised the Nigerian elections as largely peaceful."

Though this chapter has focused on the INEC's efforts at reform, it is important to add that the success of the elections went beyond overcoming strong resistance to reform. It included the steadfast focus by the INEC Chairman, Attahiru Jega, on managing a successful process. Additionally, the civil society organizations and the mass media played a strong watchdog role of monitoring polling results and publishing them as a check against the alteration of results by authorities and/or politicians and political parties.

REFERENCES

Abubakar, A. (2015, March 28). History of elections in Nigeria from independence. *Peoples Daily.* http://www.peoplesdailyng.com/history-of-elections-in-nigeria-from-independence/

Ajayi, K. (2007). Election administration in Nigeria and the challenges of the 2007 elections. *The Social Sciences, 2* (2): 142-151.

Beber, B., and Scacco, A. (2012). What the numbers say: A digit-based test for election fraud. *Political Analysis*, 20: 211-234.

Big men, big fraud and big trouble. (2007, April 26). *The Economist.* http://www.economist.com/

Boeije, H. (2002). A purposeful approach to the constant comparative method in the analysis of qualitative interviews. *Quality and Quantity*, 36: 391-409.

Boyatzis, R. (1998). Qualitative information: Thematic analysis and code development. CA: Sage Publications.

Bratton, M. (2008). Vote buying and violence in Nigerian election campaigns. *Electoral Studies*, 27: 621-32.

Campbell, I. (1994). Nigeria's failed transition: The 1993 presidential election. *Journal of Contemporary African Studies*, 12(2): 179-199.

Collier, P., and Vicente, P. (2011). Violence, bribery, and fraud: The political economy of elections in sub-Saharan Africa. *Public Choice*, 153 (1-2): 117-47.

Corbin, J., and Strauss, A. (2008). (3rd ed.). Basics of qualitative research: Techniques and procedures for developing grounded theory. Thousand Oaks, CA: Sage Publications.

Diamond, L., and Plattner, M. (2010). (Eds.). *Democratization in Africa: Progress and retreat.* Johns Hopkins University Press.

Fram, S. (2013). The constant comparative analysis method outside of grounded theory. *The Qualitative Report*, 18: 1-25.

Ibrahim, J. (2006). The rise of Nigeria's godfathers. *BBC Focus on Africa Magazine.* London.

Jega, A. (2012, July 4). Improving elections in Nigeria: Lessons from 2011 and looking to 2015. Speech made at Chatham House in London. http://www.chathamhouse. org/sites/files/chathamhouse/public/Research/Africa/040712summary.pdf

Joseph, R. (1987). Democracy and PrebendalPpolitics in Nigeria: The rise and fall of the second republic. Cambridge University Press.

Kew, D. (2010). Nigerian elections and the neopatrimonial paradox: In search of the social contract. *Journal of Contemporary African Studies*, 28(4): 499-521.

Lewis, P., and Alemika, E. (2005). Seeking the democratic dividend: Public attitudes and attempted reform in Nigeria (Working Paper No. 52). Afrobarometer Working Papers. Http: www. http://www.afrimap.org/english/images/documents/Afropaper No52-17nov06.pdf

Morrison, A. (2015, March 29). Nigeria election 2015 update: Amid violence, UN Chief congratulates country on largely peaceful voting process. *International Business Times.* http://www.ibtimes.com/nigeria-election-2015-update-amid-violence-un-chief -congratulates-country-largely-1863036

Nwokedi, E. (1994). Nigeria's democratic transition: Explaining the annulled 1993 presidential election. *The Round Table: The commonwealth Journal of International Affairs,* 83(330): 189-204.

Olarinmoye, O. (2008). Godfathers, political parties and electoral corruption in Nigeria. *African Journal of Political Science and International Relations*, 2 (4): 66-73.

Oromareghake, P. (2013). Electoral institutions/processes and democratic transition in Nigeria under the Fourth Republic. *International Review of Social Sciences and Humanities*, 6 (1): 19-34.

ENDNOTES

1. The ERC was set up by late President Umaru Yar'Adua in August 2007 to reform Nigeria's electoral process. Justice Muhammadu Uwais led a committee of 23, which submitted its final report in December 2008.

CHAPTER 2
Technology Integration and Transformation of Election in Africa: An Evolving Modality in Ghana

Matilda Yeboah-Fofie
Vice President of Operations
G. Manu & Associates, Virginia

INTRODUCTION

The democratization process in Africa is inextricably interwoven with elections. Elections give meaning to the concept of political representation, and the protection of all the rights enshrined in the Universal Declaration of Human Rights and the Constitution of Ghana. We elect representatives to govern us because we cannot all rule at the same time. Political party engagement stems from the aggregation of political ideas through political parties so that a meaningful political competition can take place. Hence, to steal in an election is to unlawfully appropriate the will of the people.

A study of conflict in African states reveals two main causative factors: ethnicity and elections. Indeed, the latter often propels the former. The regional elections in Western Nigeria in 1964, for example, were the principal trigger of political conflict that erupted into ethnic violence, and which ultimately degenerated into the Biafran War. Despite the various political and ethnic issues underscoring the conflict in Liberia, electoral rigging catapulted the nation into the carnage of the civil war, which disgraced Africa and humanity. Elections have plagued Cote d'Ivoire, Togo, Benin, Kenya, Zimbabwe, etc. The notorious phenomenon of "power sharing" can only be perceived as an ad hoc apology to a lingering cancer. Ultimately, Africa can only stabilize and deepen democracy through an electoral system that will put results beyond dispute.

BACKGROUND OF THE STUDY

Ghana was at the brink of conflict in the month of December, 2008. The National Democratic Party (NDC) complained that it had unveiled a conspiracy between the New Patriot Party (NPP) and the Electoral Commission (EC) to rig the elections. In 2012, the panic scenario was repeated. Integrity of the election process is holistic and refers to a state of completeness from the beginning to the end of an electoral cycle. An old adage is often used by election analysts that only amateurs steal elections on election day. Hence, the purity of elections must cover all stages in the process, as well as fundamental, institutional, and policy choices related to the electoral system, its competition, and outcomes.

Electoral reform is akin to continuing education. It has no immediate end, especially in fledgling democracies. The process should be professional, nonpartisan, and transparent. It must be seen as a true reflection of the people's will by politicians and the citizenry alike. It cannot be refuted that electoral reforms are imperative in Ghana today, after the Supreme Court case and judgment on the Presidential Election Petition. Justice Atuguba in his recommendation after the Presidential Election Petition stated that the Biometric Device System that was used during the electioneering period must be streamlined to avoid breakdowns and stress on the electorate involved in an adjournment of the polls. Invalidating wholesale votes for insignificant excess numbers is not the best application of the administrative principle of the proportionality test.

Electoral reform started in Ghana in 1992. The 1992 elections in Ghana generated loads of controversy, which led the New Patriotic Party (NPP), which lost the presidential elections to boycott the ensuing parliamentary elections, and published the *Stolen Verdict* to catalogue a number of pitfalls. The NPP called for reforms before it would participate in future elections.

In March 1994, an Inter Party Advisory Council (IPAC) was formed to bring representatives of the political parties together with the aim of building a consensus on electoral matters, in partnership with the Electoral Commission (EC). The following reforms have taken place since 1992: First, in 1995 the EC discarded the existing register and compiled a totally new register. Second, in 1996, photo ID cards were given to qualified voters in 10 Regional Capitals and 10 rural communities. In 1995, the EC had a better database resulting from the reforms. The voter turnout shot up from over 50 percent in 1992 to over 80 percent in 1996. Third, in the 1996 elections, opaque ballot boxes were replaced with transparent ballot boxes. Fourth, in 2000, party agents were allowed to come closer to the EC officials (earlier they were allowed only to "observe" the process from a distance). Fifth, in 2004, the EC decided to give all registered voters black-and-white ID cards, which the EC justified as being easy to scan and difficult to replicate. Sixth, the Voters' Register was developed from a state of raw data to a verifiable document. Party agents were part of the process.

Seventh, fresh registration took place in 2004 and all qualified voters were issued photo ID cards. Eighth, training sessions have been organized by the EC for agents of political parties to educate them on the rules and practices of the elections. The concept is to ensure understanding, uniformity, and a level playing field for all. Ninth, the optical mark reader (OMR) was introduced to enhance the integrity of the electoral system. The scanning of voter data or information is vital in ensuring accuracy in the process of transferring voter details on the register. It also saves time and minimizes cost. Tenth, numbered seals for ballot boxes were introduced to build trust and eliminate suspicion. Later, political parties were allowed to add their own seals if they wished. Eleventh, ballot papers are counted at polling stations and the results declared there. Movement of ballot papers to central counting points is no longer applied. Twelfth, political parties are allowed to police ballot papers in printing houses and after. And finally, biometric registration and biometric verification were introduced for the 2012 elections. However, the biometric reform, though good, also brought some challenges that resulted in electoral petition. Therefore, for effective elections in subsequent years, our electoral system could be tackled by strengthening some clearly identified areas, including the following: strengthening the legal and systemic regime that regulates elections; and examining, improving upon, and applying legal measures and sanctions that relate to elections and election offenses. More importantly, the IT Division of the EC should be revamped to keep pace with latest developments in the industry and system.

PROBLEM STATEMENT

As noted by the African Union recently, general elections, apart from being laudable hallmarks of representative democracy, also breed conflict and violence that sometimes threaten the socioeconomic development of a nation. One study noted that, despite strong economic growth over the last decade by African countries, political instability remained an ongoing concern impeding continued economic growth. Among the reasons cited for political instability is the lack of a smooth process of handover of power on the eve of political elections. In Ghana, the 2012 elections dispute was marred with disputes in court, and could have led to disruptive social conflict with dire consequences on the economy. The main problems relate to the voting process, counting of ballot papers, and collation of results at various polling stations. However, since these processes are being done manually, there could be human error that may affect the actual results. Therefore, the main objective of the research is to find out whether Information Communication Technology (ICT) can be used to minimize or resolve these electoral issues, thereby enhancing the electoral process in Ghana.

RATIONALE OF THE STUDY

Electoral justice is the cornerstone of democracy in that it safeguards both the legality of the electoral process and the political rights of citizens. It has a fundamental role in the continual process of democratization and is a catalyst for the transition from the use of violence as a means for resolving political conflict to the use of lawful means to arrive at a fair solution. An electoral justice system that resolves political conflict through different legal mechanisms, guaranteeing full compliance with the law, enables democracy to thrive. This deepens the importance of strong electoral bodies, and improves the framework within which political, administrative, and judicial institutions coexist. In consequence, it provides cognitive elements that will assure social stability.

Elections are at the core of the democratic process. The competitive and politically divisive nature of elections, along with their technical complexity, make them vulnerable to abuse, fraud, or perceptions thereof. At the same time, elections are able to achieve their key purpose of providing legitimacy to the government only if they are fully trusted and perceived to be impartial and fair, hence the need for an effective mechanism such as ICT to prevent, mitigate, or resolve disputes that are likely to arise in every electoral process, and to preserve—and when necessary, restore—the real and perceived equality of citizens and their representatives. An efficient and effective electoral justice system is fundamental to securing these objectives. Without a system to mitigate and manage inequality or perceptions of inequality, even the best management of an electoral process may lead to mistrust in the legitimacy of a democracy.

RESEARCH OBJECTIVES

The main objective of this study is to review the impact of the continuing transformation and integration of technology into the electoral processes in Africa with an evolving modality in Ghana. The specific objective is to find out whether ICT can be used to minimize or resolve electoral issues, thereby enhancing the electoral process in Ghana.

OVERVIEW OF METHODOLOGY

Descriptive research design was used for this study. According to Burns and Grove (2003:201), descriptive research "is designed to provide a picture of a situation as it naturally happens." It may be used to justify current practice and make judgment, and also to develop theories. Descriptive research design is a scientific method that involves observing and describing the behavior of a subject without influencing it in any way. It is used to obtain information concerning the current status of the phenomena to describe "what exists" with respect to variables or conditions in a situation. This was based on a cross-sectional data. Cross-sectional data, or a cross section of a study population, in statistics and econometrics is a type of one-dimensional data set (Henry, Brady & Johnston, 2008). Cross-sectional data refers to data collected by observing many subjects (such as individuals, firms, or countries/regions) at the same point in time, or without regard to differences in time (Henry et al., 2008). Analysis of cross-sectional data usually consists of comparing the differences between the subjects (Henry et al., 2008). A structured questionnaire was used for the cross-sectional data.

Both qualitative and quantitative methods were used for this study. The study adopted the quantitative approach, which comes from the deductive school of thought. This is because the study was to understand and interpret social interactions concerning workers, which falls under qualitative research. However, the questionnaire was coded in order to fit into quantitative research methods (to be specific, nonparametric research analysis). The quantitative approach of this research involved the deployment of a self-administered survey for 200 respondents. Again, the qualitative data refers to subjective data associated with the respondents' opinions, positions, views, and biases on the subject or issue under investigation.

The study was based on two sources of data; that is, primary and secondary data sources. The primary data sources include the careful collection and analysis of firsthand information from ICT professionals or experts, electoral commission officials, political party representatives, and ordinary voters in Ghana. The proposed sample size is 200 respondents. A multi-stage sampling method was used to select the sample. Since there are many categories of respondents to be studied, a disproportionate sampling method was used to select 40 ICT personnel, 10 electoral commission officials, 30 major political party representatives, and 120 ordinary voters. A purposive sampling method was also used to select the sample. This was done by finding out whether the person is an experienced ICT person, electoral commission official, or experienced voter. Some of the tools used in the primary data collection were interview, administration of questionnaires, and direct observation. The tools to be used are Statistical Package for Social Sciences (SPSS) and Microsoft Excel. A combination of inferential and descriptive statistics was used in analyzing and interpreting the data collected.

LITERATURE REVIEW: INTEGRATION OF ICT INTO ELECTORAL PROCESSES AND ITS BENEFITS

The rate of scientific and technological change has greatly increased over the last half century. Nowhere is this more the case than in the areas of ICT (Adesida, 2011). Grönlund (2011) noted that an important element in building a pluralistic society is the management of elections. This is because the credibility of an election result has many ramifications, including the central question of legitimacy of authority. It is also because the public can only be expected to gain confidence in the electoral system if it is based upon transparency, and fair, strong procedures and working methods. A well-established electoral process that is transparent can help result in a fair electoral outcome, but this is attainable only when some form of information and communication tools are applied to the electoral process.

The introduction of ICT into the electoral process is generating both interest and concern among voters, as well as practitioners worldwide, with most electoral management bodies using new technologies aimed at improving the electoral process (Nielsen, 2009). These technologies range from the use of basic office automation tools, such as word processing and spreadsheets, to more sophisticated data processing tools, such as database management systems, optical scanning, and geographic systems (International Institute for Democracy and

Electoral Assistance, 2011). In fact, the previous study further pointed out that the election and technology initiative is a response to the increasing interest in applying new information and telecommunication technologies to electoral processes.

Dill (2004) observed that the use of electronic voting in the electoral processes has improved efficiency, especially in many developed nations that enjoy a relatively stable social order that permits continued economic growth. This is because winners of elections and the entire general public are usually pleased with the outcome if it is sufficiently transparent, accurate, free, and fair. Countries such as the US, UK, and France have already deployed electronic voting widely in their electoral processes (Xenakis & Macintosh, 2003). It is against this background of huge benefits of technology in the electoral process, as witnessed by those countries, that the major stakeholders in Ghana's political system are calling on the Electoral Commission to adopt these technologies (Ekabua & Bassey, 2011).

Larvie et al. (1996) noted that strengthening ICT in electoral process is not something that is being forced on electorate's ignorance. The ground rules for elections in Ghana have been developed for over three decades. Universal adult suffrage, official registration of voters, secrecy of ballot, parliamentary elections, presidential elections where the winner requires more than 50 percent-plus-one of the valid votes cast, and permanent and independent Electoral Commission have been the attributes of the electoral system since the late 1960s. These notwithstanding, controversy surrounded the results of the 1992 and the 2012 presidential elections, culminating in the boycott of the subsequent parliamentary election and disputed results in the Ghana Supreme Court respectively. This clearly showed that putting in place the structures alone is not enough; the people must, above all, have confidence in the electoral process, and this in turn depends on how much the people understand and become familiar with the processes. In the 2012 presidential and parliamentary elections, the Electoral Commission introduced biometric voter registration. This was done in a bid to improve the system, and also to ensure that the voters registered, which formed the basis of credible electoral results that were clean and verifiable. Though its implementation encountered myriad problems, it was seen by stakeholders as a much-improved method of registration over the manual method. It is, therefore, not out of place that many Ghanaians are agitating for electronic voting (Bafo, 2012).

Mathieson (2011) probably summed up the use of ICT in elections when he indicated that ICT at the stages of the electoral cycle include the polling day, electronic voting, communications, count of ballot, and tabulation and declaration of results. Mathieson (2011) further noted that if properly organized and managed, ICT can speed up electoral work, improve accuracy, meet tight deadline constraints, and can be cost-effective. Therefore, the use of ICT in the electoral process to promote fair electoral results cannot be underestimated.

As observed by Ekabua and Bassey (2011), the use of ICT poses opportunities and threats for elections. For example, increased ICT use in the electoral process promises to bring about increased public confidence and participation in the political process, and supplies the antidote for voter apathy, a greater convenience in terms of voting time, reduced cost, and access by people with disabilities. At the same time, increased ICT use in the electoral process can become a threat to democracy by compounding existing election problems. For example, electronic voting can threaten the integrity of the elections by introducing a new set of risks, doubts, and opportunities for fraud and failure, and the technologies are often not as safe, reusable, trustworthy, or correct as promised by the suppliers.

One study ("Information Communication Technologies," 2014) has noted that a number of developing countries are at the various stages in the deployment of ICT in monitoring their elections. For example, Brazil and Chile have successfully deployed voting machines to aid in the election process. The deployment of the voting machines by those countries has resulted in faster voting and the more efficient counting of votes. A reduction in disputes after results is declared (as the representatives of political parties can check the machine and be satisfied with its performance before the actual election), as well as a reduction in the responsibilities of returning officers. One of the most powerful uses for ICT in elections is for forensic analysis, where duplicate voting is minimized, quick counts are implemented, and parallel tabulations of results is possible (Schuler, 2009). This view is supported by Laverty (2011), who noted that with no international monitors in the countryside or rural areas, national and local elections were often accompanied by significant fraud and abuses because of anonymity of the culprits in those areas.

HISTORY OF ELECTORAL PROCESSES IN GHANA

Like other Commonwealth countries, Ghana's Electoral Commission (EC) evolved as part of the institutional transfer of the superstructure of British colonial rule (Jinadu, 1995). Post-World War II political developments triggered constitutional reforms leading to multiparty politics in the Gold Coast (Austin, 1964; Apter, 1955). Since elections lie at the heart of multiparty politics, the search for an efficient system of election management became a priority. The limited suffrage and the narrow nature of the electoral system were suitable for a less complex election administrative system (Cohen & Laakso, 1997:717-710). Initially, the machinery for administering elections was located within the colonial government—a department under the Ministry of Local Government (Ayee, 1998:54). To be sure, colonial-supervised elections were devoid of political manipulations and state controls (Smith, 1960). The relatively congenial electoral environment provided by the colonial government fostered effective competition among the African political parties. The electoral regime was characterized by a relative fairness and agreements on the rules of the game that were defined and implemented by the colonial government (Debrah, 1998). This was at the core of election management efficiency and credibility.

But immediate post-independence political developments present a debilitating picture of the EC. Political control and manipulation of the EC ensured that its independent power over election management was curtailed. Under the 1960 First Republican Constitution, the chief justice whose appointment was determined and controlled by the president of the republic had oversight responsibility over elections. But the power to determine the finality of an election outcome would lie with the president. By 1964, when the single-party rule was inaugurated, the electoral commissioner had lost his sense of impartiality, independence, and neutrality on electoral matters (Debrah, 1998). The overthrow of the one-party regime of Dr. Kwame Nkrumah on February 24, 1966 opened up a long search for the most viable ways of achieving election authority credibility. To overcome the lack of independence of the EC, Justice Akufo-Addo's Constitutional Commission of 1968 recommended the establishment of an independent sole electoral commissioner with legal autonomy to manage the electoral process. Until 1992, the most preferred model of sole electoral commissioner had been experimented with.

Toward the end of the 1980s, disillusioned civil society groups and individuals emerged on the political arena to challenge the military establishment to implement the NCD's report. Though small and weak in their number and strength when they appeared, they gradually became a formidable force that the regime could not contain. On May 10, 1991, the regime grudgingly announced the time table for the return of the country to constitutional rule. Interestingly, the political systems that evolved (the executive, presidential, and multiparty system, etc.) were based on the elite's consensus. Even certain elements in the ruling class had a firm belief in it, despite Rawlings's earlier expression of disbelief in its workability. Events since 1992 appear to confirm the assertion— something most respondents in elite interviews overwhelmingly admitted—that multiparty politics and elections rather than military coups are regarded by the elite as the only legitimate route to ascending to political power (CDD, 2000). Thus, both competition for political power, and recruitment into state positions have manifested the elite consensus that the impressive holding of relatively free and fair elections is progressively attracting universal acceptance.

The fear that the executive could influence the electoral body has virtually waned. Whereas most interviewees recognize that executive manipulation of the Interim National Electoral Commission (INEC) and political controls over the Consultative Assembly (CA) undermined the attainment of credible elections, the EC has proven to be different from its predecessor. Thus notwithstanding the pervasive powers of the executive in national affairs, elite interviewees believe that the EC is free from political control and influence. On several instances, it demonstrated that it could not be influenced by either the executive or its apparatus. For instance, it refused to honor a meeting called by the Bureau of National Investigation (BNI) on grounds that the electoral security task force's meetings could only be held at the police headquarters. Similarly, neither pressure from financial donors nor civil society could sway the EC from carrying out its legitimate functions.

The EC has shown that social forces seeking to engage in the electoral process could only do so under its authority. To this end, civil society and other groups observing elections were recognized only after the EC granted accreditation to them. Only a minority thinks that the executive influence is high and could be used to undermine the EC. To them, the wanton media attacks on the EC and behavior of party activists/agents during elections can dent the EC's image. Furthermore, it is believed that the chosen political system is suitable for holding credible elections at all times.

RESEARCH METHODOLOGY

The research method focuses on the procedures or methods employed to undertake the study. It involves the sources of data, population studied, sample size, and sampling techniques, as well as the research instrument, administration of the research instrument, and data analysis.

DATA SOURCES

Two types of data were collected for the study. These comprise primary and secondary data. The primary data are those data collected by the researcher in the pursuit of the study. For this study, data were collected from respondents using a questionnaire that contained both open-ended and closed questions. Secondary data are the type of data used for some purpose other than that for which they were originally collected. The compilation of literature review was the source of the secondary source of information. These data included items from newspapers, the Internet, books, articles and journals.

POPULATION, SAMPLING PLAN, AND SAMPLE SIZE

According to Cochran (1977), if the population of interest is unknown, the following formula is appropriate in choosing the sample size.

$$n' = \frac{t^2 P (1 - P)}{e^2}$$

Where, n' = sample size with finite population
t = the number relating to the degree of confidence anticipated in the result; in this case a 95% confidence interval (t=1.96 which is the abscissa of the normal curve).
P = Expected proportion (in proportion of one), 84.615%, and
e = Precision (in proportion of one) is 0.05

Therefore:

$$n' = \frac{(1.96)^2 \times 0.84615 (1 - 0.84615)}{(0.05)^2}$$

$$n' = 200$$

Hence, the sample size is 200.

A multi-stage sampling method was used to select the sample. Since there are a lot of categories of respondents to be studied, a disproportionate sampling method was used to select 40 ICT personnel, 10 electoral commission officials, 30 major political party representatives, and 120 ordinary voters. A purposive sampling method was also used to select the sample. This was done by finding out whether the person is an experienced ICT person, electoral commission official, or an experienced voter.

DATA COLLECTION METHOD

Personal Interview
This refers to the direct interface with respondents through semi-structured or unstructured questions with the view of soliciting the respondents' personal opinions and views on the subject matter.

Administered Questionnaire
This refers to structured questions designed to solicit the respondents' views on the issue under study. The questionnaire was the major instrument used to collect the data. The questionnaire was used in order to get a standard form of answers. The number of questionnaires that the researcher sent out was much larger than the sample size chosen because provision was made for spoiled questionnaires, as well as those questionnaires rendered unusable for analysis. The departments and homes of the respondents were visited in order to distribute the questionnaires. The questionnaires were collected on the same day as and when the interview was going on. The answered questionnaires were cross checked to see whether they were filled out and answered properly.

VALIDITY AND RELIABILITY

All assessments of validity are subjective opinions based on the judgment of the researcher. The researcher validated this to come to the opinion that the survey is measuring what it was designed to measure. An instrument was developed and each question was scrutinized and modified until the researcher was satisfied that it was an accurate measure of the desired construct, and that there is adequate coverage of each area to be investigated. Face-to-face validity was used in instances where there was a likelihood that a question would be misunderstood or misinterpreted. There was a pretesting of the survey to increase the likelihood of face validity. To establish the face-to-face validity, a questionnaire was sent to a sample of about five potential respondents and their responses were evaluated.

To ensure the reliability that it was measurement that yielded consistent results over time, the questionnaire was carefully measured in order to ensure that it was not prone to random error so as to be lacking in its reliability.

In order to test reliability, a measure of internal consistency was used. An instrument, which included a series of questions, was designed to examine the same construct. The questions were arbitrarily split into two groups, which is the "split-half" reliability.

DATA ANALYSIS

Data analysis involved compiling, selecting, and entering data into computer files, inspecting it for errors, and running tabulations and various statistical tests in order to derive proper findings for this study. The Statistical Product for Service Solutions (SPSS) and Microsoft Excel software were used to analyze data obtained from the survey.

RESULTS AND DISCUSSIONS

This study sought to examine the impact of Information Communication Technology (ICT) on electoral processes in Ghana. Data analysis consisted of the various ways through which data collected from respondents and other sources was structural in a meaningful way to make it easy to understand. This involved testing of reliability of the survey items, coding, editing and statistical analysis of responses gathered from the field. To answer the research questions of the study, three hypotheses were tested. These were: (1) the relationship between ICT and reliability, timeliness, trust, and acceptability; (2) reduction in electoral riots; and (3) reduction in electoral flaws (such as duplicate registration or voting, alien voting, minor/underage voting, recording errors, collation errors, and transfer errors). The statistical tools employed in the analysis of the gathered data include Spearman's rank correlation coefficient and weighted rank mean. Presentation of the results from the analyses, together with discussions of the findings relating to the literature reviewed, have been presented in this chapter.

DEMOGRAPHIC INFORMATION OF THE RESPONDENTS

A structured survey questionnaire was employed to collect the data from the respondents sampled. Two hundred survey questionnaires were self-administered by the researcher. Due to non-response errors, 166 or 83 percent of the 200 survey questionnaires were retrieved and were found to be appropriate for the final analysis. The 166 respondents studied were comprised of 57.8 percent males and 42.2 percent females. Furthermore, the majority (57.8 percent) of the respondents were 40 years and above with the rest (42.2 percent) being between 30 to 35 years, as this study needed information from mature and well-experienced personalities.

To add to the above, a majority (52.4 percent) of the respondents hold bachelor's degrees (or HND) while 18.7 percent were master's degree holders.

This signifies that all of the respondents studied were well educated and understand the content of the questionnaire and the objectives of the study. This background of the respondents helped in securing balanced information from all angles.

Table 2.1: Description of categorical variables

Variable	Number of respondents	Percentage (%)
Gender Distribution		
Male	96	57.8
Female	70	42.2
Total	166	100.0
Age Distribution		
Between 30-35 yrs	70	42.2
40 yrs and above	96	57.8
Total	166	100.0
Highest level of academic achievement		
S.H.S/A/O-Level	31	18.7
Diploma	17	10.2
Degree/HND	87	52.4
Masters	31	18.7
Total	166	100.0

Source: Field Data, 2015

THE IMPACT OF INFORMATION TECHNOLOGY ON IMPROVING THE EFFECTIVENESS AND EFFICIENCY OF ELECTORAL PROCESSES IN GHANA.

Analysis and interpretation revolve around the impact of information technology on improving the effectiveness and efficiency of electoral processes in Ghana. The major variables considered in determining the efficiency and effectiveness of ITC on electoral processes were its reliability, timeliness, trust, acceptability, reduction in electoral riots, and reduction in electoral flaws (such as duplicate registration or voting, alien voting, minor/under age voting, recording errors, collation errors and transfer errors). The entire discussion on these very aspects is as follows:

Table 2.2: Assessment of the Impact of ICT on Electoral Processes

Areas	E (5)	VG (4)	G (3)	A (2)	P (1)	Total	Rank	Description
Reliability	138	23	2	3	0	166	4.78	Excellent
Timeliness/Speed	11	155	0	0	0	166	4.07	Very Good
Transfer of information	72	28	66	0	0	166	4.04	Very Good
Chronological updates of data	69	32	65	0	0	166	4.02	Very Good
Trust	42	72	52	0	0	166	3.94	Very Good
Acceptability of results	12	45	109	0	0	166	3.42	Good
Reduction in electoral riots	43	44	79	0	0	166	3.78	Very Good
reduction in electoral flaws (such as duplicate registration or voting, alien voting, minor/under age voting, recording errors, collation errors and transfer errors)	42	47	77	0	0	166	3.79	Very Good

Note: P=Poor, A=Average, G=Good, VG=Very Good and E=Excellent
Source: Survey Data (2015)

Table 2.2 assesses information technology's efficiency and effectiveness on electoral processes in Ghana. It appears from the study that information technology is the best solution to electoral processes in Ghana. This is because the study shows a positive relationship beween ITC and electoral reliability, timeliness, trust, acceptability, reduction in electoral riots, and reduction in electoral flaws (such as duplicate registration or voting, alien voting, minor/under age voting, recording errors, collation errors and transfer errors).

Meanwhile, currently the use of ICT in the electoral process of Ghana is limited to the registration of voters and voting procedures, though there are other equal key areas of the electoral process, such as results collation and results transmitting, where ICT can be used to ensure more free and fair elections. Even the use of ICT in the compilation of voters registered has encountered a lot of challenges, among which include limited equipment, multiple registration, and incomplete data by applicants. In this current situation, ICT use is limited to registration of voters, and voting procedures leave gaps for promoting distrust of the electoral results.

It is, therefore, against this background that ICT is being proposed for all key areas, including results collation and results transmission, of the electoral process to help enhance and strengthen the system to produce results acceptable by stakeholders. Through ICT, the system can uncover vulnerabilities such as counting of votes, collation of votes, and transmitting of results to the headquarters. This will avert incidents similar to the 2012 elections dispute, which had the potential to drag the whole country into a conflict, and significantly disrupted macroeconomic activities, creating hardships for the Ghanaian citizens.

For example, in the disrupted 2012 election, one key area that was found wanting was results transmission, where there was even an allegation against the incumbent party of having engaged the services of an "Israeli company" to collate the results outside the premises of the Electoral Commission headquarters via wireless transmission. This may also serve as an example worthy of emulation by other regions of Africa, and might prevent the national economic disasters that often plague the African continent.

ICT is a tool, not a magical solution, and like any tool, it can be misused. It therefore requires training and experience to be used properly (Mathieson, 2004). Mathieson (2004) further noted that the use of technology in elections depends on the proper design of the systems, including all the non-ICT procedures and activities. It requires steady, long-term management to make it work efficiently and cost effectively.

Dispute resolution arising from declared election results is an essential part of the election process. Most (47 percent) interviewees think that complaints are formalized per the election law. It requires an aggrieved person to notify the chairperson of the EC in writing, outlining the basis of the challenge. A majority (67 percent) of interviewees think that the EC has taken steps to address petty election disputes, and indeed, has handled minor cases through IPAC and its Registration Review Committees (RRCs).

Post-election disputes are handled by the law courts. Although the burden of proof lies on the complainant, who seeks relief from the court, the EC is the ultimate body to provide evidence to the court regarding the election case in dispute. It is fair to say that the EC has been proactive in electoral dispute matters.

There is an extremely high public trust of the EC. In all the four general elections, the EC demonstrated sufficient impartiality in handling the electoral process. It is a credible election authority that can be depended upon for all future elections. It has shown tenacity in the management of the electoral process. When the 1992 election cleaved society, the EC undertook measures that had far-reaching consequences on the subsequent credibility of the elections. EC's strategic initiatives reassured the public and engendered their confidence in the electoral process. When the EC's decision to open a fresh registration of voters in March 1995 proved contentious because the opposition distrusted the process, it overcame the suspicion of partiality and partisanship by rendering the registration process transparent. Thus, from 1995 on, a very large proportion of the citizens who possessed the electoral qualification actually registered with the EC. Undoubtedly, the high voter response to all voter registration exercises could be attributed to the growing confidence voters had in the EC and its ability to conduct free and fair elections.

CONCLUSION

The study examined the impact of Information Communication Technology (ICT) on the electoral processes in Ghana. The major variables considered in determining the efficiency and effectiveness of ITC on electoral processes were its reliability, timeliness, trust, acceptability, reduction in electoral riots, and reduction in electoral flaws (such as duplicate registration or voting, alien voting, minor/under age voting, recording errors, collation errors and transfer errors).

Though the use of ICT in the electoral process of Ghana is limited to the registration of voters and voting procedures, it appears from the study that information technology is the best solution to electoral processes in Ghana. However, there are equally other key areas of the electoral process, such as results collation and results transmitting, where ICT can be used to ensure a more free and fair elections.

RECOMMENDATIONS

In a fast-growing world, managing elections has become a complex enterprise requiring the use of the most sophisticated equipment to overcome challenges and unforeseen contingencies. This implies an initiative that integrates the EC into the technological system. To overcome electoral challenges such as unreliability, late delivery, mistrust, unacceptability, electoral riots, and electoral flaws, the following measures should be implemented:

- Procuring modern equipment with installed technological facilities would enhance EC's work in the area of voter registration, ballot printing, and election results transmission.
- The EC's staff, beyond the headquarters, must undergo technological training to acquire skills not only in ICT, but also in other specialized fields that enhance their competency in the application of new scientific ideas in election management.
- Efficient electoral management is capital intensive. Lack or delay in releasing resources can compromise the integrity of the election and democratic process. To overcome perennial inadequate financial resources for elections, stakeholders may agree, by consensus, to set up an election fund.

REFERENCES

Basedau, M., Erdmann, G. & Mehler, A. (2007). *Votes, Money and Violence: Political Parties and Elections in Sub-Saharan Africa.* Uppsala Scottsville, South Africa: Nordiska Afrikainstitutet; University of KwaZulu-Natal Press.

Bekoe, D. A. (2012). *Voting in Fear: Electoral Violence in Sub-Saharan Africa.* Washington, D.C.: United States Institute of Peace.

Collier, P. (2009). *Wars, Guns, and Votes: Democracy in Dangerous Places* (1. ed.). New York: Harper.

Daily Graphic (2013). Report on IEA workshop on review of Ghana, Daily Graphic, Accra, Ghana

_____ (2013). Saturday 31st August 2013 edition of the Daily Graphic, The Daily Graphic, Accra, Ghana

Danquah Institute (2014). Press release on limited voter register exercise, 29 may 2014 electoral system, Danquah Institute, Accra, Ghana.

Ghana Supreme Court (2013). Akufo-Addo V. Mahama and others, Accra, Supreme Court Judgment on the Presidential Election Petition.

Gillies, D. (2011). *Elections in Dangerous Places: Democracy and the Paradoxes of Peacebuilding.* Montreal: McGill-Queen's University Press for the North-South Institute.

Global Commission on Elections (2012). Report on elections, democracy and security, Global Commission on Elections, p. 5

Höglund, K. (2009). Electoral violence in conflict-ridden societies: concepts, causes, and consequences, *Terrorism and Political Violence* 21(3), 412–427.

IEA (2013). Report of the IEA-GPPP workshop on electoral reforms, The Institute of Economic Affairs (IEA), Osu, Accra, Ghana, p.8

_____ (2014). Strengthening Ghana's electoral system: a precondition for stability and development. The Institute of Economic Affairs (IEA), Osu, Accra, Ghana

Lindberg, S. I. (2009). *Democratization by Elections: A New Mode of Transition.* Baltimore: Johns Hopkins University Press.

Oquaye, M. (1993). The stolen verdict: the Ghanaian elections of 1992. The New Patriotic Party, Accra, Ghana

_____ (2004). Dissenting view, African affairs, London: *Politics in Ghana,* 1982 1992, Delhi, Thompon Press.

CHAPTER 3
E-Voting: A New Model of Democracy in Ghana

Kristie Roberts-Lewis — Troy University
Stashia Bryant Emanuel — Tennessee State University
Orok Michael — Virginia Union University

INTRODUCTION

Across the globe, social accountability has been introduced and executed as a means of ensuring transparency among a variety of organizations, officials, resources, and government. Through the means of social accountability, individuals have become empowered with knowledge as it relates to the dissemination of information to the public. According to Ackerman (2004), the accountability process is both horizontal and vertical, which translates to checks and balances that are particularly vital in relation to international politics and government, as many infrastructures are emerging and developing to empower local and surrounding communities.

Accountability is affected where there are weak checks and balances, a lack of separation of power, and the absence of rule of law (King, Owusu & Braimah, 2013). On the contrary, social accountability strategies and tools help empower ordinary citizens to exercise their inherent rights and hold governments accountable for how they exercise authority (Malena & McNeil, 2010). The concept of good governance as a necessary condition for viable development and poverty reduction has gained widespread prevalence, especially among international organizations and industrialized world nations (World Bank, 2007).

Social accountability strategies are put into place to improve institutional performance by bolstering both citizen engagement and the public's responsiveness of states. Insofar as social accountability builds citizen power concerning the state, it is a political process—yet it is distinct from political accountability, which focuses specifically on elected officials and where citizen voice is often delegated to representatives between elections (Fox, 2014). This distinction makes social accountability an especially relevant approach for societies in which representative government is weak, unresponsive, or nonexistent (Prze-worski, Stokes & Manin, 1999). Social accountability offers a way for players inside and outside the government to work together for better governance, ensuring that communities get the results they need and deserve. The act of social accountability is not about civil society to work against civil servants, but about ensuring that information from the citizens' perspective is put in the hands of the officials in charge to make their work easier and more effective. The thought of social accountability is an evolving undertaking that involves many facets. These facets of feedback, effective service delivery, transparency, regulation, and access ultimately build trust and offer valuable responses. Murphy (2005) and Synder and Shown (2012) determined that appropriate social ethics should involve high moral standards, consistent organizational goals, and strategic decisions.

On the continent of Africa, the country of Ghana has experienced a considerable amount of success as it relates to social accountability. Ghana has been widely quoted as an example of successful adjustments in Africa (Hutchful, 2002), yet there is still an overriding problem of access to information. Ghana is a low-income, developing country in sub-Saharan Africa. The country context there has exhibited discrepancies of policy decision making related to strong political power. The country itself has seen great advancement in the areas of healthcare, corporate partnerships, and global marketing, but unfortunately the area that still lacks the commitment, trust, and social responsibility from the powers that be is the electronic electoral voting process. Abela and Murphy (2008), and Kotler (2004) have all agreed that, in the wake of globalization, there is still a need for social accountability and honest interactions in order to achieve social good. The concept itself has engaged and propelled Ghana into the 21st century, allowing the country to interact and exchange in global dialogue. However, the actual process leaves much to be desired. When participants, specifically the ones that are supposed to benefit from the voting process, do not trust or have confidence in the process, and the inadequacies continue to persist, some type of measurement must be put in place to assure the people that not only is the process being reviewed, but accountable measures are created to ensure that trust is regained, accurate results are being achieved, and proper governance is to be executed. Ethical commitment and social responsibility are important business practices that should be adequately demonstrated to all (Okoro, 2012).

Ghana introduced decentralization in 1988 with the definitive purpose of accompanying participatory governance and improving service delivery and financial management to assist in the achievement of rapid socioeconomic growth (Ohene-Konadu, 2001). The World Bank (2003) has maintained that Ghana's decentralization program was not fully implemented. For decentralization to reduce poverty, generate growth, and ensure accountability, there must be the full transfer of power, competences, and resources to the Metropolitan, Municipal and District Assemblies (MMDAs) (King, Owusu & Braimah, 2013). However, securing accountability at the local level is perhaps the most disturbing problem within democratic local governments in developing countries such as Ghana, where institutions are about evolving, and the rate of illiteracy, ignorance, and poverty are extremely high, while access to information and legal means are practically nonexistent (Agyeman-Duah, 2008). Local government and decentralization in Ghana is the subject of much scholarly discourse as the subject of local government accountability remains underexplored (Deborah, 2009). When accountability fails and the state breaks its contract with the citizens, many things can go wrong, such as public services being poorly delivered or not delivered at all (Deborah, 2009).

PROBLEM

Despite Ghana's prominence as the icon of democratic governance in Africa, the country faces enormous challenges with ensuring a fair and free electoral process. Accountability and social responsibility are akin to Ghana's success in developing and sustaining valid electoral procedures; however, allegations from political parties over electoral fraud and malpractice abound. From a global context, many growing democracies utilize new technologies, infusing information and communication technology (ICT) into the electoral process. One such use of technology was introduced in Ghana's 2012 Presidential and Parliament elections, which included a high-tech voter registration process utilizing biometric technology designed to centralize voter registration information through verification of voter eligibility and authentication. Despite the high expectations of its success among Ghana's Electoral Commission, several challenges relative to the efficient management of elections were identified. These challenges included: the late arrival of election materials and personnel at some polling stations, inadequate communication devices for security forces, poor transportation networks, inaccessibility of remote constituencies (Aubyn & Abdallah, 2013), difficulty in identifying minors and non-Ghanaians, and the inability to reconcile the 23,000 polling stations in the region in sharing registration information.

The aforementioned challenges were exacerbated by the malfunctioning of the Biometric Voter Registration (BVR) and the Verification System (VS), creating a firestorm of contention and confusion among various election stakeholders. One area of concern was confusion among the populace, the Ghanaian Electoral Commission, and party stakeholders, who were not prepared for the system failures or the lack of personnel to provide assistance in addressing issues on election day. Secondly, there was also concern and confusion among political parties when election officials extended the voting period by one day due to the aforementioned access challenges. Scholars and practitioners alike agree that when new and emerging technology is introduced, it should be accompanied by a trained and prepared cadre of professionals to oversee implementation, engage in service delivery, aid in education training, and the building of networks and relationships with stakeholders. In the absence of the aforementioned practices, voters become disenfranchised with the election process, and distrustful of election outcomes and the introduction of new and emerging technology.

The introduction of information and communications technologies (ICT) into the electoral process is generating both interest and concern among voters, as well as practitioners across the globe. Yeboah (2013), in a research study, highlighted the receptivity among Ghanaians toward electronic voting, who believed that "the adoption and diffusion of electronic voting will be of a greater help to the country Ghana and perhaps help reduce electronic rigging as well" (p. 9). Moreover, respondents note that adopting electronic voting as opposed to traditional voting practices will enhance free and fair elections. This research will explore the expanded use of technology in Ghana by designing a four-prong model for implementation of technology into Ghana's electoral processes, and accountability of the electronic process and training regimen that is needed to ensure that the decentralization that took effect in 1988 is delivered with the definitive purpose of participatory governance prior to the 2016 election.

THEORETICAL FRAMEWORK

Structural functionalism is the earliest sociological paradigm based on the scientific advances of Herbert Spencer (1820-1903). This framework views society as a complex system whose parts work together to promote solidarity and stability. This approach also looks at both social structure and social function. Functionalism addresses society as a whole in terms of the function of its constituent elements; namely norms, customs, traditions, and institutions. This particular theoretical framework is being utilized as a result of the current state of the Ghanaian elections and how the many integral pieces make or create an entire system that governs the people of the country.

The voting process, which is the whole, relies on several parts in order to increase effectiveness and a representative process. In the Ghanaian electronic voting process, there are many fragmented pieces that prohibit the whole from functioning optimally. For example, the authentication system in the polling process has posed irregularities that include bloated voter registry, ballot-box theft and stuffing, voter impersonation, multiple voting, violence, and intimidation. To be more specific, demographic manipulation appears to be a common occurrence, coupled with political patronage and corruption, creating a fragmented electoral process with growing distrust of its effectiveness among the citizenry. Moreover, the results of elections are nearly fixed, favoring one party and disfavoring the others (PICAM, Electoral Reform in Cameroon, 2006).

Concomitantly, there is disenfranchisement among Ghanaians who have misgivings about the electoral process and those who are responsible for designing the system. The aforementioned decreases voter turnout and increases the likelihood of parody (Zimbabwe Election Watch, 2008). The impact of decreased voter turnout is false counting as a typical and voluntary malpractice by some leaders to rig elections and retain power (Dagne, 2009). These confluences of the myriad and diverse problems with the electoral process thwart the development of an efficient and effective voting system, or the introduction of new and emerging technologies to improve the systems. Hence, in many instances a two-tiered system is implemented with some introduction of technology and the use of traditional paper ballots.

Despite the real/perceived benefits of these processes, there are challenges with implementation and execution. For example, in some areas where paper ballots are utilized, there are flaws in the system that affect determination of the appropriate protocol for distribution of ballots and proper collection, which have delayed counting processes, leaving many to question whether their vote really counted.

In a country where there is growing distrust of the electoral process, disenfranchisement abounds amidst speculation of the validity of the outcomes (International Crisis Group, 2007). The electoral process as a whole is lethargic and encumbered, but could be strengthened with the introduction of a coordinated, unified system that is grounded in accountability, validity, and social responsibility (Jinadu, 2007). The implementation of ICTs and other forms of technology, such as electronic voting, can seek to address many of the shortcomings of the current structure. If democracy in Ghana is to succeed, it requires solutions to the basic instruments of the rigging that undermines it (Otchere-Darko, 2010).

The social structure of the electoral voting process is stressed and placed at the center of analysis, and the social functions are deduced from these structures. The voting process is a mutually interrelated system that takes the parts, and focuses on how these interrelated parts fulfill the requisites of the systemic whole. Abela and Murphy (2008) noted that there is a positive correlation between growth and ethical responsibility. In the case of the voting process in Ghana, it is possible to see a rapid growth in voter turnout if the process is perceived as politically impartial, legitimate, and efficacious. Central to structural functionalism is the inherent ability to assess the entire system through feedback and redesign. As one part of the system changes, other parts have to readjust to accommodate the proposed changes that have taken place to ensure a cohesive, unified, and integrated system of effectiveness. The Ghanaian electronic voting process, although fragmented and disintegrated, can benefit from structural functionalism and its tenets that require a clear understanding of the social, cultural, and political pieces that must be considered and carefully balanced in the development of a system that will be respected and received by both citizens and the administrative officials.

LITERATURE REVIEW

Elections in Ghana predated its independence and cannot be discussed without mentioning Kwame Nkrumah, a pan-Africanist who led Ghana's independent movement. In 1949, it was Kwame Nkrumah who set up the first political party, called the Convention People's Party (CPP), to campaign for independence. The Commonwealth of Nations reported that under Nkrumah, elections in Ghana "took place in 1951, and the following year Nkrumah became the country's first

Premier. The 1954 constitution provided for a legislative assembly of 104 direct-ly elected members, and an all-African Cabinet; the UK kept responsibility for foreign affairs and defense. The CPP campaigned for full independence. The general election of 1956 returned the CPP with a big majority." (See more at: http://thecommonwealth.org/our-member-countries/ghana/history#sthash.rtHTF S5e.dpuf)

Therefore, Ghana's representative democracy began as early as the 1950s, during the period of its struggle to transition from a colonial state under British hegemonic rule to an independent nation state. Even under a British crafted and influenced constitution, there was political will among the populace, as such between 1954 and 1957, when approximately eight political parties were in-volved in the process of self-determination. The formation of political parties did not cease even after the first military coup and the installation of dictatorial government. Between 1969 and 1972, about 12 political parties were formed to free Ghana from military rule. In fact, after Ghana freed itself from military go-vernance, there were about 11 political parties, subsequently reducing to about six prior to the military control of 1981-1992 (Ninsin, 2006). Therefore, while most countries on the African continent were still entangled in the geopolitical structure designed by the British colony, Ghana was at the forefront, plotting its separation from Britain and the relative asymmetric relationship. As a conse-quence of its earlier struggles for self-determination, it emerged successfully on the 6th day of March 1957, as the first African country with political indepen-dence, thus emancipating its geopolitical structure from the British political dogma. Even then, governance was still a British imposition. The citizens of Ghana could not still engage in the practice of representative government, where the power resided in the hands of elected citizens based upon the rule of law. Subsequently, Ghana achieved that political milestone on July 1, 1960 when it became a republic. Therefore, the process of representative government was defined in the 1960 presidential elections when Dr. Kwame Nkrumah, a pan-Africanist, won the presidential election.

Nkrumah's election became a pivotal point in Ghana's political transition from a colonial state to a republic, but still with vestiges of post-colonialism. As the country engaged in comprehensive restructuring in preparation for a well-defined constitutional rule, a substantive instrument of governance was absent. But in 1992, about 35 years after independence, the 1992 constitution was pub-lished. It provided "the basic charter for the countries fourth republic govern-ment since independence in 1957. That constitution declared Ghana to be a uni-tary republic with sovereignty residing in the Ghanaian people" (CIA, 1994).

Despite that significant accomplishment, many political pundits continued to raise the question regarding the political legitimacy and sanctity of elections and governance in Ghana before 1992. There was persistent argument that those early elections were unfair and facilitated through sectoral control. Therefore, there was the claim that the post-independence political and governance process in Ghana was very complex and challenging. The Nkrumah era witnessed a one-party presidential approach that was controversial and inundated with missteps as the new republic struggled to define itself. This "first republic experiment," as some called it, collapsed as a result of military takeover in 1966. So, dictatorial military governance dominated Ghana's politics until 1969, when a second attempt was made to reinstitute representative government with two key political parties. This too collapsed in 1972 through military overthrow. Between 1972 and 1979 there were several occurrences of successive military governance, and in 1979, the Third Republic was ushered in with the introduction of a three-party system. At this juncture, Ghana's attempt to stabilize its representative government structure took on a more dynamic posture with several intermittent governance efforts consisting of military rule and brief periods of electoral political party structure.

As with many post-independence African States, military governance became the governance approach of choice in Ghana. Elections through representative government were few and far between until 1992, when a two-party system was introduced and Jerry Rawlings of the National Democratic Congress (NDC) was democratically elected as president under a two-party system over the ruling Provisional National Defense Council (PNDC) (CIA, 2004). The transition from the PNDC to the NDC was contentious at best. Many Ghanaians, still unsure about democratic governance given their experiences with military "takeover," believed that the transition could lead to an outbreak of violence.

Many political analysts contend that the evolution of democratic transition and the election processes in Ghana between 1988 and the dawning of the Fourth Republic in 1993 should be understood through the juxtapositioning of the uncertainty and intense mutual hostility and distrust among political rivals (Richard & Claire, 1993). Regardless of how one views Ghana's election processes, whether at the presidential or local levels, the 1992 Constitution of Ghana transformed the political environment and provided the impetus for civic engagement where the citizens could influence government policies. After all, as Owono (2012) put it, "of the 43 countries (in Africa) that have engaged in a process of democratic liberalization since the early 1990s only a tiny handful, one of which was Ghana, adopted constitutions anointed by a direct referendum of the people" (p. 3).

The claim that Ghana has positioned itself as a democratic model for most of Sub-Saharan Africa cannot be contested if comprehensive and properly documented evidence is presented within an appropriate political context. After all, Ghana emerged from colonial domination with consistent political will for democratic rule and representative governance (Owono, 2012: 2). But while Ghana has engaged in representative democracy through the election processes, the perplexing concern is that there is a structural, functional cloud that encircles the election effort and the historical development of that process. Some have questioned the effectiveness of the process, especially voting practices, while others believe that the effectiveness of the process was compromised by the same corrupt and fraudulent practices noticeable in other African countries. Others argue that granting the people the opportunity to select their leaders says nothing about the efficacy of that selection or the behavior of those who participate in the selection process. This appears to account for why the 1948 Universal Declaration of Human Rights placed emphasis on elections and the utilization of a selection system that is fair and free from bias (Salomonsen, 2005). Given this postulation, it must be information that discerns how Ghanaians select their leaders.

The literature on elections in Ghana explicitly delineates the election process. First, it occurs every four years in order to elect the president and members of parliament. The electoral procedure consists of multiple processes, including voter registration, voter register exhibition, voting, vote counting, collection, and publication of the results. These manual processes were used in Ghana pre- and post-independence, prior to the introduction of the Biometric Electronic System used in the 2012 elections (see Fig. 3.1 for manual voting process) (Otori-Dwum Fuo & Paatey, 2011).

ELECTRONIC VS. MANUAL VOTING

Res. J. Inform. Technol.. 3(2): 91-98. 2011

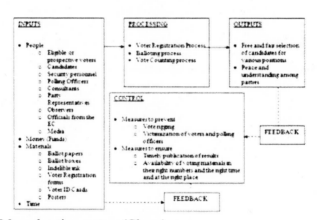

Figure 3.1 Manual voting system (Ghana)
Extracted from Research Journal of Information Technology (3)2:93

Many have argued that the manual voting system has many associated problems. These problems are not endemic to the Ghanaian system only—they are universally applicable to states where the manual voting system is still utilized. There have been problems of fraud, invalid votes, and long lines at polling stations, delays in publishing results, and in some cases violence and even death due to trampling. Given this experience, many countries have concluded that electronic voting could provide the security and procedural exigencies for fair and sustainable voting systems, which might engender an effective election process. Proponents of the electronic voting system argue that the system "ensures proper management of personal data of voters, reduces election costs, prevents double voting, ensures quick, effective and efficient processing of votes cast during elections and speeds up the release of election results" (Ofori-Dwumfio & Paatey, 2011:95). In fact, within the African context, leaders there were asked in 2012 to avoid manual voting systems and to adopt the Biometric Voter Registration System in preparation for general elections (Hassan, 2012), Additionally, in support of the electronic voting environment, and in opposition to the manual system, in 2008, the Chairman of the Supreme Council of Kenya Muslim (SUPKEM) declared that the previous (manual) system was archaic and full of flaws, and the cumbersome procedures drew numerous petitions from election losers. In fact, that same year, the National Muslim Advisory Council in Kenya, in an article published in *the Daily Nation,* 2012:2, Sheikh Ngao declared that "Ghana was a role model because of open democracy resulting from the rise of the Biometric Voting System in elections."

In contrast with the manual system of voting, there is overwhelming evidence in the literature in support of electronic voting. Ghana, therefore, appears to be the pioneer of a new approach to successful elections in Sub-Saharan Africa. While this is the case, there is a cacophony of voices decrying the problematic aspects of its utility in Ghana given other geopolitical and socio-dynamic considerations. While the supporters of the electronic (biometric) voting in Africa remain vocal, Christine Mungai (2015) sees things differently. In an article that she published in *Mail Guardian,* entitled "Dirty Hands: Why biometric voting fails in Africa — and it doesn't matter in the end," she pointed out that during the 2014 election in Nigeria, the biometric system used in that election was "marred by technical problems with electronic fingerprinting readers that were intended to verify voters' identities before being allowed to cast votes" (p. 1). Of course, as support for the biometric system continued to mount in Nigeria, the Nigerian Independent National Electoral Commission (INEC) downplayed the problem by reporting that only 25 percent of the readers had malfunctioned. In fact, she continued to report that the failure of electronic voting systems in Africa were widespread. At least 25 African countries including Ghana, Sierra Leone, Zambia, Malawi, Rwanda, Democratic Republic of the Congo, and Cote d'Ivoire, have tried the electronic system with very minimal success. Guardian (2015) contended that in December 2012 the biometric kits failed in many parts of Ghana, causing the election to be extended. In 2010, even Somalia abandoned their local election results due to inconsistencies in vote counts that were generated from the biometric voting process (Mungai, 2, 7). In his on-the-air report for Cable News Network (CNN), Jonathan Bhalla (2012) asked the question: *Can technology revolutionize African Elections?* His answer leaned toward "no" and at best "maybe." He indicated that "elections (in Africa) are portrayed as democracy at an embryonic stage ... the greatest limitation of biometric voter registration is that it only counters the symptoms not the causes of electoral fraud" (p. 3).

It is along this same line of argument that others posit that technology is only as good as the way it is deployed. Soiled data, when input into the system, will generate unreliable results. Bhalla (2012: 3, 4) further contends that "expectations about technology's role in elections must be realistic." Biometric voter registration is not a "'silver bullet" for eliminating fraud and electoral malfeasance. Where institutions are weak and perpetrators of electoral crimes are not prosecuted, politicians can find ways to achieve undemocratic ends. It is apparent that many are not convinced that biometric voting is a solution for the diverse problematic issues of elections in Africa. And Ghana is not isolated from the contrite problems. From the dearth of literature on biometric voting globally, there appears to be a general consensus that there are complexities based on the national character and the acceptance of unfamiliar approaches to elections. Bhalla (2012) suggests that in order to fully implement the electronic voting system in Africa and move toward limiting or eliminating voting irregularities and related problems, we need to look beyond the "symptoms" and seek a greater understanding of the "causes."

ANALYSIS/FINDINGS

The success experienced by Ghana with their utilization of technology in the electoral process has helped to boost support for the use of electronic voting as a tool to address challenges faced by third world countries in mitigating factors that have led to unproductive electoral processes. Electronic voting, also known as e-voting, is used to describe diverse methods of voting utilizing technology to both cast and count votes. It is a web-based application where voters can participate in the electoral process online, yet is managed by representatives of the governmental or independent electoral authorities either through the use of electronic voting machines, or remotely through the use of one's personal computer, cell phone, television, or via the Internet (please see Figure 3.2 below). The original goals of electronic voting were to ensure faster results, increased validity and accuracy in the counting process, enhance the election process with the use of innovative and emerging technology, to enhance the recruitment of poll workers, and to eliminate the effects of political patronage and spoiled votes, and arbitrary ballot interpretation.

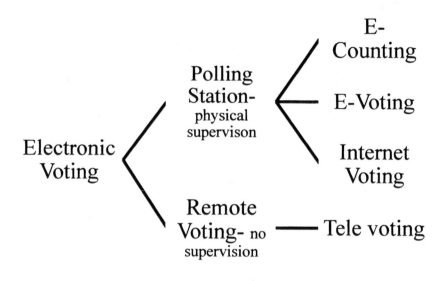

Figure 3.2. The Electronic Voting Process

Globally, many countries have experimented with various forms of electronic voting tools. Specifically, many countries have experimented with electronic voting machines (EVMs) and then later decided not to use them primarily due to their inability to implement the EVMs throughout the entire country. Currently, EVMs are being used in 20 countries, with six of these countries still piloting the technology as noted in Figure 3.2. Figure 3.3 also highlights the decline in use of EVMs in Europe and North America, while South American and Asia or steadily increasing in interest and use.

E-Voting Around the World

○ Never Used
● Piloted and Not Continued
○ Pilots Ongoing
● Currently Used in Parts of the Country
● Currently Used Nationwide
● Discontinued

Figure 3.3. The Use and Spread of Electronic Voting around the World
More Latin American countries were experimenting or using e-voting machines
in 2012. (International Foundation for Electoral Systems)
Most of Europe was not using electronic voting in 2012. (International Foundation for Electoral Systems)

In order for electronic voting to have a chance at success, it is imperative that
countries invest and acquire state-of-the-art computer systems coupled with ICT
technologies. Concomitantly, countries will need to develop processes and systems
to address issues such authentication/validation, security, robustness, performance, accuracy, and short-/long-term evaluation tools. Moreover, the short
tenure of e-voting, coupled with the cultural norms and values that govern regions where political systems are or have been associated with corrupt practices,
has caused world leaders to embark on e-voting with skepticism and trepidation
regarding what might appear to be the best practice in one part of the world, but
may not be an appropriate fit for its counterparts. As a result, scholars suggest
and highly recommend that as new systems abound, countries simultaneously
develop a diversity of evaluation tools to determine the fit and feasibility of an
e-voting system before one is deployed.

A TALE OF TWO STATES: EXAMPLES OF SUCCESSFUL MODELS OF ELECTRONIC VOTING IN EUROPE

According to Trechsel (2013) "Internet voting has gone from private military
trails to mainstream politics in two European states," referring to Estonia and
Switzerland. Both Estonia and Switzerland sought to incorporate electronic voting as not only a means to increase voter turnout, and upgrade from a modern

electoral administration to a highly technology-driven electoral process, but also to address issues of democracy and citizen engagement. Early reports note the effectiveness of the systems in both states, seen as models of success, and suggest they be replicated in other parts of Europe and around the world.

Estonia is the only country in the world that currently relies primarily on Internet voting for national elections. Electronic voting, or Internet voting, rose to popularity in Estonia in 2001 with the development of an "e-minded" coalition government under the leadership of Prime Minister Taavi Roivas. In 2005, Estonia made history when they held their first general election utilizing technology, namely the Internet. Estonian officials deemed the election a success and built on the success in the general election to utilize Internet voting in the 2007 parliamentary elections (Esteve, Goldsmith & Turner, 2012). By 2009 and as recently as 2015, Estonia continues to utilize I-voting or electronic voting in local elections, parliamentary elections, and the European parliament elections.

Estonia has a national database of all its citizens and its voters who utilize an identification card with a computer-readable microchip to cast their votes utilizing the computer (Padmanabhan, 2014). Estonia's Internet voting system is undergirded by the Estonian ID cards that are mandatory national identity documents for citizens. The voting system offers various methods to ensure voter identification, such as an ID card with PIN codes. The system requires PIN codes, a PC with Internet access, and a Smart Card reader as well as ID card software, a Digital ID (document which allows identification of a person in the electronic environment and signing with digital signature), and/or a Mobile ID. Requirements: mobile ID SIM card with PIN codes and certificates, PCs with Internet connection, mobile phone and no card reader or special software is needed (Budurushi, Neumann & Volkamer, 2012).

Estonia has built in several processes to ensure a more secure remote authentication with the use of a Smart Card and the utilization of state-supported public key infrastructure that supports a legally binding digital signature system. As a result, by 2007, in excess of 1.08 million cards were issued out of an estimated 1.32 million population (Valimiskomisjon, n.d.). Despite these efforts, nearly two-thirds of Estonia's population still chooses to visit polling stations to cast their e-ballots, even though they don't have to. Many citizens view voting as a cultural staple, a ritual of citizenship, and do not feel that it needs to be reformed.

Table 3.1 Traditional Voting Methods Vs. I-Voting "Internet Voting in Estonia" Vabariigi Valimiskomisjon, n.d. http://vvk.ee/voting-methods-in-estonia/

Traditional Voting/ Paper Voting	**I-Voting**
• A voter presents an ID document to be identified. • The voter then receives the ballot and two envelopes. • The voter fills in the ballot paper and puts it into the envelope, which has no information about the voter. • Then he encloses the envelope into an outer envelope on which the voter's information is written. • The envelope is delivered to the voter's polling location of residence. After the eligibility of the voter is determined, the outer envelope is opened and the inner (anonymous) envelope is put into the ballot box. • The system guarantees that the voter's choice shall remain secret and recording of the vote in the list of voters in the polling district of residence prevents voting more than once.	• The downloaded I-voting application encrypts the vote. • The encrypted vote can be regarded as the vote contained in the inner, anonymous envelope. • After that the voter gives a digital signature to confirm his or her choice. By digitally signing, the voter's personal data or outer envelope are added to the encrypted vote. • I-voting is possible only during the 7 days of advance polls – from the 10th day until the 4th day prior to Election Day. This is necessary in order to ensure that there would be time to eliminate double votes by the end of the Election Day. • Before the ascertaining of voting results on the evening of the Election Day, the encrypted votes and the digital signatures (i.e., the data identifying the voter) are separated. Then anonymous I-votes are opened and counted. The system opens the votes only if they are not connected to personal data.

As with any system, Estonia's electronic voting system is not without challenges. One major issue is that citizens are able to utilize Internet voting during an early voting period (typically four to six days prior to the election day) and voters have the ability to change their electronic votes an unlimited number of times. Additionally, it is possible that those who vote through the Internet can also vote in the polling stations during the early voting period, which under-mines the principle of "one person, one vote" and increases voting irregularities. However, if a voter cancels his/her electronic vote by going to the polling station to vote, it is guaranteed that only one vote is counted per voter. Estonia believed citizens should be allowed to change their minds and to cast multiple ballots to ensure that they are satisfied with their final voting decision. The state, however, instituted measures to safeguard the aforementioned from thwarting and skew-ing votes, as all polling stations are informed of the I-voters on their list of vot-ers after the end of advance polls and before the election day on Sunday. If it is found at the polling district that the voter has voted both electronically and with a paper ballot, the information is sent to the Electronic Voting Committee and the voter's I-vote is cancelled.

Switzerland, on the other hand, has a long history of citizen engagement in policy matters through elections and direct democracy instruments at the federal, cantonal, and local levels through referendums and initiatives. In addition to elections, the Swiss believe that voting methods and tools are best utilized when taking into consideration the needs and social development of citizens which are considered to be "citizen friendly," and helps to ensure high frequency of voter participation. These initiatives commence with the people's assembly and have been enhanced to include voting at the polling stations, to postal voting, and finally to Internet voting or e-voting, and a short-lived SMS voting. At the heart of the Swiss's citizen-friendly initiatives are the opportunities for at least two voting methods available in every canton: voting at the polling station and vot-ing by post. The postal voting process, adopted in the 1990s, completely libera-lized voting by introducing distant polling procedures that introduced remote voting, and is one of the main features of Swiss voting procedures (Gerlach & Gasser, 2009). Hence, the introduction of e-voting as a new process would be a logical next step to modernizing the voting process.

The story of e-voting in Switzerland began in February 1998 when the Fed-eral Council—Switzerland's executive body—adopted its "Strategy for an In-formation Society in Switzerland" and introduced an interministerial coordina-tion group labeled the "Information Society." The group implemented a plan of action that had two major priorities/projects: the "electronic desk" on the one hand, and e-voting projects on the other. The "electronic desk" was designed to promote and encourage the use of e-government in online channels for adminis-trative procedures, such as tax or military service-related procedures; the second project was aimed at the development of secure online methods for voting.

To support the aforementioned goals, ICTs were implemented in all areas of the information society (economy, democratic opinion-making, and contact with agencies, culture, education, science, and law). Switzerland's efforts to create an information society was driven by the desire to increase voter participation in general, but specifically among millennials who are more technologically savvy. Moreover, Swiss officials believed that the utilization of e-voting would en-hance civic engagement by allowing citizens to express more differentiated opi-nions on a variety of issues, policies, and services that directly affect them at every level of government multiple times a year. The vast number of elections held each year in Switzerland, and the highly structured voter registration processes that are compulsory and consistently updated, provide the most accurate information on citizens.

In 2000, the Swiss launched "vote électronique," a remote Internet voting system, in collaboration with national as well as cantonal level administrations. Three cantons developed their own remote Internet voting systems. The goal of the project was to emphasize the coordination and intergovernmental relations between the various federal levels. Since the inception of "vote électronique," in excess of 150 e-voting trials have been carried out at the federal level (Driza-Maurer, Spycher, Taglioni & Weber, n.d.). In addition, numerous trials have manifested at cantonal and communal levels. The current legal basis for e-voting in Switzerland can be found in two Federal Acts (the Federal Act on Political Rights of 17.12.1976 and the Federal Act on Political Rights of the Swiss Abroad of 19.12.1975) adopted by parliament and in two regulations. One (Ordinance on Political Rights of 24 May 1978) was adopted by the Federal Council (government) and the other (Federal Chancellery Ordinance on Electronic Voting of 15.1.2014) was issued by the Federal Chancellery (the Electoral Knowledge Network, aceproject.org/ace-en/focus/e-voting/countries).

Remote or distance voting from an uncontrolled environment (typically home) on the Internet has been tested and introduced on a limited scale and in a controlled manner since the beginning of the 2000s. It is currently being used by half of the 26 cantons that constitute the Swiss Confederation. Most of them initially offered e-voting to their citizens living abroad. In Switzerland, electronic voting has reached a place of stabilization and by 2013 it was reported that approximately 20% of the votes cast were cast electronically (Driza-Maurer, Spycher, Taglioni & Weber, n.d.).

LESSONS LEARNED FROM THESE EXAMPLES

Estonia and Switzerland have shown that it is possible to use new technology on a large scale to process election results in an efficient, effective, and expeditious manner. Moreover, both states have committed to long-term initiatives that will not only modernize and enhance current election processes, but will build bridges between the electoral process and the promotion of democratic values that will enhance citizen engagement and participation. Efforts to infuse technology in both states was driven and supported largely by their respective governmental administrators, who were supported by legislative initiatives that support the new methods while ensuring voter protection, equality in voting, and privacy and security features. Estonia, unlike Switzerland, has had greater success in expanding the electronic voting methods throughout the state, while Switzerland has only successfully implemented methods in limited places. Additionally, both have worked to ensure that processes are in compliance with the Committee of the Ministers of the Council of Europe that developed legal, operational, and technical standards for e-voting in 2004 to include at least three main goals:

- Respect for all the democratic principles, and be at least reliable and safe as the paper elections.
- The connections between the legal, operational, and technical aspects of e-voting procedures must be considered when the recommendation is applied.
- The Members States should consider a review of their legal rules following this recommendation.

Both systems have been the topic of much debate and criticism, as no system is exempt from security risks or challenges from those who wish to maintain the status quo; however, it is important to note that both systems respect the preferences of the people and have sought to create balance of e-voting processes with traditional methods that many believe are important to their cultural heritage, values, and norms. As one Estonia native notes, "Voting is an act of ritual citizenship and that is not something we want to or need to change. ... There will never be a technology which is a substitute for culture. But that does not mean we should resist technology which could transform participation."

PROPOSED MODEL FOR GHANA

As Ghana seeks to introduce technology into the electoral process beyond its current processes, the following model is being proposed. The first phase of the process will focus on training and development for Ghana's Election Commission and the introduction of e-voting.

Electronic voting encompasses several different types of voting, consisting both of electronic means of casting votes and electronic means of counting votes (Johnson, 2001). Appropriate uses of electronic voting in Ghana will include punch cards, optical-scan voting systems, and specialized voting kiosks that include self-contained, direct-recording electronic voting systems, or DREs. The voting process will also be expanded to include the transmission of ballots and votes via telephone, private computer networks, or the Internet (Johnson 2001) to ensure that citizens throughout the region have access to the electoral process. Mercouri (2002) notes the positive impact that electronic voting can have in Ghana as it will eliminate the personal voting and counting of votes, which is time consuming and subject to fraudulent activity, by utilizing a system that if implemented properly would be devoid of such issues.

Secondly, the Elections Commission will engage in implementation planning and will oversee the development of recruitment materials and training of a newly formed group of election workers. This training will utilize a variety of learning modalities to include webinars, panel experts, and case study analysis of countries where proposed processes have been effective: Congo, South Africa, and Nigeria. The Election Commission will recruit and hire election workers who will develop educational materials on the new elections process utilizing a Modified Cascade Model. The cascade model acts through training small groups of people in both voting operations, functional skills, and training techniques. These training sessions will be recorded and videos will be developed to assist in training election workers. Simultaneously, a mobile of two or more trainers visiting different geographic localities and conducting one or a number of training sessions will also be implemented to ensure that a trained professional is galvanized throughout the region.

Pre-election tests and audits should be considered during this process to assess not only the functioning of the electronic voting system, but also the access of key stakeholders to the electoral process, including the technologies in use. Findings from this assessment should be utilized in the final design of the system (Carter Center, 2007, p. 2).

Training will occur utilizing horizontal interactions (music, video clips, etc.), rather than top-down voter education efforts, in order to reach youth and other stakeholders most effectively via the Internet. Once training has occurred, individuals will then share information with citizens utilizing social media—commercials, websites, Facebook, Instagram, and Periscope—to educate the general populace. This form of training is cost-effective, easy to manage, and has a built-in evaluation component that allows trainers to assess the effectiveness of outcomes of the training and make adjustments in a timely fashion.

The third process will require a revamping of the current verification systems as the process of registering voters and producing voter lists is one of the most important and time-consuming activities. Hence, local election management bodies (EMBs) will utilize database management software, such as Microsoft Excel or Access, for storing and generating a database of registered voters. These systems will partner with educational institutions, governmental departments, the religious community, and other civic organizations to generate support and participation in the development of a voter registration database. Finally, Geographic Information Systems (GIS) will be utilized to assign voters to geographic locations, mapping out polling locations by geographic regions to alleviate issues of multiple voting opportunities. The GIS will help to create a centralized verification system that will connect the 23,000 polling stations and aid in ensuring quality and integrity of voter data.

The fourth and final phase of this strategy will require the Elections Commission to implement and utilize SMS technology, cell phones, and email to ensure that consistent communication among election workers and officials is possible prior to the election, but equally as important, on election day. Election officers and staff will disseminate policies and procedures for Election Day protocol along with FAQs, or frequently asked questions. Staff will be required to report hourly on the status of the election process, while identifying any potential issues. As issues arise, decisions will be made to address them immediately per the established protocol.

Increasing the effectiveness of the election process not only requires integrity of the election process, but is also fundamental to the integrity of the democracy itself. Ghanaian elections officials and other governmental officials will develop a joint agreement to expand the use of ICTs in the implementation of e-voting methods that will include a two-tiered system: Internet voting and remote/distance voting. This approach will enhance processes in rural areas and give the state adequate time to evaluate and propose an appropriate integration plan for areas with limited access to technology. The remote/distance voting process will include the following, as prescribed by Valimiskomisjon (n.d.):

- A voter ID document to be identified.
- The voter then will receive the ballot and two envelopes.
- The voter fills in ballot paper and puts it into the envelope, which has no information about the voter.
- Then he encloses the envelope into an outer envelope on which the voter's information is written.
- The envelope is delivered to the voter's polling location of residence. After the eligibility of the voter is determined, the outer envelope is opened and the inner (anonymous) envelope is put into the ballot box.

The system guarantees that the voter's choice shall remain secret and recording of the vote in the list of voters in the polling district of residence prevents voting more than once. Secondly, the state will need to adopt a unified voter verification system that is mandatory, but will allow for accurate tracking and verification of citizens. Thirdly, officials will need to develop training and educational services to introduce and bring awareness to the new processes. Finally, monitoring and evaluation of the overall process is essential and must be done throughout each stage of the process.

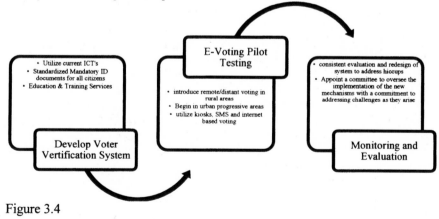

Figure 3.4

1. Ghanaian Elections Officials and the Ghanaian Administration must adopt unified voter verification system that would allow for the creation of a database to register all eligible voters.
2. All processes should embrace and consider the democratic principles and values of the various regions even if this means implementing a two-tiered system of paper and electronic voting processes
3. Consistent monitoring and evaluation must be at the heart of the new systems to address problems immediately and protect the validity of the electoral process

CONCLUSION

The acceptance and execution of the electronic voting system is based on how the modernization will be diffused, and the perceived benefits that will come from the investment of the system. Whilst Ghana takes pride in its position as successful in the voting process entering the 21st century, there are still avenues that must be effectively explored to ensure that the new process is not a quick fix, but rather an innovative beginning to a new way of handling democracy. Specific attention must be paid as it relates to the communication that is disseminated to the Ghanaian, the workers of the electronic voting process, social/cultural norms/values of Ghanaians, the political and historical context and modern-day practices, and the government as a whole. Communication is vital, as this proposed new model will be implemented to correct the wrongs of the past and propel the country's government into a new era of conducting vital business in a manner that is representative of the people it serves.

No matter how much a new system is deemed necessary, it needs support. This support ranges in various areas, but the key areas of support for this new electronic voting system are accountability, funding, and training. As this chapter has thoroughly explained, the implementation of this new voting system would create a more holistic environment for the people of Ghana, and for the betterment of the government. Mistakes are inevitable and probably will happen, but if the system is properly implemented and regulated, the mistakes will not become the norm. There are often irregularities when elections are conducted because some of the government officials may not be willing to adopt such a transparent system, but with the adoption of electronic voting, the trustworthiness of the electronic election process can be guaranteed to an extent.

Strong commitment must be given by the existing government, and willingness must be accepted. Taking responsibility and initiative for what needs to be changed, such as the IT infrastructure, is essential as this is the foundation for such an electronic system. The system has to be customized specifically for Ghana and it must meet the needs of the Ghanaian way of conducting elections. If democracy is truly to be grounded in the country of Ghana, it is important that a trustworthy election process yields results that are viewed as equitably fair by all with the outcome acknowledged even by the losing side.

REFERENCES

Abdallah, M. (2013). Ghana's 2012 Elections: Lessons Learnt Towards Sustaining Peace and Democratic Stability Mustapha Abdallah. Kofi Anna International Peace-keeping Training Centre Policy Brief 4/ 2013.

Abela, A.V. and Murphy, P.E. (2008). *Journal of Academic Marketing Journal Science*, 36:39-53.

Ackerman, J.M. (2005). Social accountability in the public sector: A conceptual discussion. *Social Development papers, 82*, 1-44.

Agyeman-Duah, B. (2008). *Ghana Governance in the Fourth Republic*. Digibooks Ghana Limited.

Amankona, E. and Paatey E. (2009) Online Voting Systems. Graduation Project, Ghana: Wisconsin International University College.

Aubyn, F. and Abdallah, M. (2013). Sustaining Peace and Stability: Appraising the Role of the National Election Security Task Force in the 2012 Elections. *Journal of African Elections*, Vol. 12, No. 2, 132-153.

Bhalla, Jonathan (2012). "Can Tech revolutionize African Elections?" CNN Special Report: Sat. November 17.

Budurushi Jurlind, Stephan Neumann and Melanie Volkamer, (2012). "Smart Cards in Electronic Voting: Lessons Learned from Applications in Legally Binding Elections and Approaches. Proposed in "Scientific Papers" *CASED/Technische Universitat Dearmstadti*, Retrieved September, 2015.

CIA (1994). Ghana; The Transition from Military Rule to Demographic Government, The Library of Congress Country Studies; Washington, DC: CIA World Factbook

Dagne, T. (2009). Kenya: Current Conditions and the Challenges Ahead. Retrieved January 7, 2016, from http://www.fas.org/sgp/crs/row/RL34378.pdf

Daily Nation (2012). Avoid Manual Voting System, IEBC told. Taken from www.nation.co.ke/news/marende+team+seeks+les+help+on+electronic+voting+system/-1056/1471500/-h8g4jd31-/index.html

Deborah, E. (2009). Assessing the quality of accountability in Ghana's district assemblies, 1993-2008. African Journal of Political Science and International Relations, 3(6), 278-287.

Driza-Maurer, Ardita, Olver Sphycher, Geo Taglioni and Anina Weber (n.d.) "E-Voting for Swiss Abroad: A Joint Project Between the Confederation and the Cantons" Federal Chancellery, Section for Political Right. Retrieved September, 2015 http://www.e-voting.cc/wp-content/uploads/downloads/2012/07/173-187_Weber_et-al_Internet-Voting-CH.pdf

Esteve, Jordi Barrat I, Ben Goldsmith and John Turner. International Experience with E-Voting. Norwegian E-Vote Project. *IFES*, June 2012.

Fox, J. (2015). Social Accountability: What Does the Evidence Really Say? *World Development 72*, 346-361

Fuglerud, K. S., & Røssvoll, T. H. (2012). An evaluation of web-based voting usability and Accessibility. *Universal Access in the Information Society, 11*(4), 359-373. doi:http://dx.doi.org/10.1007/s10209-011-0253-9

Gerlach, Jan and Urs Gasser. (2009) "Three Case Studies from Switzerland: E-Voting" Internet & Democracy Case Study Series. *Berkman Center Research Publication No. 2009-03.1*

Hunter, G. E. (2001). The Role of Technology in the exercise of voting rights. Law Techor., 34 (4): 1-14.

Hutchful, E. (2002). Ghana's adjustment experience: The paradox of reform. Geneva: Unrisd.

International Crisis Group. (2007). Nigeria: Failed Elections, Failing State? Africa Report No. 126. Retrieved January 8, 2016, from www.unhcr.org/refworld/docid/465 e88892.html

Jinadu, L.A. (2007). Matters Arising: African Elections and the Problem of Electoral Administration. *African Journal of Political Science, 2*(1), 1-11.

Johnson, D.W. (2001). *No Place for Amateurs: How political consultants are reshaping American Democracy*. London: Routledge.

King, R., Owusu, A., and Braimah, I. (2013). Social Accountability for Local Government in Ghana. Commonwealth Journal of Local Government, 13, 61-75. Retrieved July 22, 2015, from http://epress.lib.uts.edu.au/ojs/index.php/cjlg

Kotler, P. (2004). *Marketing Management*, (November/December), American Marketing Association, pp. 30-35.

McNeil, M., & Malena, C. (Eds.). (2010). Demanding good governance: Lessons from Social Accountability Initiatives in Africa. World Bank Publications.

Mercouri (2002): Boyo-2 Melina Mercouri: Elgin Marbles

Mungai, Christine. (2015). Dirty hands; Why Biometric Voting fails in Africa and it doesn't matter in the end. *Mail and Guardian Africa* (30 March1/7-7/7 National Demographic Congress (Ghana). (2004). Available www.nationaldemographic congress.com

Murphy, P.E. (2005). Developing, communicating and promoting corporate ethics statements: A longitudinal analysis. *Journal of Business Ethics, 62*(2), 183-189.

Ninsin, Kwame (2006). Political Parties and Political Participation in Ghana. A study on behalf of the Konrad Adenauer Foundation Accra/Ghana/Berlin/Germany

Ofori-Dwumfo, G.O. and Paatey, E. (2011). The Design of an Electronic Voting System. *Research Journal of Information Technology* 3 (2) 91-98 Ghana: Methodist University

Ohene-Konadu, G. (2001). Gender Analysis and Interpretation of Barriers to Women's Participation in Ghana's Decentralized Local Government System. A Paper presented at African Gender Institute, University of Cape Town, South Africa.

Okoro, E. (2012). Ethical and social responsibility in global marketing: An evaluation of corporate commitment to stakeholders. *International Business & Economics Research Journal 11* (8), 863-870.

Otchere-Darko, A. (2010). Kenya Goes E-Voting in 2012, As Ghana Dithers. Retrieved January 8, 2016 from http://www.ghanaweb.com/GhanaHomePage/politics/artikel. php

Owono, Julie (2012). Ghana: A democratic anomaly, Aljazeera. Taken from www. aljazeera.com/indepth/opinion/2012/07/201273182115464514,html

Padmanabhan, Leala (2014) "Could e-voitng be on its way in the UK?" *BBC News* Retrieved October, 2015 from www.bbccom/news/uk-politics-30234304

PICAM, Electoral Reform in Cameroon. (2006). Retrieved January 7, 2016, from http://picam.org/projects/ERC/home.htm

Przeworski, A., Stokes, S., and Manin, B., (Eds.) (1999) *Democracy, Accountability and Representations*. Cambridge: Cambridge University Press.

Richard, Jeffers and Claire, Thomas (1993). The Ghanaian Elections of 1992. *African Affairs*, 92 (368)331-366.

Salomonsen G (2005). Voting for Online Democracy. Retrieved from www.physorg. com/news4011.html (Access on: September 30, 2015).

Sergei A. K. Nikolai, L. Dennis and L. Vitaly (2011) The Guarantor: A web-centric system for organization and remote monitoring of electronic events, Transferring Government. *People, Process Policy,* 5 (1): 56-67.

Shwom, B. and Snyder, G. L. (2012). *Business Communications: Polishing Your Professional Presence*. New York: Pearson Publishers, Inc.

The Carter Center. "Developing a Methodology for Observing Electronic Voting" (2007) www.cartercenter.org Retrieved October, 2015

The Commonwealth of Nations, Ghana History information extracted on October 15, 2015 from www.Thecommonwealth.org/our-member-countries/Ghana/history (see more discussion at http://thecommonwealth.org/our-member-countries/ghana/history #sthash.rtHTFS5e.dpuf

Trechsel, Alexander (2013). "Internet Voting a success in two European Countries" *European University Institute* Retrieved from http://www.eui.eu/News/2013/02-12-InternetvotingasuccessintwoEuropeancountries.aspx

World Bank (2003). World Development Report 2004: making Services Work for Poor People. World Bank and Oxford University Press. Washington, D.C.

World Bank (2007). Source Book on Social Accountability: Strengthening the Demand Side of Governance and Service Delivery. Washington: World Bank.

Yeboah, A. (2013) "Electronic voting in Ghana: Is it the solution to Ghana's perceived electoral challenges after biometric registration?" *Journal of Information Engineering* and Applications 3 (1).

CHAPTER 4
Social Media Communication: Using Internet Radio to Transform Election Outcomes and Build Interactive Communication Among Diverse African Communities

Otis Thomas — Bowie State University
Ephraim Okoro — Howard University

INTRODUCTION

Political analysis in recent decades indicates that democratic politics, practices, and policy implementation in sub-Saharan Africa have taken a significant leap in the last five decades, and especially since a good number of African countries have gained independence. Significantly, political systems on the continent are striving consistently toward achieving a level of political sophistication that will ensure global recognition and respect. Campaigns, political parties and structures, elections, and voting processes are being reconstructed to promote democracy, good governance, peace, and stability. Several countries in the sub-Saharan region have adopted or implemented constitutional measures and reforms that support political stability, as well as strengthen democratic growth, checks and balances, and accountability in governance.

In the 21st century, achieving democratic ideals and sustainable political development is the primary goal of African countries, especially in the sub-Saharan region. The Sustainable Development Report on Africa (2008) explains that African leaders have made irrevocable commitments to human rights and the rule of law. The leadership of these countries has embraced a significant measure of international and regional human rights norms and standards, and has continued to improve human conditions on the continent. While total application of human rights and the principles of good governance are still being improved in the sub-Saharan region, there appears to be an expanded and renewed interest to uphold and ensure respect for human rights, political accountability, and administrative transparency.

As explained in the Economic Commission for Africa's (ECA's) African Governance Report (2005), political communication, freedom of the news media, and citizen awareness and participation in the democratic process must be encouraged during campaigns and elections. Furthermore, competitive multiparty democracy, free and fair elections, civil society associations, and independent groups must be allowed to contribute to the political process. Therefore, in order to sustain a commitment to transparent and inclusive governance, social media channels and Internet radio must be vigorously engaged during elections.

As African countries continue to strive toward sustainable political ideals, a guiding element must be the effective use of radio to inform and engage the rural communities in order to increase both awareness of issues, and participation in civic duties. Studies by a number of indigenous scholars have recognized the role of mass media in ensuring that citizens are adequately informed and included in the democratic process. Recent elections in sub-Saharan Africa, such as the 2011 and 2015 presidential elections in Nigeria, resulted in a range of issues and challenges that bordered on election apathy, unawareness of critical economic and social issues, sectionalism, and tribalism. These occurred as a result of a lack of information available to the grassroots population.

Studies of past decades (Dia, 2002; Nwokeafor & Okunoye, 2013; Okoro, 2010) explained the significance of radio, television, newspapers, and the new media in creating awareness and activating citizens to action. Importantly, radio is the most common source for information about election campaigns in local and rural communities because of its availability and accessibility. The importance of radio as a critical channel for disseminating information during elections cannot be overemphasized. While citizens in the cities depend on television and newspapers for election information, the rural communities listen to radio channels for information and election updates.

RADIO AND POLITICAL DEVELOPMENT IN SUB-SAHARAN AFRICA

Over the years, radio has contributed immensely to political, social, and economic progress in the rural areas, and has been quite effective as a result of its broad reach to a wide audience of people in the villages and other rural settings, where a television set is unavailable or too expensive to obtain. Historically, radio has been the most inexpensive and accessible medium to rural populations in the sub-Saharan region for disseminating development and political information. In evaluating the effectiveness of radio broadcasting in rural development in Nigeria, Akosa (2012) noted that radio is the single most important, far-reaching channel for communicating to the rural communities in sub-Saharan Africa.

While studies indicate that awareness and development cannot occur without communication, radio broadcasting has been the most effective mode for conveying news and information in the rural communities of Africa. Furthermore, radio plays a significant function in achieving many objectives of development communication in sub-Saharan Africa because of its availability and expensiveness.

As scholars noted in recent studies, development communication has been the primary focus of the mass media in Africa, primarily because of the rural nature of communities in the countries. Therefore, the role of radio in achieving the objectives of development communication distinguishes it from the functions of other channels of communication in the African context. As explained by scholars (Okorie, 2006; Nwokeafor, 2006; Okoro, 2009), development communication is greatly needed in Africa because it involves reporting and promoting messages associated with development needs and activities of rural communities. Additionally, radio accessibility to citizens in the rural areas and villages increases its value. This channel of communication accommodates the explanation of issues and activities in various languages and dialects, as well as being used to encourage citizens to understand the development goal and process.

By understanding the objectives of rural development, citizens in the local areas become more willing to participate in various development-related activities, including elections, independent and collective contributions, and engagement in agricultural efforts. Furthermore, Ekwelie (1992), together with other scholars (Moemeka, 1980; Hendy, 2000; Ndolo, 2015), emphasized that the fundamental feature of development communication is that it contributes significantly to the sustainable growth, empowerment, and sophistication of rural dwelling. Community development involves economic change for the improvement of living conditions of people in rural areas of the African continent, and evidently, radio broadcasting and content are designed with development needs of the inhabitants in mind. Through radio messages, local citizens are made aware of information about agriculture, health education, socialization, and environmental issues.

SOCIAL MEDIA COMMUNICATION: EFFECTIVE USE OF INTERNET RADIO

As eloquently stated over five decades ago by the "Father of Communication Studies" Schramm (1964), by making one section, tribe, or race of a country aware of other parts, their people, culture, traditions, and political process; by allowing and engaging the political leaders to communicate with the citizens, and citizens communicate with political leaders and with each other; by making possible nationwide discussions and debate on national policy or political issues; by explaining national objectives and goals as well as sharing political agenda and accomplishments with citizens—communication channels (radio, television, and social media), widely used, can help to connect diverse communities, disparate subcultures, races, self-centered individuals and groups, and separate units into a cohesive national and political entity.

Certainly, the quality of independent radio stations has a positive impact on societies, particularly in rural areas of Africa that depend on radio broadcasting for information and directions to participate in political activities. A number of studies by African and Western scholars respectively (Casmir, 1991; Diamond, 2004; Megwa, 2009; Okoro, 2010; Nwokeafor & Okunnoye, 2013) attest to the fact that social media and radio have a transformative impact on elections' outcomes in developing nations. The effective role of radio and new media for sustainable democracy cannot be overstressed, as it ensures and contributes to accurate election results.

Over the past few years, there has been a disconcerting national concern about the low level of voter turnout in elections conducted in the countries in sub-Saharan Africa. This voter apathy was traced to a lack of awareness and information to citizens in local communities. Research findings and conclusions clearly indicate that the mass media operationalizes issues, analyzes their implications, and ultimately sets community agenda. As a result, it is critically important that citizens in the rural communities are adequately informed, their interest aroused, and their engagement engendered through a channel that has a wider reach to both rural and urban dwellers. In a recent study entitled "Media power in elections: Evidence of the role of agenda-setting theory in political communication in Nigeria evolving democracy," Nwokeafor and Okunoye (2013) echoed and supported the role of radio and other forms of mass communication. These researchers noted that the television innovation swept Nigerian communities with amazement in 1959, which expanded the use of television and radio broadcasting simultaneously in political campaigns. Ever since then, these news sources have become an irresistible dynamic source of reporting news and conveying information about political issues and initiatives, as well as on various party candidates. Consequently, television, newspapers, and radio significantly cover political campaigns, leading to increased participation of voters. The authors noted that radio and the new media have gradually become very influential and effective in disseminating campaign updates, party platforms, and other election-related issues to the citizens. Through this awareness, voter participation and engagement has consistently increased and election outcomes reflect the opinions of a large proportion of the population.

Additional studies have noted that access to information during elections is significant to the success of democracy, especially in the sub-Saharan region, where voter participation is extremely minimal or discouraging. It is critically important that citizens have adequate information to make knowledgeable decisions and independent choices. While radios and televisions are owned by governments in African countries, radio is more affordable to the citizens, can be carried to various locations, and can be used at different times. Twenty-four-hour television broadcasting is not available to citizens in many rural areas of sub-Saharan Africa; therefore, both the knowledge level and degree of involvement of the people are limited, hence their poor turnout and consequent election outcomes. Although the role of mass media continues to be of paramount importance in the democratic process in developed countries, radio broadcasting is of immense value in developing nations of Africa because of access and the location of people in rural communities where development is much needed.

Nokoko (2013) and other scholars noted the role of radio and new information technologies in the lives of local citizens involved in violent conflicts in Zimbabwe and South Africa in 2008. The author explained that radio and new information technologies, particularly radio and cell phones, are by far the most widely used means of communication in African political and social environments, both in rural and urban communities. The radio trend continues to contribute to citizens' level of awareness, knowledge of current affairs, and raises their level of involvement in social, cultural, and political activities. Using Internet radio to transform elections' outcomes and to establish interactive communication among diverse African communities is an important objective of this chapter, because studies of the past few years strongly determined that radio broadcasting is the most pervasive medium to Africans in the rural areas (Brinkman, 2009; Bosch, 2011; Gunner, Ligaga and Moyo, 2012).

RURAL AND COMMUNITY RADIO CHANNELS AND FORUMS

Evaluating the historical and contemporary roles of radio and its use in rural communities in sub-Saharan Africa requires an analysis of the evolution of radio broadcasting in Africa and its contributions to political development. Given the pluralistic nature of the African continent and the proliferation of the contemporary broadcasting environment, it is an enormous undertaking to make a comprehensive assessment of the role of rural or public radio in political communication. Prior to the independence of many of the countries in sub-Saharan Africa, radio broadcasting was designed to provide information on health, financial education to farmers, and information for political awareness and participation. In some of the countries, radio was the source for promoting economic development enlightenment. Ilboudo (1989) identified specific examples of the role and use of rural radio in civic engagement, raising political awareness, and civic health education (Cameron in 1956, Mali in 1957, Nigeria in 1962, and Ghana in 1956).

Ilboudo's research noted that Radio Accra's dissemination of news and development information in Ghanaian languages had programs for rural activities, and Nigerian radio stations broadcasted news in different dialects to inform and empower citizens in the villages on political development matters. Radio Kano established programs encouraging farmers to adopt agricultural mechanization and to improve seed varieties. Similarly, Kenya, in 1962, produced educational training and programs through radio to advise rural farmers on improving agricultural productivity. Furthermore, in the early 1960s, Radio Dahomey designed special programs in the Fon language for encouraging and engaging rural citizens of the Benin Republic.

Over several years, before gaining independence, the role of rural and community radio was instrumental to the results of development efforts, political activities, and sophisticated educational reforms in African countries. Citizens in rural areas depended largely on radio for information regarding general lifestyle trends and current affairs. This was largely the case because of the affordability and accessibility to radio broadcasting in the rural communities. A number of studies (Bosch, 2011; Aker & Mbiti, 2010, Nokoko, 2013) emphasized that radio played a fundamental role for dissemination of critical political, social, and economic information in African countries. The authors further noted that it was of paramount importance to establish information and media policies that would enhance or increase citizens' access to radio and other news channels, especially during elections, in order to engender adequate participation in the political process.

In addition to increasing political participation, radio played critical, informative role in times of violence, tribal conflict, and regional wars. Additionally, because of the availability, affordability, and accessibility of radio broadcasting in rural and local communities, there was increased interaction among the villagers, more effective and efficient news-gathering processes, as well as promotion of participatory/collective culture and local engagement among local citizens.

Emphasizing the unique role of radio in conflict situations, Nokoko (2013) pointed out that radio broadcasting has been expanded and adopted to appropriating new media to broaden its functional scope, as well as to sustain the interest and focus of rural residents. This aspect of radio's function is significant in the development of a collective culture and for the promotion of traditional African communal cultural environment. Studies noted that a large group of African communities did not have much access to other forms of advanced modes of communication, which made radio broadcasting indispensable to the increasing political and developmental needs of the rural communities. Therefore, community and local radio remains a vital source of information essentially for mobilizing, informing, and engaging grassroots participation and support for all forms of development activities and programs.

Studies by Ekwelie (1992), Okorie (2006), and Mboho (2005) identified the specific role and function of community radio in both development and political communications. The authors noted the characteristics of radio as pervasiveness, immediacy, economic medium, portability, and presence. These characteristics distinguish radio among forms of news sources as uniquely designed for rural development, and they emphasized its usefulness in community outreach programs. Therefore, effective use of radio in disseminating and engaging citizens in rural areas can transform or improve elections' outcomes through constant reminders of events and programs. The preceding studies also explained that television and newspapers are important sources of information in Africa, but they lack the basic attributes associated with radio broadcasting in rural areas in terms of pervasiveness and immediacy. Additional functions of radio include promoting of economic knowledge, creating an understanding and wisdom among villagers, propagating of economic programs and policies, facilitating the national integration for economic progress, teaching the use of modern approaches, strategies, and standards for farming and agricultural development, and making citizens responsive, responsible, and accountable during elections.

SOCIAL MEDIA COMMUNICATIONS: THE ROLE OF RURAL RADIO IN SUB-SAHARAN AFRICA

Communications scholars have continued to evaluate the role and use of rural radio in Africa, and their assessments of radio broadcasting in political elections have been consistent. Their evaluation of the role radio channels play transcends the political context and has touched upon various aspects of national development. Other researchers have extended their analyses of radio broadcasting and have examined the agenda-setting role of news sources and radio in rural development (Nwokeafor, 1992; Ndolo, 1990; Okoro, 1993), as well as newspapers and their agenda-setting function in the political environment.

In an earlier study, Moemeka (1989) identified and analyzed the role of seven different media sources (social forums, town crier, village market, village school, newspapers, radio, and television) in determining the interest level in rural community programs such as Operation Feed the Nation, Local Government Reforms, and the Universal Free Primary Education. The study determined that 80 percent of respondents attributed their knowledge of the programs to radio broadcasting, 15 percent indicated traditional media as a significant source, and 5 percent cited newspapers as a primary channel. In other words, accessibility of radio channels to rural dwellers in Africa differentiates radio as largely instrumental to knowledge and interest in community programs. This finding clearly supports the use of Internet radio to promote elections and election-related activities in Africa.

BUILDING INTERACTIVE COMMUNICATION AMONG DIVERSE AFRICAN COMMUNITIES: RADIO AND SOCIAL MEDIA COMMUNICATION

The Center for Democracy and Governance (1999), in an analysis of the role of media in democracy, stressed that access to information is critically essential to the development of democracy both in developed and developing nations. Information allows the citizens to make authoritative decisions, and it also ensures that voters make responsible and objective choices based on knowledge provided by news channels. Further, it was noted that information provides "a checking function" that makes elected representatives accountable and transparent, which ultimately establishes a trusting relationship between voters and elected officials in democratic governance. The Center for Democracy and Governance pointed out that the media, specifically radio, is an integral part of a civil society, and free and fair elections must be conducted through objective and transparent processes that allow the citizens to make their choices. Increasingly, voter turnout, public engagement, and citizens' participation in electioneering campaigns usually would lead to better election outcomes. Collectively, the mass media plays an indispensable role in democratic elections.

In developing nations of Africa, specific news channels, such as radio, must be identified to support an election process because of the rural nature of much of the continent. For example, in many African countries, governments maintain exclusive control over the media channels, indirectly or directly, and government officials determine the coverage of events, information that should be provided, and the scope of news that will be shared with the public. The Center for Democracy and Governance (1999) noted that although the content of radio stations is equally controlled by governments, citizens in the rural areas listen to radio more than they watch television and read newspapers. Consistent with the preceding view, Nwokeafor and Okunoye (2013), in their analysis of media power in elections (evidence of the role of agenda-setting theory in political communication in Nigeria's evolving democracy) noted that the media (radio, television, newspapers, the new media, etc.) are significant to the sustainability of any democracy, and they cautioned that democratic elections and citizens' engagement would be impossible without the empowering and informative functions of the mass media. Moreover, election outcomes (free and fair elections) are not necessarily about the freedom to vote and the knowledge of how to cast a vote, but more significantly about the citizens' participation in elections in which candidates engage in open debates in order to allow voters to vote according to their impression and conscience. Nwokeafor and Okunoye concluded that the crucial watchdog role of the news media, specifically radio broadcasting, is providing adequate and timely information, explaining policies, and operationalizing guidelines to citizens in remote communities, which contributes immensely to voter confidence.

RURAL BROADCASTING, POLITICAL DEVELOPMENT, AND RURAL DEVELOPMENT IN AFRICA

Consistent with the notion of using Internet radio to improve elections' outcomes and build interactive communication among diverse African communities in the 21st century, radio broadcasting can be used effectively to transform agricultural and cultural programs in sub-Saharan Africa. For the most part, Africans depend on agriculture for their wellbeing, but agricultural activities have been largely agrarian in nature for decades, lacking the sophisticated knowledge to improve farming activities. There is no doubt that citizens' access to radio broadcasting plays a significant role in mobilizing people for elections, which also improves election outcomes due to more of a grassroots presence in democratic elections. Empirical studies (Bates, 1981; ACARSTSOD, 1991; Adedeji, 1993; Obasanjo & d'Orville, 1992) explained that radio broadcasting contributes a great deal to medical and economic awareness, just as it is expected to contribute in the democratic process.

For decades the African continent has faced an increased insecurity of food availability, along with other unfavorable or hostile circumstances, such as famine, drought, conflict, and irresponsible governments. Although Africa has a vast land mass with a relatively sparse population, it has not been well harnessed or cultivated as a result of irresponsible governance or lack of political sophistication for electing respectable and accountable leaders. Additionally, the fragility of soils and unreliability of water systems for agricultural purposes clearly indicate that the management of land and rights in land were determined by selfish colonial masters of pre-independence years, as well as by indigenous leaders who inherited corrupt and dishonest governance. It is noted that shifting and pastoralism constituted major problems for colonial rulers. Vague or unexplained rights and privileges in land ownership were addressed by appropriation or establishment of individual ownership in the colonial African environment. These challenges were some of the issues that the African continent faced, which contributed to political apathy and shortsighted economic planning. Importantly, radio broadcasting is the main medium of communication in distant places of the continent to stay informed, empowered, and engaged.

EXPANDED LITERATURE AND CONCEPTUAL FRAMEWORK

The role of radio and social media communication in sub-Saharan Africa has attracted a significant amount of scholarly interest over the past few years, primarily because of election apathy, exclusion, and misinformation, all of which occurred during elections. Authors Ronning (1995) and Nyamnjoh (2005) drew the attention of scholars to evaluate the role of radio and new media in promoting democracy, political process, and development agenda in many parts of Africa because of the wide reach of these channels of communication to rural areas of the continent. While television and newspapers are equally important in promoting democratic efforts and activities, they are not easily and readily accessible to citizens in the villages. In addition to creating awareness and participation in democracy, radio broadcasting plays an important part in conflict and war situations. For example, Ronning (1995) and Nyamnjoh (2005) identified the critical part played by radio channels during the 1994 genocide in Rwanda, in which radio broadcasting consistently exposed and analyzed the nature of the conflict, as well as public reactions. Consequently, radio messages and reporters' analyses of political issues in democracy and conflict raised public awareness, thereby mobilizing support and sympathy.

An extensive literature review was conducted focusing on the cultivation of Internet radio technological convergence to assess the capability of using the social media global network communities to generate revenue and to improve local and national communication connections. The review examined the technological advancement of Internet radio, streaming programs and information, and how this new media technological innovation is revolutionizing democracy and social equality, which is essential to people in sub-Saharan Africa, as well as people in other parts of Africa.

INTEGRATION OF RADIO AND SOCIAL MEDIA
IN CONTEMPORARY POLITICS

It is widely acknowledged in past and recent communication literature (The World Bank, 2014; Nwokeafor, 2013; Graber, 1990; Schramm, 1964) that the integration of radio and social media networks is a highly effective tool to inform and connect political citizenry to information about public policy agenda, as well as development initiatives in the quest for democratic governance and national unity. Fundamentally, radio broadcasting empowers people in a way that is faster and more pervasive than other forms of communication. It is noteworthy that election outcomes have been controversial in some sub-Saharan African countries because of people's limited access to television in the rural areas. Radio is readily available and information can reach voters in the rural areas, and it reduces dependency on television and other sophisticated news sources. Moreover, regular and constant access to radio channels encourages pluralism, simultaneous communication to young and older citizens in the rural communities, and timeliness in information dissemination.

CONCEPTUAL FRAMEWORK: RADIO-SOCIAL MEDIA BASED INTEGRATIVE MODEL

The concept of the radio-social media based integrative model was developed in this chapter as a balance for achieving sustainable political development and governance in sub-Saharan Africa. Drawing selectively from democratic governance in Nigeria and research evidence from World Bank reports (1989 & 2009), as well as findings from studies (Entman, 1989; Diamond, 2004; McCombs & Reynolds, 2009), the chapter focuses on the critical importance of using Internet radio to improve or enhance election outcomes and to establish interactive communication among diverse African communities.

The strategic advantage of the radio-based integrative model is grounded on political empowerment and participation. The model suggests that (a) establishing independent ownership of radio stations in African countries will be useful in order to encourage a more elaborate and constructive dissemination of news, development initiatives, and activities; and (b) discouraging exclusive government ownership of radio stations will affect interactive communication among diverse communities.

Potentially, the radio-based integrative model, which derives substantially from a general system theory concept, is a constructive model that enhances democratic ideals and practice, which fosters the realization of better election outcomes as a consequence of grassroots voter participation in general elections. Implicit in the radio-based model is the idea that radio broadcasting and related news sources should be considered an integral part of sustainable development objectives in Africa. The concept is not only concerned with the integration of underutilized radio channels in the African political development agenda, but also with the integration of all other news sources in mobilizing African citizenry in political campaigns and elections toward the overall goal of sustainable democratic governance.

INTERNET RADIO AND COMMUNICATION EFFECTIVENESS

Generally speaking, the social media technological process provides its users in the rural and urban communities of Africa adequate access to broadcasting networks, which can lead to community improvement and rural development awareness. As an example, the impact of convergent media can present mobile phone listeners numerous radio broadcast programs ranging from news, talk, music, entertainment, government, political, educational, and specialized formats. The power of Internet radio reaches various global audiences simultaneously, making the development of political efforts achievable and sustainable. A more specific example is that new digital audio delivers sounds and images that are formatted through customized streaming media systems, which would improve the quality of messages in African countries. Furthermore, radio audiences within rural communities are able to access programs around the world in seconds. *Bloomberg News* (as cited in Biagi, 2017, p. 119) reported that Internet radio corporation providers like Pandora and iHeartRadio are providing broadcasting opportunities for advertisers, music producers, radio station programmers, and political candidates, to reach millions of listeners both nationally and internationally through live, local broadcast programming. Through these digital distribution channels, data is collected, analyzed, and stored for marketing by companies and media organizations. These advanced digital services are able to track, engage, respond, and resonate with Internet radio consumers through innovative new terrestrial broadcasting cyberspace technologies (Biagi, 2017, p. 119).

Both academic and action research findings provide a closer look into the world of terrestrial digital media platforms with ubiquitous network transmission services. A report by EBU Technology and Development (2011) points out that terrestrial Internet digital broadcasting systems incorporate a number of technological Internet features, which utilize multiple services. The growth of mobile cell phone users and broadband networks both give subscribers shared information online and in real time. Additionally, this pooled data furnishes mobile listeners with historical opportunities to connect with larger communities and engage in discussions essential to their social, political, and cultural views and interactions. As a result, Internet radio technological and transformational broadcasting digital systems are historically significant to communities' individualization and fundamental relationships amid challenges facing independent, political, and social democracies.

RADIO POWER IN ELECTIONS: AGENDA-SETTING FUNCTIONS IN DEMOCRACY

In evaluating the role and effectiveness of mass media in political campaigns and elections, scholars (Graber, 1990; Kaid, Negrine & James, 2007; Okoro, 2010) recognized the significant position of various communication channels in defining the salience of issues by establishing public agenda. This unique role of determining and guiding citizens worldwide during elections is consistent with the functions of radio broadcasting in reaching the rural communities in Africa to make informed decisions. Fundamentally, by expanding the knowledge and awareness of citizens in rural and urban areas, they are politically empowered to vote in elections with the result that election outcomes will be grossly impacted. The "intellectual godfathers" of agenda-setting studies, McCombs and Shaw (1972), demonstrated that by stressing the critical nature of election issues, candidates' credibility, and candidates' positions on various issues, the news sources (radio, television, and newspapers) have the capacity to establish the importance of issues and topics to the listening and voting audience.

As Nwokeafor and Okunonye (2013) recently determined in their "media power in elections" research, the mass media is capable of exerting irresistible or compelling influence on voters, and news sources "have the opportunity to mold their minds and significantly influence flow of news and information and directing their thinking and selection of candidates." Citing presidential elections in Nigeria in 2015, Nwokeafor and Okunoye explained that the People's Democratic Party (PDP) positioned their presidential candidate, Dr. Jonathan, as a more electable candidate based on media presentation of the candidate's agenda, his political experience, and qualifications. The news media creatively and strategically presented Dr. Jonathan as a more capable person to be president of Nigeria, which immensely impressed voters. The perceived favorable characteristics of the candidate by the media, according to authors Nwokeafor and Okunoye (2013, p. 9), "positively influenced the opinion of the Nigerian electorate as a result of which candidate Jonathan was overwhelmingly elected the president of the nation in the April 2011 general election." The concept of agenda-setting is the strategic manipulation of public opinion and agenda by news sources (radio, television, newspapers, and the new media) in favor of a particular candidate and issues.

This mind or opinion control exerted upon the audience is what Lippmann (1922, 1962), Klapper (1960), and McCombs and Shaw (1972) consistently described as defining, emphasizing, and/or repositioning salience of political issues and developments. In recent studies, Okoro (2010) and Nwokeafor (2013) determined that the press is exceedingly influential in political environments and can control a significant segment of the social and political process that establishes political issue and event salience. As a news source largely used in rural communities of Africa, radio broadcasting is therefore quite capable of setting the agenda for the citizenry, which ultimately affects election outcomes.

EVOLUTION OF DIGITAL RADIO TECHNOLOGY: A GLOBAL ASSESSMENT

The rising growth of Internet radio and mobile technology provides a vehicle for listeners who have an inquisitive interest in local and national programs, and events which impact their cultural environment. XAPP-media (2015) reported that Internet radio growth will reach millions of listeners who are moving from traditional daily radio to spending more time accessing and downloading streaming program services. Hausman, Messere Benoit, and O'Donnell (2016, p. 347), stated that the number of Americans subscribing to Internet radio broadcasting has grown to nearly half of the U.S. population. According to their study, approximately 73 percent of individuals 12 and older listen to Internet radio and more than 90 percent of individuals 12 and older are terrestrial listeners. Similarly, Edison Research and Triton Digital (as cited in XAPPmedia 2015, p. 4) discussed the growth rate of Internet online radio over a five-year period. This report pointed out that the growth rate of Internet online radio users has dramatically increased to 13.5 percent over the last five years). Figure 4.1 below illustrates the rapid growth rate of weekly Internet online radio listeners from 2008 to 2014.

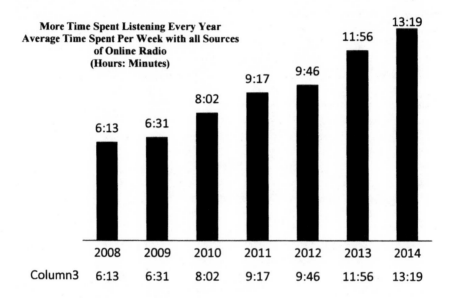

More Time Spent Listening Every Year
Average Time Spent Per Week with all Sources
of Online Radio
(Hours: Minutes)

	2008	2009	2010	2011	2012	2013	2014
Column3	6:13	6:31	8:02	9:17	9:46	11:56	13:19

Figure 4:1 Weekly Online Radio Listeners Report
Source: 2014 Edison Research and Triton Digital

Nielsen's data (2015, p. 4) reported a faster growth rate of 60.5% for Internet online radio listeners interested in streaming music and entertaining programs. Furthermore, XAPPmedia (2015) reported that Internet radio will generate billions of dollars in revenue and music will represent nearly 20 percent of the mobile audience's choice for selected entertainment. It explained that millennials between the ages of 18-34 had disposable income and would spend an estimated $200 billion annually by the year 2017, and $10 trillion during their lifetime.

Central to the XAPPmedia (2015) study is the attraction of consumers to Internet radio broadcasting. According to XAPPmedia's report, Internet radio attracts consumers who are preoccupied with a number of personal activities and mobile devices, like Smartphones and personal tablets. Moreover, Nielsen's data (2014) reported that Internet and broadcast radio audiences spend nearly 80 percent of their mobile music time listening while multi-tasking during personal, professional, and travel time.

ANALYSIS OF INTERNET RADIO UNIVERSAL COVERAGE

Internet radio broadcasting and streaming services are developing new, innovative technology for consumers to access free information and entertainment around the world. This development will benefit audiences in developed and developing countries in Africa for years to come. Consequently, broadcasting and audio engineers are researching various ways to deliver new broadcasting services to mobile consumers and listeners in sub-Saharan Africa and other African countries. Mobile users throughout the globe will have opportunities to download significant information involving government regulations, and economic, political, cultural, and historical global events.

This chapter notes the profound growth and mobile networking evolution through a very high-tech study conducted by Cisco (2016, p. 31) called "The Zettabyte Era: Trends and Analysis." This unique technological study forecasts that by the end of 2016, the annual busy hour for Internet traffic will increase by 51 percent, and that Smartphone traffic will exceed PC traffic by the year 2020. Cisco (2016) also reported that annual global IP video traffic will increase by nearly 82 percent for both businesses and consumers, and global mobile data traffic will increase by 53 percent between 2015 and 2020, reaching exabytes by 2020. Cisco (2016, p. 2) further stated that content delivery networks (CDNs) will carry nearly two-thirds of Internet traffic globally by 2020, which will immensely benefit developing countries in Africa where rural communities need more information to participate in the political process of democracy. This research pointed out that new evolutionary technology expanded the availability of Internet radio broadband and mobile video to millions of Smartphone traffic consumers with broadband speeds, which will double from 24.7 mbps to nearly 48 mbps by the year 2020.

THE DEVELOPMENT STREAMING INTERNET RADIO TECHNOLOGY

Internet radio audio content incorporates various technological mechanisms for distribution of live programming transmitted by uplinking and then downlinking to service providers throughout the world. As a result, Internet radio program files are transformed to streaming media formats and distributed to mobile Smartphones globally. Rayburn and Hoch (2005, p. 85) asserted that live webcasting is one of the most common digital components for streaming media to public and private audiences in developed and developing countries in Africa. Additionally, the studies pointed out that technological resources and new innovations are extremely important and beneficial in the process of delivering and broadcasting live events in real time. For example, some benefits include new innovative systems that provide tremendous, interesting ways for schools and cultural institutions to stream live educational content to classrooms where lectures are being conducted during actual scheduled sessions. Moreover, students are gaining insight into depths of education and information with immediacy, which wasn't previously available. Other benefits include the use of Smart-boards, Smartphones, and tablets.

The growth of Internet mobile traffic technology and development is rapidly expanding with the unprecedented demands for service and accessibility to countries in developed nations, and gradually will extend to the developing nations of Africa. Cisco's (2015, p. 2) report illustrates this rapid expansion in the Middle East and Africa. Specifically, this report asserts that:

> In Middle East and Africa, mobile data traffic was 294.5 Petabytes per month in 2015, the equivalent of 74 million DVDs each month or 811 million text messages each second. In 2015, Middle East and Africa's mobile data traffic grew 2.2-fold, or 117%. In Middle East and Africa, mobile data traffic in 2015 was equivalent to 34x the volume of Middle Eastern and African mobile traffic five years earlier in 2010. In Middle East and Africa, mobile data traffic grew 2.6 times faster than Middle Eastern and African fixed IP traffic in 2015. In Middle East and Africa, the average mobile-connected end-user device generated 231 megabytes of mobile data traffic per month in 2015, up 98% from 117 megabytes per month in 2014. In Middle East and Africa, the average Smartphone generated 835 megabytes of mobile data traffic per month in 2015, up from 519 megabytes per month in 2014. In Middle East and Africa, the average PC generated 2,478 megabytes of mobile data traffic per month in 2015, up from 1,953 megabytes per month in 2014. In Middle East and Africa, the average tablet generated 1,758 megabytes of mobile data traffic per month in 2015, up from 1,080 megabytes per month in 2014.

Internet radio digital technology has unlimited potential for universal availability. This rapidly changing terrestrial phenomenon has revolutionized the way consumers access media services through their personal computer, Smartphone, tablet, or mobile phone. In addition, Internet radio is a vital distribution network for the entertainment industry. The popularity of the social media experience, combined with consumers' increased demand for technological advancements in mass quantities, more streaming media, and high-tech media gadgets, all have placed corporations in a constant renewed and transformative position to proactively conform and respond to consumer requests, and take advantage of new technological opportunities and innovation for competitive benefit, efficiency, enhanced communication, and sustainability.

Streaming is a powerful, progressive download of live programming over the Internet for continuous local and national viewership to generate revenue, enhance communication, and improve content quality, training, and programming delivery systems in a cost-effective way. Consumers can listen to Internet radio services on satellite (either free or through subscription) anywhere they would like for personal interest and entertainment; in their cars, on their mobile phones, on their computers, on their tablets, at home, or at the office. According to Nielsen's report (as cited in Biagi, 2017, p. 150), "Americans spend an average of 31 hours a week watching traditional TV and video on the Internet. Similarly, people 50 years and over spend twice as much time watching TV and videos on the Internet."

CONCLUSION

This chapter provides a comprehensive exploration and evaluation of the role of radio broadcasting in the democratic process, social media communications, and the impact of using Internet radio to transform or enhance election outcomes and to build interactive communication among diverse communities in Africa. As civil societies and democratic nations are improving communication tools and acquiring more sophisticated channels for the purpose of ensuring that citizens are communicating effectively, there is a renewed focus on making sure that developing nations are using radio broadcasting to strategically enhance sustainable political development. Media and political communication scholars are consistent in their position that radio can be used to support elections in the rural areas of Africa, because radio is a popular channel for the rapid dissemination of fundamental and critical information in a variety of languages and dialects across geographically vast areas of the continent. Further, radio broadcasting, if properly and adequately used, can provide a constructive platform for interactive communication (dialogue and debate) among development stakeholders. It can also become an efficient channel through which rural and urban communities can express themselves on development-related issues, and to provide an avenue for raising public awareness and social mobilization among citizens in rural/local areas.

Essentially, radio and other news sources are critical to the advancement of democracy. Over the years, empirical studies strongly indicate that democratic elections will not produce a credible result without the significant role of the mass media. In an analysis of the role of media in the African changing electoral process, Megwa (2014) described political elections as highly competitive, involving transitional processes that are fraught with tension, confrontation, conflict, and instability—especially in the developing nations of Africa. The political stage involves the mass media (radio, television, newspapers, etc.), citizens, politicians, political parties, and governments at all levels who play active roles to ensure that the outcome of elections are fair and free, responsibly conducted, and widely acknowledged.

Author Megwa emphasized that in representative democracies in developed and developing nations, the mass media, more than any of the participants and groups on the political stage, are expected to play a neutral, independent, and effective role in the electoral process by objectively shaping citizens' opinions and positively influencing political behaviors and decisions. As a result of the agenda-setting function of news sources, citizens will be able to reliably utilize the information provided to make brilliant voting decisions, and can hold elected officials accountable for their actions. Internationally recognized subject-matter experts, authors across disciplines, and mass media scholars (Megwa, 2014; Nwokeafor, 2013; Langmia, 2010; Okoro, 2010; Onwumechili, 2009) agree that the single most important requirement for sustainable political development in the evolving African democracy is the presence of robust and effective Internet radio and social media, which will build interactive communication among diverse rural and urban communities. This is a critical, central point as the relationship between radio and community has been a significant concern for decades.

REFERENCES

Biagi, S. (2017). Media_impact: An introduction to mass media (12th ed.). Boston, MA: Cengage Learning.

Bloomberg News (2014). Pandora Radio Opens Listener Data on Let Musicians Target Fans. In Biagi, S. *Media Impact: An Introduction to Mass Media* (12th ed., p. 119). Boston, MA: Cengage Learning.

Bosch, T. (2011). "Talkradio, democracy and citizenship in South Africa." In Herman Wasserman (Ed.), *Popular Media, Democracy and Development in Africa*. London: Routledge.

Cisco (2016). The Zettabyte Era: Trends and Analysis. San Jose, CA: Cisco Public.

_____ (2015). Middle East and Africa 2015 Year in Review. http://www.cisco.com/assets/sol/sp/vni/forecast_highlights_mobile/index.html

EBU Technology and Development (2011, November). The Future of Terrestrial Broadcasting. Switzerland.

Edison Research and Triton Digital (2014). Time spent listening growth. In XAPPmedia. Internet radio trends report 2015: The state of internet radio and streaming services (pg. 4). Washington, D.C.: XAPPmedia.

Hausman, C., Messere, F., Benoit, P., & O'Donnell (2016). Modern radio & audio production: Programming and performance (10th ed.). Boston, MA: Cengage Learning.

Klapper, J. (1960). *The Effects of Mass Communication*. Glencoe, IL: Free Press.

Lippmann, W. (1922). *Public Opinion*. New York: Macmillan, p. 29.

McCombs, M., & Shaw (1972). The agenda-setting function of the mass media. *Public Opinion Quarterly, 36*, 176-185.

McQuail, (1990). The influence and effects of mass media in Graber, D., (1990). *Media Power in Politics* (2nd edition). Congressional Quarterly Press. Washington, DC

Moemeka, A.A. (1980). Perspectives on development communication. *Africa Media Review*, Volume 3, Number 3.

Nielsen (2015). Time spent listening growth. In XAPPmedia. Internet radio trends report 2015: The state of internet radio and streaming services (pg. 4). Washington, D.C.: XAPPmedia.

_____ (2014). The total audience report. In Biagi, S. *Media Impact: An Introduction to Mass Media* (12th ed., pg. 150). Boston, MA: Cengage Learning.

Ndolo, I.S. (1987). Radio broadcasting and the language problems of socio-political integration in Nigeria. Unpublished doctoral dissertation, Howard University, Washington, D.C.

_____ (2013). The role of radio and mobile phones in Conflict Situations. Institute of African Studies, Carleton University, Ottawa, Canada

Nwokeafor, C.U. & Okunoye, A. (2013). Media power in elections: Evidence of the role of agenda-setting theory in political communication in Nigeria evolving democracy. "International conference on ICT for Africa for 2013, Harare, Zimbabwe."

Nwokeafor, C.U. (1992). Development communications in the Nigerian mass media. A study of selected publications. Unpublished doctoral dissertation, Howard University, Washington, D.C.

Okoro, E.A. (2010). Communication, Civil Society, and Democratization in Africa: Perspectives on political development. In Nwokeafor, C. & Langmia, K. (2010). *Media and Technology in Emerging African Democracies.* University Press of America, Lanham, MD.

_____ (1993). The press and politics in Nigeria: Toward a conceptual framework for political development. Unpublished doctoral dissertation, Howard University, Washington, D.C.

Okorie, P.U. (2006). Communication challenges of reform policies in Nigeria, Aba: POU Ventures

Rayburn, D., & Hoch M. (2005). *The Business of Streaming & Digital Media.* Burlington, MA: Focal Press.

UNESCO (1968). An experiment in radio forums for rural development. Reports and papers in mass communication. Number 51, Paris.

XAPPmedia (2015). Internet radio trends report 2015: The state of internet radio and streaming services. Washington, D.C. XAPPmedia.

CHAPTER 5
Social Media and Politics in Burkina Faso

Kehbuma Langmia
Howard University
Washington, D.C.

INTRODUCTION

This chapter examines the influence of Western technological tools (social media) on the successes and failures of election practices in Burkina Faso. For decades, Africans have conducted municipal, parliamentary, senate, and presidential elections by following Western democratic tenets. They also follow the same format as in the West. There are election campaigns on the radio, newspaper, television, and in-person rallies in stadia and community halls. The onslaught of social media tools on the continent has changed the way people communicate with each other, and has prompted a change in political campaign strategies as well.

Information Communication Technology (ICT) is making headway on the continent of Africa, and this is changing communication-related activities substantially. The traditional forms of communication (newspaper, radio, and TV) are being outpaced by mobile telephony (cell phones) and Internet-driven Smartphones and tablets. Another emerging and significant platform of communication is the tendency for the younger populations to be engrossed in instant messaging using social networking sites (SNS) like Facebook and the user-generated YouTube channels. Research has shown that social media (open-source) platforms on the Internet are the new phenomenon, where information is shared between the citizens and their government. My recent publications on the use of YouTube as a medium for political electioneering in Kenya (Langmia, 2014) and Cameroon (Langmia, 2010) are testament that the future of political elections in Africa is going to be generated in the electronic republic called the Internet.

There are numerous challenges that accompany this new technology. Language barriers between nations impede the sharing of information. There are

Anglophone, Francophone, and Lusophone African countries. Additionally, these countries also have native languages that are not easy to write, read, and interpret from mobile devices using European keyboards. The digital divide, whereby only a select few are educated in Western languages, does utilize all the features on mobile devices. Gender and age gap with respect to ICT is another challenge. Some universities, especially in sub-Saharan Africa, have begun inculcating cyber knowledge on their campuses. Our organization (ictforafrica.org and ICT University), with campuses in Uganda, Nigeria, and Cameroon, will inculcate new media communicative technologies to the students in Africa. It is our intention to train future Africans through virtual means of communication using open-source systems like WebEX technology and other Internet-driven platforms like Google Hangout and Skype. We have students from all over Africa that are taking courses virtually from that university.

African governments have begun to recognize the importance of Intelligence Surveillance Reconnaissance (ISR), especially as it could help in fighting many social, economic, and educational challenges. It is not uncommon to find new ministries of information communication and technology springing up in most African countries. In fact, at the last World Summit for Information Society, most of the African delegations constituted ministers of new media communications. With the new threats being posed by Boko Haram (a new terrorist threat) and other border-related problems, and also domestic problems, African governments from either Anglophone, Francophone, or Lusophone Africa need secured "open" source platforms of sharing requisite information that will help them thwart the numerous threats they face. But the challenges they face are numerous, as already enumerated. Most of the governments already have territorial disputes and other politically driven disputes that make the matter of sharing information a daunting task.

At first, fear gripped the citizenry because the traditional media was firmly controlled by the state, and mainly governmental policy stances were allowed on the air (Alzouma, 2010). Then came multiparty politics that swept through the continent following the western winds of democracy.

The "one party rule" system that was customary in an overwhelmingly large number of African countries post-independence was toppled. Countries with long-time dictators like Bokassa of Equatorial Guinea, Mombutu Sesse Seko of Congo, Kinshasa, Samuel Doe of Liberia, Paul Biya of Cameroon, Gnassingbe Eyadema of Togo, Felix Houphet Boigny of Cote D'Ivoire, and Blaise Campaore of Burkina Faso were forced to organize national conferences or referenda for their people to choose either to remain with one-party systems or move to embrace multiparty democratic systems. There were successes and failures as the repressive regimes clamped down on the people willing to welcome change. Since the early 1990s, when this wind swept through the continent, successive means of empowering the people to stand up against the old order have continued unabated. The new tools that have given strength to the people are the social media communication platforms.

The people of sub-Saharan Africa were emboldened in 2011 when three North African dictators like Ben Ali in Tunisia, Hosni Mubarak in Egypt, and Mouamar Kadafi in Lybia were toppled by the people, galvanizing under what has now been duped the "Arab Spring" (Klein, 2014). This chapter examines the influence of social media campaigns as a way to galvanize people to vote for their favorite candidates or stand against fraud and other election malpractices in Burkina Faso. The recent action in Burkina Faso vindicates the power of social media and charts election courses and the future trajectory for other states to emulate. (http://www.oafrica.com/web/online-resources-for-the-2012-burkina-fa so-elections/)

A BRIEF HISTORY OF BURKINA FASO

The original name of Burkina Faso was Upper Volta. After the Berlin Conference of 1884, Africa was divided among the Europeans and Upper Volta fell into the hands of the French. Like other French African countries such as Togo, Benin, Algeria, Cameroon, Gabon, Congo, Zaire, and Ivory Coast, Burkina Faso experienced French direct rule from France in what is often referred to as Assimilation. Around 1904, the French appointed officials that administered the political, social, and economic affairs of Burkina Faso and other neighboring countries like Senegal and Niger. Skinner (1989) makes this observation in his 14-month-long anthropological study of the Mossi people of Ouagadougou (the capital of Burkina Faso): "This new colony was similar to the others in that it had its own administration (at Bamako), its own budget, and a Lieutenant Governor responsible to the Governor-General at Dakar" (p. 158).

The new colony here is Burkina Faso and all the administrators were French citizens. The role of the natives, called "vassals," was to collect taxes from their people and hand them over to them for effective administration of the colony. This action continued like this for all other French colonies of Africa (Adloff, 1964) until the 1960s, when most of them started gaining their independence from European hegemony.

On August 5, 1960, Burkina Faso had its first national president by the name of Maurice Yameogo. He was later succeeded by Jean-Baptiste Ouedraogo, who himself was deposed through a military coup by Thomas Sankara in 1984. When Sankara came to power, he wanted to end allegiance to French colonial masters by empowering the people to self-reliance. Before acceding to power, the country was facing serious economic crisis and foreign aid was not sufficient to solve the country's problems. According to Manning (1988), Sankara wanted "to reject international aid as a solution, arguing that a decade of aid had failed to make a dent in the country's poverty and dependence" (p. 128). His mantra was, "He who feeds you controls you" (Akomolafe, 2014, pp. 66-67).

It was under Sankara that the country assumed a new name, Burkina Faso. His populist stance did not augur well with his former colonial masters, and so his demise was eminent. His successor, Blaise Campaore, organized a bloody coup that toppled him in 1987. Campaore assumed power and was toppled not by a military coup in 2015, but by popular riots because he wanted to change the constitution of the state to allow him a limitless term to run for power. His overthrow has been attributed to popular uprising on the streets as well as on social media.

THE FORCE OF SOCIAL MEDIA TECHNOLOGY

When the Arab Spring was about to ebb, speculation was rife that sub-Saharan Africa was certainly going to catch a cold. Apparently, the sneezing could not penetrate the other southern parts of the continent in the way that it did in Tunisia, Egypt, and Libya. Nonetheless, social media platforms have been instrumental in disseminating pivotal information that has rallied the masses to political and economic action. The recent presidential election in Kenya (Langmia, 2014) and the petroleum riots in Nigeria (Adeiza, 2011) saw the prominent role that social media contributed to making the citizens and netizens[1] aware. The reason as to why there is an apparent slow penetration rate is multifarious:

1. The continent of Africa has, since the 1960s, witnessed periods of arms as well as civilian conflicts. The cases of Congo, Kinshasa, Chad, Ethiopia, Eritea, Mozambique, Rwanda, Burundi, Angola, and Zimbabwe gave rise to dictatorships. These ruthless leaders were firmly entrenched in power for long periods of time, thereby stalling any attempts at democratic change. It may take some time for these psycho-political and economic effects to lessen their grip on the people and its leaders.

2. The presence of many tribes, especially on the southern part of the continent, has created subcultures. These subcultures are rivals with deep historical differences that prevent mass mobilization and actions that could include all the constituent members of the state.

3. Religion could be another factor. The fact that Islam is the dominant religion in Tunisia, Lybia, and Egypt created a sense of unity and purpose. They could rally under a certain social spirit. But sub-Saharan Africa has many religious affiliations: Christianity, Islam, and Africanity. Even among Christians, there is Catholicism with their leader, the Pope in Rome. This is not the case with Anglican Christians, Presbyterians, Baptists, Pentecostals, Born Agains, etc. They all have different rituals of worship. This is also a factor in the mobilization movements if social media platforms have to be used to rally people for protest. Their different schools of thought and approaches to conflict resolution maybe a hindrance.

Be that as it may, there are in-roots that are being paved by social media communication. Given that there is a rise of mobile phone subscriptions on the continent, there is hope on the horizon that one day the fever from the Arab Spring in North Africa and the Middle East will get to the sub-Saharan folks. In the meantime, some countries, such as Burkina Faso, have just deposed their leader through a mass protest. Election of the country's president took place on November 29, 2015 with the election of Marc Christian Kabore as their new leader. The former deposed president, Blaise Campaore, is hiding in the neighboring Cote D'Ivoire. The election officials did not include members of his team on the ballot for elections, and that prompted the presidential guards that were still loyal to him to detain the interim president and prime minister for about two weeks. This gave rise to internal as well as external protests. Many African governments, including the International community, were quick to denounce the coup d'état and demanded that the interim government be installed immediately. It was not until the country's military decided to stage a march to the nation's capital, Ougadougu, that Deandre, the self-imposed leader of the coup, decided to hand back power to the previous regime. As a result, the election that was to take place was rescheduled for November 29. Citizens then decided to use social media, especially in the city center, to sensitize the public.

YOUTUBE CAMPAIGNS

YouTube has singled itself out as one of the prominent social media platforms at the mercy of the public and election candidates in Africa to campaign, promote party slogans, galvanize people to the polls, and record live events at polling stations to avoid fraudulent activity. It should be recalled that Burkina Faso is not the first country in the post-social media era to skillfully use YouTube as a valuable tool to sensitize the public. Cote D'Ivoire's Alassane Ouattara owes his rise to the helm of power in that country to YouTube, and other social media platforms like Facebook and Twitter, by the people of that country at home and abroad (Amutabi & Nasang'o, 2013). When Laurent Gbagbo was declared winner of the presidential election by the constitutional council in 2010, his supporters, and those of Ouattara at home and abroad, took to social media to shower their support to their candidates (Shumann, 2015). This would have been unprecedented in the pre-social-media era, because a lot could have been swept under the rug. As already discussed, traditional media (radio, television, and newspapers) post-independent Africa were under the firm grip and control of the regime in power (Eribo and Tanjong, 2002). It was a propaganda machine and that has not changed significantly today. What has neutralized the situation is the liberation of the media market in most of sub-Saharan Africa, and the plethora of social media communicative tools on mobile phones on the continent. Candidates for parliamentary, municipal, and presidential elections need not wait for traditional media outlets to get their messages across to their supporters. In fact, a good number of these candidates have their own websites and social media sites. This would have been unthinkable in the '60s, '70s and '80s.

The other country in sub-Saharan Africa that also benefitted from the new digital media technology—which influenced massive groups of people, especially young people, to go to the polls—was Kenya. The victory of Kenyatta, in spite of the fact that he was embroiled with war crimes at the Haque, was thanks to YouTube campaigns by his supporters at home and abroad (Langmia, 2014). Other leaders on the continent have also seen the power of social media technology, and are aggressively pursuing it to help them increase turn-out numbers on election days, or to transmit their messages.

Christian Kabore, the presidential candidate for Mouvement du people pour le Progres (MPP); and Ze´phirin Diabare, the opposition candidate for L'Union Pour Le Progres (UPC), used YouTube and Twitter to urge followers to cast ballots for them on November 29. This new form of technology has gained a fever pitch in Africa in the last 10 years, and the rate of mobile phones on the continent has equally increased. One of the advantages of using YouTube video clips to get to supporters is that users can react by clicking the thumps-up or thumbs-down icon to show their love or displeasure with the candidate. There is also room for them to write down their sentiments about the candidate, which would not be possible with traditional media. Another significant benefit to social media like YouTube is that viewership is not limited by space. Any upload on the Internet can be viewed by all and sundry within and beyond the boundaries of Burkina Faso. This is one of the most important contributions of new technology to electioneering practices in Africa.

FACEBOOK

Facebook, Twitter, and YouTube are the most popular social media sites in Africa. As seen in Table 5.1, there has been a steady rise in the rate of subscription by countries in the sub-Saharan region of the continent.

Table 5.1
GROWTH OF FACEBOOK USE IN AFRICA
Oct. 2011

CONGO	783,840	56%
ANGOLA	284,840	54%
SOMALIA	32,300	50%
MOZAMBIQUE	157,660	49%
ETHIOPIA	370,040	40%
TANZANIA	360,140	39%
BENIN	127,640	32%
NIGERIA	3,886,260	30%
CAMEROON	435,580	30%
MALI	120,200	27%
MAURITANIA	76,260	25%
GHANA	1,111,320	23%
SENEGAL	581,100	22%
BURKINA FASO	85,940	20%
KENYA	1,197,560	15%

Carrie Cockburn/The Globe and Mail
Source: African Center for Strategic Studies

From table 5.1, it can be seen that Burkina Faso had a subscription rate of over 85,940, representing 20 percent of all the other countries in the sub-region. There is no doubt that six years later, the number should have risen much higher.

Christian Kabore, who won the November 29 election, has a Facebook page (https://www.facebook.com/groups/1489932191278327/). This page has over 2,000 members and is open to the public. In it you will find a plethora of activities and discussions geared toward supporting the presidency of Kabore, and many other discussions praising him as the new leader of Burkina Faso. The majority of the submissions are in French, but a click on the translation button will open the English version. This is a novelty, and gives the opportunity to those both in and outside the country to contribute to the democratic process.

It is now necessary to have offices of social media personnel in most governments, which would have been unthinkable decades ago. During the traditional media epoch, public voices of dissent were never welcomed on the government-controlled radio/television stations (Alzouma, 2010). Another important benefit of having a Facebook page is that photographs, texts, audio, and video transmissions can be uploaded with ease and consumed instantly by followers around the world.

Facebook, like many other social media outlets, is a convenient forum whereby page owners can invite everyone to subscribe to their group and become members. The Kabore Facebook page automatically sends a request to the administrator about subscribing you to the group. Since the setting is made public, there is little room for the censorship that one would ordinarily have with government-controlled media—a fact that is quite evident by the campaign speeches, rallies, and party slogans seen on Kabore's Facebook page. When these audio-visual and textual data are uploaded, people all over can discuss as freely as they please. This is now the new norm for present and forthcoming election practices in Africa. Gone are the days for restricting dissent and encouraging sycophancy. According to Bax (2015) Twitter and Facebook are helping the youthful populations to galvanize and organize protests, which was unheard of before. The event to push Campaore out of power was initiated by youthful protest that was viewed by some political analyst as West Africa's Arab Spring (Louw-Vaudran, 2014).

CHALLENGES TO "E-GOVERNANCE"

Burkina Faso, like most other African countries that have been poorly governed by dictators since independence, face the daunting task of providing ICT amenities to strengthen relationships between government and the governed. Albert (2009), in his article on e-government in Africa, reiterates the view that infrastructural problems are the hindrance to effective e-governance in Africa. E-governance is the tendency for the populace to have online amenities at their disposal to contribute to ongoing debates on issues that can be legislated, or where executive action by the head of state is needed. It is imperative that the voices of the citizens, coming directly from the citizens, can be heard not exclusively through their representatives. This is why governments in Burkina Faso, or any other part of sub-Saharan Africa, should not create websites simply for uploading government decrees and legislative actions. Having a website of that nature can never be considered acts of initiating e-governance. For such an initiative to succeed, there has to be investment on ICTs to provide enough bandwidth for synchronous and asynchronous information sharing between various branches of government and the people. Attitudes toward technology use have to change, and more importantly, those on the helm of power ought to recognize that the voices of their citizens count. Without such initiatives, accountability cannot be assured and therefore e-governance can hardly function effectively. Now that the rate of ICTs is growing exponentially on the continent, this is the time for such initiatives to be undertaken. If they are not, the people, especially the youths, will take to social media technology, either through their handheld phones or in an Internet café, to force governments to act on their demands. This was evidenced in Burkina Faso with the ouster of Blaise Campaore, and the other dictators aforementioned in North Africa who suffered a similar fate.

Another challenge that Burkina Faso, like other African countries, faces is the question of transparency. It is not because a two-way dialogue can be established between the public and the government that trust can immediately be restored between the two entities. With respect to Burkina Faso, Blaise Campaore refused to cede power when the youths came out marching to the presidency. It was not until they had attacked the National Assembly buildings that they realized that revolution was indeed real. This force of social media, though limited in a country like Burkina Faso, still had a significant effect as captured below:

In the few days following Compaoré's ousting, the hashtag #BurkinaSpring began to appear on social media. The basic scenario of all the Arab Spring events in North Africa in 2011 were mass protests by frustrated youth to remove a long-serving head of state from power, with the acquiescence of the international community, or sections of it. (Louw-Vaudran, 2014)

This is a case where it was no longer transparency, but accountability. This was a clear example to the Campaore regime that time was no longer on their side because they had not been transparent with the people; therefore they decided to take down the entire regime. The hashtag galvanized people to Tweet about the recent events in the country. If left to traditional media outlets like radio, newspapers, and television, maybe this hashtag would not appear. Therefore, the challenge that governments in Africa will face in the coming years is how to control the new media sensation that has gripped other regions of the world. It means laws have to be passed in the parliament to authorize government surveillance.

The digital divide is a serious impediment to achieving success with electronic communication between the people and the government. Given the fact that the digital divide is the tendency to have only a handful of people with access to the new media technology, the situation in most countries in sub-

Saharan Africa is acute. The vast majority of the population lives in the rural setting with little or no access to formal education, let alone technology. This is the situation as observed by Mazrui (1986):

> Some African rulers sought to be taught western technology rather than import Western goods. In Ethiopia, Lebna Dengel in the seventeenth century and Te-wodros in the nineteenth century wrote to European rulers for assistance in industrialization. In the eighteenth century King Agaja Trudo of Dahomey thought the best way of stopping the slave trade was to industrialize west Africa with European help. Opoku Ware of Asante in the nineteenth century also tried to innovate industrially. *In each case, Europe refused help* [emphasis mine] (Mazrui, 1986, p. 165).

This is the fate that Africa has been bearing since Western industrial education was implemented. The implementation of the Internet will be no different, and so education, being the key to circumvent the challenges of new media access and knowledge, could not be attained by Africans. The same educational challenges still exist today. Another heartbreaking educational challenge that faces Africa was equally carried out by Ali Mazrui in this scenario:

> At Navrongo in rural Ghana, I have witnessed the slow death of a village school. The desks which broke were not replaced. Those which remained were carefully stored away during vacations. Some of the walls began to crumble, the hinges came off doors and windows; the desks were fewer each year. And yet that was not the worst of it. Africa is quite familiar with schools without walls, classroom in the open. Teaching can go on without desks, learning can take place without walls, but teaching without teaching materials is a different matter. An entire term had taken place at this school without the basics of writing, without paper, without pens. Someone complained, 'why not write to the head of state?' Someone retorted, 'write? With what?' (Mazrui, 1986, p. 204).

These are the challenges that are still present today in some parts of Africa, making it difficult to achieve general access and literacy with respect to new media technology. Governments may have to devote resources to invest in schools so that the next generation of kids will be proficient with new technologies.

CONCLUSION

Statistics from the African Center for Strategic Studies, as seen above, indicate that information communication technology, commonly referred to as ICT, is growing at an astronomical rate in Africa. In fact, the growth and penetration rate of ICT facilities in Africa has made the continent second to none in the world. The rate of adoption is growing mostly in the mobile sector. The question is whether this is the panacea to Africa's social, economic, and cultural malaise that could not be resolved through colonization and modernization. The industrial revolution transformed the West, and in their quest for raw materials and finished products for their goods and services, they came to Africa for labor (Mazrui, 1986). This is what helped cripple the continent economically, socially, and culturally. Misery and poverty skyrocketed because average citizens could not afford the prices of goods and services imported from the West. Socially, they were no longer a communal society living side by side with brothers and sisters, mother and father, cousins, nephews, aunts, uncles, stepfathers, stepmothers, and stepsons.

Today, Western social ways of life abound throughout the continent, creating confusion and disharmony in certain parts, as argued by Ali Mazrui. Politically, governments are now forced to reckon with the new normal of social media communication that galvanizes people in a split second to congregate and stage open protests, as was the case in Tunisia, Libya, Egypt, Cote D'Ivoire, and now Burkina Faso. Though these movements are limited to the youths mostly resident in the urban centers of Africa, there is little doubt that later the seeds of this revolution will sprout and spread to the hinterlands, especially as the rate of ICT penetration on the continent is growing geometrically. There is no doubt, however, that these Western social, economic, and cultural ways of life, with the introduction of information communication technologies (ICTs) in Africa, have permeated the political sphere.

It was the intention of this chapter to examine how this Internet revolution is affecting Africa, and how the new term "globalization of media technology" championed by social media communicative platforms such as YouTube and Facebook is impacting political lives in Burkina Faso, especially following the overthrow/resignation of Blaise Campoare and the election of Marc Christian Kabore.

REFERENCES

Adeiza, M. (2013). The trouble with social media in Africa. *New African, p. 28-79*

Adloff, R. (1964). *West Africa: The French-Speaking Nations.* Holt, Rinehart and Winston, Inc.

Akomolafe, F. (2014). Burkina Faso: You cannot kill ideas. *New African*, pp. 66-67.

Albert, I. O. (2009). Whose e-governmence? A critique of online citizen engagement in Africa. *African Journal of Political Science and International Relations, 3 (4),* pp. 133-141

Alzouma, G. (2010). Media, technology and democracy in Niger: What did the advent of ICTs change? In C. U. Nwokeafor and K. Langmia (Eds.) *Media and Technology in Emerging African Democracies.* Lanham, MD: University Press of America, pp. 23-42

Amutabi, M. N. & Nasang'o, S. W. (2013). *Regime Change and Succession Politics in Africa.* New York, NY: Routledge.

Bax, P. (2015, May17). Protests threatening leaders fueled by economic problems; Social media played a big part in protests. *Sunday Tribune,* South Africa.

Langmia, K. (2014). Cock-crow in the electronic republic: Social media and Kenya 2013 presidential election. In K. Langmia, T. Tyree, P. O'Brien and I. Sturgis (Eds.) *Social Media: Pedagogy and practice.* Lanham, MD: University Press of America, pp. 255-275

Langmia, K. (2010). The role of online media technology and democratic discourse in Cameroon: A case study of The Post and Cameroon Tribune. In C. U. Nwokeafor and K. Langmia (Eds.) *Media and Technology in Emerging African Democracies.* Lanham, MD: University Press of America, pp. 65-82.

Louw-Vaudran, L. (2014, Nov. 16). Iss Burkina Faso-West Africa's Arab Spring? Retrieved from http://www.issafrica.org/iss-today/burkina-faso-west-africa-arab-spring.

Manning, P. (1988). *Francophone Sub-Saharan Africa.* New York, NY: Columbia University Press.

Mazuri, A. (1986). *The Africans: A Triple Heritage.* Boston, MA: Little Brown and Company.

Shumann, A. (2015). The war of images in the Ivoirian post-electoral crisis: the role of news and online blogs in constructing political personas. In J. Gallagher (Ed.) *Images of Africa: Creation, Negotiation and Subversion.* Manchester, UK: Manchester University Press, pp. 144-166

Skinner, E. P. (1989). *The Mossi of Burkina Faso.* Chicago, Illinois: Waveland Press.

York, G. (2011, Nov. 14). Democratic yearning takes root in Africa. *International News,* p. A3.

ENDNOTES

1. Netizens are those engaged in dialogue in the cyberspace and citizens are outside the cyberspace.

CHAPTER 6
Technology Integration in Elections: The Nigerian Transformation Experience

Cosmas Uchenna Nwokeafor
Bowie State University

INTRODUCTION

The Internet has come to play an important role in elections worldwide, including Africa. From making it easier for voters to find information, to enabling the exchange of views, to increasing voters' engagement with decision makers and vice versa, the World Wide Web has, in many ways, changed how African voters approach the polls. This was evident in the March 28 and April 11, 2015 general elections in Nigeria. As the country went to the polls to elect their leaders—ranging from the president and members of the national assembly to the governorship and state legislators—voters passionately searched for information on candidates, parties, and polling units. To help voters find all necessary political information about various candidates to enable them to make their choices, January data and an information repository were launched in Nigeria to avail voters the opportunity to retrieve valuable information necessary to make decision on whom to vote for. The most essential of these data repositories was the Nigeria Elections, which was updated with news and information on a regular basis. Google hangouts and videos were also put in place for the purpose of providing a variance of information hubs that would be an easy source of information and data abstraction about the politicians and Candidates vying for an elected office. In addition to the established information hubs, a great number of local organizations were established, and various initiatives aimed at encouraging Nigerian voters to take part in the electoral process, enabling them to make informed democratic decisions.

PRESIDENTIAL ELECTION AND PARTY PRIMARIES

People's Democratic Party (PDP)
It had long been assumed that incumbent President Goodluck Jonathan would run for re-election. Despite declining approval ratings, he was still thought to be popular and had several high-profile supporters. Jonathan officially confirmed his candidacy on November 11, 2014 at a rally in Abuja, announcing to cheering supporters: "After seeking the face of God, and in the quiet of my family, and after listening to the clarion call of Nigerians, I have accepted to present myself to serve a second term." Jonathan ran unopposed in the People's Democratic Party (PDP) primaries on December 10, 2014, receiving the nomination of the party. However, this was against an unwritten rule that the PDP's presidential candidacy should alternate between Muslim northerners and Christian southerners, and opposition to Jonathan's candidacy led to the defection of dozens of PDP Members of Parliament (MPs) in the House of Representatives to the All Progressive Congress (APC).

All Progressive Congress (APC)
Prior to the elections, the All Progressives Congress was formed as an alliance of four opposition parties: the Action Congress of Nigeria, the Congress for Progressive Change, the All Nigeria Peoples Party, and the All Progressives Grand Alliance. Its primaries, also held on December 10, were won by Muhammadu Buhari, who defeated Kano State Governor Rabiu Kwankwaso, former Vice President Atiku Abubakar, Imo State Governor Rochas Okorocha, and newspaper editor Sam Nda Isaiah. On December 17, APC chose Professor Yemi Osinbajo as the running mate of Muhammadu Buhari. As of February 2015, "Though the APC's voter base is in the north, it enjoys support all over the country, unlike the opposition in 2011."

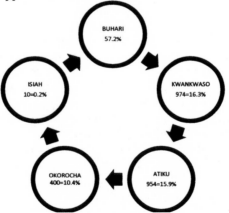

Figure 6.1 APC Candidates Running for Presidency in the Primary

Table 6.1 May 2015 Presidential Election Candidates According to Party

Candidate	Running Mate	Party	Acronym
Allagoa Chinedu	Arabamhen Mary	People's Party of Nigeria	PPN
Ambrose Albert Owuru	Haruna Shaba	Hope Party	Hope
Adebayo Musa Ayeni	Anthony Ologbosere	African People's Alliance	APA
Chekwas Okorie	Bello Umar	United Progressive Party	UPP
Comfort Oluremi Sonaiya	Seidu Bobboi	KOWA Party	KOWA
Ganiyu Galadima	Ojengbede Farida	Allied Congress Party of Nigeria	ACPN
Godson Okoye	Haruna Adamu	United Democratic Party	UDP
Goodluck Jonathan	Namadi Sambo	People's Democratic Party	PDP
Mani Ahmad	Obianuju Murphy-	African Democratic Congress	ADC
Martin Onovo	Ibrahim Mohammed	National Conscience Party	NCP
Muhammadu Buhari	Yemi Osinbajo	All Progressive Congress	APC
Rufus Salawu	Akuchie Cliff	Alliance for Democracy	AD
Sam Eke	Hassana Hassan	Citizens Popular Party	CPP
Tunde Anifowose- Kelani	Ishaka Ofemile	Accord Alliance	AA

Source: Independent National Electoral Commission (INEC).
www.inecnigeria.org

The candidates' standing after the APC primary recorded Muhammadu Buhari leading with a 57.2 percent of the total votes cast, which represents 3,430 votes with Rabin Kwankwaso with 16.3 percent representing 974, Atiku Abubakar with 15.9 percent representing 954 votes, Rochas Okorocha with 10.4 percent of the poll representing 400 votes, and Sam Nda Isaiah with 2 percent representing 10 votes with a total of 5,992 (http://www.nigeriamasterweb.com).

May 2015 Candidates Who Contested For The Presidential Election

There are 14 candidates from the 14 registered parties who contested the election. Among them, the main opposition Goodluck Jonathan faced was Muhammadu Buhari of the APC. While inaugurating a 250-bed orthopedic hospital in Wamakko, Buhari said: "We will stop corruption and make the ordinary people, the weak and the vulnerable our top priority."

National Assembly

The People's Democratic Party (PDP) has dominated Nigerian politics since democracy was established in 1999. While opposition parties have failed to present any serious opposition in the past, the All Progressives Congress (APC) is now being viewed as a serious challenge to the PDP in national elections. After a botched governor's election in Anambra State, there were serious concerns that the election would not go smoothly. The country's election commission had promised a better election process, hoping that combating electoral fraud would prevent the violence that had plagued previous Nigerian elections (http://www.inecnigeria.org). Despite this, a pre-election poll by Gallup noted that only 13 percent of Nigerians had confidence in the honesty of elections. The Socialist Party of Nigeria (SPN) filed for registration as a political party in order to contest the election, but the Independent National Electoral Commission (INEC) refused the registration. The SPN sued the INEC at the Federal High Court, claiming that the INEC had failed to respond to their petition within 30 days as prescribed by law, and that thus it would have to be registered automatically.

The presidential election was a trending topic in Nigeria on Twitter—one social media platform reflecting public opinion—although Goodluck Jonathan of the PDP may simply have had better support on social media, which is not representative of the population as a whole (http://www.inecnigeria.org). According to Impact Social, based on data from 40,000 tweets, Facebook messages, blogs, and other Internet outlets that mention PDP or Goodluck Jonathan, 70 percent of public opinion toward President Jonathan was positive, but messaging on the economy took up 6 percent of election conversation and was seen as a key PDP strength. Social media support for Buhari of the APC was a bit "noisier" without a single issue leveraged by the campaign to gain traction. There was general frustration that the campaign lacked consistency, content, and focus on the important issues at hand (http://www.inecnigeria.org).

Brief History of the Conduct of the 2015 General Election

The 2015 general election in Nigeria was the fifth quadrennial election to be held since the end of military rule in 1999. During this election, Nigerian voters elected the president, the governors, and members of the Senate and House of Representatives (National Assemblies). During this election circle, Goodluck

Jonathan, the incumbent president, sought his reelection for a second and final term. The elections were first scheduled to be held on February 14, 2015; however, the electoral commission postponed it by six weeks to March 28, mainly due to the poor distribution of Permanent Voter Cards (PVCs), and also to curb ongoing Boko Haram insurgency in certain northeastern states in the country. The government closed its land and sea borders from midnight on March 25 until the end of the polling date. The election was extended to March 29 due to delays and technical problems with the biometric card readers (http://www.guardianngr.com).

This election was rated the most expensive election ever held on the continent of Africa. Nigeria, Africa's most populous country, has Africa's largest economy and is its leading oil producer, a characteristic that places her on the apex of the pedestal in the comity of nations. Opposition candidate Muhammadu Buhari won the presidential election by more than 2.5 million votes, resulting in the incumbent President Goodluck Jonathan conceding defeat on March 31, before the results from all 36 states had been announced. The election marks the first time an incumbent president has lost re-election in Nigeria. According to Article 134 (2) of the Nigerian Constitution, "a presidential candidate will be duly elected after attaining both the highest number of votes cast, and having received at least a quarter of the votes at each of at least two-thirds of the 36 states and the Federal Capital Territory (FCT). If no candidate satisfies the requirement, a second election will be held between the two leading candidates within seven days from the pronouncement of the result." Candidate Muhammadu Buhari, having attained the stipulations on Article 134 (2) as stated on the nation's constitution, was elected by the INEC and was sworn in on May 29, 2015 (http://www.inecnigeria.org).

CREDIBILITY OF ELECTION ATTRIBUTED TO SMART CARD READERS AND PVC

In view of the analysis and detailed review of the presidential election won by the candidate of his party, the All Progressive Congress (APC), the director of the Electoral Planning and Monitoring of the APC Presidential Campaign Council, Theodore Ekechi, opined that the use of the Smart Card removed the chances of manipulating the 2015 election process. Ekechi referred the challenges witnessed during the election with the integration of the card reader and the PVC as human-driven, and antics employed by persons that wanted to scuttle the overall election process. Ekechi (2015) summarized the integration of the card reader and the PVC as follows:

> The fact that we have a card reader that did not function perfectly does not mean that it is not a good process. I think what we need to do is to improve on it. We can tell you that most of the problems encountered with the card reader were man made.

He further noted that despite the challenges, the use of the card-reader technology was an addition that should be sustained and improved.

> It created the sanity we have today and the fact is that we are going to have less court cases related to elections. Every genuine democrat should make the sacrifice of patience that the use of card reader and the PVC process demands.

The chairman of the Independent National Electoral Commission (INEC), Professor Attahiru Jega, clearly stated that the biometric card readers and the PVCs accelerated the election processes and helped tremendously in stopping rigging and other malicious election malpractices that had consistently marred a free and fair election in Nigeria. Jega further stated that he had no regrets, insisting on deploying the biometric card readers and PVCs for the conduct of the general election, adding that he knew that the decision would attract attacks on his integrity as a person. He maintained that it is only those that hitherto nurtured plans to fraudulently manipulate the outcome of the elections that have been crying foul over the introduction of the technology, which he said would only add credibility to the electoral process in the country. The INEC had perfected all its strategies and put every apparatus in place with a view to ensuring a hitch-free poll that will reflect the choice of Nigerians (Jega, 2015).

The biometric card-reader machines and PVCs were tremendously helpful to the INEC and its staff in all 36 states in addressing all the irregularities, starting from the accreditation of voters at all the polling units, and several other integral parts of the election process, including the collating, and of course, the announcement of the election results. The integration of this new technology made it difficult to manipulate the election when all the information with regard to the number of voters that turned out at every polling unit was automatically captured and transmitted by the card-reader machines (Jega, 2015).

The integration of the biometric card readers and the use of the private voter card (PVC) have made rigging impossible for those who intended to plunge the general election into chaos and scuttle the entire process. The technology integration legitimizes the process, and led to a more credible outcome as there was no way the total number of votes cast at a specific polling unit could exceed the number of accredited persons. Such discrepancy in figures would be immediately spotted. This technology will further make it impossible for any corrupt electoral officer to connive with any politician to pad-up results (Jega, 2015).

The past practices of dubious INEC officials involved the delay of the entry of a number of accredited voters until the end of voting, so as to have the leeway to tamper with results. This was a very devastating and deplorable problem which has been obviated by the introduction and usage of the biometric Smart Card readers and the PVCs. In the recent articulation of the INEC's best practices, both the card readers and the result sheets would be taken to the ward levels. Once there is evidence of tampering, the information saved in the card reader will be retrieved. It is as a result of such a transparent process that many of the political pundits and party stalwarts opposed the use and integration of technology during the 2015 elections. The corrupt strategies fraught with manipulation of election results, snatching of voters boxes and intimidation, all common practices in the past, was reduced to a minimum with the integration of technology.

The Independent National Electoral Commission (INEC) put a very formidable peg on the report of election results whereby all the results coming to local government collection centers will be scanned, transformed to PDF format, and uploaded on their website so that anybody can go there and confirm results from his polling unit. This transparent reportage mechanism added value to the INEC's performance process and thereby paved the way for a credible result.

The biometric card readers have been rated as the best for accreditation and the process of conducting elections in Nigeria, despite the challenges attributed to its usage. According to the European Union Chief Election Observer in Nigeria, Mr. Santiago Fisa, who monitored the presidential elections in the Maitama district of Abuja, despite its challenges, the card readers and PVCs were still the best form of accrediting voters. He commended the courage of Nigerians to exercise their rights to vote and opined that although the accreditation of Nigerian voters was slow, the biometric card readers ensured the integrity of the election processes.

REVIEW OF THE IMPACT OF TECHNOLOGY IN THE 2015 GENERAL ELECTIONS IN NIGERIA

The March 28 presidential election, previously scheduled for February 14, 2015, was peacefully conducted, with only minor and sometimes technological hitches here and there in various polling stations across the country. Prior to the initial date of February 14, the most influential participants on the political stage were finding ways to manipulate and subvert the conversation in their favor. Every trick in the book was in play—spoof Twitter accounts, viral smear campaigns, blatant astroturfing, etc. In response, civil society was trying to mobilize and use technology to cut through the noise and help citizens engage productively. The obvious war on who held the most dignified or most high-performance technology gadget was on, and the airwaves did not make the matter of this war of party and personal interest—orchestrated by the use of the most appropriate handset and or information technology-enhancing mechanism that money can buy—easier to follow. The stage was set as the days drew nearer. The various political caterpillars had drawn their ammunition for a victory on their side. In this war of interest, there were various ways by which technology and the Internet had already impacted Nigeria's 2015 general elections.

Election Monitoring

Local cell-phone developers have designed mobile applications and websites that can aggregate real-time updates from polling units from across Nigeria, some of them with geo-tagging functions to track election updates by location. Nigeria Elections was a mobile application in itself. It aggregates news around the election polling units across the entire country and also provides a listing of polling booths, national constituencies, presidential candidates, and their running mates. The results of the election are uploaded on the applications when they are officially announced. The INEC, Nigeria's electoral umpire (Independent National Electoral Commission) allows users to get information on polling units, the election process, and the status of their PVC. Other similar election monitoring applications are EiE's Revoda, Pollwatchng.com and Nigeriadecide.org. These are websites which allow voters/observers to submit situation reports about the elections in their local polling units. Users can upload images with cursory comments about the situation being reported (Onalaja, 2015).

Online Conversations and Campaigns

Traditional media (print, television, and radio) remained the major sources of information dissemination in Nigeria, until enormous mobile penetration, data availability, and cheap access to the Internet and the world wide web (www. com) pages. The growth of access and Internet usage in Nigeria had since been rated at 16 percent in 2014, making a total of about 37.53 percent of Nigerians with Internet access. Politicians have joined the growing online community, which contributed to a much-desired platform upon which to sell their respective campaign agenda in the form of a manifesto, and allows them to cash in by fund-spending and flashy words. Political office hopefuls and their supporters have taken to Twitter and sent out political messages with hashtags like #GEJ_WINS, # CHANGE, etc. (Onalaja, 2015). To show that they #get it, both front-running political parties—the APC and PDP—have staged Google Hangouts. The All Progressive Congress's (APC's) Vice Presidential Candidate, Professor Yemi Osinbajo, and Lagos State Governor Babatunde Fashola, answered questions from Nigerian youth. The PDP's Google Hangout session was staged for its Lagos governorship candidate, Jimi Agbaje.

An overwhelming torrent of websites and applications, designed by political parties and their stalwarts to reach supporters, were put in place. Forwardnigeria.ng and Apcgm.mb.ca.org are affiliated with the PDP and APC presidential candidates respectively. They have also embraced candidate-specific applications such as the Muhammadu Buhari and the APC Situation Room for the APC presidential candidate, Muhammadu Buhari and the others for his party, APC. Forward Nigeria was for the incumbent president and PDP presidential flag bearer, Goodluck Jonathan. Individuals and civil organizations are also driving conversation via the Internet. Enough Nigeria Coalition's eie.ng is a website that provides information on candidates vying for political offices, as well as beams INEC's press releases. Sterling and Greenback, a Lagos-based enterprise, also created a sentiment machine that measures the level of support for different parties (Onalaja, 2015).

Online Advertising

Online advertising, also called online marketing or Internet advertising, is a form of marketing and advertising that uses the Internet to deliver promotional marketing messages to consumers. It includes email marketing, search engine marketing (SEM), social media marketing, many types of display advertising (including web banner advertising), and mobile advertising. Like other advertising media, online advertising frequently involves both a publisher, who integrates advertisements into its online content, and an advertiser, who provides the advertisements to be displayed on the publisher's content. Other potential participants include advertising agencies who help generate and place the ad copy, an ad server that technologically delivers the ad and tracks statistics, and advertising affiliates who do independent promotional work for the advertiser (Business Dictionary.com). In 2011, Internet advertising revenues in the United States surpassed those of cable television and nearly exceeded those of broadcast television. In 2013, Internet advertising revenues in the United States totaled $42.8 billion, a 17 percent increase over the $36.57 billion in revenues in 2012. U.S. Internet ad revenue hit a historic high of $20.1 billion for the first half of 2013, up 18 percent over the same period in 2012.

Online advertising is widely used across virtually all industry sectors, including politics. Since the communication software (browser) reveals sufficient information about the site's visitors, online advertising can be custom-tailored to match user preferences. The usage of online advertising in politics may be new, but has tremendously strengthened the process of bringing political awareness, candidates, and their messages to the electorate, as was glaring in the 2015 general elections in Nigeria.

In the early days of the Internet, online advertising was mostly prohibited. For example, two of the predecessor networks to the Internet, ARPANET and NSFNet, had "acceptable use policies" that banned network "use for commercial activities by for-profit institutions." The NSFNet began phasing out its commercial use ban in 1991.

Email

The first widely publicized example of online advertising was conducted via electronic mail. On May 3, 1978, a marketer from DEC (Digital Equipment Corporation), Gary Thuerk, sent an email to most of the ARPANET's American West Coast users, advertising an open house for a new model of a DEC computer. Despite the prevailing acceptable use policies, electronic mail marketing rapidly expanded and eventually became known as "spam" (Business Dictionary.com).

During the just-concluded general elections in Nigeria, sponsored posts were very popular and were popping up at every click of the mouse, as there was a good possibility of encountering a political ad, thanks to AdSense, while watching a YouTube video or just reading through your favorite blog. Social media brand promoters known as pirates of Nigerian Twitter are also part of the online advertising stratagem. They are throwing their online weight behind the highest bidding political party. Various scripted messages, like those promoting the incumbent president for his accomplishments or speaking positively of Muhammadu Buhari, become too popular on Twitter.

Crowdfunding

Crowdfunding is the practice of funding a project or venture by raising monetary contributions from a large number of people, typically via the Internet. The Oxford Dictionary and the Merriam-Webster Dictionary both define crowdfunding as the practice of funding a project or venture by raising money from a large number of people who each contribute a relatively small amount, typically via the Internet. The crowdfunding model is fueled by three types of participants: 1) the project initiator, who proposes the idea and/or project to be funded; (2) individuals or groups who support the idea; and (3) a moderating organization (the "platform") that brings the parties together to launch the idea. In 2013, the crowdfunding industry grew to be over $5.1 billion worldwide.

The All Progressive Congress (APC), challenging the incumbent party PDP and waxing very strong, has sought to crowdsource funds for their campaign. The party has employed means ranging from ringtones, premium SMS, scratch cards, and e-transactions to get supporters to contribute financially to its political cause. The Nigerian Communications Commission (NCC) later banned the APC's mobile crowdfunding short code, but this decision has been struck out by a federal high court sitting in Lagos. The court also ruled that the NCC and the telcos involved pay N500 million ($2.5 million) in damages to the party (Onalaja, 2015). Gboza Gbosa Technology recently launched a broad-based fundraising platform, SpeaksForUS, to help organizations with crowd-sourced fundraising. The website has a category for political donations where you can make donations by buying political posters, bags, and other party-branded items, with prices ranging between N48 ($0.25) to N10,000 ($50) naira (Onalaja, 2015).

Fact-Checking

Fact-checking is the process of checking factual assertions in nonfictional text, usually intended for publication in a periodical, to determine their veracity and correctness. The job requires general knowledge and the ability to conduct quick and accurate research. The resources and time needed for fact-checking mean that the work is not done at most newspapers, where reporters' timely ability to correct and verify their own data and information is chief among their qualifications. Publications issued on a weekly, monthly, or infrequent bases are more likely to employ fact-checking. Fact-checking, known as "research" at many publications, is most critical for those publishing material written by authors who are not trained reporters—such writers being more likely to make professional, ethical, or mere factual mistakes. Fact-checking methods vary. Some publications have neither the staff nor the budget needed for verifying every claim in a given article. Others will attempt just that, going so far as communicating with the authors' sources to review the content of quotations. According to the *Columbia Journalism Review*, German weekly *Der Spiegel* runs "most likely the world's largest fact-checking operation," employing the equivalent of 80 full-time fact checkers as of 2010. Factchecki.ng is a website that cross-checks dubious information in circulation, debunks myth, and verifies fact. On fact-checking, you can submit questions, facts, and lies. However, the platform only caters to facts related to the APC presidential aspirant, Muhammadu Buhari (Onalaja, 2015).

Tech-driven Data Crunching is the Future of African Politics/Elections

Data is distinct pieces of information, usually formatted in a special way. All software is divided into two general categories: *data* and *programs*. Programs are collections of instructions for manipulating data. Data can exist in a variety of forms—as numbers or text on pieces of paper, as bits and bytes stored in electronic memory, or as facts stored in a person's mind. A nation's budget basically determines how well the government can function. Budgit is a website that allows you to simulate the Nigerian budget. Budgit simply breaks down the Nigerian budget and allows you to "become the finance minister for a day," thereby coming up with your own budget structure. Although Budgit was not created for the 2015 election, it could make the electorate better informed and lead to a sound analysis of the promises of the electoral candidates. Even though it took the electoral body about three days to collate and announce official results, Nigerians on social media had already received the tentative results of the elections on social media from media platforms such as Sahara Reporters, and the opposition party, the APC, which had a very big election situation center in Lagos. Citizens only stayed glued to TV sets to find out whether the results had been tampered with, while the electoral officials made their way to the International Conference Center in Abuja from across the 36 states of the federation.

One of the defining moments that pointed to the fact that technology-driven data crunching is the future of politics and Africa's electoral process was when agents of the PDP said the electoral body chairman, Attahiru Jega, had already shared the results of the election with the APC; and the results, being gradually announced by the INEC, were similar to those that were already on the website of the APC. Even though Jega exonerated himself from the allegation and claimed the commission's officially declared results were the real ones, the fact that each party had at least an agent at each polling unit nationwide pointed to the fact that, armed with just mobile phones, results announced at the polling units across the country could be sent to a situation room, collated, computed, analyzed, and published within a few hours after elections had been conducted in Nigeria or elsewhere. This is the future of elections and politics in Nigeria and across Africa. The days of relying on big forms and old-school calculators to compute election results are numbered. Its strong voice is gradually disappearing as Nigerians herald the emergence of its next president with loud shouts of Sai Baba, Sai Buhari! (Onalaja, 2015).

Online Polls

The advent of online technologies during the 1990s has led to the development of numerous new automated data collection techniques and preconfigured web polls (Ostendorf, 1994). These tend to emulate hand-held keypad systems used for anonymous polling in political and advertising research (Baggaley, 1997).

Uses of the term "poll" differ widely, depending on the context and for what reasons they are being used. Mancinelle (2003) suggests that polls refer to a single question, while surveys are more complex. An earlier report in the current series (Technical Report XII) has recommended the use of the term "online polling" in referring generally to "questionnaires, quizzing, survey and assessment products" (Baggaley, Kane & Wade, 2002).

The online format typically associated with these activities is one in which participants place closed-ended "votes" in response to fixed questions or statements, and in which the votes are counted. The current use of "polling" as a generic term is thus consistent with the definition of "polling" provided by the Oxford Dictionary (Sykes, 1976) as being associated with voting and mediated by the counting of ballots. For the purposes of the current discussion, an online polling system may be further defined as an asynchronous or real-time process of information gathering, obtained via responses to question(s) mediated by web-based formats (Oxford Dictionary). Email polls embedded in the body of the message have been found to produce a five-fold increase in response over those sent as attachments (Moss & Hendry, 2002). According to Kehoe and Pitkow (1996), "implementation of HTML forms turned the web into a two-way medium to contact the audience directly."

Online polling is regarded as having advantages over the pencil-and-paper alternative, including savings of time and money, and fewer data collection errors (Solomon, 2001). It has been described as yielding faster responses, permitting adaptive responses whereby the questions can be changed according to the users' input (Watt & Van Den Berg, 1995), and reducing fatigue by the use of easy click-response methods and color graphics (Bonk, 2003). Handverk, Carson, and Blackwell (2000) have suggested that web respondents seem more comfortable with providing comments than mail-in poll respondents, possibly owing to "an additional sense of confidentiality." Carbonaro, Bainbridge, and Wolodko (2002) describe advantages of online polling, such as built-in security methods and user-friendly editing features (e.g., copy/paste, data processing, storage and display). Hitherto, web polling has been regarded as less suspect than telephone surveys in terms of hidden sales motivations (Yun & Trumbo, 2000), although this may change. A cost-effectiveness benchmark favoring online polling over more traditional methods has been provided by Dillon (2001).

In anticipation of the forthcoming elections in Nigeria, media houses came up with online presidential polls. Three of these polls were more popular and were held by Sahara Reporters; President Jonathan's social media aide, Reno Omokri; and AIT. These online pollsters crunched poll numbers to Nigerian citizens regarding the standing of their candidates, but they were marked by controversies, accusations of double voting, and biased umpires. Whatever the case may be, it was clear that all parties involved in these elections didn't want to look like they were falling behind in the digital popularity race. Nigeria Decide 2015 and NaijaPolls are applications that allow registered voters to read the bios of their preferred candidates and vote for them across the nation.

Table 6.2
Nigeria Decide 2015 Polls Result – Have you Decided?

Candidate	Party	Polls Result
Allagoa Chinedu	Peoples Party of Nigeria (PPN)	0%
Ambrose A. Owuru	Hope Party (Hope)	0%
Adebayo Musa Ayemi	African Peoples Alliance (APA)	0%
Chekwas Okorie	United Progressive Party (UPP)	0%
Comfort Oluremi Sonaiya	Kowa Party (Kowa)	1%
Ganiyu Galadima	Allied Congress Party of Nigeria (ACPN)	0%
Godson Okoye	United Democratic Party (UDP)	0%
Goodluck Jonathan	Peoples Democratic Party (PDP)	24%
Mani Ahmad	African Democratic Congress (ADC)	0%
Martin Onovo	National Conscience Party (NCP)	0%
Muhammadu Buhari	All Progressive Congress (APC)	71%
Rufus Salawu	Alliance for Democracy (AD)	1%
Sam Eke	Citizens Popular Party (CPP)	0%
Tunde Anifowose Kelani	Accord Alliance (AA)	1%
	Labor Party (LP)	2%

Source: Independent National Electoral Commission (INEC).
www.inecnigeria.org

Electronic Smart Card Readers

Nigeria's electoral regulatory body, INEC, hoping to curb irregularities and fraudulent malpractices associated with the electoral process, employed the use of Smart Card readers to verify the authenticity of the permanent voters' card at the polling booths. The biometric Smart Card reader—a product of TECHEDGE company from Atlanta, Georgia, in the United States of America—doesn't just authenticate the card, it also allows for the biometric authentication of the legitimacy of the Smart Card holder—at least in theory. In view with its best practice, INEC has reportedly indicated that in cases where the biometric authentication fails, it would revert to the manual authentication of voters to make sure that every voter's right is not disenfranchised.

The integration of technology in the electoral process as a tool for social change in Nigeria is new and booming (Onalaja, 2015), but it had hardly matured as subsequent usage and practices over time will tell. The needle is twitching, but just barely, with strong hope of a much brighter future.

Reducing Rigging to a Bare Minimum

Rigging during elections is a fairly popular electoral tactic in Nigeria (Adepoju, 2015). "Rigging" is the word used to describe the major electoral malpractice in which votes are massively cast for a candidate. For example, during previous elections, some regions of the country that didn't have up to one million voters used to present an "amplified" total number of votes reaching as high as two to three million. This was done by hijacking electoral materials and/or by printing their own ballot papers. Looking at the 2015 elections, the Nigerian electoral body, the Independent National Electoral Commission (INEC), introduced the permanent voter card (PVC) reader—something that unsettled several politicians who allegedly relied on rigging to win.

The first thing the card reader did during the 2015 election was to authenticate voter cards and match each card to the holder via confirmation and matching of thumbprints. Since not all registered voters will eventually vote, it introduced new indices, including the total number of accredited users, which means no matter how much the politicians rig, they cannot go above the total number of accredited voters that are verified by the card readers, or such results would be cancelled (Adepoju, 2015).

Social Media's Impact

In the previous elections, social media was not taken very seriously because the playmakers extensively believed that only a few Nigerians used the medium. But the 2015 general elections were probably won and lost on social media, even before the citizens got the ballot papers. Muhammadu Buhari's associated topics trended more easily on Twitter than Goodluck Jonathan's, forcing the PDP social media camp to sponsor trend topics on Twitter and several posts on Facebook. It also promoted its Twitter handles and Facebook pages, not to mention numerous Google ads, even though comparatively the APC's social media team did not do much sponsored social-media promotion. The Buhari social media topics were also more fun-filled and got the attention of even the president's supporters on Twitter. A good example is the *#BabaWhileYouWereGone* topic that trended when Buhari traveled to London, while moments after he was declared winner, *#BabaNowThatYouAreThere* became a trending topic—and an opportunity for Nigerians, especially his fans, to tell him the changes that they desired (Adepoju, 2015).

Mobile Video

The high penetration rate of Smartphones positively impacted the political race and empowered citizens with an instrument-turned-powerful-medium that they could use to accurately tell stories without holding degrees in journalism. They also got to stay anonymous. There is video evidence circulating on social media platforms to support claims of electoral malpractice. Some of the videos were so boldly taken that you sometimes ask yourself whether they were staged, or whether the persons that recorded them had a death wish. They've become powerful tools in the hands of online debaters with which they can win arguments without saying anything apart from introducing the video and providing information on where the videos were taken and names of the participants (Adepoju, 2015).

Internet and Live TV Can Make It Easy to Go Viral and Gain Popularity Within Minutes

Prior to the morning of Tuesday, March 31, 2015, many Nigerians did not know anything about Peter Godsday Orubebe, although he is a former federal minister. But when he attempted to create confusion and ultimately (and abruptly) end the collation of the election's results live on international TV, he became an instant Internet sensation, leaving behind several memories that will not be forgotten easily. Within a few minutes, he became the number-one trending topic in Nigeria, and 24 hours later, he remained among the top 10. His Wikipedia page was also swiftly updated to feature his special moment of shame on TV. The video, which has already gone viral, is available on various platforms and the memes flying around are hilarious (Adepoju, 2015).

THE M2SYS TECHNOLOGY'S IMPACT IN NIGERIA'S 2015 ELECTION

M2SYS Technology is a global biometric identification management company that provides biometric identity management software and hardware, along with enterprise software applications to several vertical markets, including public safety, workforce management, point of sale, healthcare, education, child care, transportation security, banking, membership management, and in the case of Nigeria, the biometric card reader technology that cut fraud risk in the 2015 polls that elected Muhammadu Buhari the president. They offer software development kits to software vendors that wish to add biometric identification to their applications, and solutions directly to end users (https://www.M2SYS.com/m2-

S.htm). The name "M2SYS" is short for "Mind to System," and was coined by CEO Mizan Rahman to describe the flow of development ideas into a tangible, market-ready, biometric recognition software engine and ancillary products. M2SYS was incorporated in 2001 as a small software company that developed supply chain software. As the company explored other areas of technology innovation, it later pursued fingerprint biometric research and development after the invention of Bio-Plugin. M2SYS established its headquarters in Atlanta, Georgia, United States, where it continues to operate. In 2007, they added an Asian office located in Dhaka, Bangladesh, and in 2013, a South America office in Lima, Peru (https://www.M2SYS.net/store/pc/msg.asp).

M2SYS works closely with its clients, enabling them to capitalize on the benefits of using biometrics for security and accelerating their return on investment (ROI). These case studies of multi-modal biometrics security deployments for various verticals show how biometric security software solutions can protect the welfare of citizens, stop corruption and fraud, and create efficiency (http://www.M2SYS.com/M2-S.htm). This technology seems to have created a very unique political atmosphere in Nigerian politics, most importantly among the opposition party APC, who won the presidential election and majority seats in the national assembly, as well as the gubernatorial elections. It has no doubt impacted the 2015 elections and the electoral process as never before, and may have created a clear-cut avenue for technology to take control of future Nigerian elections.

CONCLUSION

The M2SYS technology provided the Nigerian government with 10,000 fingerprint scanners and biometric software to help register over 20 million of 71 million voters for their biometric voter registration exercise in the 2015 general elections (http://www.M2SYS.com/M2-S.htm). Millions of Nigerian voters registered with the biometric voter registration technology that assisted in providing free and credible elections without fear of corruption, bribery, or duplicate voters. In the past, the use of outdated voter registration systems cast a shadow of doubt over election results because of corruption, cheating, irregularities, and accusations of fraud at the polls. The impact of these outdated modalities, coupled with duplicate registrations, proxy voting, and the absence of a credible mechanism to verify the true identity of voters—which promotes fraud and illegal practices—have jeopardized democratic principles and institutions in the country. In order to establish a free and credible election, the Nigerian electoral body, the Independent National Electoral Commission (INEC), seeks a technology solution that would help to promote the "one citizen, one vote" mandate.

In the process of seeking a technology solution, an Atlanta, Georgia, company, TECH EDGE, answered the call with the provision of a human-recognition technology that allows computers to identify fingerprints. The impact of this technology resulted in an election and electoral paradigm shift preventing the fraud and irregularities that continued to prevail in subsequent elections in Nigeria.

The Nigerian government's investment in the M2SYS biometric solution technology was a milestone in the history of elections in the country. Capturing millions of eligible voters, the use of the technology (biometric identities) allowed election agencies to maintain full control of the voting process and acted as a preventive measure for potential illegal manipulation of the voting polls by incumbent leaders or political parties. The use of the M2SYS technology, which was spread out at hundreds of voting registration centers throughout the country, helped to capture and verify millions of voter identities with the Independent National Electoral Commission (INEC). It also helped in coordinating effectively the accreditation of voters and the counting and reporting of votes.

Through the application of this technology-driven voting platform, the federal government of Nigeria has established a political legitimacy that has resulted in the establishment of a free and fair election paradigm absent of fraud and corruption, thereby positioning Nigeria as a model of democracy for the entire region.

Technology appears to have played a decisive role in ensuring that Nigeria's fraught elections were more credible than they have been in the past. Western diplomats and civil society activists have suggested that the party's real worry was that the technology, designed to lock automatically as soon as the full quota of eligible voters at each polling station have been accredited, would do what it was meant to, which is prevent fraud and present a free, fair, and credible election that would result in a meaningful democratic dispensation where the leaders are credibly elected and not selected, as was the case in the past.

Despite the multiple glitches here and there during the 2015 election, the Atlanta, Georgia, technology appears to have curbed the multiple voting and ballot stuffing that marred previous elections in the Africa's most populous country, Nigeria. According to Nasir el-Rufai (2015), the governor of Kaduna State, and a closer adviser to Muhammadu Buhari, "Whatever one can say about INEC, they must be commended for introducing the technology to improve the election process in Nigeria."

REFERENCES

Adepoju, P. (2015). Five ways technology impacted the Nigerian elections: Africa News. April http://www. Apcgm.mb.ca/org Apcgm.mb.ca.org. Association of Professional Engineers & Geoscientists of Manitoba (APEGM). Geomatics Directory Canada.

Baggaley, J., Kane,T; & Wade, B. (2002). For online polling comparison information. Journal of Online and Teaching.

Baggaley, J. (1997). Cross-cultural uses of media research technology. European Association for International Education, Amsterdam, Netherlands, pp.33-45 http://www.businessdictionary.com/ BusinessDictionary.com OnlineBusinessDictionary

Bonk, C. J. (2003). Blended learning environment. www.aect.org. Association for Educational Communications and Technology, http://www.cjr.org/ Columbia Journalism Review. Columbia Journalism Review – Encouraging Excellence in Journalism. Bi-monthly publication of the Columbia University Graduate School of Journalism

Carbonaro, Bainbridge & Wolodko (2002). Online Polling as a Collaborative Tool, http://www.irrodl.org. Describe advantages of online polling such as built-in security methods and user-friendly editing features.

Dillion (2001). Dillon's CV-2001 Vibratory Case Cleaner: Case Preparation. https://www.dillonprecision.com/.../Dillon__039_s_CV_2001_Vibratory

Ekechi, T. (2015). The Director of Planning for the All progressives Congress's campaign team, Dr. Theodore Ekechi, says he is optimistic that President Muhammadu Buhari of Nigeria will be able to block the leakages in the oil sector in Nigeria and reduce corruption. https://WWW.YOUTUBE.COM/WATCH/ v=FSAU4AYTIUW. May 29.

Factcheckin.ng (2015). https://www.*factcheck.org*/Monitors the factual accuracy of what is said by major U.S. political players in the form of TV ads, debates, speeches, interviews, and news releases.

Forwardnigeria.ng Journalist101, http://www.forwardnigeria.ng/ Facebook *https://www.facebook.com/Journalist101/posts/350207398500138*. Forward Nigeria is working to continue the progress made under President Goodluck Jonathan and help our country fulfil its potential.

Gbosa Gbosa Technology Ltd. Gboza Gbosa Technology Ltd., Nigeria's First Ecommerce...*gboza.net*/ SpeaksForUs provides social campaigners with the ability to raise funds for their cause using targeted crowdsourced ecommerce. Targeted crowdsource. http://www.guradianngr.com How Goodluck Jonathan lost the Nigerian election *www.theguardian.com › World › Nigeria.*

Handverk, Carson, & Blackwell (2000). Online Polling as a Collaborative Tool. www.irrodl.org › Home › Vol 4, No 2 (2000). Have suggested that Web respondents seem more comfortable with providing comments than mail-in poll respondents. http://www.inecnigeria.org inecnigeria.org How To Register For Voter Card - Elections. *www.electionin.org › Nigeria* Apr 10, 2015 - inecnigeria.org How to Register for Voter Card: Independent National Election Commission Nigeria. Sponsored Links. Organization

Jega, A. (2015). Apr 1, 2015 Jega vowed to reform Nigeria's electoral process to ensure free and fair elections

Mancinelle, (2003). Online Polling as a Collaborative Tool www.irrodl.org › Home › Vol 4, No 2 (2003) suggests that polls refer to a single question, while surveys are more complex. An earlier report in the current series

Merriam-Webster: Dictionary and Thesaurus. https://www.merriamwebster.com

Moss, J. & Graham, H. (2002). British Educational Communications and Technology Agency.

M2-S Fingerprint Reader, USB Fingerprint Scanner https://www.youtube.com/watch?v=ssmiMcsxXwE Nov 3, 2009 - Uploaded by M2SYS.

The M2-S fingerprint reader (http://www.m2sys.com/M2-S.htm) is a durable fingerprint scanner. http://www.M2SYS.net/store/pc/msg.asp.

M2-EasyAccess Fingerprint Access Control m2sys.net. https://www.m2sys.net/ store/pc/viewPrd.

http://www.M2SYS.net. Biometric. M2SYS. Retrieved 4 November 2015

http://www.M2SYS.net. TAG Names Top 40 Innovative Technology. Tagonline.org. Retrieved 4 November 2015

http://www.nigeriamasterweb.com Nigeria 2015 Presidential Election Results Live Report, nigeriamasterweb.com/.../nigeria-2015-presidential-el..."It's the first time we are using this technology, PVCs (permanent voters' card), card readers. Mar 28.

Ostendorf, M., Wightman, C. W. (1994). Automatic labeling of prosodic patterns. IEEE Trans.

Oxford Dictionary. www.oxforddictionaries.com/us OxfordDictionaries.

Pitkow, J. E. & Kehoe, C. (1996). Advertising and the World Wide Web. *https://books. google.com/books?isbn=1135672377*. Journal of Broadcasting and Electronic Media, 34, 17–36.

Santiago, F. (2015).Elections leadership.ng/news/.../elections-what-difference-did-card-readers-make Credibility of Election Attributed to Smart Card Reader. European Union chief election observer in Nigeria, Mr. Santiago Fisa, said that despite the hiccups in the use of card readers, it was still the best election.

Solomon, D.J. (2001). Conducting web-based surveys. pareonline.net/getvn. asp?v=7&n =19. Conducting web-based surveys. Practical Assessment, Research & Evaluation, 7(19). Retrieved February 15, 2016.

Speech and Audio Processing, Vol. 2, No. 4, pp. 469-481. www.cs.tufts.edu/~ jacob/ isgw/Ostendorf.html HTML - Tufts University Computer Science

Sykes, (1976). "Sykes" Bath (TV Episode 1976) IMDb www.imdb.com/ title/tt0714 718/Internet Movie Database

Thurk, Gary. Gary Thuerk, American marketer, Britannica.com, www.britannica.com/ biography/Gary-Thuerk Encyclopedia Britannica: The origin of spam dates to 1978, when Gary Thuerk, a marketing manager for the now defunct computer company Digital Equipment Corporation Onalaja, P. (2015). Nigeria's Vice President says the administration plans to build more technology hubs. http://www.techcabal.com Ecosystem Features News

http://www.vanguardngr.com/2015/04/Nigerian-2015-elections-in-search-of-god-of-technology

Wallis, W. (2015). Card reader technology cuts fraud risk in Nigeria poll. Africa, March 31.

Watt, J. H. & Van den Berg, S. A. (1995). Principles of research design research notes.maksl.com/index.php?Watt...van_den_Berg.(1995), Boston:Allyn and Bacon. August.

Wiley Online Library. onlinelibrary.wiley.com/doi/10.1111/1467.../pdf http://www. M2S YS.com/M2-S.htm.

Yun,G. W. & Trumbo, C. W. (2000). Comparative Response to a Survey. Some internet users are familiar with contact customization (Yun & Trumbo, 2000), the intrusion of data processing. https://www.researchgate.net/.../22043773

CHAPTER 7
An Evaluatory Discourse on the Role of ICT in the Conduct of the 2015 Nigerian General Elections

Tayo Popoola & Oloruntola Sunday
University of Lagos Akoka – Yaba

INTRODUCTION

The probing thesis in this study is anchored on the indispensability of Information Communication Technology (ICT) in the democratization process in Nigeria. In post-independent Nigeria, elections have taken place in 1964/65, 1979, 1983, 1993, 1999, 2003, 2007, 2011, and 2015. Most elections conducted in the country before the 2015 elections resulted in serious violence, while the outcomes were the subject of litigation. This study, therefore, sought to inquire as to whether the introduction of ICT devices such as the Permanent Voters Card (PVC), Card Readers (CRs), and production of biometric voters' register could assist in the task of conducting a credible, hitch-free, free and fair election. Using the technological determinism theory as theoretical underpinning, and in-depth interviews with 100 respondents across the 20 local government areas of Lagos state (which included top management staff of the Independent National Electoral Commission [INEC]), the study found that technology played a great role in the conduct of the elections and recommended perfection of observed lapses before future elections in the country.

BACKGROUND OF THE STUDY

Since 1922, when Nigerians had a taste of completive elections courtesy of the Hugh Clifford's Constitution of 1922, democratic navigation in the country has yet to be perfected. Rather than perfection, democracy in Nigeria had become a deadly business. There have been instances in which empty coffins were placed in strategic places during voting to frighten voters from exercising their franchise. There have been instances in which curses were used to induce voters to vote in a particular way. There were instances in which incantations were used to influence voters' decisions. Acts of hooliganism, abduction, killings, violence, ballot box snatching, and illegal thumb printing are similarly regular occurrences. These are notable actions that obstruct or prevent the smooth conduct of elections in Nigeria.

Since the first post-independent elections of 1964/65, conducting a hitch-free, credible, free and fair election remains a goal yet to be fully achieved. Even though the country, in the words of Diamond (1995:417) gave a picture of enthroning vigorous democratic pluralism, an epicenter of democratic energy with the freest press on the continent, the country is now infamous for all forms of anti-democratic behavior.

In the context of Diamond (1995:417), in Nigeria, "Political rules are meaningless and raw power is the only object and arbiter of political affairs." Olurode (2015) similarly says, "Nigeria's electoral landscape is filled with diverse unbelievable acts of impunity by political players. Political parties breach their constitutions and rules with impunity. Internal party democracy is rarely allowed while imposition of candidates by godfathers is a common phenomenon." These are part of the reason why the democratic process in Nigeria is usually a sad commentary. However, in a bid to rescue the Nigerian democracy from collapsing, stakeholders—especially the civil society groups, international elections observers, and opposition parties—canvassed for electoral reform. Government, acting on the popular call, instituted the Justice Uwais Commission. Therefore, the introduction of Permanent Voters Card (PVC) and Card Readers (CRs) were some of the innovations that made the 2015 elections in Nigeria a new beginning.

Prior to their introduction, every election in Nigeria was a rerun of the old tricks: rigging at vote count, banditry, hijacking of ballot boxes, etc.; hence, some scholars described Nigeria as a "regressive state based on the fact that the country has failed to deepen democracy." According to Adekanye and Iyanda (2011:45), quoting Ken Nnamani, Nigeria's former Senate President, "Since the return of democracy in 1999, succeeding election is worse than the previous one." Williams (2011:4) similarly remarked that "since the return of civil rule in 1999, Nigerian elections have produced increasingly cruel travesties, leading to democratic regression rather than the consolidation of the democratic process. Civil rule in Nigeria has produced electoral results which cannot stand scrutiny or the elementary test of integrity."

STATEMENT OF PROBLEM

Conducting a credible, free, and fair election in Nigeria remains a goal yet to be fully realized. At present, it has been very problematic to conduct a hitch-free election as most of the elections conducted in the post-independent era ended in violence, tears, and sorrow (Popoola, 2015). It is also instructive to add that rarely was there any election in post-independent Nigeria that did not end with serious disputes and litigation. Hence, Lindeerg (2006) pointed out that "Only 30 percent of African elections were free and fair."

The political class tends to have perfected various strategies to influence electoral outcomes by thwarting the wishes of the electorates as expressed through the ballot box. The strategy constitutes electoral malpractice, described in various ways by political scholars. To Anifowose (1982), it is "vote switching," while Ogunsanwo (2003) described it as "massive rigging." Onuoha (2003), on his part, says it is "electoral malpractices" amongst others. This chapter, therefore, looks at the introduction of the New Permanent Voters Card and the Card Reader to the voting system in Nigeria during the 2015 general elections in the country.

AIM AND OBJECTIVES

The aim of this chapter is to canvass the deepening of the democratization process in Nigeria through the technological application of ICT in the election process. The specific objectives of the chapter are:

- To find out whether introduction of ICT devices during the 2015 elections minimized the intensity of political contestation and cleavages, as well as the do-or-die attitude of Nigerian politicians during elections.
- To find out whether the ICT tools used by election umpires during the elections reduced the commissioning of electoral crimes, especially multiple voting, voting by proxy, and other electoral crimes.
- To ascertain whether the introduction of ICT devices made election outcomes more credible than in previous elections.
- To determine necessary policy measures that could promote and preserve the gains of conducting ICT-driven elections in Nigeria.

RESEARCH QUESTIONS

1. Do ICT devices introduced in the conduct of the 2015 general elections minimize the intensity of political contestation and cleavages, including the do-or-die attitude of Nigerian politicians?
2. Do ICT devices used during the elections reduce commissioning of electoral crimes, especially multiple voting, voting by proxy, and other electoral crimes?
3. Does the application of ICT in the conduct of the elections make election outcomes more credible than the previous elections?
4. What policy measures are necessary to promote and preserve the gains of conducting ICT-driven elections in Nigeria?

LITERATURE REVIEW

Democracy thrives on the sanctity of the ballot box when the principle of franchise (i.e., one person, one vote) is respected. It is equally assumed that a conducive political atmosphere that is devoid of any harassment, intimidation, or molestation of the electorate prevails. However, most elections in Nigeria in the post-independent era are devoid of these principles.

Reflecting on his experiences on a voting day in Nigeria, Buba (2013:123) identified a number of factors that made it difficult to conduct credible, free, and fair elections in Nigeria.

First, he identified monetary inducement of voters at polling stations. According to him:

> A money bag is stationed somewhere away from the polling station while his agents lure voters to thumb print in favour of his party in the open as against the secrecy provided by law. This is normally done outside the cubicle and they display such votes cast to the public. The agent then signals the money bag and some amount of money is thereby released to the voter. The amount ranges from N300-N500 per vote.

Buba further states that at times, GSM handsets are used to capture the voter's choice as evidence before payment. He similarly identified the outright purchase of voter cards prior to elections as another problem. "This is a device to disenfranchise some voters perceived to be sympathetic towards an opposition party."

To worsen the situation, Buba (2013:124) laments that many electoral crimes were committed in the full glare of security agents. In his words:

> The security agents at polling stations adopt a sit-down-and-look attitude. The inaction of the security agents to a clear breach of procedures at polling stations may not be unconnected with inducement by political parties for them to turn a blind eye to the glaring electoral malpractices.

Furthermore, he listed three other embarrassing conducts of the Nigerian security agents on voting days:

1. Compromise to aid and abet electoral fraud. The issuance of security tags to top government officials such as state commissioners, special advisers, etc. to disguise themselves as security agents or observers in order to move freely during elections, thereby contravening the restriction order.
2. Connivance between politicians and security agents to disrupt polls in areas/polling stations where they have weak support.
3. Security hurdles/difficulties created by security agents to scare election observers/monitors from certain areas.

The enumerated problems listed above are part of the major problems that may not make the citizens' votes count at any election.

Adekanye and Iyanda (2011:31) similarly identified the inadequacy of the Nigerian police to provide adequate security on voting day as another problem. According to them, although the police are constitutionally vested with the central responsibility of policing and securing elections, the Nigerian police have historically not been adequate for that role.

With a current police/population ratio of about 370,000 members to 150,000,000 citizens (or 1:405) Nigeria is one of the world's most under-policed states. The police are also poorly funded, ill-equipped, not well-armed, corrupt, undisciplined, and not always ably led (Adekanye & Iyanda, 2011:31).

Maitambari (2011:79) equally identified falsification of the voters' register as one of the major problems of elections in Nigeria. He noted specifically that:

> In 1983 and 2007, there was large scale falsification of voters' registers. Under-aged persons were registered. Names of non-existent persons were inserted in the registers. The practice degenerated to the point that the names of well known citizens of other nations such as Bill Clinton and Mike Tyson appeared in voters' registers in Nigeria.

Popoola (2015:25), however, attributed the various problems enumerated above to the inability of succeeding Nigerian governments to heroically and courageously confront such problems in an objective and impartial fashion. Quoting Uche (1989), in what he described as a prelude or background to these politics of desperation, Popoola (2015:26) contends that the demise of public confidence and trust in government-owned media in Nigeria started during the first post-independent election of 1964 in the Western Region. He noted that the election was very controversial, with various contentious issues regarding allegations of rigging throughout the region, which were substantiated and proved beyond doubt. In spite of this, Uche (1989:53) asserts that "the Nigerian Broadcasting Corporation (NBC) still went ahead to broadcast the results of the discredited election. This angered some people in the Region who reacted sharply by cutting off their rediffusion boxes which related the false election results."

In a related perspective, Anifowose (1982:220-221), writing on the "switching of results," says that in several cases during the election, the United Progress Grand Alliance (UPGA) candidates were declared elected by the Returning Officer and accordingly issued certificates, only to hear over the radio that their opponents were declared elected. He cited two prominent examples to buttress his assertion. The first was the rigging at Ilesha Urban constituency, in which both the NBC in Lagos and the Western Nigeria Broadcasting Service/Western Nigeria Television (WNBS/WNTV) in Ibadan announced the defeat of Olowofoyeku, a former Attorney General in the region. "However, the same radio station and the Electoral Commission later announced him as the victor."

The second example happened in Alhaji Adegbenro's constituency at Egba South, in which counting did not take place. However, Anifowose said, "The Eastern Nigeria Broadcasting Service (ENBS) which had a mobile station at the Oke-Ado residence of Chief Awolowo, in Ibadan, broadcast one set of results while the WNBS/WNTV and the NBC in Lagos and Ibadan broadcast another set."

In spite of the various laws and ethics of journalism and political campaigns, this trend has not changed today. Ologbenla (2003:80) attributed the above political trend in Nigeria to the nature and structure of the Nigerian state, the petty-bourgeoisie who run its apparatus, and their poor economic base. They seek to use state power to accumulate wealth in a primitive manner within the Nigerian political economy. Thus, gaining access to political power is a do-or-die affair and violence, assassinations and ethnicity is often used to gain access to power and to sustain it. (Ologbenla, 2003:80)

Popoola (2009:45), quoting Gutmann and Thompson (1997), alluded to Ologbenla's assertion. He pointed out that consistently, since the first post-independent elections of 1964/65, public officials in Nigeria have been fond of using means such as violence and threat of violence to achieve a set goal. In addition, Anifowose (1982:218) added boastful and unguarded utterances as additional means. Citing pre-election speeches of political leaders during the Western Regional elections of 1965 as examples, Anifowose (1982:201) quoted the Premier of the Region, Chief S.L. Akintola, who reminded the opposition party through a press statement that his re-election was a forgone conclusion. According to Anifowose, Chief Akintola further reminded the opposition of the fact that in the previous 15 years, no Regional Government in Nigeria had lost an election. Chief Akintola's deputy, Fani-Kayode, was further quoted by Anifowose (1982:219), stressing that his party would be returned to power whether or not the electorate voted for the Nigeria National Democratic Party (NNDP). "If people did not come to vote... the angels would vote for the NNDP."

While literature on politics and elections in Nigeria is not lacking, literature on the angle of ICT to secure elections, and gather reliable, effective, and efficient voters' registration, including voting procedures, is not prolific. This is the lacuna that this study intends to fill.

THEORETICAL FRAMEWORK

This study is anchored on the Technological Determinism Theory. Leading communication scholars, notably Lowery and DeFleur (1995), Grossberg et al. (1998), Baran and Davis (2009), Burton (2010), and McQuail (2010) argued that the technological determinism theory was propounded by Marshall McLuhan in the 1960s. Explaining the theory, Lowery and DeFleur (1995:ix) say it is anchored "on the belief that technology is the cause of social change in society."

Grossberg et al. (1998:48) further explained that McLuhan's theory clearly assumes that technology determines everything else in history, and moreover that communication technology is a crucial invention for mankind. "McLuhan argued that the forms of communication technology (oral, print, electronic) available to people at a particular historical moment determine the ways they can perceive reality and the logic they use to understand it."

In a similar contribution, Baran and Davis (2009:219) say McLuhan is said to be a technological determinist because "he argued that technology inevitably causes specific changes to how people think, how society is structured, and in the forms of culture that are created."

Burton (2010:201) enumerates features of the theory thus:

> McLuhan advanced ideas about the power of technology within a new electric culture. He spoke up for television at a time when it received a lot of bad press, critically speaking. He saw television as a medium which engages the senses. He was interested in effects as much as in causes. He saw the media as extension of the senses. He saw the media as being more than mere carriers of content, the medium itself was the message.

A similar scholarly contribution came through McQuail (2010:103), in which he put forward four main propositions (1) Communication technology is fundamental to society; (2) Each technology has a bias to particular communication forms, contents and uses; (3) The sequence of invention and application of communication technology influences the direction and pace of social change; and (4) Communication revolutions lead to social revolutions.

McLuhan (1964:24) himself says, "Technology is the change of scale or pace or pattern that it introduces into human affairs." Giving an example of the railway, he says, "The railway did not introduce movement or transportation or wheel or road into human society, but it accelerated and enlarged the scale of previous human functions, creating totally new kinds of cities and new kinds of work and leisure."

Along same reasoning, he says, "The airplane, on the other hand, by accelerating the rate of transportation, tends to dissolve the railway form of city, politics, and association quite independently of what the airplane is used for."

McLuhan's theory, however, has been criticized by communication scholars. Quoting Raymond Williams (1975), Grossberg et al. (1998:48) says the assumption that technological invention is accidental, and that it is the result of an internal process of research and development, are both false. They anchor their position on the fact that "communication technologies have always been sought in the context of solving particular social needs. These needs were often military and political, not economic and cultural." To back up their argument, Grossberg et al. said, "For instance, radio communication was first used by the Navy for ship-to-shore communication, and only later exploited for commercial purposes."

Baran and Davis (2009:119) similarly contend that even though McLuhan drew on critical cultural theories, such as the political economy theory, to develop his perspective, "his work was rejected by political economists because it failed to provide a basis on which to produce positive social change."

The above criticisms, however, do not reduce the relevance of the theory to the study. The fact remains, as Maitambari (2011:82) pointed out, elections are data-driven events, and the accuracy and protection of such data from unauthorized access should be accorded priority. The trend in progressive democratic African states today such as Ghana, Botswana, Mozambique, and Sierra Leone, which have been described as "success stories of electoral governance in Africa," was primarily motivated by the introduction of technology to the conduct of elections. Nigeria, even though it had challenges using technology in the conduct of the 2015 elections, need not retreat, but rather should forge ahead with this approach in future elections.

METHODOLOGY

The study uses an in-depth interview method in gathering data from purposely selected 100 respondents who are political stalwarts of the registered political parties in Nigeria, across the 20 local government areas of Lagos state listed in the 1999 Constitution of the Federal Republic of Nigeria. The respondents were interviewed based on their perceived political knowledge, as well as their involvement in the conduct of the 2015 elections.

DATA PRESENTATION, ANALYSIS, AND DISCUSSION

Across the world, elections have become a technology-driven political activity. The inability to move in this direction was largely responsible for some of the avoidable political conflicts that wrecked democratic governance in Nigeria in the past. Popoola (2013:4), for instance, recalled that it took six days for the defunct Federal Electoral Commission (FEDECO) to release the final results of the 1979 presidential election.

While noting that the election took place on August 11, 1979, he stated that the final results were released on August 16, six days after voting. Twenty years later, Popoola (2013:5) stated that another presidential election, which took place on February 27, 1999, was similarly delayed. According to him, the results were not released until March 1; that is, four days after the election was held. Popoola observed that every stage in the conduct of any election should be technologically driven.

It is against this background that this study sought to evaluate the role that ICT played in the 2015 general elections in Nigeria. The study used open-ended questions to extract responses from respondents across the 20 local government areas of Lagos state. The choice of open-ended questions was determined by the manageable size of the interviewees coupled with the need to provide them an opportunity to express themselves. Furthermore, the sample size can easily be handled through unstructured questions. In all, views of 100 respondents were sought on the basis of two per local government. The responses of the interviewees are hereby presented.

Table 7.1: ICT and Political conduct during the 2015 elections

	Options	Frequency	Percentage
RQ1: Do ICT devices introduced in the conduct of the 2015 general elections minimized intensity of political contestation and cleavages including the do-or-die attitude of Nigerian politicians?	Yes	80	80
	No	20	20
	Total	100	100%

Eighty percent of the respondents claimed that the application of ICT devices, such as the Permanent Voters Card and Card Readers, helped in minimizing the intensity of political contestation and cleavages, including the do-or-die attitude of Nigerian politicians during the elections.

Lai Olurode (2015), an INEC, national commissioner, says that a new biometric register of voters that was used during the elections eliminated names that were not registered in the previous register. He stresses that the new register contained names, addresses, fingerprints, and other details of the eligible voters. "It was a much cleaner register of voters than the previous ones." The biometric register of voters was therefore the first step in the direction of minimizing election troubles.

Senator Anthony Adefuye, a stalwart of All Progressives Congress (APC), says the PVC and Card Readers played significant roles in minimizing political contestation. He stressed that, "It is now very difficult for desperate politicians to tamper with the voters registers. If you do, the card readers will detect."

Another politician, Prince Adeniyi Jafojo (2015), says that for the first time in the political history of Nigeria, the electoral umpire made a bold attempt at eradicating rigging and other electoral crimes. He expressed the hope that, sooner than later, Nigerians in the diaspora will be able to participate in future elections by voting through technological devices.

A member of the House of Representatives, Ayo Omidina (2015) was of the view that the application of the card readers would bring credibility into the elections. The Peoples Democratic Party (PDP) described the card readers as instruments that will authenticate the PVCs:

> The whole essence of the card reader is to ensure that you are who you say you are and the card that you are holding is the genuine card from INEC. It would prevent technological rigging because we hear that some people are buying voters cards and we don't know what they plan to use it for. They probably want to give them to some people to vote for them. However, when we heard that card readers would be used, we were happy because the card reader would not allow any form of irregularities. It is better to have genuine 100,000 people casting their votes for their preferred candidates than have 500,000 people, out of which 400,000 are fake (Omidina, 2015, field interview).

Olurode (2015), an INEC national commissioner, further corroborates Hon. Omidina's view. Going down memory lane, he stated that stakeholders put forward an argument for a proposal concerning a compilation of a biometric register of voters in a bid to rid it of the double registration of voters. The proposal was accepted by the INEC and the register, and thus became a "sanitizer" as over four million duplicated names were removed when the automatic finger identification scanner (AFIS) was implemented.

> From a figure of over 73 million registrants collected during the 2011 registration, by 2015, after subjecting the register to cleaning and other scientific screening, the figure came to 68.8 million, 82 percent or 54,460,968 of those who were issued with PVC for participation in the 2015 elections. The deployment of the card reader was therefore particularly helpful in navigating Nigeria's turbulent electoral landscape (Olurode, 2015, field interview).

Osita Okechukwu, (2015), a chieftain of All Progressives Grand Alliance (APGA), on his part, says the biometric registration system contributed significantly in making the 2015 elections credible. "The use of PVC during the elections gave way for conscious steps toward the stability of Nigerian democracy as it made the choice of leadership truly representative as the wishes of the people."

A member of the Labour Party (LP), Kenneth Ehensekhe (2015), applauded the introduction of the PVC Card reader by INEC. He pointed out that the violence that usually characterized Nigeria's elections in the past was reduced to the barest minimum. "The international community praised the efforts of INEC for recording such a feat."

Chief Martins Adegboyega (2015), of the All Nigeria Peoples Party (ANPP), expressed a similar view. He stated that the PVC and CRs saved the country from post-election violence, loss of life, and destruction of property.

Dr. Chris Iyimoga (2015) of the Accord Party contends that the deployment of card readers provided what he called "a disaggregated data of all accredited voters, male/female, youth/elderly which could be used for national research and planning purposes."

> The beauty of the card reader is that after accreditation before voting, data of all the accredited voters could be sent to its central server in Abuja, thus equipping the Commission with information that could be used to audit figures subsequently filed from the polling units by electoral officials and determine if fraudulent alterations had been made. (Iyimogba, 2015, field interview)

Alhaji Jimoh Ishola (2015) of the Unity Party of Nigeria (UPN) said, while acknowledging the impact of the PVC & CRs in the conduct of the elections, that "many technology experts in Nigeria who monitored the elections were full of praises for INEC, for using the machines. It is the best thing that has ever happened to the Nigerian electoral process in the area of election transparency."

A councilor from the Ibeju-Lekki Local Government areas of the state, Hon. Shoyemi Sewedo (2015) of the APC, said the PVC and CRs eliminated serious electoral crimes that characterized the conduct of the previous elections in the country, especially the problem of ballot-box snatching and multiple-ballot thumb printing.

Meanwhile, as earlier presented through table 7.1, 20 percent of the respondents dismissed the claim that the introduction of the PVC and CRs during the elections minimized intensity of political contestation and cleavages, including the do-or-die attitude of Nigerian politicians.

Honourable Dapo Adesina (2015) said the delay that many electorates encountered during accreditation was very frustrating and discouraging. "This heightened political tension as many politicians were alleging foul play." Adesina traced the frustration to the period of collection of the PVC and stressed that it was as if the INEC was not ready for the poll.

Alhaji Fatai Sunmonu (2015) similarly recalled that many electorates complained that the card reader rejected their fingerprints or that it could not recognize them. Others similarly complained that the card reader was slow, leading to the INEC jettisoning its usage in some places and therefore resorting to manual registration.

Barrister Chukwudi John (2015) further observed that adequate test running of the card reader was not done to eliminate many of the problems that were observed on voting days.

In a related development, Honourable Bello Gidado (2015), another leader of the PDP in the Oshodi Isolo area of Lagos State, said many eligible voters who duly registered were unable to get accredited and consequently were disenfranchised. "Also, some duly registered voters misplaced their PVC and could also not vote."

Another politician in the Ajeromi Ifelodun Local Government, Honourable Tunji Oseni (2015), said there were reported cases of malfunctioning of the card readers across the country, which made several politicians who initially objected to the usage of PVC and CRs agitated and restless.

Table 7.2: Evaluating role of ICT in checkmating electoral crimes during the 2015 elections

	Options	Frequency	Percentage
RQ2: Do ICT devices used during the elections reduce commissioning of electoral crimes, i.e., voting by proxy, and other electoral crimes?	Yes	82	82
	No	18	18
	Total	100	100%

Eighty-two percent of the respondents were of the view that application of ICT devices in the conduct of the 2015 elections reduced commissioning of various electoral crimes, which brought into question the credibility of the previous elections in the country, while 18 percent disagreed. Such election crimes include multiple voting or voting by proxy, snatching of ballot boxes/ballot papers, thumbprinting of ballot papers, stuffing ballot boxes with fraudulent ballot paper, etc.

Part of the reasons adduced by the 82 percent of respondents was that deployment of technology in the production of voter register reduced the magnitude of the above-listed electoral fraud. The Honourable Tunji Oseni (2015), who earlier expressed reservations over the reported cases of malfunctioning card readers, described the biometric compilation of the voters' register, as well as the voting procedure, as a technological revolution. According to him:

> The deployment of ICT in generating a biometric voters register with the subsequent issuance of the PVC whose authenticity were verified through the card readers on voting days were bold measures which drastically reduced the commissioning of electoral fraud (Oseni, 2015, field interview).

Olurode, (2015), an INEC national commissioner, said on voting day in Nigeria that it is not uncommon for those he called "political rascals" to snatch election result sheets and write their own scores on it, and subsequently get them announced. "Connivance with election staff was a common practice. Indeed, a typical election day in Nigeria is a real fiasco as it is also very chaotic and may be disordered" (Olurode, 2015, field interview).

Olurode, a Professor of Sociology at the University of Lagos, further stated that to worsen situation, "election management bodies are rarely trusted even with the new electoral reforms, the question of trusting election management bodies has not abated."

Theodore Ekechi (2015) on his part opined that prior to the introduction of the new permanent voters' card and card readers, election outcomes were usually predetermined, but that the introduction of the PVC and card readers has checkmated such habits. According to him, "The introduction of the PVC and card readers has restored fidelity in some aspect of election administration in Nigeria."

Amongst the top views expressed by the 18 percent respondents was the fact that, following reported cases of malfunctioning of the card readers in parts of the country, the INEC resorted to Plan B, which was reverting back to the manual voting system. It was therefore asserted that through such a manual approach, the various forms of electoral crimes that the reforms were meant to checkmate could still be introduced.

Table 7.3: Appraising role of ICT in election outcomes during the 2015 elections

	Options	Frequency	Percentage
RQ3: Does the application of ICT in the conduct of the elections made election outcomes to be more credible than the previous elections?	Yes	84	84
	No	16	16
	Total	100	100%

Based on the statistical information in Table 7.3, RQ 3 above, 84 percent of the respondents claimed that the application of ICT in the conduct of the 2015 elections in Nigeria made election outcomes more credible than the previous elections, while 16 percent disagreed.

Many of the respondents, while applauding the deployment of ICT in the conduct of the elections, said that we live in a technology-dependent world and many African countries—notably Ghana, South Africa, and Kenya amongst others—are deeply involved in the application of ICT in the conduct of elections, and that Nigeria, being the giant of Africa, cannot afford to be left behind.

The top reasons put forward by 84 percent of the respondents are:

1. The PVC and card readers helped in reducing both ghost voters and those who are fond of indulging in multiple voting. A respondent said this is probably due to the wide publicity given by the INEC on the functions of the card readers on voting day. It then means that many people with cloned cards did not have the courage to show up on election day. The news must have gotten around that, after the field test running of the card readers, only voters with PVCs issued by the INEC would be allowed to vote. Such measures made election outcomes very credible.
2. The use of PVC for accreditation similarly reduced the number of people voting. Following elimination of multiple registrations, the voters' register became more real and manageable than the previous ones.

Professor Lai Olurode, an INEC national commissioner, said during the 2011 elections, in which temporary voters' cards were used, the total number of voters who voted during the presidential election was 39,469,484; whereas, during the 2015 presidential election, the figure dropped to 29,432,083—a difference of more than 10 million (10,035,401). He asked:

How could over 10 million voters disappear between 2011 and 2015? The card reader had evidently helped to screen off fake voters. A related point is the margin of defeat between the two leading candidates in 2011 and 2015. In

2011, Jonathan defeated Buhari by about 10 million votes whereas in 2015, Buhari defeated Jonathan by just 2,571,759.

Olurode (2015) further contended that glaring proof that ICT made the outcome of the election more credible is the number of losers who were willing to go to court in 2015 compared to 2011. He stated that in 2003, 560 election petitions were filed before election tribunals, while in 2007, the figure was 1,250, and 400 in 2011, and less than 150 cases in 2015.

Meanwhile, the Goodluck Jonathan Lagos Grassroots Project has said that the introduction of the PVC and card readers was most ill-advised. The group claims that there was no test-running of the card readers before they were used on voting day to ensure error-free results. However, media news reports were to the contrary, as *Punch*, in its lead story on Saturday, March 7, said, "INEC tests Card Readers today amid controversy." The paper went further and published states of the federation as well as the local government areas designated for the exercise.

A chieftain of the Peoples Democratic Party (PDP), who came in third at the party's governorship primary, Adedeji Doherty (2015), described the card reader as the modern-day tool or template that opposition parties in modern day Africa use to rig out incumbent governments.

RQ4: What policy measures are necessary to promote and preserve the gains of conducting ICT-driven elections in Nigeria?

All of the respondents, irrespective of their position on whether or not they support the introduction of the technological innovations used in the conduct of the Nigerian 2015 elections, agreed on the need to reform and improve electoral administration in Nigeria. They all believed that the country must move forward. Therefore, it was not difficult to extract suggestions on the urgent policy measures that should be introduced by the government before the next general elections in 2019. The first policy measure, widely canvassed by 70 percent of the respondents, concerned the need for the decentralization of the production of the permanent voters' cards. It could be recalled that a major reason for the postponement of the 2015 elections from February to March 28 and April 14 was due to the late distribution of the PVCs by the INEC. Even at the point of the INEC's presentation before the National Council of State on the preparedness of the electoral umpire to go ahead with the elections as scheduled, many voters' cards were yet to be printed.

The second policy measure suggested by the respondents was the need to adequately test run all the technological devices to be used in the conduct of all future elections, in order to promptly tackle any problem that could threaten the conduct of a hitch-free election.

The third policy measure put forward by the respondents was the need to devise ways by which Nigerians in the diaspora, as well as those who had relocated from their places of abode to a new location, would be allowed to vote during future elections.

The fourth policy measure worthy of consideration and execution concerned a systematic and continuous registration of voters by updating the voters' register. As people are dying, more and more qualified Nigerians eligible to vote should be encouraged to register without stress.

DISCUSSION, CONCLUSION AND RECOMMENDATIONS

> But we thank God for technology, the PVC and card readers. It not for this luck we had with technology and insistence of constituencies to make sure they were used, in two political zones where they mere subverted, the people wanted to vote but they were not allowed to vote. They continued with what they used to do. Go to their party offices or their sitting rooms, write the results, go to radio house and television house and announce the result and say whoever does not want the result should go to court. (President Buhari, *The Punch*, May 7, 2015)

There is no better way to open up the last segment of this paper than the above quotation of President Muhammadu Buhari, reflecting on the conduct of the 2015 general elections in Nigeria. As stated elsewhere in the paper, most elections conducted in Nigeria in the post-independence era before the 2015 polls, were a rerun or reenactment of the old, discredited tricks, such as rigging at vote count, banditry, falsification of voters' registers, purchase of voters cards, broadcast/dissemination of false results, snatching/destruction of electoral materials, invalidation of ballot papers, multiple voting, substitution of results, and collusion between security personnel/electoral officials with party agendas, etc.

Leduc et al. (1996:1) once remarked that the 20th century may be seen by future historians as a period of dramatic political change due to the global surge toward democracy. In a similar fashion, the 2015 general elections in Nigeria will go down in history as the election that brought a real change to Nigeria.

As McLuhan propounded in the technological determinism theory, technology is the cause of social change in society, and the introduction of technological devices brought about a much-cherished change in Nigeria. As Grossberg et al. (1998:48) revealed while alluding to the technological determinism theory of McLuhan, "Technology determines everything else in history" and that "communication technology is the crucial invention for mankind." This is exactly what has happened in Nigeria as far as the 2015 elections are concerned. Nigeria cannot afford to look back, but must step forward and smoothen all the rough edges by correcting noticeable lapses in the application of ICT during the last elections.

While confronting these lapses, cognizance must be taken of the various policy measures canvassed by the respondents in the preceding section of this paper, in order to improve the voting system.

It was equally observed that many innovations were introduced within a short period during the last elections. This should be avoided during future elections, to checkmate the fire-brigade approach of Nigerians to serious national assignments. That the U.S. Ambassador to Nigeria applauded the INEC on the use of the PVC and card readers during the elections, to the extent of saying it is better than what was obtained in his home state. The U.S. is an indication that Nigeria should strive to explore all other technological angles that could help in conducting a credible national election.

Earlier, the study put forward four research questions. RQ1 sought to establish whether ICT devices introduced in the conduct of the 2015 elections minimized the intensity of political contestation and cleavages, including the do-or-die attitude of Nigerian politicians. Going by findings from the study through the majority of the respondents (80 percent), the answer is in the affirmative though pre-election violence occurred across the country, and snatching of election materials was equally noticed in places where card readers malfunctioned. All the same, the evidence through the respondents was that ICT reduced the intensity of political struggle in the post-election period.

RQ2 similarly sought to know whether the ICT devices used during the elections reduced the commissioning of various electoral crimes that rendered the outcome of the previous elections in Nigeria useless. The answer, going by the findings, is also in the affirmative.

RQ3 asked whether the ICT devices used in the elections made election outcomes more credible than the previous elections in the country. From the incumbent president of Nigeria, Muhammadu Buhari, and the U.S. Ambassador to Nigeria, as well as a majority of the respondents, the answer is also positive.

RQ4 asked for necessary policy measures that could promote and preserve the gains recorded through the ICT-based elections of 2015. Various measures were put forward by the respondents, among which were the urgent need for the decentralization of the production of PVCs, test-running of ICT devices before election days, as well as devising ways by which Nigerians in the diaspora, Nigerians who have relocated to new places, INEC ad hoc staff, security agents, and those in prison and hospitals, could exercise their franchise.

Based on the above, the authors of this chapter puts forward the following recommendations:

1. The decentralization of the production of permanent voters' cards (PVCs) to fast-track the process of production and distribution. This could be done through each of the six geopolitical zones of Nigeria.

2. That all the existing technological devices that were used in the conduct of the 2015 elections (i.e., the biometric production of the voters' register, the PVC, and the Smart Card Readers, along with other technological devices/innovations that will be used in the conduct of the future elections) should adequately be tested before voting day so as to avoid a repeat of the 2015 election pitfalls during future elections.

3. That Nigerians in the diaspora, including those who have relocated to new locations, be allowed to vote, including security agents, INEC ad hoc staff, prisoners, as well as those on admission in hos-

pitals, who were disenfranchised during the 2015 elections. Apart from the fact that it is their fundamental right, in highly competitive elections, their votes could decide the winners.

4. The voters' register should be updated from time to time in a bid to extend franchise to Nigerians who are now of the voting age.

REFERENCES

Adekanye, B. & Iyanda, R. (2011). "Security challenges in election-management in Nigeria: An Overview" in Lai Olurode & Attahiru Jega (eds.) *Security Challenges of Election Management in Nigeria.* Abuja: The Independent National Electoral Commission (INEC).

Akinboye, S. O. & Popoola, I.S. (2010). "Role of ICT in election coverage by the Nigerian print media: A study of the 2007 General Elections," in Cosmas U. Nwokeafor & Kehbuma Langmia (eds.) *Media and Technology in Emerging African Democracies.* New York: University press of America

Alechenu, J. (2015). Buhari pledges electoral reforms, good governance, Lagos: Punch Nig Ltd.

Alechenu, J. (2015). Buhari pledges electoral reforms, good governance, Lagos: Punch Nig Ltd.

Anifowose, R. (1982). *Violence and Politics in Nigeria, Tiv and Yoruba Experience.* New York: NOK publishers Int.

Baran, J. S. & Davis, K. D. (2009). *Mass Communication Theory* (5th ed.) Australia: Wadsworth CENTAGE Learning

Buba, A. (2013). "New security challenges of election management in Nigeria: Towards 2015" in Lai Olurode (ed.) *Election Security in Nigeria: Matters Arising.* Abuja: Frederick –Ebert-Stiftung

Burton, G. (2010). *Media and Society, Critical Perspective.* Berkshire, England: Open University press.

Diamond, L. (1995). "Nigeria: The Uncivic Society and the descent into preatorianism," in Larry Diamond, Juan J. Linz & Seymour Martin Lipset (eds.), *Politics in Developing Countries* (2nd ed.) London: Lynne Rienner publisher.

Grossberg, L., Ellen, W. & Whitney, D.C. (1998). *Media Making, Mass Media in a Popular Culture.* London: SAGE publications Ltd.

Jinadu, L. A. (2011). "Comparative analysis of security challenges of elections in Nigeria", in Lai Olurode & Attahiru Jega (eds.) *Security Challenges of Election Management in Nigeria.* Abuja: The Independent National Electoral Commission.

LeDuc, L., Niemi, R.G., and Morris, P. (1996). *Comparing Democracies, Elections and Voting in Global Perspective* London: SAGE publications.

Lindeerg, (2006), *Democracy and Elections in Africa.* Baltimore: the John Hopkins University Press.

Lowery, S.A. & DeFleur, M.L. (1995). *Milestones in Mass Communication Research.* (3rd ed.) New York: Longman publishers.

Maitambari, U. (2011). "Emerging patterns of security challenges: some reflections on 1983 and 2007 elections". in Lai Olurode & Attahiru Jega (eds.) *Security Challenges of Election Management in Nigeria.* Abuja: The Independent National Electoral Commission.

McLuhan, M. (1964). *Understanding Media: The Extension of Man* London: New American Library.

McQuail, D. (2010). *McQuail's Mass Communication Theory.* (6th ed.). London: SAGE publications ltd.

Ogunsanwo, A. (2003). "Keynote Address" in Remi Anifowose & Tunde Babawale (eds.) *2003 General Elections and Democratic Consolidation in Nigeria.* Lagos: Friedrich Ebert Stiftung.

Oketola, D, Fabigi, !., Oba, E, Ogundele, K., Akasike, C., Opara, E & Adeoye, G. (2015). INEC Card Readers today amid controversy, Lagos: Punch Nig Ltd.

_____ (2015). "INEC test-run Card Readers today amid controversy," Lagos: Punch Nig Ltd.

Ologbenla, D. (2003). "Political Instability, Conflict and the 2003 General Elections" in Remi Anifowose & Tunde Babawale (eds.) *2003 General Elections and Democratic Consolidation in Nigeria.* Lagos: Friedrich Ebert Stiftung.

Onuoha, B. (2003). "A Comparative Analysis of General Elections in Nigeria," in Remi Anifowose & Tunde Babawale (eds.), *2003 General Elections and Democratic Consolidation in Nigeria.* Lagos: Friedrich Ebert Stiftung.

Popoola, I.S. (2009) "Unequal Media access and elections in Nigeria: A commentary on the 2007 elections", in Lai Olurode, Solomon Akinboye & Rasheed Akinyemi (eds.) *Nigerian 2007 elections: The crises of political succession.* Lagos: Rebonick publications Ltd.

_____ (2015). "Political Reporting and Electoral violence in Nigeria," 1999 – 2011, a Ph.D. Thesis submitted to the School of Post Graduate Studies, University of Lagos.

Popoola, T. (2013). "ICT and political Reporting: A comparative analysis of press coverage of the Nigerian 1979 and 1999 presidential elections," paper presented at a Ph.D seminar organized by the Department of Political Science, University of Lagos on July 12.

_____ (2013). ICT and political Reporting: A comparative analysis of press coverage of the Nigerian 1979 and 1999 presidential elections, paper presented at a PH.D seminar organized by the Department of Political Science, University of Lagos on July 12.

Uche, L.U. (1989). *Mass Media, People and Politics in Nigeria.* New Delhi: Concept publishing company.

Williams, A. (2011). "Democratic Transition in Nigeria: Perils and Prospects," in A. Maja-Pearce (ed.) *A Handbook for April 2011 Elections in Nigeria.* Lagos: The Anchor newspapers.

MEDIA NEWS REPORTS
"Card Readers Failure: We warned the Nation" Punch, March 29.

CHAPTER 8
Technology and Election Coverage: A Study on Selected Presidential Elections in Nigeria

Tayo Popoola
University of Lagos, Nigeria

INTRODUCTION

This study focuses on the role of Information Communication Technology (ICT) in election coverage with specific reference to press coverage of selected presidential elections in Nigeria. The study notes that the mass media are indispensable tools in the political process as their involvement in election coverage enables the citizenry to have timely information about pre-election campaign and related activities, the election, as well as post-election political developments. While noting that timely information is necessary at every stage of the political process, the study notes that the ability of the press to offer such information is hamstrung by the unavailability of state-of-the-art technology necessary for prompt dissemination, especially on the part of the electoral umpire. Using the historical method and cybernetics theory, the study found out that the delay in the prompt release of the final results of presidential elections in Nigeria was due to nonapplication of the state-of-the art technology, and consequently recommended upgrading of all equipment used by the electoral umpire in the conduct of future elections in the country.

This study focuses on the first, fourth, and eighth presidential elections in post-independence Nigeria. Thus far, presidential elections have taken place in Nigeria in the following years: 1979, 1983, 1999, 2003, 2007, 2011 and 2015 (prior to 1979, the first post-independence elections took place in 1964). That was a period when Nigeria operated under the British parliamentary system of government. Following the collapse of Nigeria's First Republic on January 15, 1966, the parliamentary system of government collapsed with it. Thirteen years later, when the military restored democratic governance, it was under a new presidential system of government.

The 1979 presidential election, which took place on August 11, was therefore the first presidential election in post-independence Nigeria. The final results of the elections were released on Thursday, August 16, six days after it was held. Twenty years later, the 1999 presidential election took place, specifically on February 27, while its outcome was released on March 1, four days after it was conducted. The 2015 presidential election took place on March 28, and its outcome released after three days. During these delays after the conduct of these elections, uneasy political tension gripped the entire country with rumors and speculation spreading like wildfire. This study is therefore curious about the circumstances responsible for such unhealthy delays.

While the 1979 elections were conducted by the Federal Electoral Commission (FEDECO), the 1999 and 2015 elections were conducted by the Independent National Electoral Commission (INEC).

STATEMENT OF THE PROBLEM

Extracting timely information by members of the press has been a major problem confronting media professionals in Nigeria during elections. While local and foreign media representatives usually thronged the federal and state offices of the electoral umpire for information about who had won, the electoral body in turn was not able to respond to the yearnings and aspirations of media professionals due to the fact that necessary ICT facilities that would have aided collation and promoted the prompt release of election results were not available.

Societal expectations from the media are that of prompt dissemination of election outcomes once an election has taken place. The *Punch* newspaper edition of July 10, 1979, through a front-page editorial, captured the perplexing situation thus: "It is now three days since the senatorial elections were held and Federal Electoral Commission (FEDECO) has been able to announce barely half of the results. We dare say that delay in counting and announcing results open the whole exercise to abuse."

In a related development, the newspaper's lead story of August 13, 1979 says: "The results of the governorship elections in Borno and Gongola states were not released until more than nine days after the elections were held." The newspaper attributed the delay in the release of the final results of the presidential election to communication problems encountered by FEDECO officials in parts of the northern states. To rescue the electoral umpire from the mess, Nigerian Air Force planes were dispatched to those areas to help the situation by collecting ballot boxes from remote areas and taking them to collating centers. This trend, as will be observed later in this study, changed only slightly in more recent times, when technology was introduced to critical aspects of election administration in the country.

AIMS AND OBJECTIVES

This study aims to advocate full application of technology to every phase of election administration in Nigeria so that the citizenry can have timely information. While it was six days before the public was notified of the final results of the 1979 presidential election, the results of the 1999 election did not come until four days after the election was held. The results of the 2015 election took three days to be released. In some states of the federation, Borno and Gongola for example, the results of the governorship elections in 1979 were not released until after nine days. The objectives of the study therefore are:

1. To ascertain the role, if any, played by ICT in FEDECO/INEC operations during the 1979, 1999, and 2015 presidential elections.
2. To assess the use of ICT in print media operations, especially in the area of editing of political news/pictures of the various political contestants during the 1979, 1999, and 2015 presidential elections.
3. To ascertain the ICT facilities available at the disposal of the defunct FEDECO and INEC for the gathering, collation, and dissemination of election results during the 1979, 1999, and 2015 presidential elections.
4. To examine the ICT facilities used by the Nigerian print media in the coverage of the 1979, 1999, and 2015 presidential elections.

RESEARCH QUESTIONS

1. What role did ICT play in the late release of the results of the 1979, 1999, and 2015 presidential elections?
2. What role did ICT play in print media operations, especially in the area of editing of political news/pictures used by the Nigerian press during the 1979, 1999, and 2015 presidential elections?
3. What were the ICT facilities available at the disposal of FEDECO and INEC for the gathering, collation, and dissemination of election results during the 1979, 1999, and 2015 presidential elections?
4. What were the ICT facilities used by the Nigerian print media in the coverage and reportage of the 1979, 1999, and 2015 presidential elections?

LITERATURE REVIEW

Information Communication Technology (ICT) has attracted commentaries from several academics in recent times. According to Evans (1990), cited in Akinboye and Popoola (2010:45), "While some abbreviate it as IT, others would rather prefer to call it Info Tech." In the words of Muchie and Baskaran (2006:26), "ICT has become one of the main driving forces of globalization ... like the first machine-driven industrial revolution, the ICT revolution has generated fundamental changes in the socio-economic life of people and nations across the world."

Muchie and Baskaran (2006:26) further argued that ICT is unique mainly in two aspects. First, they contended that "it affects almost every country on the face of the earth and almost every aspect of life"; and second, they pointed out that "unlike other technologies, ICT as an enabler has significant potential to build both social and technological capabilities in developing countries."

Burton (2010:37), quoting McQuail (2000), identified four main characteristics of ICT. They are: 1) Interpersonal communication media, such as e-mail; 2) interactive media play (i.e., computer games); 3) information search media, such as Net search engines; and 4) participatory media, such as Net rooms.

Of the above four characteristics, the most strategic and indispensable in the quest for an efficient and prompt release of election results in Nigeria is that of interpersonal media. The electoral body needs it in order to communicate within and outside the organization. During the 1979 and 1999 elections, when the need arose to invite political reporters to FEDECO or INEC functions, press invitations were distributed manually. It took almost a day for such invitations to be distributed among the media houses that were located at various locations in the state or country. The trend changed a little during the 2015 elections, where, through the Internet, all the media establishments could be reached within five minutes. Therefore, with ICT, you gain speed, you incur fewer costs, you eliminate risk of accident or auto crash, and above all, you reduce stress drastically.

Therefore, in considering a technological device that could create, store, and distribute election information, the ICT tool that readily comes to mind is indisputably the computer. In the words of Mohammed (1990:9), "the computer is the most pervasive of all the new communication technologies." Besides satellite, he stresses that "it is about the only device that has a hand in all the pies of communication: print, radio, television, telephone, fiber optic, film, photography, cinema, etc."

Within the ICT department of Lagos State INEC, the talk during the 2015 elections was about the information superhighway or broadband network, communicating through electronic mail, sending election results from local INEC offices to the head office, or posting election results on the INEC website. None of this would have been possible without computers.

Scholars disagree on the exact time when the computer originated. Parker, cited in Pool (1983:620) traced its origin to 3,500 BC when it was used as a simple adding machine. Pelton (1981:25), while contributing, says the "oldest one that springs to mind is a Babylonian computer that dates from 1,921 BC." Hofbaver (1990:22) asserts that "the history of computers can be traced roughly from the year 1812, when the English mathematician, Charles Babbage, designed what he called a different machine which could automatically work out trigonometric and logarithmic function."

The role of the media at a period of election has been the object of serious attention by communication scholars. Semetko (1996:269) says that at such periods, people use the media for strategic purposes. Both the candidates and the electorates are involved in the strategic use of the news media. According to him:

> For the vast majority of people living in democratic societies, election campaigns are experienced through the media. Politicians gear their daily campaign

activities to meet the constraints and deadlines of the news. They know that far more people turn to print or broadcast sources for information than turn out for political rallies in the town square.

While this assertion is true to some extent, the fact remains that most political parties in Nigeria hardly structure their campaign activities in a way that would meet the deadline of media establishments covering the campaign. That is why you find them at campaign venues by 6:00 p.m., still campaigning. The implication is that most print audiences read their stories two days after the event. However, if a political party is buoyant enough, live coverage of the campaign by radio and television stations may help in getting the stories across fresh and unedited.

Articulating the basic role of the media in a democracy, Odunewu (2000:7) says the role of the press in a democracy "is to nurture the government of the people by the people," adding that in this context, "the press is the very oxygen of democracy."

Gana (2000:11) says the media in a democracy should aspire to carry out five core functions. He argued that the media have a vital role to play in promoting the culture of peace, promoting development, promoting people's participation, and promoting positive virtues, as well as promoting a stable polity—all necessary imperatives for the sustenance of democracy.

Justice Sawant (2000:25) says that the press is the only institution that can keep people, as well as those in authority, informed on all matters and at all times of the day, adding that:

> It is the media which enables the people to perform their three-fold functions in democracy—to participate in the day-to-day affairs of the society, to take informed decision, and to keep a check on the authorities who rule on their behalf.

For these reasons, Justice Sawant (2000:32) described the press as the lifeline of democracy, as well as the "ears" and "eyes" of the people.

> The press is a powerful institution in a democracy. There is no subject on which it cannot comment and there is no institution which can escape its criticism. The media helps to preserve and promote democracy by safeguarding the independence of its institutions including' of itself and ensuring accountability of them all.

As a former American statesman, Abraham Lincoln understood the centrality and critical role of the media in democracy. Edwards (1996:192) quoted Lincoln as saying, "With public sentiment, nothing can fail, without it, nothing can succeed. Consequently, he who moulds public sentiment goes deeper than he who enacts statutes or pronounces decisions."

Akinfeleye (2011:12-13) similarly quoted a renowned American philosopher, democrat, and president, Thomas Jefferson, who declared poignantly that if he were to choose between having a government without a newspaper, he would not hesitate to choose the latter. It is therefore stating the obvious in the context of North (1967:301) once more, that politics cannot exist without communication through the press.

In a related development, Edwards (1996:10) argued that the press performs a dual role in every democratic society. First, he contends that "the press occupied a position that is analogous to that of a middleman providing necessary information about the affairs of the state and politics." He states further that as a watchdog, it carries out investigation into activities of public officials and exposes scandals. He was, however, quick to add that the founders of the U.S., especially former American statesmen such as Washington, Jefferson, and Madison, never anticipated a scenario in which the watchdog role of the press would turn into an attack by engaging in what U.S. political scholar Larry Sabato calls "a feeding frenzy"—that is, a situation where a critical mass of journalists pursue the same story intensely, excessively, and sometimes uncontrollably. Said he: "They did not foresee that journalists would seize the center stage in the political process, creating, not reporting, the news and altering the shape of politics and the contours of government."

A similar scenario was witnessed in Nigeria after the 1979 presidential elections concerning the 12 2/3 saga. To date, many Nigerians believe ex-president Sheu Shagari stole the presidency in active collaboration with the military as a result of the way the press portrayed the matter. However, a major reason why the press wielded such enormous power was given by Helge through a piece entitled "Democracy, civil society and the media in Africa in the nineties." According to Helge (1995:335), the media are at the center of the democratic process and their situation can be used as a barometer for explaining the depth of political change. His words: "Citizens' participation through the media is indispensable in order to carry out coherently the economic and cultural development of society."

In the last decade, the electioneering process across the world has been experiencing a dramatic change, and this change is largely being induced by the amazing impact of ICT on reporting. Edwards (1996:33) vividly captured the global impact of ICT on reporting when he said, "The leader of every nation, north and south, rich and poor, democratic and authoritarian, acknowledges the awesome power of the media, especially electronic media to shape the politics of his nation."

Edwards (1996:33) further presented the views of the foremost European leaders Lech Walesa and Jiang Zemin, when confronted with a similar question. While Lech Walesa, a Polish leader, said "Would there be Earth without the Sun?" Jiang Zemin, the General Secretary of the Chinese Communist Party, said, "The power of the media is so enormous that chaos could result if the tools of public opinion are not tightly controlled in the hands of true Marxists." Edwards similarly quoted a Chilean opposition that upset Augusto. Pinochet, in a plebiscite, said: "In 15 minutes' television time, we destroyed 15 years of government publicity for the dictators."

The reality of global politics today is that the arrival of ICT has brought remarkable changes to politics. Edwards (1996:188) further contended that the greatest impact of ICT on political reporting has been greatest on the office of the president. While noting that John F. Kennedy was the first TV president in 1960, he added that Ross Perot was the first talk show presidential candidate in 1992. It could be recalled that both used television to talk directly to the voters without being filtered or mediated through journalistic editorial processes.

Back home in Nigeria, several newspapers and magazines wrote after the first presidential television debate between the late Basorun M.K.O. Abiola of the defunct Social Democratic Party (SDP), and Alhaji Bashir Othman Tofa of the defunct National Republican Convention (NRC), that the SDP candidate was better material for the office of president. Some political pundits were also of the view that the results of the 1979 presidential election won by Alhaji Sheu Shagari of the National Party of Nigeria (NPN) would have been different had there been a live presidential election debate featuring all the five presidential candidates who contested the election, namely: Alhaji Sheu Shagari, Chief Obafemi Awolowo, Dr. Nnamdi Azikiwe, Malam Aminu Kano, and Alhaji Waziri Ibrahim.

Up to Nigeria's Second Republic politics (1979-1983), party candidates used to be picked behind closed doors by party bosses or through a consensus arrangement. Through media insistence, the political parties now embrace primaries; that is, events covered live by television to decide the party's flag bearers. Such insistence is in line with the primary obligation of the mass media in any political community with regard to feeding the citizenry with information about occurrences in their environment. Whitney (1975:69), while re-echoing the three major activities of the mass media, narrowed down this function to "surveillance of the environment, correlation of parts of society in responding to the environment and transmission of the social heritage from one generation to next."

Surveillance has to do with the primary responsibility of the media with regard to combing the environment for useful information that would make life meaningful for the people. *Correlation*, on the other hand, involves interpretation of information collected from the environment. When editorial, news analyses, or commentaries are published, government may be forced to take some positive action to redress the perceived problems. Transmission of social heritage from generation to generation is the socializing function of the media through conscious education and enlightenment.

THEORETICAL FRAMEWORK

This study is anchored on the communication theory, otherwise known as cybernetics. According to Gauba (2003:98), the theory represents another model of political analysis derived from the concept of political systems. According to Gauba, the chief exponent of the theory is Karl Deutsch, who sought to use the approach in analyzing the political system. Quoting Norbert Wiener, cybernetics major developer, Isaak (1981:293) says, "It is the study of communication and control in all types of organizations, from machines to large-scale organization."

Deutsch, a leading proponent of the theory, was said to be less concerned with the *bones* or *muscles* of the body politic than with its nerves, its channels of communications, and decisions. Deutsch, according to Gauba, further argued that, "It might be profitable to look upon government somewhat less as a problem of power and somewhat more as a problem of steering, i.e., directing the course of its activity which is the main function of communication."

Conducting elections in any democratic society is a task requiring specific and decisive steering. First, there must be communication between the electoral umpire and the political parties. The electoral commission must put in place a mechanism for transmitting messages and obtaining reactions or feedback. The input and output communication mechanism must take cognizance of environmental stress, distortion, gain, and feedback.

Isaak (1981:294-295) provides insight to each of these core communication concepts in relation to the conduct of elections in a democratic polity. He contends that every institution, including electoral body, exists within an environment. This environment places stress on the system. This stress is otherwise called *load*. Load is a burden. If a load on the system increases without deliberate efforts to reduce or manage it, it would be difficult for the system to adjust and meet aspirations of the people in the environment. If load is poorly managed, there would be *lag* in the system. Therefore, *lag* is the fallout or an offshoot of load. It refers to the time between the reception of information and the reaction or reply to it. Thus, the greater the lag, the less efficient the system.

A system must be able to maintain itself. The ability to promptly respond to information or demand accurately enhances the efficiency of a system. Once lag sets in, rumor and gossip will take over. In the context of Blake and Haroldsen (1975:30), "rumour is a widespread report from an unknown source." Quoting Shibutani (1966), they contend further that, "It develops as men caught together in an ambiguous situation attempt to construct a meaningful interpretation of the situation by pooling their intellectual resources." They further described gossip as unverified news that is transmitted through the interpersonal channels.

A recurring problem in post-independence elections in Nigeria is the problem of *distortion*. Distortion is defined as the changes that take place in information between the time it is received and the time it is reacted to. While Anifowose (1982:220) refers to this as "switching of results," Ologbenla (2003:91) says it is "electoral malpractices," while Onuoha (2003:59) described it as "winning at all cost."

Gain, therefore, is a product of learning. Part of the reason the 1983 general elections were riddled with crises was due to the fact that FEDECO did not learn from mistakes of the past, especially from the 1979 elections. Maitambari (2011:71) while buttressing this fact, says, for instance, rather than FEDECO adhering to the 1979 election timetable, FEDECO exposed itself to allegations of bias and manipulation by scheduling the presidential election to be held first, which all parties except the NPN opposed. "The opposition alleged that the sequencing of the election was to produce a bandwagon effect to the benefit of the NPN." The ruling party, NPN, ignored feedback from the opposition parties. When treatment or attention is given to every load a system receives, it is bound to strengthen the system as it would produce positive feedback. Whenever an incoming load to the system is handled in the right manner, the system would then be in a position to predict future states of the environment. This is the whole essence of cybernetics, to transfer information through communication. In other words, information is what flows through the channels of communication. When received, it is analyzed and reacted to.

In the course of receiving and reacting to load, there are lessons to be learned. Adjustment will come in a manner analogous to an anti-aircraft gun correcting or adjusting its goal to the speed and flight pattern of its target. The overall result of the changes and adjustments is that the system would be in top shape to predict the future state of the environment. In this manner, the system could anticipate certain developments and therefore make adequate provisions in advance to address it.

METHODOLOGY

To enrich the historical method of analysis used in this study, whose population consists of 57 print media establishments identified by Akinfeleye (2003:47-57) and Komolafe (2004:107-112), 10 members of staff in the ICT department of Lagos State INEC, 29 ICT members of staff of Abuja INEC, and three senior journalists were specifically chosen from the professional body. The three senior journalists were deeply involved in the coverage of the 1979 presidential election in particular.

SAMPLE SIZE

The sample size for the study is 20 print media establishments in Lagos, extracted from the population of 57 print media establishments in the country identified by Akinfeleye (2003) and Komolafe (2004). It is instructive to stress that two-thirds of Nigerian print media establishments are based in Lagos. The 20 represent 64 percent of the 33 Lagos-based print media establishments currently in circulation in the country. Those ignored and no longer in circulation at the time the fieldwork was conducted include *National Concord, Sketch, National Interests, The Monitor, The Democrat, TNT, Classique, Tempo,* and *Lagos Horizon,* among others. In all, the sample size consists of 80 practicing senior journalists of editor rank, three former editors, and the head of the ICT department of Lagos State INEC and Abuja Headquarters of INEC.

DATA PRESENTATION AND ANALYSIS

Table 8.1

Q1: What role does ICT play in the late release of the results of the 1979, 1999, and 2015 presidential elections?

Option	Frequency/percentage					
	1979	%	1999	%	2015	%
Maximum	-	-	70	87.5	80	100
Minimal	13	16	10	12.5	-	-
Nil	67	84	-	-	-	-
Total	80	100	30	100	80	100

The Federal Electoral Commission (FEDECO) conducted the 1979 presidential election on Saturday, August 11. FEDECO withheld the results until Thursday, August 16, six days after it was held.

The 1999 presidential election, on the other hand, was held on February 27. Its outcome was not made public until March 1, four days after it was conducted. The 2015 presidential election similarly took place on March 28. Its results were released on March 31, three days after it was held. The respondents, having been involved in the coverage of the electoral process from the stage of party primaries, campaign, voting, and collation, had the results but could not publish the story on the winner of the election because the law empowered the electoral body to release it first officially, following which they could then disseminate the information.

As can be seen from table 8.1 above, only 16 percent of the respondents agreed that ICT played a minimal role in the gathering and processing of political news/election results during the 1979 presidential elections, while 84 percent poignantly declared that ICT played no role. During the 1999 presidential elections, 87.5 percent of the respondents claimed that ICT played a maximum role while 12.5 percent said it played a minimal role. In the 2015 election, all the respondents claimed ICT played a maximum role.

Available ICT facilities identified by the 16 percent of the respondents used in the news gathering, processing, and reporting of election news/results during the 1979 elections were: telephone (analog), compugraphics, radio/tape recorder, TV set, telex machine, typewriters, cameras, and midgets (micro-tape recorders).

Apart from asserting that ICT played a minimal role in the coverage of 1979 elections, they also attributed the delay in the release of the final results of the presidential election to nonavailability of up-do-date, modern, and efficient ICT facilities at the disposal of FEDECO. However, all the 80 respondents said ICT played a maximum role in the gathering, processing, and reporting of the results of the 1999 and 2015 presidential elections. They further claimed that the press was far ahead of the INEC in 1999 concerning the acquisition of ICT gadgets needed for their operations.

Table 8.2

Q2: What role did ICT play in print media operations, especially in the area of editing of political news as well as pictures used by the Nigerian press during the 1979, 1999, and 2015 presidential elections?

| Option | Frequency/percentage | | | | | |
	1979	%	1999	%	2015	%
Maximum	-	-	80	100	80	100
Minimal	-	-	-	-	-	-
Nil	-	-	-	-	-	-
Total	-	-	80	100	80	100

Going by the statistical figure in table 8.2 above, it can be seen that all the respondents claimed that ICT played no role in the editing of stories/pictures of political personalities that were used to spice political news during the 1979 elections. However, all of the respondents agreed that ICT played a maximum role in the editing of political news/pictures during the 1999 and 2015 presidential elections. One of the three senior journalists chosen from the professional body, Prince Henry Odukomaiya—a former Managing Director/Editor-in-Chief of *Champion* newspapers—recalled that a major editing style in the newsroom during the colonial days, still in vogue during the 1979 election, was that of "cut and paste" system which ICT has completely eliminated today. In his words: "The computer has completely eliminated the cumbersome, dirty and frustrating processes of newspaper production during the colonial era through compugraphy." Prince Odukomaiya further recalled with nostalgia that under the outdated compugraphic system, stories were composed on compugraphic machines. After composition, you use bromide to start developing it like photographic film. "After developing the film, it goes to the graphic artist, who will do the paste up with the aid of cow gum; following which the material will go to lithographers who in turn will patch the film before mounting it on the exposing machine to produce the plate."

Odukomaiya argued that it could take a whole day to produce a newspaper during the colonial period up to the first republic, unlike now when a newspaper can be produced in a few hours.

Furthermore, the former Editor-in-Chief of *Champion* recalled that a lot of embarrassing developments took place while producing a newspaper prior to the arrival of ICT. He said, for example, pasted headlines may unintentionally fall off during movement from the graphic artist to the lithographers. Prince Odukomaiya, however, pointed out that ICT has eliminated all the problems.

> It is a different story altogether today. All you need doing is just to sit down before the computer, type your story, edit straight on the computer, with the aid of spell check and produce an error-free copy. The job today is 99.9% error free in that you no longer experience the possibility of one line dropping or one line falling in the process of carrying compugraphic bromide from one point to another. Whatever you have corrected on the computer nowadays is exactly what will come out. If you do a good job, it comes out good. If you did a bad

job, it comes out bad. Computer has eliminated what we used to call the printer's devil in the newsroom.

The former editor of the *Daily Times,* Prince Tony Momoh, says that ICT has greatly enhanced photo editing. He recalled that during the colonial era until the 1979 elections, photo editing was done in a crude way. Momoh, the second senior journalist chosen from the professional body, said as an example, whenever the need arose for cropping, a common practice then was that the photograph was folded to extract the personality needed. He pointed out that the greater effect of cropping during the period was that it could damage the picture and consequently reduce its lifespan. The former Minister of Information, however, stressed that today, ICT has eliminated the crude system of photo editing, pointing out that "with scanner and the page maker, photo editing can be done with a touch of class."

He further noted, "You know nowadays, once the picture is placed on the scanner, it is previewed to capture the details with the aid of your mouse, you can then crop the picture to what you desire. As a matter of fact, photo editing is done for three reasons: cropping, scaling and sizing."

Innocent Okoye, the third former editor purposively chosen from the professional body, says that the arrival of the Internet has made it very easy for political reporters, feature writers, editorial writers, sports writers, and even subeditors to locate information on a wide variety of topics. He stressed that through the Internet, background information, facts and figures, and expert opinions, among others things, can easily be sourced. According to Okoye, "Suppose you want to write an article on Kosovo, but there is no library with up-to-date materials on the subject, you can easily find a source that is sufficiently knowledgeable on the subject through the Internet. You can then send an e-mail to him, asking him your questions and he can reply through e-mail."

RQ3: What were the ICT facilities available at the disposal of FEDECO and INEC for the gathering, collation, and dissemination of election results during the 1979, 1999, and 2015 presidential elections?

The study established a little contradiction between the responses of the Lagos state INEC and the Abuja headquarters of the electoral body to the above question, which was tackled by the ICT units of the electoral umpire. While the Lagos state INEC declined listing any ICT facilities and categorically stated that ICT was nonexistent then, the Abuja head office listed computers and printers. Curiously, the Abuja office of the INEC admitted that ICT played little or no role in 1979 elections.

In a related development, while the Lagos state INEC attributed the delay in the release of the results of the 1979 presidential election to nonavailability of ICT equipment, leading to a situation whereby results were manually counted from all the states of the federation, the Abuja head office of INEC said, "The delay was caused by logistics problems." The Abuja head office of INEC further said the delay had nothing to do with nonavailability of ICT.

Furthermore, while the Lagos INEC listed digital radio transmitters and NI-TEL telephone lines as available ICT for the compilation of results of the 1999 presidential elections, the Abuja INEC listed computers and printers. The Lagos INEC further argued that "in 1999, ICT was not much in existence save for only NITEL telephone lines and radio rooms which was used for the transmission of results." The Abuja head office of the INEC says ICT was used in the computation of results. The two offices, however, agreed that press invitations were distributed physically by hand whenever they needed media coverage during the 1979 and 1999 elections.

The two offices equally agreed that INEC could release presidential election results within 24 hours if INEC offices are well stocked with ICT equipment. The deepening of ICT equipment in the state as well as all the local government offices of the federation will go a long way in helping INEC to promptly release election results.

The two offices agreed that the biometric computation of voters registered for the 2015 elections, coupled with the introduction of the Permanent Voters Card (PVC) and Card Readers (CR), helped in injecting credibility to the electoral system.

RQ4: What were the ICT facilities used by the Nigerian print media in the coverage and reportage of the 1979, 1999 and 2015 presidential elections?

The respondents claimed that, among other, the following ICT facilities were at the disposal of the Nigerian print media for the coverage and reporting of the blow-by-blow account of the 1999 elections. They are: Internet, desktop/laptop computers, digital cameras, flash drives/DVD, digital midgets/audio recorders, online editing of political stories, electronic printers, Fax machines, IPADS/Smartphones (i.e., Blackberry), cable television, recorder pens with hidden cameras, etc. The available ICT facilities for the coverage of the 1979 presidential election were listed previously in RQ1.

Among the prominent roles played by ICT in the timing of the release of the results of the 1999 and 2015 presidential elections, Obadare Obafemi (2015), editor of *Saturday Punch*, says "It ensures early release of results as it aids collation, just as it also ensures transparency." Chiawolamoke Nwankwo (2015), another editor, says "use of ICT tape recorders helped political reporters to quote those interviewed accurately."

Lekan Olufodunrin (2015), editor of *The Nation On-line,* says "it hastens compilation of results across the states of the federation." A similar view was expressed by Robert (2015) Obioha, news editor of *The Sun* newspaper, who claimed that "it enabled journalists to gather, process and disseminate political news fast." Another editor in the same medium says, "ICT has helped in reducing electoral violence and malpractices."

Thomas Imonikhe (2015), weekend editor of *Champion* newspaper, says "it helped journalists file their stories faster and with relative ease."

Mideano Bayagbon (2015), deputy editor, *Vanguard* newspapers, added the dimension of breaking news, adding that "ICT has eliminated late arrival of stories across the federation and that stories are now being served to media audience fresh."

Jahman Anikulapo (2015), editor of the *Sunday Guardian,* further contended that "ICT provides an opportunity for Nigerians to observe or monitor the conduct of elections across the country and consequently send their views to the media houses for publications."

Roland Ogbonaya (2015), deputy editor of *This Day Saturday Desk,* expressed a similar view, pointing out that "with ICT, one can cover events, send election results and pictures straight to the newsroom from either the polling centres or collation centre."

Habib Haruna (2015), news editor of the *Daily Independent,* says it "makes the job of reporters easier and effective."

Some of the respondents, however, said those ICT facilities were available in limited quantity.

DISCUSSION

Implicit from the data presentation section of this paper is the fact that the performance of the press in Nigeria varied under the three presidential elections covered in this study. The performance was at an optimum level during the 2015 elections. The fluctuating performance of the press during the elections must have been dictated by the acquisition of technological devices that aided efficient and prompt service delivery.

Another influencing factor was the fact that the media industries across the world are going through a transitional period, and the media in Nigeria cannot afford to be left behind. Reflecting on the transition, Dizard Jr. (1997:4) says, in the context of this transition, old technologies are being adapted to new tasks. This is exactly what happened, as some of the ICT facilities used in the coverage of 1979 elections were adapted to new roles during the 1999 and 2015 elections.

The press, being the tool by which INEC, political parties and other stakeholders tell their stories, has equally gone through technological advancement. Baus and Lesly (1978:408), while reflecting over such changes, argued that as various weapons of war have advanced in scope, power and efficiency from the archaic spears and swords of the olden days to the various missiles and weapons of mass destruction today, so also have the media advanced from letters and signs and speeches to include radio, television, the Internet, and Short Message Service (SMS), among others. It is interesting to note that, unlike the 1979 and 1999 presidential elections, the political class used SMS effectively to reach out to the public during the 2015 elections. Therefore, the media environment in 2015 was an entirely different ball game altogether.

Writing on the new media environment, Severin and Tankard Jr. (2001:4) say, "We are living in a time when communication systems are evolving rapidly." Wingston (2009:30) similarly says, "The emergence of new media technologies over the past 20 years has dramatically changed the media environment that many of us have been familiar with." He stressed further that the Internet in particular has changed the way in which most of us work and live.

Hofstetter (2001:37), quoting Dick Brass, Vice President of Microsoft, even projected a technological communication trend by 2020. He predicted that by the year 2018, the newspaper on paper could become extinct. He stresses that "the future is electronic, the past is paper." The Microsoft chief further asserts that by 2020, *Webster's Dictionary* would have changed its first definition of a book to "a substantial piece of writing commonly displayed on a computer or other personal viewing device."

With the world going technological and becoming more and more sophisticated, it is expected that election coverage will similarly be technologically driven in furtherance of the emergence of the global village. During the 1979 and 1999 presidential elections, there was no online medium in Nigeria. However, during the 2015 elections, there were many online media. Going by the trend observed during the fieldwork for this study, some of the print media surveyed are fast switching over to online. Several factors are forcing publishers to rest their print publications and embrace online publications.

It is expected that electoral umpire would similarly be affected by the technological wave. If this happens, whenever elections are conducted, the public might have the results within 24 hours, as envisioned by the electoral umpire in this study. In virtually all the progressive democratic societies today, technology is perceived as an enabler that can assist in realizing the national objectives of conducting credible, free, and fair elections. Maitambari (2011:82) pointed out that elections are data-driven events, and the accuracy and protection of such data from unauthorized access should be accorded priority. The trend in progressive democratic African states such as South Africa and Tanzania, which Jinadu (2011:58) described as "success stories of electoral governance in Africa," is in the direction of technologically driven elections. Technology is the nerve system of the political process. If we remove technology from the political engineering of conducting any national election, the system is bound to be chaotic, nasty, and violence prone, as there would be lots of distortions (otherwise called rigging, manipulation of results, and falsifications). The system would then be forced to carry too much load, which, if care is not taken, can endanger the survival of the system. Therefore, the trend in progressive democratic societies is in cybernetics, through the effective utilization of technology, to gather, collate, and dispatch information online.

CONCLUSION AND RECOMMENDATIONS

The study identified the nonavailability or insufficiency of ICT facilities as a major factor responsible for the delay in the release of the final results of all the presidential elections covered by this study. The study further discovered that the inability of the Nigerian press to provide timely information concerning the final results of the elections to their teeming audience was due to late rerelease of the results by the electoral body.

The study showed that during the 1979 presidential election, political reporters sent their stories to their respective newsrooms through telex, radio message, and telephone. Others in out-stations used public transport. However, the existence of cyber cafés and business centers afforded political reporters the opportunity of either sending their stories to the newsroom through e-mail or fax machine, or calling through mobile phones during the 2015 elections.

The contradictions between the Lagos INEC and Abuja head office of INEC is an indication that most times, government officials resort to deliberate falsehood in a bid to cover up their failures or shortcomings. The study revealed the existence of more ICT facilities at the disposal of the Nigerian press during their coverage of the 1999 and 2015 presidential elections, unlike that of 1979. This enabled the evening tabloids, such as "PM News" and "TNT," to promptly carry the news as soon as the result was released by the INEC.

Based on the above, this chapter puts forward the following recommendations:

1. That all INEC offices throughout the federation be linked with Internet facilities as well as other ICT equipment which is highly indispensable in the organization and conduct of credible, free, and fair elections.
2. That the INEC should make it a deliberate policy henceforth to store strategic information over lessons (gain) learned in the conduct of every election so that future researchers can have access to such information, and for the improvement of the organization.
3. That deliberate efforts be made by media owners in the country to adequately equip the press with up-to-date ICT facilities in a bid to raise the standard of election coverage in Nigeria to that of the U.S.
4. That government institutions, especially the INEC, should adhere strictly to provisions of the Freedom of Information Act (FOIA) by releasing information to media men over any story under investigation in order that public interest is better served at all times.

REFERENCES

Akinboye, O. S. & Popoola I. S. (2010). "Role of ICT in Election coverage by the Nigerian Print Media: A study of the 2007 General Elections" in *Media and Technology in Emerging African Democracies*, Cosmas U. Nwokeafor& Kehbuma Langrmia (eds.). New York: University Press of America Inc.

Akinfeleye, R. A. (2003). *Fourth Estate of the Realm or Fourth Estate of the Wreck: Imperative of Social Responsibility of the Press*. Lagos: University of Lagos Press.

_____ (2011). *Essentials of Journalism, an Introductory Text*. Lagos: Malthouse press Ltd.

Anifowose, R. (1982). *Violence and Politics in Nigeria. Yoruba & Tiv Experience*. New York: Nok publisher Int.

Baran, J. S. & Davis, K. D. (2009).*Mass Communication Theory* (5[th]ed) Australia: Wadsworth CENGAGE Learning.

Baskaran, A. & Muchie, M. (2006)."The problem of integrating ICT within National Systems of Innovation: Concepts, Taxonomies and strategies" in *Bridging the*

Digital Divide Angathevar Baskaran & Mammo Muchie (eds.).London: Adonis & Abbey publishers ltd.

Blake, H. R. & Haroldsen, O. E. (1975), *A Taxonomy of Concepts in Communication.* New York: Hastings House Publishers.

Burton, G. (2010). *Media and Society, Critical Perspective.* Berkshire, England: Open University press.

Deutsch, K. (1963). *The Nerves of Government.* New York: The Free Press.

Edwards, L. (1996). "Reshaping the World of Politics" in *Mass Media* (Joan Gorhaned)

Folarin, B.(1998). *Theories of Mass Communication, An Introductory Text.* Ibadan: Stirling Horden publishers.

Gana, J. (2000). "The media and democracy" in *Media and Democracy.* Abuja: Nigerian Press Council.

Gauda, Q. P. (2003). *An Introduction to Political Theory.* New Delhi: Palgrave Macmillan India Ltd.

Grossberg, L., Ellen, W. & Whitney, D. C. (1998).*Media Making, Mass Media in a Popular Culture.* London: SAGE publications Ltd.

Helge, R. (1995). "Democracy, civil society and the media in Africa in the nineties, A discussion of the emergence and relevance of some analytical concepts for the understanding of the situation in Africa," in The *European Journal of Social Sciences* Vol. 8, Issue 4.

Hofbaver, M. (1990). "Information Technology: Hardware and Systems" in Desmond, Evans (ed), *People, Communication and Organization,* London: Pitman Publishing.

Hofstetter, T. F. (2001). *Multimedia Literacy* (3rd edition) Boston: McGraw-Hill Irwin.

Isaak, C. A. (1981). *Scope and Methods of Political Science, an Introduction to the Methodology of Political Inquiry.* Illinois: The Dorsey Press.

Jinadu, L.A. (2011). "Comparative analysis of security challenges of Elections in Nigeria" in Lai Olurode & Altahiru Jega (eds) *Security Challenges of Election Management in Nigeria..* Abuja: Independent National Electoral Commission.

Komolafe, F. (2004). *Nigerian Journalists Directory.* Lagos: Friedrich Ebert Stiftung

Maitambari, U.(2011). "Emerging pattern of security challenges: some reflections on 1983 and 2007 elections" in *Security Challenges of Election Management in Nigeria.* Lai Olurode and Attahiru Jega (eds.). Abuja: The Independent National Electoral Commission.

McQuail, D. (2010). *McQuail's Mass Communication Theory* (6thed.)London: SAGE publications Ltd.

Mohammed, M. (1990). "Traditional Forms of Communication in Borno State." An unpublished paper presented at international communication conference, May 10, University of Maiduguri, Nigeria.

North, C. R.(1967). "The analytical prospects of communications theory," in James C. Charles worth (ed.) *Contemporary Political Analysis.* New York: The free press.

Odunewu, A.(2000). "Welcome Address" in *Media and Democracy.* Abuja: Nigerian Press Council.

Ologbenla, D.(2003). "Political Instability, Conflict and the 2003 General Elections," in 2003 *General Elections and Democratic Consolidation in Nigeria.* Remi Anifowose &Tunde Babawale (eds) Lagos: Firedrich Ebert Stiftung.

Onuoha, B.(2003). "A Comparative Analysis of General Elections in Nigeria," in 2003 *General Elections and Democratic Consolidation in Nigeria.* Remi Anifowose & Tunde Babawale (eds) Lagos: Friedrich Ebert Stiftung.

Pelton, J. (1981). *Global Talk: The Marriage of the Computer World Communications and Man.* London: The Harvester Press Ltd.

Pool, I.D. S. (1983). *Technologies of freedom* Massachusetts, USA: Harvard University Press.

Roger D & Dominick J. R. (2006). Mass *Media Research, An Introduction* (8th ed.) New York: Wadsworth cengage learning.

Sawant, P. B. J. (2000). "Media and Democracy: A Global View," in *Media and Democracy:* Abuja: Nigerian Press Council.

Semetko, H. A. (1996). "The Media" in *Comparing Democracies, Elections and Voting in Global Perspective.* Lawrence Leduc, Richard G. Niemi &Pippa Norris (eds.) London: SAGE publication

Severin. J. W. & Tankard, W. J. (2001). *Communication Theories: Origins, Methods and Uses in the Media.* New York: Addison Wesley Longman. Inc.

Whitney, C. F. (1975). *Mass Media and Mass Communication in Society.* Iowa: Win C. Brown. Wimmer.

MEDIA NEWS REPORTS

"Obasanjo Wins", *Vanguard,* Mon. March 1st

"Results from II states released," *The Punch,* Tuesday, August 13,

FEDECO, lead us not into darkness," *The Punch* editorial, Tuesday, July 10.

CHAPTER 9
Technology and Elections: A Look at Electoral Integrity, Results and Management in Nigeria

Chike Patrick Chike
Bowie State University

INTRODUCTION

The International Republican Institute headquartered in Washington, D.C., United States, cites democratic elections as the foundation of a representative government which fosters peaceful rotation of power, ensuring that citizens choose their own leaders from a group of competing political entities. Such democratic elections, the Institute argues, must ensure recurring, transparent, and open competitions where all voters can participate freely without any form of intimidation or harassment (IRI, 2016). Yves Leterme, Secretary General of the International Institute for Democracy and Electoral Assistance (McCormick, 2016) characterizes technology as a tool which, when rightfully utilized, ignites electoral innovation.

Nigeria, with a population of 177 million people (World Bank, 2016) has been democratic for only 26 years of its checkered, post-independent history (1960-1966; 1979-1983; 1999-present). Nigeria's elections have been far from transparent, as they are marred in bribery, fraud, and stolen electoral ballot boxes and materials, followed by stampedes, riots, arson, and the cutting-down of rivals. Successive elections in Nigeria since 1960 have been mired in political turmoil and violence. The 1959 general elections, which ushered in the first republic, were not free and fair. There were accusations and allegations of rigging and ethnic favoritism. The 1964 elections did not fare better, resulting in violence and mass killings, particularly in Western Nigeria, hence legitimizing the "Wild Wild West" metaphor. The military, buoyed by the crisis, stepped in on January 15, 1966 to sack the first democratic government under the guise of salvaging the country from political precipice, but did not relinquish power on October 1, 1979 to a democratically elected government.

Ironically, the 1983 elections went down in flames. Arson, mass killings, maiming of opponents, and free-for-all fighting became the order of the day as parties and candidates rejected election results. The resident electoral commissioners became demigods, having the powers to announce election results in their domain. The main source of information was the local radio. There was no Twitter, Facebook, cell phones, or Internet. Whatever results the state-run radio stations and newspapers announced or published became final, leaving little room for verification or validation by the electorate. Few households at that time had television sets, through which information and content, controlled by the state apparatus, was delivered.

As in 1966, the military struck again on December 31, 1983, with the message to cleanse Nigeria from corrupt political godfatherism, bribery, and corruption. So continued Nigeria's march to political hara-kiri and wilderness for another 16 years; a period marked by coups and countercoups. The electorate watched helplessly and hopelessly as their powers were trampled and decimated. The scenario described above captured the contributions and effects of illiteracy, poverty, lack of technology, and social media in the psyche of the ordinary Nigerian in what could be described today as the Dark Ages, given the current proliferation of modern technologies such as digital cameras, Smartphones, iPads, BYODs, Wi-Fi, Facebook, Google and e-mails etc.

Nowhere in the history of Nigeria's democracy had the electorate been more resolute, cohesive, and unified than in the 1993 and the 2015 general elections; the latter ushering in President Muhammadu Buhari and the former annulled by the military dictator General Ibrahim Badamasi Babangida. Nowhere in the annals of Nigeria had an incumbent president handed over the reins of power to a rival after failing to win a second term in office in a general election, as when Dr. Goodluck Ebele Jonathan passed the torch of leadership to his rival Buhari after a resounding defeat at the polls.

So, what is the difference between the 1993 and 2015 general elections? The difference is very clear. The potency of technology, such as the Internet and social media, played a huge role in the 2015 elections. The electorate and media tapped into digital technology, making it harder for corrupt election officials to alter the results per usual. Live feeds from polling booths were relayed. Smartphones, cable channels, radio stations, Facebook, Twitter, blogging, voice recorders, newspapers, and e-mails were at work.

Rewind to 1993. Had it been that all these technological resources and technology-driven electorates were available in the 1993 elections, when Nigerians gave their mandate to the late Moshood Kolawole Abiola for president, the military leadership would have found it very difficult to cancel the results. It was an election that had global trappings and implications. It was adjudged as the freest election Nigeria ever had. General Babangida would have shot to the status of a global icon, a local hero, and respected statesman had he and his acolytes jettisoned their personal ambitions, grandiose and "Maradonic" tactics to transfer the reins of power to the presumed winner of the election, M.K.O. Abiola. Thus, perhaps Nigeria's free-fall to utopia would have been salvaged.

General Babangida would go down in history as the autocratic and self-styled military president who almost single-handedly canceled Nigeria's freest and fairest election, plunging the country into political quagmire and a state of economic coma. If 1993 were today, with all the trappings of digital technology and sophisticated social media, could Babangida and his group have canceled the elections? Perhaps not.

Electoral transparency is achievable in Nigeria, as the 2015 elections have shown. Development of Information and Communications Technologies (ICT) and network infrastructure across the country can serve as the vehicles of electoral transparency. Improved ICT will give rise to improved communications technology, such as mobile phones, SMS applications, e-voting systems, enrollment, and the storage of biometric data of citizens. The use of the Internet in promoting citizen advocacy helps to promote government transparency and accountability not only in electoral processes, but in all sectors of governance. As the National Democratic Institute (NDI) rightly puts it, the use of the Internet and related technologies enhances communications and improves access to critical data, thereby strengthening democratic processes and increased effective governance (NDI, n.d.).

The role of technology and social media was evident in the 2011 Nigerian elections, and got better in the 2015 elections as the Independent National Electoral Committee (INEC) actively deployed information technology and fostered citizen participation through social media engagement, which facilitated the successful conduct of the elections (Ehidiamen, 2015). Ehidiamen (2015) reported the fusion of various innovative mobile apps with social media, enabling election officials and observers to report incidents from a wide range of polling units, and minimizing electoral fraud and manipulation of election results. Some mobile applications, such as Revoda and Nigeria Elections, were locally developed during the 2015 elections to aggregate real-time updates from polling units across the country (Ehidiamen, 2015; Fadoju, 2015).

Nigeria can leverage ICT to effectively improve her electoral processes if she deploys appropriate technologies and trained manpower. ICT can provide a slew of information, such as an online database of voters and their demographics, in a variety of ways, including voter information and identification, e-voting, processing of results, and the use of open-source technology in election management (IDEA, 2015). Utilizing cell phones for domestic election observation/monitoring is instructive as a SMS text-message-based reporting system enhances the integrity of elections by alerting authorities of problem areas that can be corrected in a timely manner (NDI, n.d.). The advancement of technology will certainly stimulate its inevitable use in elections.

THE NARRATIVE CALLED NIGERIA

Nigeria is a source of intrigue and connotes different meanings to different people. To some people, it is the product of an illegitimate marriage of the Northern and Southern Protectorates. Others refer to it as an awkward creation of the British colonial masters to further their expansionist movement in Africa. Yet others define Nigeria in terms of its population strength, people, strategic regional economic power, and political resilience. There is also a set of people who define Nigeria as a nation of corruption, thievery, violence, and maladministration. Although Nigeria has been written off as a state in critical distress, despite being one of the fastest-growing economies in Africa (Obado-Joel, 2014), the former U.S. Ambassador to Nigeria, John Campbell, did not hesitate in 2010 to hand Nigeria a death knell, predicting its imminent collapse and disintegration (Joseph, 2010a, 2010b).

Irrespective of the negative connotations, definitions, and assumptions about Nigeria, there is a common denominator for the country. Nigeria and its people are resilient and not unlike shock absorbers. The country has passed through difficult times, from coups and countercoups, military rebellions, secession that culminated in a 30-month civil war, repressive military regimes and impoverishment of the state, austerity measures, underdevelopment, and successive kleptomaniac democratic governments. Yes, Nigeria is still going strong! It remains the giant of Africa! It is a regional power. Nigeria draws its strength from its diverse ethnic population. Like a virus, its strength, weakness, or collapse infects the rest of the continent in no small measure.

Nigeria, with a population of 183 million people, is the most populous country in Africa. The Population Division of the United Nations Department of Economic and Social Affairs (UNDESA) ranks Nigeria's population seventh largest in the world (UNDESA, 2015). However, Nigeria's population is growing the most rapidly among the 10 largest countries in the world, and it is on target to eclipse that of the United States by 2050, making it the world's third largest country (UNDESA, 2015). It is projected that Nigeria—alongside China, India, Indonesia, Pakistan, and the United States—will be the sixth of the 10 largest countries in the world, to exceed 300 million people, by 2050 (UNDESA, 2015). (See Table 9.1)

Nigeria is a West African country with a land mass of 923,768 square kilometers (356,669 square miles) and is subdivided into six geo-political zones and 36 states (Bamgbose, 2012; BBC News, 2016). (See Table 9.1)

Table 9.1: Nigeria's six geo-political zones showing member states

Geo-Political Zone	Constituent States
South East	Abia, Anambra, Enugu, Imo, Ebonyi
South South	Bayelsa, Akwa Ibom, Cross River, Delta, Edo, Rivers
South West	Ekiti, Lagos, Ogun, Ondo, Osun, Oyo
North East	Adamawa, Bauchi, Borno, Gombe,Taraba, Yobe
North Central	Benue, Kogi, Kwara, Nasarawa, Niger, Plateau
North West	Jigawa, Kaduna, Kano, Katsina, Kebbi, Sokoto, Zamfara

The oil-rich country is bounded on the south by the Gulf of Guinea, Cameroun in the east, Chad in the northeast, Niger in the north, and the Republic of Benin in the west. It comprises more than 250 ethnic groups. Ten of these groups (Hausa, Fulani, Yoruba, Ibo, Kanuri, Tiv, Edo, Nupe, Ibibio and Ijaw) make up approximately 80 percent of the total population (Nwokeafor, 2013). With its major languages as English (official), Ibo, Hausa, and Yoruba; and major religions as Christianity, Islam, and indigenous beliefs; the life expectancy in Nigeria is 52 years for men and 53 years for women (BBC News, 2016). The Central Intelligence Agency rates Nigeria as Africa's largest economy, with a 2015 gross domestic product (GDP) estimation of $1.1 trillion (CIA, 2016).

While the author does not attempt to turn this chapter into a history lesson about Nigeria, the following section will delve into the elections organized in Nigeria before its independence from Britain in October 1, 1960.

THE BIRTH OF POLITICAL PARTIES PRE-INDEPENDENT NIGERIA

The march to Nigeria's political consciousness was conceived by African students in London in the 1920s. The ideological influence and inspiration of Pan Africanists such as Booker T. Washington, Marcus Garvey, and W.E.B. Du Bios gave birth to the founding of the West African Students' Union in London in 1925, which became critical of colonialism and agitated for self-government (Metz, 1992). The 1920s also witnessed the rise of nonpolitical associations, such as the Nigerian Union of Teachers, anchored by trained leadership; and the Nigerian Law Association, a group of Western-educated lawyers (Metz, 1992). On the other labor flank was the Nigerian Produce Traders' Union, whose able leader was Obafemi Awolowo. However, ethnic and tribal unions had started to gain mainstream acceptance, and by the mid-1940s the Igbo Federal Union and the Egbe Omo Oduduwa, a Yoruba cultural organization led by Awolowo, had emerged.

Herbert Macaulay, often regarded as the father of Nigerian nationalism and the architect of political consciousness, capitalized on the 1922 constitution, which had provided Nigerians with the opportunity to elect their representatives to the Legislative Council in Lagos. He formed the Nigerian National Democratic Party. The NNDP would dominate elections in Lagos until the birth of the National Youth Movement (NYM) in 1938. Future Nigerian leaders, such as H.O. Davies and Dr. Nnamdi Azikiwe (Zik) leveraged their Western education to agitate for improved education and elevating Nigeria to the same status as Canada and Australia in the British Commonwealth of Nations. Internal wrangling and ethnic distrust forced Zik and his Igbo compatriots to leave the party, paving the ascendancy of Awolowo as the de facto leader. The NYM metamorphosed into Action Group, which was a predominantly Yoruba political party. The Igbo-Yoruba political rivalry and distrust featured prominently in the early political landscape of Nigeria, and has continued to influence political calculations.

The National Council of Nigeria and the Cameroons (NCNC; from 1960 known as the National Conventions of Nigerian Citizens) formed in 1944 on the ideals and appeals of the defunct NYM to weld Nigeria under one solid bloc for self-government. Anchored by the able leadership of Herbert Macauley and Nnamdi Azikiwe, it was the first Nigerian political party to have a national appeal. However, it would degenerate to an eastern-region-dominated party, just as the Action Group in the western union. Sir Ahmadu Bello (Sarduana of Sokoto) and Sir Abubakar were the pillars of the Northern People's Congress (NPC), dominated by the northerners. The emergence of these three political parties along geo-political and ethnic lines bred politics of distrust and rancor.

In 1954, the British colonial masters were compelled to establish a measure of compromise in conflicting agitations for autonomy and central government, having seen the composition of the various political parties along ethno-political lines. The arrangement conceded two parallel governments—the federal government at the center and the regional governments with significant autonomy (Institute of Security Studies, n.d). The federal government was allocated powers such as defense, police force, custom duties, communications, national trade, finance, and banking, while political powers rested with the regions responsible for health, agriculture, education, and economic development (Awa, 1960; ISS, n.d.; Metz, 1992). The Macpherson Constitution promoted regionalism, while the Lyttleton 1954 Constitution established the federal principle and divided Nigeria into three regions (Eastern, Western, and Northern) including the Federal Territory of Lagos, and set in motion Nigeria's path to independence in 1960 (Awa, 1960; Metz, 1992). The Eastern and Western regions were granted internal self-governing in 1957, followed by the Northern region achieved in 1959 (Awa, 1960; Metz, 1992).

In preparation for independence, the British deliberately made political maneuvers to favor the North against the rest of the country by allocating the North 174 seats out of the total 312 seats in the Federal House of Representatives, based on larger population of the North. The East got 73, West 63, and the Capitol Territory of Lagos, 3 (Awa, 1960; Metz, 1992). The same formula was also adopted for the apportionment of the 44-member Senate. The results of the 1952-1953 census had given the North 54 percent of the country's population. The East and the West Regions had accused the North of fraud and rejected the results on the basis of figure inflation.

The 1963 census did not fare better, as it showed the North with greater population strength. The rest of the country cried foul and accused the North of manipulation. Regardless, the federal government adopted the figures and the legislative allocation remained unchanged. Thus, regional hostilities became a feature at the inception of Nigeria's independence, partly due to an imbalance of the population, which paved the way for the Northerners to control not only their own regional assembly, but also the federal government and instrument of political power (Awa, 1960). The issue of the controversial Northern population has continued to dog Nigeria's political landscape to date (Metz, 1992).

In his book *Federal Elections in Nigeria*, Professor Eme Awa asserted that "the combination of threat with violence and the appeals of tribalism make it difficult to evaluate the weight of tribalism as far as elections are concerned, but it is these three forces—tribalism, violence, and threats which primarily determined the results of the elections" (Awa, 1960, p. 110).

In the 1959 parliamentary elections, the NPC and allies won 148 out of 174 seats in the Northern region, the NCNC/NEPU 8, and AG and allies 25. In the Western region, NPC captured 6 seats, NCNC/NEPU 21, and AG and allies 35. In the Eastern region, NPC won one seat, NCNC/NEPU 58, and AG 14. In Lagos, NCNC won 2 seats and AG won 1. The total results showed NPC 148, NCNC 89, and AG 75, meaning the NPC in the North had won a plurality in the election. However, none of the parties could form a government, resulting in the NPC under Sir Abubakar Tafawa Balewa entering an alliance with Dr. Nnamdi Azikiwe's NCNC to form a coalition federal government. On October 1, 1960, Nigeria achieved independent status with Balewa as prime minister, Azikiwe as governor-general, and Awolowo as the leader of the opposition (Metz, 1992).

TRIBALISM AND DISTRUST IN POLITICS

The 1959 parliamentary elections exposed tribalism and distrust as the hallmark of Nigerian politics and elections. It also strengthened the need for the creation of additional regions for the minorities (Awa, 1960; Metz, 1992). The Midwestern region was carved out of the Western region in 1963 through a plebiscite (Awa, 1960; Meltz, 1992). The NPC's unwillingness to extend its tentacles outside the confines of the Northern region confirmed the fears that the party was marked by regional orientation, religion, and traditions, given the fact it performed very poorly in other regions, when compared with other regions (Metz, 1992). No sooner had Balewa become the prime minister than he stated his party's impending launch of a political battle to conquer the southern regions, thus carrying the political battle across regional tribal lines (Awa, 1960). Awa had predicted tribalism as the greatest obstacle that would confront the young democracy (Awa, 1960). He asserted that:

> The victories of AG and NCNC outside their home bases occurred mainly in the minority areas of the order regions and these confirms not merely the existence of a strong demand for the creation of more regions, but also the great influence of tribalism in the elections, for in each region it was the minority groups principally that voted for the "invading" party" (Awa, 1960, p. 111).

There were high-level suspicions of distrust among the regional parties. This played on the eve of independence, when no party won the majority to form the central government, necessitating the formation of a coalition. There was lots of internal wrangling in the parties. It could have made sense for the southern parties of the NCNC and AG to form an alliance to counter the North, but the West showed too much disdain toward the NCNC, as exemplified in Chief Festus Okotie-Eboh (former finance minister). The AG could not work with the APC either. It took some political whipping and maneuvering before the NPC would team up with the NCNC to form the Balewa government on October 1, 1960.

HISTORY OF ELECTORAL BODIES IN NIGERIA

The 1954 parliamentary elections were held in 1954. However, the Electoral Commission of Nigeria (ECN) was established to conduct the 1959 parliamentary elections that would usher in the newly independent Nigeria under the leadership of Sir Abubakar Tafawa Balewa as Prime Minister and head of government, and Dr. Nnamdi Azikiwe as Governor-General and head of state. The ECN was the precursor that set the stage for the establishment of the electoral commissions in Nigeria.

This was followed by the Federal Electoral Commission (FEC), commissioned in 1960 by the Balewa government, to conduct the federal and regional elections in 1964 and 1965 respectively. The commission was led by Sir Kofo Abayomi, and later by Chief Eyo Ita Esua (Ekundayo, 2015). Later, the Balewa government renamed the commission as the Federal Electoral Commission (FEC). It was the FEC, under the chairmanship of Chief Esua, that conducted the 1964 general elections and the 1965 Western Region elections (Ekundayo, 2015). The elections were mired in controversy. The failure of the FEC to conduct the free, fair, and credible elections in 1964/1965 precipitated violence that largely accounted for the collapse of the first republic, and set the stage for military intervention in Nigeria politics in January 1966 and beyond (Ekundayo, 2015; Oyeweso & Amusa, 2015).

Chief Michael Ani, a trade unionist, was appointed chairman of the Federal Electoral Commission (FEDECO) in 1976 by General Olusegun Obasanjo. He was to conduct the 1979 general elections that ushered in the second republic with Alhaji Shehu Usman Shagari as the first executive president of Nigeria (Ekundayo, 2015; Oyeweso & Amusa, 2015; Vanguard News, 2010). The elections were the presidential, national assembly (Senate and House of Representatives), gubernatorial (state governors), and state assembly. At the state levels, 19 executive governors were elected. These elections were also flawed by a series of electoral fraud and irregularities, and would become one of the most controversial elections in the history of Nigeria with the acceptance by FEDECO the infamous NPN formula of 12 2/3 (Oyeweso & Amusa, 2015).

Justice Victor Ovie-Whiskey was appointed as FEDECO chairman by President Shehu Shagari in 1980, and served from 1980-1983. FEDECO conducted the 1983 general elections that re-elected Shagari of the National Party of Nigeria (NPN) to a second term. There were allegations of massive rigging, riots, looting, and violence leading to the creation of a new electoral lexicon of "landslide victory" in Nigerian politics (Ibrahim & Garuba, 2010; Oyeweso & Amusa, 2015; Vanguard News, 2010). Electoral officers were accused of rigging, bribery, and compromise. This paved the way for the December 31, 1983 coup led by Major General Muhammadu Buhari of the Nigerian Army, which seized power. FEDECO was dissolved and the military would not relinquish power until the return of the Fourth Republic in 1999.

The Federal Electoral Commission (FEDECO) was renamed to National Electoral Commission (NEC) in 1987 by the military government of General

Ibrahim Babangida, who appointed Professor Eme Awa as its chairman (Ekundayo, 2015; Oyeweso & Amusa, 2015). Awa resigned his chairmanship in 1989 after a dispute with Babangida, leading to his replacement with Professor Humphrey Nwosu as the chairman (Ekundayo, 2015; Oyeweso & Amusa, 2015). Eme Awa was Humphrey Nwosu's mentor in the Department of Political Science at the University of Nigeria, Nsukka. Professor Nwosu served as the INEC's chairman from 1989-1993, and was widely known for the conduct of the 1993 presidential election that produced Chief M.K.O Abiola as the presumptive winner. The election was annulled by General Babangida (Ekundayo, 2015; Oyeweso & Amusa, 2015). General Babangida then appointed Professor Okon Uya of the University of Calabar as the chairman of the NEC at the end of his administration in 1993, and could not organize any election before he was sacked by the new military head of state, General Sani Abacha, in November 1993 (Ekundayo, 2015; Oyeweso & Amusa, 2015).

INEC's chairman from 1989-1993, and was widely known for the conduct of the 1993 presidential election that produced Chief M.K.O Abiola as the presumptive winner. The election was annulled by General Babangida (Ekundayo, 2015; Oyeweso & Amusa, 2015). General Babangida then appointed Professor Okon Uya of the University of Calabar as the chairman of the NEC at the end of his administration in 1993, and could not organize any election before he was sacked by the new military head of state, General Sani Abacha, in November 1993 (Ekundayo, 2015; Oyeweso & Amusa, 2015).

The General Abacha regime scrapped the NEC and established the National Electoral Commission of Nigeria (NECON) with Chief Summer Dagogo-Jack as its chairman. Dagogo-Jack presided over the elections to the 1994 Constitutional Conference, and other legislative elections that never saw the light of the day (Ekundayo, 2015; Oyeweso & Amusa, 2015; Vanguard News, 2010). His tenure ended with the death of General Abacha in 1998. General Abudsalami Abubakar, as the new commander-in-chief, established the Independent National Electoral Commission (INEC) with Justice Ephraim Akapata as its chairman. The INEC conducted the 1999 general elections that midwifed the fourth republic with Chief Olusegun Obasanjo as the president. Upon the death of Justice Akpata in 2000, Chief Obasanjo tapped Dr. Abel Guobadia to head the chairmanship of the INEC, which would conduct the 2003 general elections that re-elected him to a second term (Ekundayo, 2015).

In 2005, Professor Maurice Iwu became the INEC chairman and conducted the general elections that produced President Musa Yar'Adua. His tenure ended in 2010, upon which time President Goodluck Jonathan, who took over from Yar'Adua after his death, anointed Professor Attahiru Jega as the INEC chairman. The INEC conducted the 2011 elections that returned Goodluck Jonathan to power. The INEC, under Jega, would conduct the 2015 general elections that tossed up former General Muhammadu Buhari as president. In 2016, President Buhari tapped Prof. Mahmood Yakubu as the fifth chairman of the INEC.

Table 9.2: Past Electoral Commission Chairmen

Name	State of Origin	Year of Service	Name of Commission	Appointed By Head of Government	Election Conducted
-	-	1959	Electoral Commission of Nigeria (ECN)	Tafawa Balewa	1959 – Elected Tafawa Balewa
Mr. Eyo Ita Esua	Cross River	1960-1966	Federal Electoral Commission (FEC)	Tafawa Balewa	1964 & 1965- Elected Tafawa Balewa under a Republic
Mr. Michael Ani	Cross River	1976-1979	Federal Electoral Commission (FEDE-CO)	General Olusegun Obasanjo	1979 - Elected Shehu Shagari
Justice Victor Ovie-Whiskey	Delta	1980-1983	Federal Electoral Commission (FEDE-CO)	Shehu Shagari	1983- Re-elected Shehu Shagari to second term
Prof. Eme Awa	Abia	1987-1989	National Electoral Commission (NECO)	General Badamasi Babangida	None
Prof. Humphrey Nwosu	Anambra	1989-1993	National Electoral Commission (NECO)	General Badamasi Babangida	1993 - Election Annulled
Prof. Okon Uya	Akwa Ibom	1993-1993	National Electoral Commission of Nigeria (NECON)	General Badamasi Babangida	None
Chief Summer Dagogo-Jack	Rivers	1994-1998	National Electoral Commission of Nigeria (NECON)	General Sani Abacha	(Un-inaugurated) Local Government & National Assembly
Justice Ephraim Akpata	Edo	1998-1999	Independent National Electoral Commission (INEC)	General Abdulsalami Abubakar	1999- Elected Olusegun Obasanjo
Sir Abel Guobadia	Edo	2000-2005	Independent National Electoral Commission (INEC)	Olusegun Obasanjo	2003 – Re-elected Obasanjo to second term
Prof. Maurice Iwu	Imo	2005-2010	Independent National Electoral Commission (INEC)	Olusegun Obasanjo	2007 – Elected Shehu Yar'Adua
Prof. Attahiru Jega	Kebbi	2010-2015	Independent National Electoral Commission (INEC)	Goodluck Jonathan	2011 - Elected Goodluck Jonathan 2015 – Elected

					Muhammadu Buhari
Prof. Mahmud Yakubu	Bauchi	2015-	Independent National Electoral Commission (INEC)	Muhammadu Buhari	None

The history of Electoral commissions in Nigeria is traceable to the pre-independence era, when the Electoral Commission of Nigeria was established to conducted the 1959 parliamentary elections.

ROLES OF SUCCESSIVE ELECTORAL COMMISSIONS IN NIGERIA

According to Alayinde (2016), elections are a vital tool in every democracy, which enfranchises the citizens to elect their leaders of choice. The backbone of sustainable democracy is the conduct of free, fair, and credible elections. Currently, the Independent National Electoral Commission (INEC) conducts Nigerian elections at the national and state levels. The INEC has a chairman, 12 national electoral commissioners, 36 resident electoral commissioners (for each state), and a resident electoral commissioner for the federal capitol territory (Thurston, 2015). The powers and functions of the INEC, as contained in Part I of the Third Schedule of the Constitution of the Federal Republic of Nigeria, are to:

- Organize, undertake, and supervise all elections to the offices of the President and Vice President, the Governor and Deputy Governor of a state, and to the membership of the Senate, the House of Representatives and the House of Assembly of each state of the Federation.
- Register political parties in accordance with the provisions of this Constitution and an Act of the National Assembly.
- Monitor the organization and operation of the political parties, including their finances.
- Arrange for the annual examination and auditing of the funds and accounts of political parties, and publish a report on such examination and audit for public information.
- Arrange and conduct the registration of persons qualified to vote and prepare, maintain, and revise the register of voters for the purpose of any election under this Constitution.
- Monitor political campaigns and provide rules and regulations which shall govern the political parties.
- Ensure that all Electoral Commissioners, Electoral and Returning Officers take and subscribe to the oath of office prescribed by law.
- Delegate any of its powers to any Resident Electoral Commissioner.

Table 9.3: 12 December 1959 House of Representatives Election

Registered Voters	9,036,083	
Total Votes (Voter Turnout)	Not Available (N/A)	
Invalid/Blank Votes	Not Available	
Total Valid Votes	7,185,555	

Party/[Coalition]	Number of Seats (312)	
Northern People's Congress (NPC) & Allies	148	
	Northern People's Congress (NPC)	134
	Mabolaje Grand Alliance (MGA)	6
	Igala Union (IU)	4
	Igbira Tribal Union (ITU)	1
	Niger Delta Congress (NDC)	1
	Independents	2
National Council of Nigeria and the Cameroons-Northern Elements Progressive Union [NCNC-NEPU]	89	
	National Council of Nigeria and the Cameroons (NCNC)	81
	Northern Elements Progressive Union (NEPU)	8
Action Group (AG) & Allies	75	
	Action Group	73
	Independents	2

Like what is obtained in most developing democracies, the electoral process is laced with various challenges that span institutional, operational, and technological considerations (Aderemi, 2015). An enduring democratic culture has been lacking since independence. The electoral processes in Nigeria are designed to fail and can be traced to the colonial masters that designed and ensured the North won the 1959 elections, and hence controlled the federal government. It was a calculated attempt by the colonial government to force Northern oligarchy on the rest of the country, starting with the manipulation of the 1952/1953 census figures that gave the North 54 percent of the Nigerian population, followed by an allocation of 174 seats in the Federal House of Representations based on the strength of North's larger population (Awa, 1960; Metz, 1992).

In an interview with Dr. Sylvester Ugoh, Nigeria's erstwhile minister of science and technology during the Shagari era, population is seen in Nigeria only as a means of controlling power, and not as a means of creating—meaning that a larger population enjoys a larger representation in the National Assembly, and hence control decision making therein. Ibrahim and Garuba (2010) took a cursory look at Nigeria's electoral process, asserting that the Nigeria political system is constructed in such a way as to produce repeated patterns of failed elections. Successive electoral commissions have been in the pockets of the government in power and lack any form of autonomy, independence, or cohesion as they become stooges of the government that establish and fund them.

While the pre-independence 1959 parliamentary elections were riddled with rigging, fraud, and violence, the 1964/1965 parliamentary and regional elections conducted by the Federal Electoral Commission (FEC) under Chief Eyo Ita Esua did not fare better, and threatened federal unity as violence spread across the country along ethnic lines. The December 1964 general elections were marked by massive, nationwide electoral fraud, violence, and political intimidation and political thuggery (Ibrahim & Garuba, 2010). The Tiv tribe of the Benue-Plateau, who had sought autonomy from the North, launched an insurgency against the NPC and NCNC, leading to the call of the Nigerian Army to quell the riots (Institute of Security Studies, n.d). In the Eastern region, there were talks of succession. The 1965 Western Regional Elections were heavily rigged against the dominant Action Group to favor the breakaway minority the Nigeria National Democratic Party (NNDP). The West was engulfed in violence, bloodshed, and the breakdown of law and order that necessitated the Balewa central government to send in battalions of troops to restore peace. Like the local proverb that whoever harvests ant-infested firewood invites the visitation of lizards, the invitation of the military to quell the "Wild Wild West" violence of 1965 was the straw that broke the camel's back. It proved too costly for the nation as it provided a fertile ground and good reason for the army to strike and sack the first republic on January 15, 1966.

Table 9.4: 30 December 1964/18 March 1965 House of Representatives Election*

Party/[Coalition]		Number of Seats (312)
Nigerian National Alliance [NNA]		198
	Northern People's Congress (NPC)	162
	Nigerian National Democratic Party (NNDP)	36
	Midwest Democratic Front (MDF)	-
	Dynamic Party (DP)	-
	Niger Delta Congress (NDC)	-
	Lagos State United Front (LSUF)	-
	Republican Party (RP)	-
United Progressive Grand Alliance [UPGA]		109
	National Council of Nigerian Citizens (NCNC)	84
	Action Group (AG)	21
	Northern Progressive Front (NPF)	4
	Kano People's Party (KPP)	-
	Northern Elements Progressive Union (NEPU)	-
	United Middle-Belt Congress (UMBC)	-
	Zamfara Commoners Party (ZCP)	-
Independents		5

*Due to a boycott of the 30 December 1964 elections in the Eastern Region as well as in some constituencies of Lagos and the Mid-Western Region, supplementary elections were held in these areas on 18 March 1965.

The military incursion into the politics of Nigeria put democratic and electoral processes in peril. On assumption of office after the January coup, one of the first acts of Major General Thomas Aguiyi-Ironsi as Head of State was to suspend the constitution and abolish the Federal Electoral Commission. The electoral process would remain in limbo until 1976, when General Olusegun Obasanjo's regime established the Federal Electoral Commission (FEDECO) in

1976 in preparation for the 1979 general elections, which welcomed the second republic. A new constitution, drafted in 1978, created an executive presidency and a separation of power among the three tiers of government—executive, legislative, and judiciary. FEDECO, under the leadership of Chief Ani, was tasked with the registration of political parties, delimitation of constituencies, and conduct of the general elections. As with previous elections, the 1979 elections, which elected Alhaji Shehu Shagari as president, were fraught with incompetence, rigging, forgery, manipulation, and the use of the military and police to intimidate the electorate. The elections became one of the most controversial elections in the country. One of the many failures of FEDECO in the 1979 elections was its interpretation of two-thirds of 19 states, which the citizens saw as daylight robbery to award Shehu Shagari the throne of the presidency, even when the Supreme Court upheld his elections (Institute of Security Studies, n.d.; Oyeweso & Amusa, 2015). Shagari got the 25 percent mandatory vote in 12 rather than 13 of the 19 states.

Table 9.5: July 1979 National Assembly Election

Senate (7 July 1979)

Registered Voters	48,633,782
Total Votes (Voter Turnout)	12,532,195 (25.8%)
Invalid/Blank Votes	Not Available
Total Valid Votes	12,314,107

House of Representatives (14 July 1979)

Registered Voters	48,633,782			
Total Votes (Voter Turnout)	14,941,555 (30.7%)			
Party	Senate		House of Representatives	
	Number of Votes	% of Votes	Number of Seats (95)	Number of Seats (449)
National Party of Nigeria (NPN)	4,032,329	32.75%	36	168
Unity Party of Nigeria (UPN)	2,835,362	23.03%	28	111
Nigerian People's Party (NPP)	2,145,849	17.43%	16	78
Greater Nigerian People's Party (GNPP)	1,847,019	15.00%	8	43
People's Redemption Party (PRP)	1,453,538	11.80%	7	49

Table 9.6: 11 August 1979 Presidential Election

Registered Voters	48,633,782		
Total Votes (Voter Turnout)	Not Available (N/A)		
Invalid/Blank Votes	Not Available		
Total Valid Votes	16,846,633		
Candidate (Party)		Number of Votes	% of Votes
Shehu Shagari (NPN)		5,668,857	33.77%
Obafemi Awolowo (UPN)		4,916,651	29.18%
Nnamdi Azikiwe (NPP)		2,822,523	16.75%
Aminu Kano (PRP)		1,732,113	10.28%
Waziri Ibrahim (GNPP)		1,686,489	10.02%

However, the 1983 general elections, headed by Justice Victor Ovie-Whiskey, were characterized by large-scale rigging and fraud that escalated to riots, violence, arson, and looting across the country. The elections were a disaster as there were various allegations and counterallegations at all levels of the elections—from state assemblies, gubernatorial, national assembly (house of representatives and senate) and presidential. Shehu Shagari was re-elected to a second term. Ondo and Oyo states were worst hit with arson, looting, killings, and maiming. Akin Omoboriowo of the NPN was declared winner of the Ondo gubernatorial race only to be shoved aside later with the declaration of his former boss, Chief Michael Ajasin of UPN as the rightful winner. Then, the thugs took over and the sight was gory. The same pattern played out in Oyo state, when Dr. Victor Omololu Olunloyo of the NPN won the gubernatorial election against the UPN incumbent governor, Bola Ige. The electoral tribunals set up across the country to resolve electoral disputes proved to be a sham, as they were used as tools to foist unpopular and failed candidates on the people. As in 1966, the confusion, lawlessness, and disorder created by the elections provided a cover and safe haven for the military to stage yet another coup that toppled the Shagari government on December 31, 1983. The second republic was aborted.

Table 9.7: 6 August 1983 Presidential Election*

Registered Voters	65,304,818	
Total Votes (Voter Turnout)	Not Available (N/A)	
Invalid/Blank Votes	Not Available	
Total Valid Votes	25,430,096	
Candidate (Party)	Number of Votes	% of Votes
Shehu Shagari (NPN)	12,081,471	47.51%
Obafemi Awolowo (UPN)	7,907,209	31.09%

Nnamdi Azikiwe (NPP)	3,557,113	13.99%
Hassan Yusuf (PRP)	968,974	3.81%
Waziri Ibrahim (GNPP)	643,805	2.53%
Tunji Braithwaite (NAP)	271,524	1.07%

*Due to the disputed nature of this election, results tend to differ by source.

Table 9.8: August 1983 National Assembly Election

Senate (20 August 1983)

Registered Voters	65,300,000 (approx.)
Total Votes (Voter Turnout)	Not Available (N/A)

House of Representatives (27 August 1983)

Registered Voters	65,300,000 (approx.)	
Total Votes (Voter Turnout)	Not Available (N/A)	
Party	Senate	House of Representatives
	Number of Seats (96)	Number of Seats (450)
National Party of Nigeria (NPN)	55	264
Unity Party of Nigeria (UPN)	12	33
Nigerian People's Party (NPP)	12	48
People's Redemption Party (PRP)	5	41
Greater Nigerian People's Party (GNPP)	1	-
Vacant*	10	64

*In two states, Ondo and Oyo, elections to the National Assembly were delayed due to outbreaks of violence. The delayed polls were held in September 1983 to fill the vacant seats. The final composition of the National Assembly after the elections was as follows: Senate-NPN (60), UPN (16), NPP (12), PRP (5), GNPP (2), and (1) vacant seat; House of Representatives-NPN (306), UPN (51), NPP (48), and the PRP (41). Results for the (4) remaining seats were unavailable.

Major General Muhammadu Buhari, upon assumption of office as the military Head of State, abolished all democratic institutions and suspended the constitution, and was shoved aside in August 1985 by Major General Ibrahim Babangida in a power tussle. In 1987, General Babangida established the National Electoral Commission (NECO), headed by Professor Eme Awa and later Professor Humphrey Nwosu. The 1993 elections were organized into various legislative and executive positions at the state and federal levels, and adopted the Option A4, or Open Ballot System. The elections, which produced Chief Moshood Abiola as the presumptive president, were adjudged as the fairest and freest elections ever conducted in Nigeria. General Babangida would later annul the presidential election, throwing the nation into political turmoil and quagmire. Students, traders, civil servants, and common citizens took to the streets to protest the annulment. It created chaos, angst, and commotion across the country. To counter the protests, General Babangida hurriedly appointed Professor Okon Edet Uya as the chairman of NECON to replace Professor Nwosu, who had resigned. But the damage had been inflicted and was too much to overcome. General Babangida was forced to step aside, but not before he had installed a political stooge in Chief Ernest Shonekan as the head of the transitional government, which provided a three-month temporary respite before General Sani Abacha removed him via a palace coup.

Table 9.9: 4 July 1993 National Assembly Election*

Senate

Registered Voters	38,866,336
Total Votes (Voter Turnout)	Not Available (N/A)
Invalid/Blank Votes	Not Available
Total Valid Votes	15,800,776

House of Representatives

Registered Voters	38,866,336					
Total Votes (Voter Turnout)	Not Available (N/A)					
Invalid/Blank Votes	Not Available					
Total Valid Votes	16,905,871					
Party	Senate			House of Representatives		
	Number of Votes	% of Votes	Number of Seats (91)	Number of Votes	% of Votes	Number of Seats (593)
Social Democratic Party (SDP)	7,494,228	47.43%	52	8,354,791	49.42%	314
National Republican Convention (NRC)	8,306,548	52.57%	37	8,551,080	50.58%	275
Vacant	-	-	2	-	-	4

*Soon after the Presidential Election, the Babangida administration annulled the election results. This led to his resignation after widespread protests and an Interim National Government, led by Ernest Shonekan took power.

The impact of the cancelled 1993 presidential election produced the General Abacha Abacha regime in November 1993, which shoved Chief Shonekan aside. Abacha went ahead to set up the National Electoral Commission of Nigeria (NECON) under the chairmanship of Chief Summer Dagogo-Jack. The electoral body registered five political parties that endorsed General Abacha as the sole presidential candidate. Elections were conducted at local councils and the National Assembly, but could not be inaugurated before Abacha died in 1998, aborting the transition program to democracy.

Table 9.10: 25 April 1998 National Assembly Election*

Senate

Registered Voters	Not Available
Total Votes (Voter Turnout)	Not Available (N/A)

House of Representatives

Registered Voters	Not Available
Total Votes (Voter Turnout)	Not Available (N/A)

Party	Senate	House of Representatives
	Number of Seats (80)	Number of Seats (282)
United Nigeria Congress Party (UNCP)	61	229
Democratic Party of Nigeria (DPN)	9	39
Congress for National Consensus (CNC)	6	6
Grassroots Democratic Movement (GDM)	2	4
National Centre Party of Nigeria (NCPN)	2	4

*These elections were held during the military regime of General Sani Abacha in which all political parties participating were affiliated with the government while the true opposition was prevented from participating in the poll. The results above are based on figures released by the National Electoral Commission of Nigeria (NECON) and are likely incomplete. Voter turnout was extremely low and the result was soon after annulled by the authorities.

The mantle of leadership fell on General Abdusalami Abubakar, who scrapped NECON and established the Independent National Electoral Commission with Justice Ephraim Akpata as the chairman. General Abubakar quickened the return of democracy as he moved to set the machinery in motion to realize the goal. The 1999 general election, with all its flaws, returned democracy to the country with Chief Olusegun Obasanjo as the president. Across the country, the state assembly, gubernatorial, and national assembly were successfully conducted, and like previous elections, were marred with violence, multiple voting, bribery, fraud, and the manipulation of electoral results.

Table 9.11: 20 February 1999 National Assembly Election

Senate

Registered Voters	57,938,945
Total Votes (Voter Turnout)	24,386,247 (42.1%)

House of Representatives

Registered Voters	57,938,945
Total Votes (Voter Turnout)	23,573,407 (40.7%)

Party	Senate		House of Representatives	
	% of Votes	Number of Seats (109)	% of Votes	Number of Seats (360)
People's Democratic Party (PDP)	56.4%	59	57.1%	206
All People's Party (APP)	31.2%	29	30.6%	74
Alliance for Democracy (AD)	12.4%	20	12.4%	68
Vacant/Undeclared Seats	-	1	-	12

Table 9.12: 27 February 1999 Presidential Election

Registered Voters	57,938,945	
Total Votes (Voter Turnout)	30,280,052 (52.3%)	
Invalid/Blank Votes	431,611	
Total Valid Votes	29,848,441	
Candidate (Party) [Coalition]	Number of Votes	% of Votes
Olusegun Obasanjo (PDP)	18,738,154	62.78%
Olu Falae (AD) [AD-APP]	11,110,287	37.22%

The INEC, under the leadership of Dr. Abel Guobadia, conducted the 2003 general elections that re-elected Chief Obasanjo to a second term. The elections were flawed and lacked transparency and credibility. Local and international monitors condemned the elections and reported massive rigging, ballot-box stuffing, underaged voting, falsification of results, and the use of police and other law enforcement to harass and intimidate the electorate.

Table 9.13: 12 April 2003 National Assembly Election

Senate

Registered Voters	60,823,022
Total Votes (Voter Turnout)	29,995,171 (49.3%)
Invalid/Blank Votes	965,064
Total Valid Votes	29,030,107

House of Representatives

Registered Voters	60,823,022
Total Votes (Voter Turnout)	30,386,270 (50.0%)
Invalid/Blank Votes	1,153,200
Total Valid Votes	29,233,070

Party	Senate			House of Representatives		
	Number of Votes	% of Votes	Number of Seats (109)	Number of Votes	% of Votes	Number of seats (360)
People's Democratic	15,585,538	53.69%	76	15,927,807	54.49%	223

Party (PDP)						
All Nigeria People's Party (ANPP)	8,091,783	27.87%	27	8,021,531	27.44%	96
Alliance for Democracy (AD)	2,828,082	9.74%	6	2,711,972	9.28%	34
United Nigeria People's Party (UNPP)	789,705	2.72%	-	803,432	2.75%	2
National Democratic Party (NDP)	459,462	1.58%	-	561,161	1.92%	1
All Progressives Grand Alliance (APGA)	429,073	1.48%	-	397,147	1.36%	2
People's Redemption Party (PRP)	204,929	0.71%	-	222,938	0.76%	1
Others	641,535	2.21%	-	587,082	2.01%	-
Vacant	-	-	-	-		

Table 9.14: 19 April 2003 Presidential Election

Registered Voters   60,823,022
Total Votes (Voter Turnout) 42,018,735 (69.1%)
Invalid/Blank Votes   2,538,246
Total Valid Votes   39,480,489

Candidate (Party)	Number of Votes	% of Votes
Olusegun Obasanjo (PDP)	24,456,140	61.94%
Muhammadu Buhari (ANPP)	12,710,022	32.19%
Chukwuemeka Odumegwu Ojukwu (APGA)	1,297,445	3.29%
Jim Nwobodo (UNPP)	169,609	0.43%
Gani Fawehimi (NCP)	161,333	0.41%
Sarah Jubril (PAC)	157,560	0.40%
Ike Nwachukwu (NDP)	132,997	0.34%
Christopher Okotie (JP)	119,547	0.30%
Balarabe Musa (PRP)	100,765	0.26%
Arthur Nwankwo (PMP)	57,720	0.15%
Emmanuel Okereke (APLP)	26,921	0.07%
Kalu Idika Kalu (NNPP)	23,830	0.06%
Muhammadu Dikko Yusuf (MDJ)	21,403	0.05%
Yahaya Ndu (ARP)	11,565	0.03%
Abayomi Ferreira (DA)	6,727	0.02%
Tunji Braithwaite (NAP)	6,932	0.02%
Iheanyichukwu Nnaji (BNPP)	5,987	0.02%
Olapade Agoro (NAC)	5,756	0.01%
Pere Ajuwa (LDPN)	4,473	0.01%

Mojisola Adekunle Obasanjo (MMN)	3,757	0.01%

Professor Maurice Iwu led the INEC, and conducted the 2007 general elections that produced the presidency of Alhaji Umaru Musa Yar'Adua of the People's Democratic Party (PDP). Domestic and foreign observers regarded the elections as a sham. Reports of unprecedented electoral malpractice, such as multiple thumbprinting, smuggling of ballot materials, intimidation and harassment of voters, and opposition parties were deafening. The elections were characterized by the insufficient supply of voting machines, inadequate number of registration and polling centers, shortages of registration materials, and underaged registration. Many voters were disfranchised due to lack of functional voting machines (Ibrahim & Garuba, 2010). All these deficiencies opened a floodgate of electoral fraud, collusion, rigging, and violence.

Table 9.15: 21 April 2007 Presidential Election*

Registered Voters	61,567,036
Total Votes (Voter Turnout)	Not Available (approx. 58%)
Invalid/Blank Votes	Not Available
Total Valid Votes	35,397,517

Candidate (Party)	Number of Votes	% of Votes
Umaru Musa Yar'Adua (PDP)	24,638,063	69.60%
Muhammadu Buhari (ANPP)	6,605,299	18.66%
Atiku Abubakar (AC)	2,637,848	7.45%
Orji Uzor Kalu (PPA)	608,803	1.72%
Attahiru Bafarawa (DPP)	289,224	0.82%
Chukwuemeka Odumegwu Ojukwu (APGA)	155,947	0.44%
Pere Ajuwa (AD)	89,241	0.25%
Christopher Okotie (FRESH)	74,049	0.21%
Patrick Utomi (ADC)	50,849	0.14%
Asakarawon Olapere (NPC)	33,771	0.10%
Ambrose Owuru (HDP)	28,519	0.08%

Arthur Nwankwo (PMP)	24,164	0.07%
Emmanuel Okereke (ALP)	22,677	0.06%
Lawrence Adedoyin (APS)	22,409	0.06%
Aliyu Habu Fari (NDP)	21,974	0.06%
Galtima Liman (NNPP)	21,665	0.06%
Maxi Okwu (CPP)	14,027	0.04%
Sunny Okogwu (RPN)	13,566	0.04%
Iheanyichukwu Nnaji (BNPP)	11,705	0.03%
Osagie Obayuwana (NCP)	8,229	0.02%
Olapade Agoro (NAC)	5,752	0.02%
Akpone Solomon (NMDP)	5,664	0.02%
Isa Odidi (ND)	5,408	0.02%
Aminu Abubakar (NUP)	4,355	0.01%
Mojisola Adekunle Obasanjo (MMN)	4,309	0.01%

*The figures in the table are based on final results announced by Maurice Iwu, Chairman of the Independent National Electoral Commission (INEC), on 23 April 2007. Final results were also published on the INEC website, but the figures differ from those in the table above.

Table 9.16: 21 April 2007 National Assembly Election

Senate

Registered Voters	Not Available
Total Votes (Voter Turnout)	Not Available (N/A)

House of Representatives

Registered Voters	Not Available	
Total Votes (Voter Turnout)	Not Available (N/A)	
Party	**Senate**	**House of Representatives**
	Number of Seats (109)	**Number of Seats (360)**
People's Democratic Party (PDP)	87	263
All Nigeria People's Party (ANPP)	14	63
Action Congress (AC)	6	30
Progressive People's Alliance (PPA)	1	3
Accord Party (ACCORD)	1	-
Labour Party (LP)	-	1

Dr. Goodluck Jonathan stood for election and won as an incumbent president in 2011 upon Yar'Adua's demise in 2010. The INEC, under the leadership of Professor Attahiru Jega, recorded significant improvement in the conduct of the 2011 elections over previous elections. The INEC had introduced the voters' register, an electronic compiled register and card reader designed to curb electoral fraud. Although the elections were given fair mark by local and international observers, the Nigeria political system is designed to produce repeated failed elections. There were reports of multiple thumbprinting, fraud, collusion with INEC officials, riots, thuggery, violence, looting, killing, and maiming across the six geo-political zones, fueled by the poor conduct of the elections (Bamgbose, 2012; David, Manu & Musa, 2014; Nwangwu, 2015). However, it must be recalled that, unlike the previous elections that had bedeviled the country, the conduct of 2011 elections gave Nigerians a glimpse of hope of the sanitization, reformation, and credibility of electoral process (Oyeweso & Amusa, 2015).

The INEC's conduct of the 2015 general elections under the helm of Professor Jega received praise from the International Monitoring Group (IMG) as being free and credible, although it had catalogues of flaws and challenges. In its bid to improve on its 2011 performance at the polls, and to reduce electoral fraud to a minimum, the INEC introduced the biometric PVC and card-reader machine, which were meant to validate the authenticity of the PVC. The card reader reads biometric data in the embedded chip of the PVC, which displays the voters' names and facial images, as well as authenticates their fingerprints (Nwangwu, 2015).

Table 9.17: April 2011 National Assembly Election*

Senate (9 April 2011)

Registered Voters	Not Available
Total Votes (Voter Turnout)	Not Available (N/A)

House of Representatives (9 April 2011)

Registered Voters	Not Available
Total Votes (Voter Turnout)	Not Available

Party	Senate	House of Representatives
	Number of Seats (109)	Number of Seats (360)
People's Democratic Party (PDP)	45	123
Action Congress of Nigeria (ACN)	13	47
All Nigeria People's Party (ANPP)	7	25
Congress for Progressive Change (CPC)	5	30
Others	4	9

*Preliminary (incomplete) results, as posted on the Independent National Electoral Commission (INEC) website. Due to logistical problems, elections in 15 Senatorial and 48 House constituencies will take place on 26 April 2011.

Table 9.18: 16 April 2011 Presidential Election

Registered Voters   73,528,040
Total Votes (Voter Turnout) 39,469,484 (53.7%)
Invalid/Blank Votes   1,259,506
Total Valid Votes   38,209,978

Candidate (Party)	Number of Votes	% of Votes
Goodluck Jonathan (PDP)	22,495,187	58.89%
Muhammadu Buhari (CPC)	12,214,853	31.98%
Nuhu Ribadu (ACN)	2,079,151	5.41%
Ibrahim Shekarau (ANPP)	917,012	2.40%
Mahmud Waziri (PDC)	82,243	0.21%
Nwadike Chikezie (PMP)	56,248	0.15%
Lawson Aroh (PPP)	54,203	0.14%
Peter Nwangwu (ADC)	51,682	0.14%
Iheanyichukwu Nnaji (BNPP)	47,272	0.12%
Christopher Okotie (FRESH)	34,331	0.09%
Dele Momodu (NCP)	26,376	0.07%

Solomon Akpona (NMDP)	25,938	0.07%
Lawrence Adedoyin (APS)	23,740	0.06%
Ebiti Ndok (UNPD)	21,203	0.06%
John Dara (NTP)	19,744	0.05%
Rasheed Shitta-Bey (MPPP)	16,492	0.04%
Yahaya Ndu (ARP)	12,264	0.03%
Ambrose Owuru (HDP)	12,023	0.03%
Patrick Utomi (SDMP)	11,544	0.03%
Christopher Nwaokobia (LDPN)	8,472	0.02%

The 2015 elections scored a major point in the political history of Nigeria as Mr. Muhammadu Buhari was declared winner of the presidential election over incumbent President Goodluck Jonathan. Never before in the history of Nigeria has a sitting president been defeated in an election. President Jonathan, in his magnanimity, handed over the instrument of power to Buhari. One other uncommon feat of the 2015 elections was the reduction of violence, rioting, arson, and killings. Nigerians from all corners of the country voted overwhelmingly for Buhari for change of leadership. President Buhari has reconstituted the INEC and appointed Professor Mahmood Yakubu as the chairman.

Table 9.19: The 2015 Presidential Election

Candidate	Gen-Der	Party	Votes	Remark
Muhammadu Buhari	M	APC	15,424,921	ELECTED
Goodluck Ebele Jonathan	M	PDP	12,853,162	
Ayeni Musa Adebayo	M	APA	53,537	
Alh. Ganiyu O. Galadima	M	ACPN	40,311	
Chief Sam Eke	M	CPP	36,300	
Rafiu Salau	M	AD	30,673	
Dr. Mani Ibrahim Ahmad	M	ADC	29,666	
Allagoa Kelvin Chinedu	M	PPN	24,475	
Chief Martin Onovo	M	NCP	24,455	
Jci Sen. Tunde Anifowose Kelani	M	AA	22,125	
Chief (Dr.) Chekwas Okorie	M	UPP	18,220	
Comfort Oluremi Sonaiya	F	KOWA	13,076	
Godson Mgbodile Ohaenyem Okoye	M	UDP	9,208	
High Chief Ambrose N. Albert Owuru	M	HOPE	7,435	

Source: INEC, 2015

Table 9.20. Voter's Turnout from the March 28, 2015, 2015 Presidential and National Assembly Elections

S/N	Name of States	No of Registered Voters	No of Accredited Voters	% Voters' Turnout
1	Abia	1,349,134	442,538	33
2	Adamawa	1,518,123	709,993	47
3	Akwa Ibom	1,644,481	1,074,070	65
4	Anambra	1,963,427	774,430	39
5	Bauchi	2,053,484	1,094,069	53
6	Bayelsa	605,637	384,789	64
7	Benue	1,893,596	754,634	40
8	Borno	1,799,669	544,759	30
9	Cross River	1,144,288	500,577	44
10	Delta	2,044,372	1,350,914	66
11	Ebonyi	1,071,226	425,301	40
12	Edo	1,650,552	599,166	36
13	Ekiti	723,255	323,739	45
14	Enugu	1,381,563	616,112	45
15	Gombe	1,110,105	515,828	46
16	Imo	1,747,681	801,712	46
17	Jigawa	1,815,839	1,153,428	64
18	Kaduna	3,361,793	1,746,031	52
19	Kano	4,943,862	2,364,434	48
20	Kastina	2,842,741	1,578,646	56
21	Kebbi	1,457,763	792,817	54
22	Kogi	1,350,883	476,839	35
23	Kwara	1,181,032	489,360	41
24	Lagos	5,827,846	1,678,754	29
25	Nasarawa	1,222,054	562,959	46
26	Niger	1,995,679	933,607	47
27	Ogun	1,709,409	594,975	35
28	Ondo	1,501,549	618,040	41
29	Osun	1,378,113	683,169	50
30	Oyo	2,344,448	1,073,849	46
31	Plateau	1,977,211	1,076,833	54
32	Rivers	2,324,300	1,643,409	71
33	Sokoto	1,663,127	988,899	59
34	Taraba	1,374,307	638,578	46
35	Yobe	1,077,942	520,127	48
36	Zamfara	1,484,941	875,049	59
37	FCT	886,573	344,056	39
TOTAL		67,422,005	31,746,490	

Source: Adapted from Election Monitor (2015), 2015 General Elections Observation Report, a Publication of Election Monitor.

To sum up this section, the following illustrates the periods of ragtag incursion of the military into the Nigerian politics since independence.

1960-1966: Democracy
1966-1979: Military Regime
1979-1983: Democracy
1983-1989: Military Regime
1989-1993: Restricted Democratic Practice under Military Regime
1993-1998: Military Regime
1998-1999: Transitional Government under Military Regime
1999-Date: Democracy

THE NIGERIAN ELECTORAL PROCESS

Dye (2011) defined elections as a vital tool for the recruitment of political leadership in a democratic society, the key to participation in a democracy, and the means of giving consent to the government. There are two types of elections—primary and general elections. A *primary* election is conducted at the party level to choose a candidate from a field of candidates who will represent the political party in the general elections. Once a primary candidate is elected, the party endorses him or her to stand for the general election. On the other hand, a *general* election is conducted to choose among candidates that have been nominated by their political parties for local, state, or federal office. The general elections serve to make the final choice among the other candidates who have also been nominated by their parties to represent them. Once a victor emerges from the general election, the INEC issues a certificate of return to the elected candidate.

Elections play paramount roles in a true democracy, and are powerful and critical mechanisms by which the people elect their leaders to public office to represent them and serve their interests for a period of time. This process legitimizes the elected government and gives the power to the electorate to hold the government and the elected leaders responsible and accountable for their actions. To put it succinctly, elections assist in shaping and sharpening the political accountability between the electors and the elected through mutual exchange of ideas. This process does not hold any relevance in Nigeria. Unfortunately, Nigerians have embraced lexicons such as "arranged" or "staged" elections, and "the anointed," "the chosen one," "godson/goddaughter" or "godfather." To an average Nigerian, it simply means that whoever carries any of those connotations has already been "elected" to the office even before the elections.

In Nigeria, it appears that electoral malpractice is ingrained as part of a culture. The INEC had suggested using electronic voting (e-voting), but the idea has been shut down by the political elite for fear of transparency and loss of elections. As the current political structure remains apathetic to e-voting, only electoral reforms, voter reorientation, and allowing the INEC's use of its authority in the conduct of elections can change the culture. Rigging is an endemic situation in Nigeria elections, dating back to the colonial era. Rigging of elections has produced bad politicians who would do anything to win an election using threats, intimidation, manipulation, thuggery, vandalism, arson, or violence. Opposition candidates are kidnapped, maimed, or killed, even before the elections. These politicians use their wealth, power, and connections to compromise the police and electoral officers to do their bidding. This is accompanied by voter harassment by the police and other law enforcement agents, ballot box snatching, ballot-box stuffing, unauthorized declaration of election results, underaged voting, illegal thumbprinting of ballots, multiple voting, falsification of results, and other electoral vices.

The electorate has lost faith in politics and elections due to electoral fraud. Godfatherism has become the order of the day, where people who have "good connections" are allowed to stand and win elections at all cost, at the expense of a good and trustworthy candidate. Elections which are held with the intent of holding the office-holders responsible and accountable to their constituents have eroded. There is no more accountability on the elected. How can it work when they paid their way to their juicy positions?

On a wider perspective, there is a deep-seated distrust among the different parts of Nigeria. Each section will resort to all sorts of electoral malpractice to win an election. One can conclude that distrust makes elections in Nigeria a matter of life and death. The desire to control power at all costs leads to corruption, rigging, arson, and violence. People will do anything that will make their kith and kin candidate win. If people were convinced that there would be fairness, irrespective of who is in charge, there wouldn't be much clambering to control power at all costs, or for the president, governor, senator or assemblyman to come from their own areas.

Elekwa (as cited in Idike, 2014) identified the various phases of an electoral process, which can be grouped into three main phases:

Phase 1: Pre-election phase: This phase includes delimitation of electoral boundaries, voter registration, registration of political parties, nomination of candidates, election campaigns, media and civic and voter education.

Phase 2: This phase encompasses election day activities such as polling stations, secrecy of ballot, ballot papers, ballot boxes, election materials, election monitoring and observation, and counting of votes.

Phase 3: This phase includes the announcement of results, post-election review, and post-election disputes.

In established democracies, McKenzie (as cited in Legborsi, 2011) posited four conditions for the conduct of free and fair elections, and they include the following:

- An independent judiciary to interpret the electoral laws.
- An honest, competent, nonpartisan electoral body to manage the elections (INEC for example).

- A developed system of political parties.
- A general acceptance by the political community of the rules of the game.

Sadly, none of these tenets is observed in the Nigerian context, where elections are seen as do-or-die affairs because of the influence, pay package, and political trappings such offices attract.

ELECTIONS AND THE ROLE OF TECHNOLOGY

Although traditional media (print, radio and television) still remain a powerful force in information dissemination in Nigeria, mobile technology and the Internet have taken the country by storm in the last decade. The increasing global reliance on technology for daily activities has altered the business, educational, political, legal, and social media landscapes. People all over the world are relying heavily on Smartphones (with cameras), personal computers, GPS for directions, Internet banking, and social media outlets such as Facebook, Twitter, Instagram, SMS and MMS (text messaging), blogs, etc. Nigeria is not an exception. The truth is, these social media technologies seem to overshadow the traditional print, radio and television media. Social media has revolutionized communication and access to media that used to be the exclusive preserve of the government, the political class, and the rich.

Social media—regarded as the new kid in town, or dubbed as "citizen media" or "consumer-generated media"—allows people to generate and share information easily and quickly. As Omeruo (2010) noted, Facebook Causes, a Facebook application, connects people with common interests, just as videos from YouTube allow people and organizations from diverse backgrounds to connect and promote political and social causes in their society. The citizens have used various social media platforms to register their dissatisfaction with certain government policies, and these platforms have proven to be effective.

Akpojivi (2012) cited competition and participation as the two cardinal elements in a democracy and the bedrock of any democratic society—meaning that in a society where these two elements are lacking, the media and democratic process will wobble. The media consists of print, electronic, and communication technology. Newspapers, radio, and television have played vital roles in Nigeria's electoral process, dating back to the colonial days. The media organizations tend to convey the messages or reflect the wishes and aspirations of their influential owners and financiers. The Lagos-based *West African Pilot*, controlled by Nnamdi Azikiwe (Zik), was the NCNC's platform and mouthpiece for executing their political agenda and reaching the voters.

The Nigerian Broadcasting Corporation (NBC) was established in 1956 by a bill of the House of Representatives to care for radio broadcasts in the country. The NBC was established to be independent and politically neutral, but the federal government in power hijacked the establishment alongside the *Daily Times*, to serve as its mouthpiece in propagating its political propaganda to the people in order to win elections. In the west, Awolowo and the Action Group used the state-controlled Western Nigerian Broadcasting Service (radio and TV), and later, the *Nigerian Tribune,* to engage the people in political propaganda to curry votes and win elections. The Eastern Nigeria Broadcasting Service (ENBS) was established in Enugu in 1960, followed by the Broadcasting Corporation of Northern Nigeria (BCNN) in 1962.

Because of massive illiteracy at the time, radio and television were the most effective ways for successive governments and political parties to engage the people in politics. The broadcasts were made in English and main local languages (Hausa in the North, Igbo in the East, and Yoruba in the West). The newspapers also recorded a significant impact in elections. These media were deployed in the 1959, 1964/65 elections, and they proved effective. In preparation for the transition to democracy, the Federal Radio Corporation of Nigeria (FCRN) was established in 1978, and later the Voice of Nigeria (VON) for external service. However, the creation of 19 states out of the former four regions allowed each state to establish its own radio and TV stations.

The government controlled by the National Party of Nigeria (NPN) did not waste time in establishing the Nigeria Television Authority (NTA) and Radio Nigeria in all the states, and effectively used them to their advantage in the 1983 general elections. The electoral umpire (FEDECO) would announce election results through the government-controlled TV and radio houses. The poor electorate had no idea whether their votes counted. At the state levels, the party in power would use the state-controlled media (TV, radio, and newspapers) as instruments to rig and win elections at all costs. Privately-owned newspapers such as *The Guardian, Vanguard, Concord,* etc. played major roles in informing and educating the electorate. The mass media lost its compass and bearing during the administrations of Major General Buhari and General Ibrahim Babangida between 1984 and 1993, as many reporters, journalists, and publishers were jailed for the flimsy excuse of criticizing the government.

The Buhari government imprisoned Nduka Irabor and Tunde Thompson in 1984 under Decree Number 4 of 1984. Chris Anyanwu of TSM (*The Sunday Magazine*) and others were clamped in jail during the General Babangida regime. Many media houses were either restricted or closed during this reign of terror. It must also be recalled that the administration of General Babangida witnessed the commercialization and privatization of some segments of the economy, which produced the establishment of private radio and television houses. With an increase in literacy and the proliferation of print and electronic media, the Nigerian electorates became wiser. The conduct of successive Nigerian general elections would get better, but lacked credibility and transparency. They are still bedeviled by large-scale rigging, corruption, fraud, and violence.

The media played a huge role in the 1993 presidential election that would have produced Chief M.K.O. Abiola as president. The National Electoral Commission (NECON) adopted the Option A4 model, which was seen as transparent across the country. The reduction of the political parties to two—the Socialist Democratic Party and the National Republican Convention—made the elections easier and credible. The local and international monitoring observers that swamped the nooks and crannies of Nigeria to ensure the elections were free and fair deployed various technologies to relay information to the world.

Internet and information communications technology were in their infancy in Nigeria during the 1999 general elections. The elections were popular and received wide coverage, and attracted local and international monitoring and observation. The restriction of mass media had been lifted. The proliferation of television and radio stations, along with limited Internet, helped with voter orientation and education. While the presidential election was convincingly won by Chief Obasanjo, the same cannot be said of other local, state, and national assemblies as they were flawed, rigged, and manipulated to favor one candidate over another.

Although technology and the mass media had gotten better leading up to the 2003 and 2007 general elections, their impact on the credibility of the elections was minimal as the period marked significant levels of rigging, manipulation of results, arson, violence, and political assassinations. It was a dark period for the elections in Nigeria. The INEC, rising from the 2007 horse-whipping elections, made some improvements leading to the 2011 elections. While the role and impact of the traditional media cannot be overemphasized, the social media added a dimension of transparency to the Nigerian electoral process. As in the previous elections, when the social media was not taken very seriously, the 2011 general elections were different. The social media played a pivotal role in the 2011 general elections and altered the trajectory of information dissemination in the country.

The rapid growth in Internet, broadband, mobile phones, e-mails, YouTube, and computerized databases to access technologies, as well as satellite capabilities, also proved powerful tools that positively impacted the elections (Nwokeafor & Okunoye, 2013). According to Judith Asuni and Jacqueline Farris of the Shehu Musa Yar'Adua Foundation (Abuja, Nigeria), social media tools have also revolutionized the efficiency of election observation by local and international observers, and come with increased coverage and reporting at minimal cost (Asuni & Farris, n.d). The use of social media in the 2011 elections enabled greater voter participation as citizens had access to information directly and more accurately. The period of the 2011 presidential elections marked a high record of 25 million hits on INEC website (Ed.)

The advantages of Internet technology allowed the free flow of information. The availability of social media technologies, such as mobile phones, Facebook, SMS, and Twitter allowed Nigerians and people all over the world to monitor the elections and reduce incidents of rigging and falsification of results. President Goodluck Jonathan, who was standing election to complete the term of Yar'Adua (who had died a year earlier), had a Twitter account to connect directly with millions of followers. Although he won the presidential election due to his popularity at the time, there were still many reports of election malpractice in state and national assembly elections across the country.

Leading into the 2015 general elections, President Jonathan and his People's Democratic Party (PDP) had overstayed their welcome. The other minor political parties had united to form a stronger All Progressive Congress (APC) to confront Jonathan and the PDP. The social, print, radio, and television media tapped into the unfolding drama as top politicians cross-carpeted from the ruling party PDP to the APC. This was an evil fire that blew the PDP no good. Buoyed by social media, the INEC began to show some signs of independence by engaging in voter education and orientation through the media. It became easy to access INEC documents and programs. Young Nigerians, who constitute more than two-thirds of the population, leveraged social media technology to include live streaming of panel discourse prior to elections, and used mobile apps to report live incidents from various polling stations nationwide (Ehidiamen, 2015).

Ehidiamen (2015) further stated that the aggregation of various innovative mobile apps (such as Ravoda) with social media by these young citizens facilitated the mobilization and reporting of incidents from different polling units with a view to curbing manipulation and electoral fraud. Ravoda allowed the electorate to directly report election activities in real time.

Bartlett, Krasodomski-Jones, Daniel, Fisher, and Jesperson (2015) stressed that between March 18 and April 12, 2015, there were 13.6 million tweets posted by 1.38 million unique users associated with the presidential and state elections. However, INEC deployment of innovative permanent voters' cards (PVCs) added some transparency and helped reduced voter impersonation. With all of these technologies at the disposal of the electorate, the odds were stacked against Jonathan and the PDP at the elections. It was not hard to discern how the party, which had been in government for 16 years, could perform so poorly at the elections and lose power to the opposition party APC.

ELECTION MANAGEMENT AND CHALLENGES OF THE ELECTORAL PROCESS SYSTEMS

From all indications, it is clear that electoral malpractice is a bane in the Nigerian political culture that continues to delay Nigeria's hope for a consolidated democracy. This Hydra-headed monster has become so endemic in Nigeria's political consciousness that the electorate has also bought into it and regards it as a norm, while still crying foul. It makes no difference if an election is transparent and credible as long as it produces a victor. Consolidation of power entails that the government in power must be legitimate (Jawan, 2011). Nigeria, as an emerging democracy, has no reliable and consistent infrastructure in place to conduct successive transparent and credible elections at the local, state, and federal levels.

The politicians are corrupt and see elections as a do-or-die affair. Where they are not standing for elections, they impose their acolytes, cronies, and stooges upon the electorate, and go to great lengths to ensure their victory. A case in point is former president Olusegun Obasanjo's public admission of imposing the late President Umaru Yar'Adua and Goodluck Jonathan on the people in 2007. The norm is for governors and local government chairmen to anoint their successors and use state resources and apparatus to ensure their victory with the collaboration of INEC commissioners, officials, and the police.

Nigeria has had no credible population census since independence, and there is no political willingness of the government to conduct a transparent and credible population census. The system is always rigged with inflated figures to favor the North. There must be something fishy about the census figures in Nigeria, because there is no attempt on the part of the government to get accurate figures, which is very vital for national planning and development.

The INEC lacks independence and autonomy, as it is always in the pocket of the government in power. How can the INEC conduct voters' registration exercises and elections where the voter has no identification card to confirm his or her age eligibility? Fictitious names and names of the deceased are used to register and cast votes, making room for underaged voting and rigging. The idea to introduce electronic voting was shut down by politicians who were used to rigging. In past elections, paper-based balloting posed problems for various successive electoral commissions, as politicians and thugs indulged in snatching the ballot boxes and altering the election results (Omolaye, Daniel, & Orifa, 2015).

Various electoral commissions were plagued by the diversion of election materials by officials, equipment malfunctions, and inept or untrained staff. Voter orientation and education was shallow at best, or nonexistent. The management of the election process in the country is weakened by the INEC's inability to effectively regulate the campaign procedures of the various political parties. Not even the social welfare and security of the people are addressed during the electioneering campaigns (Moveh, 2015).

Ibrahim (as cited in Osinakachukwu & Jawan, 2011) outlined different dimensions of how elections are rigged in Nigeria, and they include the following:

- Illegal printing of voters' cards
- Compilation of fictitious names on voters' lists
- Illegal compilation of separate voters' lists
- Harassment of candidates, agents, and voters
- Change of list of electoral officials
- Illegal thumbprinting of ballot papers
- Underaged voting
- Illegal possession of ballot boxes
- Stuffing of ballot boxes
- Falsification of election results
- Deliberate refusal to supply election materials to certain areas
- Box switching and inflation of figures
- Illegal printing of forms used for collection and declaration of election results
- Unauthorized announcement of election results

- Announcing results in places where no elections were held

Unfortunately, legitimate voters stay at home to avoid confrontations with dirty politicians, hired thugs, and security and other law enforcement officers who are bribed to affect illegal arrests, and detention of their opponents and "uncompromising" voters. The spectacle is scary, even though it appears that everyone has resigned to this fate.

Aside from the issues raised above, there are other challenges facing the INEC and the electoral systems, and they include delay in electoral justice, godfatherism, conflicting election tribunal decisions, pervasive grand corruption, nonprosecution of election-related offenses, and electoral disenfranchisement. There are many delays in resolving electoral disputes, and it may take several months or years to resolve them, as is evidenced in the 2003 gubernatorial elections in Anambra State between Dr. Chris Ngige and Mr. Peter Obi. It took almost two years before Mr. Obi could reclaim his mandate. Godfatherism has eaten deep into the political consciousness of the Nigerian polity. Cronies and allies are handpicked to run and win elections irrespective of their experience, brain power, and willingness to serve the constituents.

Mismanagement of resources and absolute corruption pervade the entire nation. Election officials are compromised, bribed, and used as tools for rigging elections by politicians. The legal system in Nigeria is so conflicted that a lower court will not honor the judgment of the upper court. As Odusote (2014) noted, conflicting decisions of courts in electoral matters are sore points, as orders and counterorders have become embarrassing to the judiciary. The lack of financial autonomy for the INEC has helped to complicate matters, as the body relies on the federal government for subvention. The state INECs also rely on state governors for financial assistance, coupled with the fact that chairmen and other members of the electoral bodies are appointed by the president and governors respectively (Odusote, 2014). This makes the INEC a ready tool of manipulation by the governments.

RECOMMENDATIONS

The use of technology in improving Nigerian elections cannot be relegated to the background. Social media clearly provides an excellent means for the citizens to contribute to both election monitoring, and the education of the citizens, if deployed appropriately—especially for monitoring and educating the masses. Prior to elections, the INEC could use social media to educate the citizens and mount positive campaigns for voter registration and participation. During the elections, social media can be used to identify and understand emerging events, and to analyze social media to identify multimedia-citizen-generated information about events (such as the Revoda mobile app). Automated Twitter analyses can also be deployed to identify citizen reports about electoral misconduct (Bartlett et al., 2015).

Election rigging could be curbed if the INEC could implement full electronic voting (e-voting). The body should exhibit a high level of preparedness and ensure the equipment and electoral devices are reliable and durable, and that competent staff is put in place to conduct the elections. Smartphones can empower the citizens to have access to valuable election information at any time, at any place. It is necessary that the INEC is independent and maintains its autonomy. State INECs should be eliminated, as they have become ready tools for governors to hijack for election purposes. The INEC should instill motivation and professionalism in the staff. Most of the staff are poor and are easy targets for the politicians to use for election rigging. Finally, there has to be a comprehensive electoral reform to fix the current and broken electoral system.

CONCLUSION

Analyzing this chapter, it is clearly evident that elections in Nigeria are not free and fair. They lack transparency, credibility, and integrity. The citizens have lost faith in elections and have devised methods to cheat, rig, and win elections at all costs. Democratic values remain impaired, while the integrity of the elections continues to be questionable (Idike, 2014). Successive Nigerian electoral commissions have failed to deliver credible elections to the people, despite improved technology. The argument is that while improved use of technology in Nigerian elections has impacted the electoral process to a certain degree, it may have also produced the same results when it was lacking. However, there is no denying that the use of social media in the last decade has also influenced the conduct of elections during the same period, as was evidenced in the 2015 presidential elections. The common denominator is the people, not the technology.

Elections in the Nigerian context are a do-or-die affair due the benefits and prestige of the office. The Nigerian political elite, the officers of the electoral bodies, and the general electorates have the same attitude toward elections. When an election has been bought, fixed, or arranged, or an order comes from "above" to manipulate it, it will produce a different outcome despite the amount of technology used to protect it. For example, in 2007, Senator Ifeanyi Ararume won the PDP's primary election to contest the gubernatorial election in the general elections, but his party, under President Obasanjo, decided to award the governorship position to Ikedi Ohakim of the Progressive Peoples Alliance (PPA).

A major challenge of the INEC is corruption at all levels of the government. Social media and other modern technologies deployed in the electoral process can only have maximum impact in elections if Nigerians change their orientation and attitude toward elections and nation building. When elections are already decided before they are conducted, it does not bode well for the country. When the electoral officers at the helm of office are compromised, it trickles down. If elections are conducted along ethnic, tribal, or geopolitical lines, they tend to produce different results. Technology can only have limited impact.

If today's modern technological advancements had been utilized in the previous elections in Nigeria, could they have produced better results? The answer is relative, as no one can be sure. In order to answer this question, let's step back and take a cursory look of all the elections conducted since independence. They were all marked by massive rigging, violence, thuggery, and forgery. The INEC and its predecessor are part of the problem. Unless the INEC frees itself from the shackles of the governments in power, and calls for electoral reforms, Nigeria will continue to produce failed elections. This can be achieved by a comprehensive electoral reform. The problem of failed elections in Nigeria is Nigerians!

No one is even sure whether the Nigerian socio-economic standing would have improved if Chief M.K.O. Abiola had become president. The same system and government that produced him were also corrupt. Could he have done better, being a reputed businessman with no political experience? It is left for posterity to judge. Corruption is an attack vector of the Nigerian electoral system, and must be tackled head-on in order for the country to take its place in the comity of nations as a giant of Africa.

REFERENCES

Adebiyi, O. M. (2015). "Kudos or knocks": Assessing the performance of INEC in the 2015 general elections in Nigeria. Retrieved from http://www.inecnigeria.org/wp content/uploads/2015- /07/Conference-Paper-by-Oluwashina-Adebiyi.pdf

Aderemi, A. (2015). The voracity effect and electoral integrity: The challenges of managing elections in Nigeria. Conference Paper,. Retrieved from http://www.inec nigeria.org/wp-content/uploads/2015/07/Conference-Paper-Adewale-Aderemi.pdf

Akpojivi, U. (2012). Media freedom and media policy in new democracies: An analysis of the nexus between policy formation and normative concepts in Ghana and Nigeria (Doctoral dissertation, University of Leeds).

_____ (2013). Looking beyond elections: An examination of media freedom in the re-democratization of Nigeria. In Olurunnisola, A. A. & Douai, A., *New media Influence on Social and Political Change in Africa.* doi:10.4018/978-1-4666-4197-6.ch006

Alayinde, Z. O. (2016). An examination of institutional framework of administration of election in Nigeria. *Journal of Law, Policy and Globalization*, 45. Retrieved from http://iiste.org/Journals/index.php/JLPG/article/view/28480

Asuni, J. B., & Farris, J. (n.d.). Tracking Social Media: The social media tacking centre and the 2011 Nigerian elections. Retrieved from http://yaraduacentre.org/files/tracking.pdf

Awa, E. O. (1960). Federal Elections in Nigeria, 1959. *The Indian Journal of Political Science, 21*(2), 101-113. Retrieved from http://www.jstor.org/stable/41853826

Bamgbose, J. A. (2012). Electoral violence and Nigeria's 2011 general elections. *International Review of Social Sciences and Humanities.* 4(1), 205-19. Retrieved from http://irssh.com/yahoo_site_admin/assets/docs/22_IRSSH-329-V4N1.3211029 53.pdf

Bartlett, J., Krasodomski-Jones, A., Daniel, N., Fisher, A., & Jesperson, S. (2015). *Social Media Election Communication and Monitoring in Nigeria.* London: Demos.

Retrieved from http://www.demos.co.uk/ wp-content/uploads/2015/11/Social-Me dia-in-Nigerian-Election.pdf

BBC News. (2016, February 11). Nigeria country profile. *BBC News*. Retrieved from http://www.bbc.com/news/world-africa-13949550

Campbell, J. (2011). Technology, social media, and Nigeria's elections. Retrieved from http://blogs.cfr.org/campbell/2011/07/06/technology-social-media-and-nigerias-elections/

Central Intelligence Agency (CIA). (2016). The World factbook. Retrieved from https://www.cia.gov/library/publications/the-world-factbook/geos/ni.html

Council on Foreign Relations (CFR). (n.d.). Nigeria dancing on the brink. Retrieved from http://www.cfr.org/nigeria/nigeria-dancing-brink/p22833

David, N. A., Manu, Y. A., & Musa, A. (2014). Elections, electoral process and the challenges of democratization in Nigeria's Fourth Republic. Research on Humanities and Social Sciences, 4(17), Retrieved from www.iiste. org/Journals/index.php/RHSS/article/download/14863/15506

Dye, R. T. (2001) *Politics in America*. New Jersey, NJ: Prentice Hall, Upper Saddle Rivers Edutech402. (2012). Origin of radio and television in Nigeria. Retrieved from http://edutech402.blogspot.com/2012/12/origin-of-radio-and-television-in.html

Ehidiamen, J. (2015). Leveraging technology in the Nigerian elections. A Harvard Kennedy School Student Publication. Retrieved from https://apj.fas.harvard.edu/leveraging-technology-in-the-nigerian-elections/

Ekundayo, W. J. (2015). A critical evaluation of electoral management bodies in Nigeria and the perennial problem of electoral management since independence in 1960. *International Journal of Public Administration and Management Research*, 2(5), 49-54.

Faduju, L. (2015). 8 ways technology is influencing Nigeria's 2015 elections. Retrieved from http://techcabal.com/2015/03/26/8-ways-technology-is-influencing-nigerias-20 15-elections/

Ibrahim, J., & Garuba, D. (2010). A study of the independent national electoral commission in Nigeria. Retrieved from www.codesria.org/IMG/pdf/Jibrim_Nigeria-2.pdf

Idike, A. N. (2014). Democracy and the electoral process in Nigeria: Problems and prospects of the e-voting option. *Asian Journal of Humanities and Social Sciences*, 2(2). Retrieved from http://ajhss.org/pdfs/Vol2Issue2/15.pdf

Institute of Security Studies. (n.d.). Nigeria–History and Politics. Retrieved from https://www.issafrica.org/Af/profiles/Nigeria/Politics.html

International Institute for Democracy and Electoral Assistance (IDEA). (2015). About the ICTs in elections database. Retrieved from http://www.idea.int/elections/ict/about-the-database.cfm

International Republican Institute (IRI). (2016). Strengthening Electoral Processes Retrieved from http://www.iri.org/program/strengthening-electoral-processes

Joseph, R. (2010a, October). *Elections and Democracy in Africa: Restoring Nigerian Leadership*. A lecture delivered at the Yar' Adua Center, Abuja, Nigeria. Retrieved from http://nigeria.usembassy.gov/pr_10082010.html

Joseph, R. (2010b). Nigeria's 2011 elections: Impending catastrophe or transformative moment? Retrieved from http://www.cfr.org/nigeria/nigeria-dancing-brink/p22833

Legborsi, N. A. (2011) Election Process and Mandate protection in Nigeria: The peoples power option. A paper presented at the Niger Delta Relief Foundation workshop held in Saakpenwa-Tai, Ogoni on Thursday 17th march, 2011.

Mason, B. (2007, August 9). Britain rigged election before Nigeria independence. A BBC Documentary. Retrieved from https://www.wsws.org/en/articles/2007/08/nige-a09.html

McCormack, C. B. (2016). Democracy rebooted: The future of technology in elections. Retrieved from http://publications.atlanticcouncil.org/election-tech/index.php

Metz, H. C. (1992). *Nigeria: A Country of Study.* (5th ed.). Washington, DC: Library of Congress.

Moveh, D. O. (2015). INEC and the administration of elections in Nigeria's Fourth Republic: The 2015 general elections in perspective. A paper prepared for presentation at the National Conference on the theme: The 2015 General Elections in Nigeria: The Real Issues. Organized by The Electoral Institute, July 2015. Retrieved from http://www.inecnigeria.org/wp-content/uploads/2015/07/Con-ference-Paper-by-Dr.-D.O-.MOVEH-.pdf

National Democratic Institute (NDI). (n.d.). Democracy and technology. Retrieved from https://www.ndi.org/democracy-and-technology Nigeriamuse.com. (2006).

Federal elections Nigeria results. Retrieved from http://www.nigerianmuse.com/nigeria watch/?u=federal_elections_nigeria_results.htm

Nigeriamuse.com. (2010). Past INEC chairmen of Nigeria. Retrieved from http://www.nigerianmuse.com/20100609221510zg/nm-projects/electoral-reform-project/past-inec-chairmen-of-nigeria/

Nwangwu, C. (2015). Biometric voting technology and the 2015 general elections in Nigeria. Retrieved from http://www.inecnigeria.org/wp-content/uploads/ 015/07/Conference-Paper-by-Chikodiri-Nwangwu.pdf

Nwokeafor, C. U. (2013). *The Dreams of the Founding Fathers.* USA, Instant Publisher.com.

_____ (2013). Media power in elections: Evidence of the role of agenda-setting theory in political communication in Nigeria evolving democracy. Conference paper presented at the International Conference in ICT for Africa in Harare, Zimbabwe, February 20-23, 2013.

Obado-Joel, J. (2014). Economic growth in failing states of sub-saharan Africa. Retrieved from https://www.researchgate.net/publication/262449711_Jennifer_Obado-Joel_E conomic_Growth_in_Failing_States_of_Sub-Saharan_Africa

Odusote, A. (2014). Nigerian democracy and the electoral process since amalgamation: Lessons from a turbulent past. IOSR Journal Of Humanities And Social Science, 19(10), 25-37. Retrieved from http://iosrjournals.org/iosr-jhss/papers/Vol19-issue 10/Version-6/E0191062537.pdf

Ofeimun, O. (2012, November 2). Awolowo and the forgotten documents Part 2. *Vanguard.* Retrieved from http://www.vanguardngr.com/2012/11/awolowo-and-the-forgotten-documents-of-the-civil-war-by-odia-ofeimun-2/

Omeruo, K. (2010). Social Media effect and the 2011 elections in Nigeria. Retrieved from http://www.techtrendsng.com/social-media-effect-and-the-2011-elections-in-ni geria/

Omolaye, O. P., Daniel, P., & Orifa, A. O. (2015). Systemic evaluation of semi-electronic voting system adopted in Nigeria 2015 general elections. *American Journal of Information Systems,3*(1), 15-21. doi: 10.12691/ajis-3-1-2

Osinakachukwu, N. P., & Jawan, J. A. (2011). The electoral process and democratic consolidation in Nigeria. *Journal of Politics and Law,* 4(2), 128-136, Doi:10.5539/jpl.v4n2p128

Orwenjo, D.A., Oketch, O., & Tunde, A. H. (2016). *Political Discourse in Emergent, Fragile, and Failed Democracies.* Pershey, PA: IGI Global.

Oyeweso, S., & Amusa, S. (2015). Institutional constraints on effective performance of INEC in the 2015 general elections. Retrieved from http://www.inecnigeria.org/wp-content/uploads/2015/07/Conference-Paper-by-Siyan-Oyeweso.pdf

The Columbia Electronic Encyclopedia. (2012). "Nigeria." Retrieved from http://www.infoplease.com/encyclopedia/world/nigeria-history.html

Thurston, A. (2015). Background to Nigeria's 2015 elections. Retrieved from https://csis-prod.s3.amazonaws.com/s3fs-public/legacy_files/files/publication/150126_Thurston_NigeriaElections_Web.pd

United Nations Department of Economic and Social Affairs (UN DESA). (2015). World population prospects: The 2015 revision, key findings and advance tables. Retrieved from https://esa.un.org/unpd/wpp/publications/files/key_findings_wpp_2015.pdf

Vanguard News. (2010, August 21). Past electoral umpires and their pre-election disposition. Retrieved from http://www.vanguardngr.com/2010/08/past-electoral-umpires-and-their-pre-election-disposition/

World Bank. (2016). Population 2014. Retrieved from http://databank.worldbank.org/data/download/POP.pd

CHAPTER 10
The History of Election and the Integration of Technology in the Electoral Process: A Review of Uganda's 2016 Election Outcome

Cosmas Uchenna Nwokeafor
Bowie State University

INTRODUCTION

The presidential and parliamentary general election, in which an estimated 10.3 million Ugandan citizens cast their votes at more than 28,000 polling stations across the country, was held on February 18, 2016. According to the Ugandan Electoral Commission, the election recorded a voter turnout estimated at about 63.5 percent, which was a significant increase from the 57.1 percent turnout in the 2011 general elections. The 2016 election was considered peaceful, and was one of the most competitive in Ugandan history. Incumbent President Yoweri Museveni won with 60.75 percent, defeating a long list of seven other contenders that included the leading opposition candidate Dr. Kizza Besigye, who finished in second with 35.37 percent (Nackerdien, 2016). Although Uganda avoided electoral violence, which was a major concern, as well as the large-scale malpractice and corrupt engagements that have been synonymous with previous polls, some domestic and international election observers reported a number of procedural and political challenges. Despite all the reported shortcomings, the electoral commission also experienced some positive developments, which includes the successful deployment of new and important election technologies and a 1.3 million increase in the total number of registered voters relative to the 2011 elections. The electoral commission strongly promised to build upon the peaceful outcome of the 2016 general election and to use it as a platform in planning and preparation for upcoming by-elections in the near future (Nackerdien, 2016).

A BRIEF HISTORY OF UGANDA

The history of Uganda began about 500 B.C., when Bantu-speaking peoples migrated to the area now called Uganda. By the 14th century, what today is Uganda was dominated by three kingdoms: Buganda (meaning "state of the Gandas"), Bunyoro, and Ankole. Uganda was first explored by Europeans, as well as Arab traders, in 1844. The 1890 Anglo-German agreement declaration made Uganda a part of British influence in Africa, and the Imperial British East Africa Company was chartered to develop the area (Appiah & Henry, 2010). In 1894, due to financial challenges that made it difficult for the company to prosper, a British protectorate was proclaimed, which resulted in the permanent settlement of some of these Europeans in Uganda. This attracted many Indians, who became important players in Ugandan trade and commerce.

On October 9, 1962, Uganda became an independent nation. Sir Edward Mutesa, the king of Buganda (Mutesa II), was elected the first president, and Milton Obote the first prime minister of the newly independent country (Appiah & Henry, 2010). With the help of a young army officer, Colonel Idi Amin, Prime Minister Obote seized control of the government from President Mutesa four years later. On Jan. 25, 1971, Colonel Amin deposed President Obote, who went into exile in Tanzania. Amin expelled Asian residents and launched a reign of terror against Ugandan opponents, torturing and killing tens of thousands of people. In 1976, he proclaimed himself "President for Life." In 1977, Amnesty International estimated that 300,000 may have been killed under his rule, including church leaders and recalcitrant cabinet ministers (Appiah & Henry 2010).

After Amin held military exercises on the Tanzanian border in 1978, angering Tanzania's president, Julius Nyerere, a combined force of Tanzanian troops and Ugandan exiles loyal to former President Obote invaded Uganda and chased Amin into exile in Saudi Arabia in 1979. After a series of interim administrations, President Obote led his People's Congress Party to victory in the 1980 elections, which opponents charged were rigged. On July 27, 1985, army troops staged a coup and took over the government, and Obote fled into exile. The military regime installed General Tito Okello as chief of state (Appiah & Henry, 2010).

The National Resistance Army (NRA), an anti-Obote group led by Yoweri Museveni, kept fighting after it had been excluded from the new regime. On January 29, 1986, Museveni seized Kampala and was declared president. Museveni has transformed the ruins of Idi Amin and Milton Obote's Uganda into an economic miracle, preaching a philosophy of self-sufficiency and anticorruption, which led to a massive influx of Western countries into Uganda to assist him in the transformation of the country.

Despite the intensive effort made in collaboration with the expatriates' contributions, Uganda still remains one of Africa's poorest countries. In 1996, a ban on political parties was lifted and the incumbent Museveni won 72 percent of the vote, reflecting his popularity due to the country's economic recovery (Hodd & Roche, 2011).

Uganda has waged an enormously successful campaign against AIDS, dramatically reducing the rate of new infections through an intensive public health and education campaign. Museveni won re-election in March 2001 with 70 percent of the vote, following a nasty and spirited campaign. Close ties with Rwanda (many Rwandan Tutsi exiles helped Museveni come to power) led to the cooperation of Uganda and Rwanda in the ousting of Zaire's Mobutu Sese Seko in 1997; and a year later, in efforts to unseat his successor, Laurent Kabila, whom both countries originally supported but from whom they grew estranged. But in 1999, Uganda and Rwanda quarreled over strategy in the Democratic Republic of the Congo and began fighting each other. The two countries mended their differences in 2002. Uganda also signed a peace accord with the Congo in September of 2002, and finally withdrew its remaining troops from the country in May 2003 (Middleton, 2008).

In July 2005, parliament amended the constitution to eliminate term limits, thus allowing President Museveni another term in office. In August, a multiparty political system was reinstituted after a 19-year absence. In Feb. 2006, Museveni was re-elected with 59 percent of the vote (Middleton, 2008).

THE THREAT OF THE LORD'S RESISTANCE ARMY

Uganda's 18-year-long battle against the brutal Lord's Resistance Army (LRA), an extremist rebel group based in Sudan, showed signs of abating in Aug. 2006, when the rebels agreed to declare a truce (Shillington, 2005). Between 8,000 and 10,000 children have been abducted by the LRA to form the army of "prophet" Joseph Kony, whose aim was to take over Uganda and run it according to his vision of Christianity. The boys are turned into soldiers and the girls into sex slaves (Shillington, 2005). Up to 1.5 million people in northern Uganda have been displaced because of the fighting and the fear that their children will be abducted. Shillington (2005) recorded that Kony and three other LRA leaders have been indicted on charges of crimes against humanity by the International Criminal Court. The LRA and the government signed a permanent cease-fire in February 2008; however, Kony failed to show up to sign the landmark agreement several times in 2008, dashing hopes for formalized peace. The rebels, however, sought a cease-fire in January 2009, after the armies of Uganda, Southern Sudan, and Congo attacked their bases (Shillington, 2005).

Parliament introduced the Anti-Homosexuality Bill in November 2009, which resulted in a legislation implementing the death penalty on gay individuals. The proposed bill met fierce condemnation from the European Union and the United States. Parliament did not act on the bill, and it became increasingly unpopular following the January 2011 murder of Ugandan gay-rights activist David Kato. In May, the government shelved the bill (Shillington, 2005).

In July 2010, about 75 people watching the final game of the World Cup in a Kampala restaurant were killed in an explosion. The Somali militant Islamist group Al-Shabab claimed responsibility for the bombing, saying the attack was aimed at discouraging countries from supporting the transitional government in

Somalia. Al-Shabab has been battling Somalia's weak, Western-backed government for power for several years. Uganda contributes troops to an African Union force that has been propping up the government in Somalia (Shillington, 2005).

PRESIDENT MUSEVENI'S TERMS IN OFFICE

The incumbent President Museveni was elected to a fourth term in the February 2011 election, taking 68.4 percent of the vote. Opposition leader Kizza Besigye garnered 26 percent and alleged fraud in the election. In late April, protests over rising food and fuel prices and corruption broke out in Kampala. The government responded with disproportionate force, killing five people and wounding dozens. Besigye, who was a leading figure in organizing the protests, was arrested and shot (Middleton, 2008). He fled to Kenya upon release from jail for medical treatment. His return to Kenya coincided with Museveni's inauguration, and Besigye's supporters far outnumbered those for the president. The opposition led by Besigye launched the largest antigovernment protest ever had in Uganda, and in Oct. 2011, Uganda's foreign minister and two other members of the ruling party resigned to face corruption charges.

The recent discovery of large oil reserves has put further strain on a government famous for fraud. Following allegations that oil companies paid bribes to ministers, President Yoweri Museveni denied that his government engaged in fraud when handing out oil contracts. Meanwhile, parliament voted to suspend all pending oil deals until a national oil policy could be put in place (Middleton, 2008).

In May 2012, one of the Lord's Resistance Army's top military strategists and commander, Caesar Acellam, was captured by Ugandan soldiers near the Central African Republic's border with Congo. Although Acellam is not one of those indicted along with Joseph Kony for crimes against humanity, Middleton (2008) reported that the capture of Acellam provided valuable intelligence to the military, which in turn brought Kony one step closer to judgment before the International Criminal Court. Lawyer Amama Mbabazi served as prime minster from May 2011 until Sept. 2014, when he was dropped from the Cabinet and was succeeded on September 18, 2014 by a physician, Dr. Ruhakana Rugunda, who has served in a variety of cabinet posts in Uganda since 1986.

POPULATION AND GEOGRAPHICAL LOCATION OF UGANDA

Uganda, with its capital and largest city Kampala with a population of about 1.659 million, is twice the size of Pennsylvania. It is located in East Africa with a boundary on the west by Congo, on the north by Sudan, on the east by Kenya, and on the south by Tanzania and Rwanda. The country, which lies across the equator, is divided into three main areas—swampy lowlands, a fertile plateau with wooded hills, and a desert region. Lake Victoria forms part of the southern border with a total land area of 91,135 square miles—about 236,040 square kilometers. With a growth rate of about 3.24 percent, a birth rate of about 44.17

per 1000, infant mortality rate of 60.82 per 1000, and a life expectancy of 54 years, Uganda's population, according to a 2014 census figure, is estimated at 35.9 million (Bakama, N. & Bakama, B., 2011).

BIOMETRIC TECHNOLOGY AND THE 2016 GENERAL ELECTIONS IN UGANDA

The urgent and growing pressure to embrace and integrate new technology in elections in continental Africa, most importantly in Uganda, after protracted years of wasteful military rule has resulted in the creation of a new modality in conducting elections. The use of this new modality, such as the biometric card reader, makes finding a suitable solution challenging for every citizen in the country, including lawmakers and election officials in a country known for its election fraud and malpractices. In some instances, welcoming new technology as a gateway to the February 2016 general elections in Uganda was among the visions of President Museveni to improve election efficiency, effective electoral communication processes, streamline program delivery, integrate various electoral systems, lower costs of operating and conducting elections, and minimizing manpower requirements (Yard, 2016). In other circumstances, the plan to integrate biometric technology for the purpose of modernization and automation of election processes is spurred by a sense of urgency to overcome the longevity of the crude and corrupt election practices of the past that continue to create insurmountable problems in Uganda.

Integration, use of Smartphones, and the power of social media have empowered individuals, election staff, and government officials in Uganda to monitor the election processes from the voting booths to the collation arena, spread timely information, and send pictures and video in real time as the election exercise evolves. By integrating these forward-looking technology tools, the International Foundation for Electoral Systems has become a leader in the use of technology that enhances efficiency and transparency of election administration around the world. As of February 2016, this includes Uganda, as Kenya, Ghana, South Africa, and most recently Nigeria in 2015 had already utilized such technology to their advantage. The production and supply of technology-assisted paraphernalia that is currently improving election processes in Africa, most essentially in the just-concluded Ugandan 2016 general election as well as in Nigeria in 2015, are committed to empowering the citizens through innovative use of technology that maximizes impact through proper application and transparent results.

According to Yard (2016)—who serves as Kenya and Uganda chief of party and is a recognized international election administration and technology expert with over 25 years of experience—provided authoritative technical assistance on election technology and systems for voter and candidate registration. He saw the desired need for the integration of technology to the Ugandan election. Yard has also served in the interests of political finance tracking and reporting, procurement, logistics, fleet management, vote tabulation, and results dissemination in

Uganda, where he strongly advocated for the integration of biometric card readers and other technology-driven tools for effective and efficient outcome of voter results. He joined the IFES as a technical manager in Ghana in 1994. He has also consulted on projects throughout Africa, Eastern Europe, Central and South Asia, South America, and the Middle East. He has worked on voter registration, database and data-entry projects with Election Reform International Services, the United States Agency for International Development, and the United Nations Election Administration Division. Reviewing institutional development in his books *Direct Democracy: Progress and Pitfalls of Election Technology* and *Civil and Voter Registries: Lessons Learned from Global Experiences*, both published by the IFES, it is stated thus:

> Across the world, public and private institutions are vital for meeting the social, economic and political needs of citizens. Since 1987, the International Foundation for Electoral Systems (IFES) has implemented programs aimed at developing electoral and political institutions in order to provide credible and transparent elections. IFES has worked with election management bodies around the world to develop their capacity to conduct elections in a professional, efficient and independent fashion.

The Ugandan Electoral Commission (EC), prior to all the recognized political parties registered to participate in the February 18 general elections, announced that it will use the Biometric Voter Verification Kit (BVVK) during the voter verification process, and the Electronic Results Transmission and Dissemination System (ERTDS) to transmit presidential and parliamentary results in the scheduled elections (Wafula, 2016). The Electoral Commission saw the need to improve the management and conduct of the elections by using the BVVK, which authenticates and identifies voters using fingerprints to match the details in the systems.

The use of new technology in elections in Uganda guided the Electoral Commission to ensure that only registered persons vote during the elections, and that such persons (voters) do not vote more than once for the same election (Wafula, 2016). According to the Electoral Commission (EC), the integration of this technology "will also assist the voter to locate the polling station within their district."

In order to familiarize the electorate and sensitize them with the new technology and the process of its usage, the commission held a demonstration of how the BVVS will work for party leaders, presidential candidates, and the electorates in Uganda. A public demonstration of the technology was held in the country on January 30 in all the districts—a grassroots effort to sensitize the entire nation on the innovative election voting platform. These awareness campaigns tailored toward a diverse sensitization were among the government's efforts not only to modernize the election processes, but to improve the scheduled general elections in Uganda as well (Wafula, 2016).

Wafula (2016) opined that the national readiness to utilize the new technology includes (a) the acquisition of 32,334 machines to cater to more than the

28,000 polling stations in Uganda during the elections; (b) the training of field staff on the use of Biometric Voter Verification equipment, which has been going on at national and regional levels; and (c) the training of the presiding officers and one polling assistant by the end of January. There was also the urgent need by the Electoral Commission to procure Electronic Results Transmission and Dissemination System (ERTDS) to transmit presidential and parliamentary results to the candidates and the general public, after the results were tallied from the districts to the National Tallying Center at the Mandela National Stadium in Nambole (Wafula, 2016).

As is evident with change and the introduction of an innovation, people always show some resentment. The expression of concerns by the people as to how the new technology will work, and the mass media reports alleging plots to tamper with the operation of the Biometric Voter Verification Kit (BVVK) and the Electronic Results Transmission and Dissemination System (ERTDS) with a view of sabotaging the success of the Electoral process as scheduled, are only wishful thinking because the systems were secured (Wafula, 2016). Despite the resentments and challenges resulting from the integration of the technology-assisted modalities to conduct the election, the electoral commission went ahead and partnered with Smartmatic, the world's leading electronic voting technology company, to use the biometric voter authentication technology solution that validates the identity of voters prior to ballot casting. These technologies developed a central system in which to store and manage the biographic information of all registered voters (Wafula, 2016).

The system Wafula (2016) reported is synchronized with Uganda's National ID database. It performs control and integrity checks, and converts all the data into a format that can be used to process votes and administration of the electoral processes with accuracy and speed on the day of the election. Elections in most African countries, including Uganda, have always come with unique challenges that sometimes result in questionable transparent outcomes. As is usual with all elections where technology is infused into the election process, voter identity management is always very critical. The partnering with Smartmatic provides Ugandan election field operators with the technology, services, and knowledge necessary to guarantee a successful and transparent election. According to the Secretary of the Uganda Electoral Commission, this practice helps in validating the identity of each voter with the use of biometrics with accuracy and speed, which resulted in the practice of "one voter, one voice" (MacDonald, 2016). Smartmatic, founded in the USA in 2000, supplied and configured all hardware and software to run the biometric voter verification platform with some 30,500 biometric devices deployed across 30,000 polling stations. In addition, equipment warehousing, maintenance and dispatch, project management, and election training were provided to poll workers and election officials. With biometric verification technology becoming more and more widely used around the world, Uganda has now become one of many nations taking steps to combat one of the most pervasive forms of election fraud—voter impersonation—with a result of credible election outcomes (MacDonald, 2016).

THE IMPORTANCE OF THE 2016 UGANDA'S ELECTION

The February 2016 general election should be President Museveni's fifth presidential election since his National Resistance Movement (NRM) came to power in 1986. Some political scientists and pundits have argued that repeated elections can feed into a virtuous circle, consolidating democratic values and promoting crucial electoral reforms. But in Uganda, the reverse scenario seems to be at work. Successive elections have seen little to no significant electoral reform; instead, President Museveni has repeatedly deployed and perfected a varied set of strategies to ensure victory (MacDonald, 2016).

As Uganda's electoral process under President Museveni continued to thrive with the stipulations of the old modality, there was need for a change to allow for a systemic process that would accommodate more than a party system. The change resulted in a referendum for a reform, which led to a most significant electoral reform under the NRM. This reform came with a 2005 referendum that reintroduced multiparty politics after nearly two decades of a "no-party" system in Uganda. However, Rwakoojo (2016) noted that the simultaneous removal of presidential term limits dimmed opposition prospects from the beginning, and the necessary attempts made to secure additional electoral reforms in Uganda were not successful.

Uganda's National Resistance Movement (NRM), led by President Museveni, has been in control and has dominated the Ugandan political landscape since it was founded in 1986. However, after the 2005 referendum that reintroduced multiparty politics in Uganda, national elections have become more competitive. As a result of the referendum, Rwakoojo (2016) opined that the opposition party strengthened its grassroots organization and the NRM itself began to display signs of infighting and moderate fragmentation, including the defection of former NRM Secretary General Amama Mbabazi, who then chose to run for president in 2016 under a different party banner (Rwakoojo, 2016). President Museveni therefore viewed the 2016 election as an opportunity to reassert the NRM's political dominance and achieve a third consecutive presidential term, since parliament had removed term limits in 2005. This move by an incumbent president was considered to be a highly politicized scheme to retain his presidency; a fight he fought diligently and was politically sustained as he won the election convincingly.

The 2016 elections were also a chance for the opposition to re-establish electoral significance after a setback in 2011, when the primary opposition leader Kizza Besigye received only 26 percent after a much stronger 37 percent showing in 2006. Besigye's party, the Forum for Democratic Change, also suffered a weaker showing in 2011, while other opposition parties made only moderate parliamentary gains of between one and four seats. The 2015 defection of Mbabazi therefore raised hopes that the opposition might strengthen its grassroots influence and perhaps even form a more coherent, united front. However, internal mistrust, political scheming, propaganda tailored toward the opposition, and lingering rivalries ultimately prevented the various opposition movements from coalescing around a single presidential candidate (Rwakoojo, 2016).

Given Uganda's prior electoral challenges, many citizens within civil society and the opposition called for significant electoral reforms in the years leading to the 2016 election. These recommendations included disbanding the electoral commission and changing the nomination process for its commissioners, which, under the existing constitution, allows the incumbent, President Museveni, to nominate the commissioners for the parliament to approve (Rwakoojo, 2016). Many Uganda citizens and key political activists claim that the process whereby the president and parliament nominate and approve electoral commissioners is exclusive, lacks transparency, and increases the electoral commissioners' vulnerability to influence the election outcomes from the president and the NRM. However, despite a lengthy debate over such reforms in parliament, no action was taken prior to the 2016 election (Rwakooro, 2016).

POLITICAL CLIMATE AND SECURITY SITUATION IN UGANDA BEFORE AND DURING THE ELECTION

According to Rwakooro (2016) reports on the situation of things on the ground prior to, during, and after the elections indicated that the pre-election period in Uganda was not only tense, but unpredictable, with instances of periodic reports of incessant intimidation of opposition activists. Many opposition rallies were shut down and the leading opposition candidate, Dr. Kizza Besigye, was arrested multiple times. Under the pretext of being cautious and taking preventive measures to avoid instability and violence, Besigye was placed under house arrest during and after election day. On a legal level, the relatively weak regulatory framework for campaign finance enabled campaign spending on a scale never before witnessed in Uganda. Some accused President Museveni and the ruling NRM of improperly using state funds and resources for campaign activities (Rwakooro, 2016). Moreover, the Electoral Commission itself was the subject of criticism by some participants for its purported lack of independence from the NRM. However, although many civil society groups and the opposition criticized the political environment, the election period was relatively peaceful. It was reported by Rwakooro (2016) that on the day of the election, an estimated 150,000 police officers, soldiers, and other security forces were deployed throughout the country to ensure the safety and security of election staff, as well as the safety of the more than 10 million Ugandans that stood in line to vote. According to newspaper articles—mostly from the two major newspapers in Uganda, the *Daily Monitor* and *New Vision*—prior to the election, Ugandan police reportedly trained up to 1.5 million civilians, primarily male youth, to provide additional support for public order during the election. This move was criticized by some Uganda citizens and political pundits as an attempt to deploy additional pro-regime "officials" to intimidate voters (*Daily Monitor*, 2016). On the other end of the spectrum, Dr. Kizza Besigye's opposition, Forum for Democratic Change (FDC), formed youth groups called "Power 10" with the sole purpose of protecting the party's votes on election day. Despite these concerns and documented cases of intimidation by the security forces, and to a certain extent the opposition, Uganda largely avoided electoral violence before and during the poll (New Vision, 2016).

THE ROLE OF THE INTERNATIONAL FOUNDATION FOR ELECTORAL SYSTEMS (IFES) IN UGANDA'S 2016 ELECTION

The International Foundation for Electoral Systems (IFES) has worked diligently to strengthen electoral processes and credibility in Uganda since 2011, with funding from the U.S. Agency for International Development (Rushdi, N., 2016). For the 2016 elections, the IFES built upon their previous support to further strengthen electoral technologies, promote widespread voter participation in the process, and improve electoral integrity. Specifically, the IFES supported the EC to activate an interactive SMS platform to allow citizens to check and verify their polling station locations. According to Rushdi (2016), in his publication titled "Taking Stock of Uganda's 2016 General Elections," more than 1.1 million voters sent a message to the Electoral Commissioner's SMS platform and received an immediate automated response with location information for the requester's polling station.

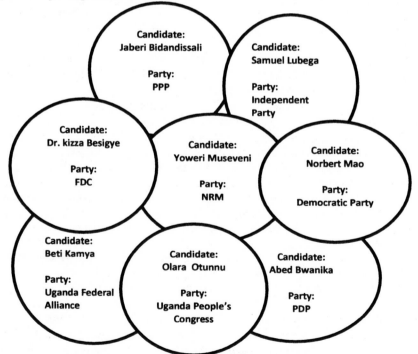

Figure 10.1: 2011 Uganda's Presidential Election Candidate and their Political Party

This system helped to increase turnout and reduce Election Day confusion, particularly given that all social media sites were blocked during the election. Upon request from the EC, the IFES developed a web application to expand the capabilities of the commission's web-based voter register, which allowed voters to check on their polling station locations and view the online national voter register by polling station (or download the register, if needed). Finally, recognizing the paramount importance of voter education, and given new technologies and the desire to increase turnout, the IFES assisted the Electoral Commission to develop voter-education materials and disseminate them through 34 radio stations, nine newspapers, widespread posters and leaflets, and online (Rusdi, 2016).

ASSESSMENT OF THE CONDUCT OF THE 2016 GENERAL ELECTIONS

Despite the tense political environment, more than 10 million Ugandan citizens waited patiently in line to cast their ballots for one of eight presidential candidates and representatives to serve within the 290-seat parliament. Procedurally, the EC's performance received mixed reviews. On the positive end, the EC successfully deployed all of its new election technologies, with only minor and sporadic challenges. After encountering numerous problems in other regional countries, most notably Kenya, the new biometric voter registration and verification system in Uganda performed well (Rusdi, 2016). Although there were delays in procurement and training, most polling station officials effectively utilized the system to verify voter registration; and in places where the system encountered problems, polling officials successfully utilized the back-up paper vote register. Moreover, the EC's SMS and web-based platforms for polling station identification were utilized extensively in a short period of time, providing the EC with a useful model to build upon for by-elections and future general elections.

At the polling stations themselves, counting was transparent, with the polling staff showing each ballot paper to the party agents during the counting process. In addition, voters waiting outside of the polling stations were allowed to enter polling stations to observe the counting of the votes. After the count, results sheets were signed by party agents and the party agents got copies of these results sheets (Rusdi, 2016).

Unfortunately, other elements of the polling process experienced challenges. Widespread delays in transporting election materials resulted in late openings in numerous polling stations in some cases, and stations did not open until late morning or even early afternoon. The EC responded by extending the voting hours from 4 p.m. to 7 p.m., and even allowed 32 polling stations to resume voting the following day. There were also sporadic, yet unverified, reports of prechecked ballots entering polling stations. During results transmission and aggregation, some key fraud mitigation and transparency measures were underutilized or not used at all, including inattention by many presiding officers to key pretransmission results forms that reconciled polling station ballot numbers, and the inconsistent distribution of printouts at the tally centers of results at the polling station level (New Vision, 2016).

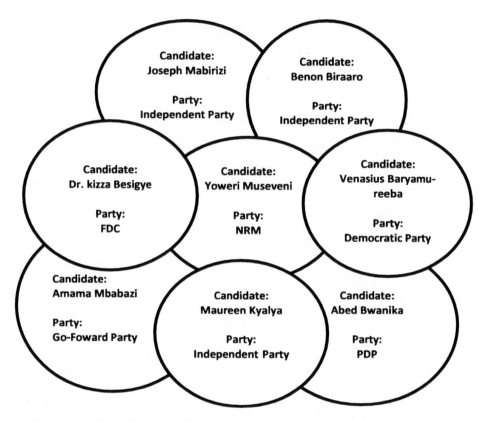

Figure 10.2: 2016 Uganda's Presidential Election Candidates and their Political Party

ELECTION OBSERVERS REPORT ABOUT THE CREDIBILITY OF UGANDA'S 2016 ELECTION

Many national and international organizations deployed missions to observe the elections in Uganda, including the European Union, the African Union, the East Africa Community, and the Citizens Election Observers Network-Uganda (CEON-U), among others. The domestic observer network CEON-U was perhaps the most critical of the 2016 elections, reporting that the "context in which Uganda holds its elections cannot allow for free, fair and credible elections" (New Vision, 2016). The EU mission also noted the widespread presence of intimidation, and it was particularly critical of the state's use of resources to create an unbalanced political playing field amid an environment that lacks campaign finance regulations. The continental and regional observation missions were less critical of the political environment, but still did note some procedural shortcomings. All observers praised the peaceful environment on Election Day itself and the relatively calm and orderly nature of the polling stations. However, Ugandan media announced that opposition presidential candidate Kizza Besigye, while under house arrest, rejected the outcome of the polls and called for an independent audit of the results by an international commission (Daily Monitor, 2016). Besigye's party, the FDC, immediately announced that it would gather evidence to legally challenge the outcome. However, the FDC did not successfully submit the challenge within the legal window for electoral appeals. Article 104(2) of Uganda's constitution provides candidates with the right to lodge a complaint in the Supreme Court within 10 days after the declaration of the election results. Although Besigye and his party—the most prominent opposition group—did not successfully lodge an appeal, former NRC Secretary General and opposition presidential candidate Amama Mbabazi formally submitted his own electoral challenge on March 1. Per the Presidential Elections Act from 2005, the Supreme Court then had no more than 30 days to issue a judgment on the petition. Although it is unlikely that the Supreme Court would overturn the results, in the event that the election is in fact annulled, the EC must hold a new election within 20 days of the date of the Supreme Court's decision. The EC's Chairman, Badru Kiggundu, has insisted that the election results were credible (*Daily Monitor*, 2016).

Table 10.1 2016 General Electoral Commission Information as recorded

Candidates	Party	Votes	%
Abed Bwanika	PDP	89,005	0.90
Amama Mbabzi	Independent	136,519	1.39
Baryamureeba Venansius	Independent	52,798	0.54
Benon Buta Biraaro	FPU	25,600	0.26
Kizza Besigye Kifefe	FDC	3,508,687	35.61
Mabirizi Joseph	Independent	24,498	0.25

Maureen Faith Kyalya Wa- luube	Independent	42,833	0.43
Yoweri Kaguta Museveni	NRM	5,971,872	60.62
Valid Votes		9,851,812	-
Invalid Votes		477,319	4.62
Total Votes Cast		10,329,131	67.61
Spoiled Votes		29,005	-

HISTORICAL OVERVIEW OF TECHNOLOGY IMPACT ON ELECTIONS

The 2016 presidential election in the United States of America has picked up considerable speed as presidential candidates are working diligently in making sure that all possible inroads are made to connect with the electorate through campaigns and town meetings. The primary voting and results are strategically going on from state to state. Over the past decade, political discussions have migrated from water coolers and dinner tables to Smartphones and social media. Here are just some of the ways technology has dramatically changed the race for the presidency in a short period of time in the United States of America, and many other developed nations of the world. These changes, brought about by the advent of the new technology, have created results through a more defined and structural manner such as:

(a) Social Influence — resulting in Twitter and Facebook transforming the way candidates interact with their constituencies. Ten years ago, campaigns were drastically different, as candidates interfaced with their constituencies and the electorate differently. In the early to late 1990s, there was hardly any social media and Facebook and Twitter were not there for the general public to use. The presidential candidates during this time were George Herbert Walker Bush, incumbent president, and his challenger, Bill Clinton. During that election, candidates didn't speak directly to the public via social channels, and everyday people didn't have as many outlets to share and debate their political views. Today, social media gives candidates a direct line of communication to the American people. That's a positive change. However, on the flipside, social media is an uncontrolled, democratized soap box where individuals can spread opinions that are not substantiated, which can change the public's view of a candidate overnight (Cutler, 2015).

(b) Smarter Campaigns — In a civilized nation like the United States, political parties and candidates running for elected offices always relied on polls to give them insight on where they stood with the public and what they should change about their campaigns. With the rise of big data and analytics, candidates running for an elected political office can now understand much more deeply what's working and what's not in their campaigns. With this information, campaigns become more effective and can be tailored to garner the votes, funds, or public opinion needed from a particular region or constituency (Cutler, 2015).

According to Cutler (2015), technology itself brings new issues to the debate floor that candidates must know about, speak about, and take a position on. Topics such as net neutrality and cybersecurity are important to constituents, and candidates need to be informed. In addition, candidates need to keep up-to-date with technology, otherwise they will be viewed as outdated and irrelevant. Candidates who don't use Twitter, for example, won't be taken seriously. The more in touch candidates are with technology, the more people they will reach. Understanding new technologies and trends is now a key part of connecting with voters and running a successful campaign (Cutler, 2015).

(c) Threat of Virality — In an election season in a developed society such as the United States, party candidates are carefully watched and mirrored under strong and sharp lenses, mostly by the mass media, who are always on their respective necks to dig out dirt from their past that could be used against them. Today, the threat of virality brought about as a result of social media is obvious. Social media runs in real time and with the variety of channels, from Twitter to YouTube, candidates' words are replayed, dissected, and played again. Once something hits the web, it stays there forever (Cutler, 2015). There is always a preconceived notion by politicians, mostly party candidates, that there is always someone with a Smartphone, camera, microphone, or other recording device capturing their actions to share with the world. While this constant monitoring of candidate activity has brought more transparency to elections, Cutler (2015) opined that it has also brought more sensationalism and often reduced political coverage to paparazzi-style reporting. According to Cutler (2015), nothing is off limits anymore as political candidates, their friends, and family members are under the microscope as well, and most of the time targeted on social media where their words, utterances, actions, and sometimes body language are misrepresented and echoed on live media coverage. Examples could be drawn from the CNN political unit publication of 10 debate moments that mattered (2012) from the days of the first television coverage of presidential debate between Kennedy and Nixon in 1960, until most recently in the 2016 presidential election debates among candidates in the United States.

1960 — Kennedy vs. Nixon: First TV debate
Just having Kennedy on the same stage as an experienced vice president made a difference for JFK, because he could hold his own with Nixon. But then, of course, when it was listened to on the radio, it made it seem like it was pretty equal, and even some people giving an edge to Nixon. But he looked so terrible. His makeup was bad. He wasn't feeling well. He looked sallow, he looked scornful. And people just reacted to that image of a vigorous, young Kennedy, and an almost sick-looking Nixon. And from then on, somehow JFK became a figure (CNN political unit publication).

1976 — Carter vs. Ford: No Soviet domination of Eastern Europe?
Ford had done well in the first debate, but in the second debate he was asked a question about Soviet domination of Eastern Europe. And he answered it in-

comprehensibly. There was already a perception, a vulnerability, that he wasn't intelligent. And then this thing just got parodied, just got talked about, and became a huge event. When ordinary people watched that debate, they didn't feel the Ford had screwed up. But when it was pointed out that he didn't understand what was happening in the Cold War in Eastern Europe, then suddenly they had shifted their minds, and he seemed much worse than it had seemed at that moment (CNN political unit publication).

1980 — Reagan vs. Carter: "There you go again."

In 1980, Carter was primed to go after Reagan about his record, especially on Medicare. He was going on the offensive: 'You did this! You voted this way! You said that!' And Reagan, just with humor and subtlety, said, 'There you go again.' And it somehow relaxed Reagan and it took the offensive away from Carter. It was a brilliant answer to a really serious critique of Reagan's past that might have been troubling for him (CNN political unit publication).

1980 — Reagan vs. Carter: "Are you better off now than you were four years ago?"

There was no more brilliant closing than Reagan's 'Are you better off now than you were four years ago?' What it did was to make people think, 'Yes. That's what's happened to me. My economic life, my family life, my working life, has been hurt by the economy over these last four years.' And once they realized that, it almost gave a poster to the entire campaign. It wasn't just a great moment in the debate, it became a theme encapsulated in just a few sentences. And in the end saying, 'if you are better off, then you vote for Mr. Carter. If you're not, you do have another choice. Me.' And at the same time, Carter gave a very weak closing statement (CNN political unit publication).

1984 — Mondale vs. Reagan: "I will not exploit ... my opponent's youth and inexperience."

In the first debate between Reagan and Mondale, Reagan had appeared old. He was the oldest candidate in history at that time. He seemed confused by some of the questions, his answers had wandered, and the issue of age really became a large question among the press. So when he comes back in the second debate, and they ask him, 'Do you think age is a problem?' He had that answer prepared, and boy did he nail it. It was subtle, it was humorous, and Mondale knew, he said right then, that he had not only lost the debate, but probably the election (CNN political unit publication).

1988 — Dukakis vs. George H.W. Bush: "If your wife, Kitty Dukakis, were raped and murdered?"

The question asked to Michael Dukakis in 1988 was a difficult one. I mean, 'What would you do, given your feelings about the death penalty, if your wife, Kitty Dukakis, were raped and murdered?' And what you would've expected might have been a home run, where Dukakis would've said, 'I would've wanted to kill that person who murdered my wife. But we have a country of laws and that would be wrong.' But instead, he answered in a policy-wonkish way about the death penalty that underscored a vulnerability that he already seemed to be without emotion and without passion (CNN political unit publication).

1988 — Bentsen vs. Quayle: "You're no Jack Kennedy."

During the campaign, Quayle had already been saying many times that he had as much experience as Jack Kennedy did, so Bentsen was primed for that and when he mentioned it again in the debate, I'm sure Bentsen was saying 'Yay! Here comes my line!' And again, Quayle handled it OK and said it probably wasn't called for but it was such a zinger of a line that people loved it and told one another about it and it became the line of that debate (CNN political unit publication).

1992 — George H.W. Bush looks at his watch

It looked like he was bored, that he didn't care about the debate and that underscored the feeling that he wasn't connected to the problems of the people and the country. He later said when he was looking he was looking at his watch he was thinking, 'I hate these debates, I'm so glad it's almost over.' In that debate Clinton showed his empathy—he was wandering around the stage. He talked to the people, almost wrapped their arms around them. The debate format in that year was perfect for Clinton because they could wander away from the microphones. When Bush is seen stiffly to be looking at his watch and seemed not engaged, and not connected, it underscored Clinton's enormous capacity to emotionally connect (CNN political unit publication).

1992 -- Stockdale vs. Gore vs. Quayle: "Who am I? Why am I here?"

When [Ross] Perot had chosen [Adm. James] Stockdale as his [running mate], Stockdale appeared to in that debate to be stunned; he almost didn't seem to belong there. He looked like an observer of the other two candidates and that was underlined when he said, 'who am I, what am I doing here?' What it underscored was a problem of judgment on Perot's part — how could he have chosen somebody who himself was wondering, 'Why am I here?' It made no sense to the audience and it hurt Perot's credibility as a presidential candidate (CNN political unit publication).

2001 — Al Gore vs. George W. Bush: Constant sighing and intimidating look

Focus groups right after Al Gore and George W. Bush debated seemed to give a slight edge to Gore because he was more articulate, he had better answers, but once the television cameras caught that sighing, that constant look on his face where he seemed annoyed by the whole idea of having to be there with Bush, it seemed to underscore, as somebody said, as a teacher's pet who knew all the answers but was annoying and irritating. And they kept playing it over and over again and it became parodies on the comedy shows and late night TV. Then people began to project onto Gore a personality trait of just annoyance and irritation of people in general and it became devastating for him to live that down (CNN political unit publication).

2016 — Senator Marco Rubio pausing to take a drink of water

Sen. Marco Rubio in the ongoing 2016 Republican Party Presidential debate had his own meme created when he took a pause in a televised speech to take a drink of water. Think about that — he paused to drink water, and the Internet went crazy. Every little word candidates speak or action they take has the potential to go viral (CNN political unit publication).

CONCLUSION

Literature has shown that the integration of technology in the just-concluded presidential and parliamentary elections in Uganda was predicted to contribute tremendously in easing some of the frustrations and corruption practices associated with elections in Uganda in the previous years. The incumbent administration of President Museveni did everything politically correct in making sure that an adequate security system was put in place to protect the Electoral Commissioners, election staff, politicians, and the entire nation both during and after the election. Voting started off to a rocky start, with severe delays at many polling stations around the capital city of Kampala. Facebook, WhatsApp, and Twitter were blocked, while news had it that about 150,000 security officers, including military troops, were trained and deployed across the country. He provided Ugandans with the adequate resources to allow technology-driven strategy to assist in the handling of the elections. However, the 2016 presidential and parliamentary elections in Uganda were seen as the most competitive yet for the country's long-time incumbent Yoweri Museveni. They nonetheless look set to extend his 30-year reign, while his leading opposition rival, Dr. Kizza Besigye, has been arrested for the third time in a week (*Daily Monitor,* 2016).

A considerable number of citizens and mostly foreign observers saw the urgent need in the Ugandan administration under the leadership of President Museveni to have consulted and utilized the technology in the process of conducting the election, but looking at the history of past elections in Uganda, the integration of technology in elections fell short in meeting the people's expectations because the old, corrupt practices were very evident during the 2016 election.

The opposition party, as well as some of the foreign observers, such as the Commonwealth of Nations led by the former President of Nigeria, Chief Olusegun Obasanjo, with a 13-member group of monitors, saw the election outcome as a sham.

Obasanjo's group was concerned over the increased prevalence of money in politics, the misuse of state resources that led to significant advantages for the incumbent, and a freewill that resulted in the accusation of the Electoral Commission's inability to manage the election processes effectively and impartially. They also reported the inexcusable delays of the supply of materials to polling stations, particularly in Kampala and its environs, and other deficiencies in the process, which seriously detracted from the fairness and credibility of the result of the elections (Ugandan Newspaper Online-www.onlinenewspaper.com/Ugandan.htm).

The European Union observers reported a mixed reaction to the election and stated that voting was conducted in a calm and peaceful environment in the vast majority of the country, but noted that the Electoral Commission lacked "transparency and independence." The EU's observers added that, "The National Resistance Movement's (NRM's) domination of the political landscape distorted the fairness of the campaign, and state actors were instrumental in creating an intimidating atmosphere." A Kenyan representative who also monitored the election, Senator Peter Anyang' Nyong'o, claimed that the election had been "badly rigged" and that "evidence of stuffed ballot boxes is rampant." The state shut down social media to curtail information on the rigging, and delays in opening up polling stations denied millions of voters' access to ballot boxes.

On Friday February 19, the United States Secretary of State John Kerry called President Museveni, and according to a statement from the U.S. State Department, "urged President Museveni to rein in the police and security forces, noting that such action calls into question Uganda's commitment to a transparent and credible election process free from intimidation" (www. onlinenewspaper.com/Uganda.htm).

REFERENCES

Appiah, A & Gates, H. L. (ed), (2010). *Encyclopedia of Africa*. Oxford University Press.

Bakama, N. & Bakama B. (2011) *A Contemporary Geography of Uganda.* African Books Collective.

Collard, M. (2016). How Uganda's government steered another state controlled election. Feb, 19.

Cutler, Z. (2015). Four ways technology has impacted presidential elections in the United States of America. Entrepreneur Coaching. July.

CNN Political Unit Publication (2012). 10 debate moments that mattered. October 3.

Daily Monitor (2016). Uganda News, Politics, Business, Travel ...*www.monitor.co.ug/*

Hodd, M. and Roche, A. (2011). *Uganda Handbook.* Bath: Footprint.

MacDonald, A. (2016). Uganda Deploys Biometric Technology to Improve General Election Transparency

Middleton, J. (ed). (2008). *New Encyclopedia of Africa*. Detroit: Thompson-Gale.

New Vision (2016). Uganda news www.newvision.co.ug/

Rushdi, N. (2016). Taking Stock of Uganda's 2016 general elections

Rwakoojo, S. (2016) http://www.ec.or.ug/?q=content/2016-general-elections-statistics#sthash.TjaNFKUV.dpuf

Shillington, Kevin (ed). (2005). *Encyclopedia of African history.* CRC Press. Selected books.

Ugandan newspapers: Newspapers from Uganda. www.onlinenewspapers. com/Uganda. htm

Wafula, B. (2016). Uganda to introduce technology in February Elections. Citizen Digital. January.

Yard, M. (2016). Modernizing Election Processes: The Ugandan Experience. January Encyclopedias

CHAPTER 11
Integration of Electronic Voting System in an Electronic Process: Types, Procedures, Benefits and Challenges

Ayoade Olusola Bamidele
Emmanuel Alayande College of Education, Oyo

INTRODUCTION

Electronic voting is a type of vote done through electronic systems. Electronic voting, also known as e-voting, features technology for optical scanning vote systems, punch cards, and voting kiosks, which includes transmission of ballots and votes via telephone, Internet, or private computer networks (Bravenewballot, 2008). These voting kiosks include a self-contained, direct-recording electronic voting system, also known as DRE. There are two types of electronic voting, which can be identified as: 1) e-voting, which is supervised physically by independent electoral authorities or governmental representatives, such as the machines at polling stations; and 2) remote electronic voting, which is where the vote is not physically supervised by government or independent representatives, such as voting from a personal computer, mobile phone, or television via the Internet, also known as i-voting (Bravenewballot, 2008).

Nowadays, electronic voting has become more popular around the world. Some of the countries that use electronic and voting online are: United States, Brazil, Australia, Canada, Belgium, Germany, Romania, France, Venezuela, Philippines, the European Union, Switzerland, Italy, Norway, Romania, and the United Kingdom (Bravenewballot, 2008). Electronic voting is very accessible for individuals with disabilities, as they have the ability to use joysticks, earphones, sip-and-puff technology, foot pedals, etc. These machines have touch screens that display the information in several languages, and voting choices in audio for visually impaired voters. These features make voting easier and more comfortable for people with disabilities (Bravenewballot, 2008).

The e-voting system has some inherent advantages over paper-based voting. Besides being robust, secure, and safe, it decreases voting errors substantially (Ahmad, Bt Abdullah, & Bt Arshad, 2015). Abu-Shanab, Knight, and Refai (2010) conformed that using e-voting improves the convenience, efficiency, and effectiveness of the election process; reduces the cost of organizing elections, increases participation, and provides alternative options as it improves the integrity of election process in general. Limitations associated with accuracy, security, and verifiability inherent in the conventional paper-based methods make the e-voting system an appealing option (Ahmad, Bt Abdullah, & Bt Arshad, 2015). This is owing to the manual operation of the former, concerning casting and counting votes.

According to Kozakova (2011) modern democracy would maximally benefit from effective implementation of electronic voting technology. If compared to traditional methods, the e-voting system increases the chance of counting each vote and broadens the number of potential voters (Ahmad, Bt Abdullah, & Bt Arshad, 2015).

Today's e-voting allows voters to use modern technologies such as optical scanning machines, paper ballots, and direct-recording electronic (DRE) voting machines to cast ballots. Electronic voter registration databases are used to manage the voter rolls; therefore, much of the time involved in registering new voters or making address adjustments is taken up by data entry from handwritten paper records. Registration data can be transferred electronically from the motor vehicle agency to the election offices. These activities can be accomplished via real-time transfer or by using a form of batch input (i.e., accumulating registration data over a period of time into a "suspense queue" and updating the registration files in batches). By receiving registrations electronically, election officials can save valuable time in registering citizens to vote while reducing potential errors encountered during the manual transfer of data. In some of these systems, the voter can make all of the changes to their registration file. While some systems still require the information in paper form, some allow the voter to input the information electronically (*The Quick Start Management Guide on Technology in Election*, 2010).

E-voting enables tracking of absentee ballots electronically. The ballot is scanned at various points during its life cycle, which creates a record of where the ballot has been. Jurisdictions with high rates of absentee voting use ballot-sorting machines to sort incoming and outgoing ballots into precincts. Some sorting machines can be linked to the voter registration database to facilitate matching voters' signatures; however, the signature match is not 100 percent accurate. Most systems are set to flag suspect signatures for further manual evaluation (*The Quick Start Management Guide on Technology in Election*, 2010). Radio-frequency identification (RFID) chips can be used to track equipment or supplies. In jurisdictions using this technology, a chip is placed in every supply box and the boxes pass through a special tunnel to record their deployment and return. The technology makes it easier to see which polling places/precincts have not yet returned their materials at the end of election day (*The Quick Start Management Guide on Technology in Election*, 2010).

TYPES OF ELECTRONIC VOTING TECHNOLOGIES

Many different types of e-voting have been in existence, such as:

Ballot Scanning Technology:

Ballot scanning technology uses a ballot paper that is either marked by a voter him or herself, or with assistance of a ballot-marking device in a polling station, which is then inserted into a scanning device and counted by electronically "reading" the voter's mark on the ballot. Such devices can be located in polling stations or counting centres, which are under controlled environments (OSCE/ODIHR, 2013). Ballot scanning technology offers the possibility of a manual recount. The ability of such devices to scan the voter's choice depends on the voter marking the ballot properly, is subject to the device's margin of error, and reliant on a legal definition of a valid ballot (OSCE/ODIHR, 2013).

Direct Recording Electronic (DRE) voting systems:

The DRE is also referred to as an electronic voting machine (EVM). DRE systems use a keyboard, touch screen, mouse, pen or other electronic device to allow a voter to record his or her vote electronically. DREs are used in nonremote, supervised polling stations. The DRE system captures the voter's choices and stores an electronic record of their vote in the machine (Goldsmith & Ruthrauff, 2013). The data captured by each individual DRE unit is then transmitted by either electronic means (i.e., Internet, cellular network or memory card) or manually (i.e., by printing the results from each machine and tabulating them) to capture the total number of votes cast for specific parties or candidates (Goldsmith & Ruthrauff, 2013). DRE systems may or may not produce a paper record to allow the voter to verify their voting choices. This paper record, also called a voter verified paper audit trail (VVPAT), has been implemented in multiple ways in different countries. DREs with VVPATs are perceived to have an advantage over DREs without VVPATs, because paper trails provide greater transparency to the voter, which can engender greater trust (Goldsmith & Ruthrauff, 2013). DRE voting without VVPATs, which is a form of "black box voting," does not provide sufficient means for voters and stakeholders to verify that votes have been accurately recorded. DREs with VVPATs provide election management bodies (EMBs), and provide oversight with the potential to audit the results or conduct a meaningful recount (Goldsmith & Ruthrauff, 2013). However, DREs with VVPATs also introduce greater technological complexity into the process, which may result in greater challenges for EMBs in terms of reliability of the machine, training for staff, and sustainability of the overall system (Goldsmith & Ruthrauff, 2013).

Electronic Ballot Printers (EBPs):

EBPs are similar to DREs in the sense that the voter uses a DRE-type interface for the act of making voting choices. However, unlike DREs, an EBP does not store vote data. Instead, it prints out a paper receipt or produces a token containing the voting choices (Goldsmith & Ruthrauff, 2013). The voter then takes this receipt or token and places it into the ballot box, which may be electronic and automatically counts the vote. EBPs are considered easier to understand and more user-friendly for the voter than DREs, as they split the actions of marking the voter's choice and casting the ballot in the same way a voter marks and casts a ballot in traditional paper voting (Goldsmith & Ruthrauff, 2013). The first machine (ballot printer) only marks the voter's choice, but does not record the vote, while the second machine (ballot scanner or "electronic ballot box") only records and tallies the votes. Like the DREs with a VVPAT, the voter can verify their vote, either on a printed paper ballot or by inserting the ballot token into another voting machine (Goldsmith & Ruthrauff, 2013). There is the possibility of a recount of the paper receipt or token if the electronic results are challenged or audited. However, because they involve two separate machines, EBP systems may entail higher costs, require greater IT capacity from EMBs, and encounter more challenges to ensuring sustainability than other systems (Goldsmith & Ruthrauff, 2013).

Optical Mark Recognition (OMR):

OMR counting machines combine aspects of paper-ballot voting with electronic counting. The voter uses a pen or pencil to mark his or her choices (usually by filling in an oval or connecting an arrow) on a special machine-readable paper ballot (Goldsmith & Ruthrauff, 2013). The ballot is then read by an OMR machine that tallies votes using the marks made by the voter. There are two methods used to tally votes using an OMR system. The tallying can be done at the polling station with the voter feeding the ballot into the machine, or votes can be tallied at a central/regional counting facility where votes from more than one polling station are counted. OMR systems provide greater ability for recounts than DREs without VVPAT (Goldsmith & Ruthrauff, 2013). Generally, OMR systems cost less than DREs and may put less strain on EMBs in terms of sustainability of the systems. On the other hand, these systems entail significant focus on details such as ballot design, type of ink used, paper stock thickness, and other factors that may inhibit the ability of OMR machines to accurately count votes. OMR machines are always used in a supervised, nonremote location (Goldsmith & Ruthrauff, 2013).

Internet Voting System:

In an Internet voting system, the voter casts his or her vote using a computer with access to the Internet. Internet voting generally takes place in an unsupervised, remote location, from any computer that has Internet access, such as a voter's home or work. It can also take place in supervised, nonremote locations if, for example, electoral authorities provide Internet kiosks at polling stations (Goldsmith & Ruthrauff, 2013). Convenience and greater access are the two key benefits cited for a move to Internet voting. In terms of access, Internet voting is perceived to provide access to specific populations that may have difficulty in voting at polling stations, e.g., persons with disabilities and eligible voters living outside a country (Goldsmith & Ruthrauff, 2013). However, Internet voting from unsupervised locations requires voting systems to place a greater emphasis on voter authentication to avoid impersonation, and also elicits concerns about the secrecy of the ballot. Internet voting also raises security concerns with regard to hacking into the system or other ways of corrupting data (Goldsmith & Ruthrauff, 2013). Similar to DREs without VVPAT, Internet voting also raises questions about verifiability, may not allow recounts, and presents challenges for adjudication of electoral complaints. Finally, transparency in Internet voting systems may be compromised to an even greater extent than with DREs. Such challenges are not beyond solution, but to date remain significant (Goldsmith & Ruthrauff, 2013).

Vote-by-Mail:

A vote-by-mail solution has the ability to enhance the convenience of voting for both resident and nonresident electors. It can also eliminate or reduce the cost of voting places and temporary election officials, depending on whether it is employed as a primary channel or as part of a multichannel approach along with physical voting places (Labelle & Clerk, 2013). As paper ballots are used, it also most closely resembles a traditional precinct-based model, which provides for a good audit trail. In vote-by-mail solutions, errors may occur as a result of the mail distribution process. For instance, during the mail distribution process, electors may mistakenly receive voter packages as well as ballots intended for another individual (Labelle & Clerk, 2013). There is also room for error in relation to the method of returning voters' packages to the Returning Office. There are documented examples within vote-by-mail elections where voters have returned their ballots improperly marked and/or inadvertently disclosed their identity by returning their declaration form and ballot in the same envelope (Labelle & Clerk, 2013). Furthermore, unlike electronic solutions, there can be no automatic controls established in order to prevent a spoiled ballot (for example, by over-voting). Although a central count scanner/tabulator can assist in deciphering voter intent as part of a vote-by-mail solution, it would still be required to automatically spoil votes for an office that is improperly marked, as the voter would not be present at the time of tabulation. Depending on the size of the electorate, there can be significant postage costs related to supporting a vote-by-mail solution (Labelle & Clerk, 2013).

Telephone Voting:

Telephone voting is most commonly employed as part of a multichannel voting solution in conjunction with remote Internet voting. Telephone voting provides for an enhanced level of convenience as it allows voters to cast their ballots remotely from anywhere they have access to a phone line, at any time within a defined voting period (Labelle & Clerk, 2013). A telephone-based system could be programmed to disallow a voter from proceeding to the next office if their current selection resulted in an over-vote. This all but eliminates unintentional spoiled ballots, a control which can also be engaged on vote scanners/tabulators. Certain voting systems allow for a voter to complete their ballot interchangeably by using the Internet as well as the telephone (Labelle & Clerk, 2013). With most technology solutions, the overall cost of telephone voting can fluctuate based on the scale and composition of the system. Often, the largest contributor to cost in this regard relates to the capacity of the system to be able to support high volumes of traffic, and its ability to provide for an adequate back-up system (Labelle & Clerk, 2013).

ISSUES RELATING TO DESIGNING THE ELECTRONIC VOTING SYSTEM

OSCE/ODIHR (2013) suggested that the following issues must be critically examined when assessing the designing of the e-voting system:

Security and Secrecy of the Vote and Integrity of the Results

Safeguarding the secrecy of the vote and ensuring the integrity of the results in a verifiable manner must be part of the fundamental design of the e-voting system. The integrity of the process is violated when the system does not record the choice made by the voter properly, or does not count it properly. For instance, this could occur if an incorrectly calibrated touch-screen device records a choice for candidate A, when the voter has touched the button for candidate B, or if ballot-scanning devices do not record voter choices correctly. The e-voting system must include robust security measures against potential threats, and legal framework and regulated measures must be taken against such attacks. In addition, the overall protection of the information systems from unauthorized external access through the use of dedicated transmission lines, firewalls, and overall security concepts, should be implemented to the e-voting system. The e-voting system must include the necessary procedures to prevent manipulation of data by election officials, vendors, or technicians, so they do not compromise the system.

Usability

E-voting systems should be designed in such a way that they are easily understandable for voters and relatively simple to use. The usability of e-voting systems will generally be correlated to the overall computer literacy within a country, the scope of voter-education efforts, and the opportunity for public testing of devices prior to elections. The physical design of the e-voting systems should facilitate the voting process. They should not allow voters to switch off the device or to undertake any action that would prevent them from casting their ballots. The size of the screen, brightness, and legibility of the display should all be considered. If touch screens are used, the ease with which selections can be made should also be considered, as well as any potential over-sensitivity of the system that could result in the recording of erroneous choices. Voters should receive clear feedback and prompts while interacting with the technology. The voter should be made aware of when the electronic ballot is about to be cast and should then receive confirmation that the vote has, indeed, been cast and that the voting process is over. The e-voting systems should clearly indicate what choice a voter has made before the ballot is cast, and allow the voter to correct mistakes. If the recording or transmission of the vote takes time to complete, the e-voting systems should inform the voter accordingly, so that she or he does not inadvertently terminate the process.

Ballot Design

Ballot design is very crucial in the design of the e-voting system, and design problems can potentially cause voter confusion or bias in favour of certain parties or candidates. Voters should not experience any difficulties in voting due to the format adopted for ballot design. In general, the same principles that apply to the design of paper ballots apply to the design of electronic ballots. The candidates or parties must be presented equitably on the ballot and all information required by law presented. All candidates or parties in the election should be given an equal amount of space on the electronic ballot and it should be possible to see all of the available choices at the same time before the ballots are cast. Ballots that exceed the size of the screen, thus requiring the voter to scroll or change screens to see the entire range of choices, have the potential to confuse voters and create bias in favor of contestants that are displayed first.

Voter Accessibility

One of the advantages of e-voting systems is that they can increase access for voters, especially those with special needs. The system should be designed to allow voters with disabilities to cast their ballots without assistance. Consideration should also be given as to whether a voter may use e-voting systems in a minority language. Where it is possible to vote in a minority language, systems should be implemented with the minority language ballot that contain the same information as that of majority-language ballot. Any special modalities, such as audio ballots for the visually impaired or the use of ballots in a minority language, should not have the potential to compromise the secrecy of the vote. This means that the content of the vote should be electronically recorded independently of the method used to "mark" the electronic ballot.

Reliability

E-voting system devices must be able to function for the entire duration of the voting process. The e-voting system device must be protected against foreseeable malfunction, and election officials must be adequately trained to deal with problems that may arise. For Internet voting, in which server failures or other system unavailability could prevent large numbers of voters from casting their ballots, proper measures must be in place on the system to ensure the availability and usability of the system.

Public Testing

Public testing is a process to test the functionality of a given e-voting system without requiring any knowledge of its inner design or logic. It is an important part of the implementation of the e-voting system. However, the value of testing depends, in part, on the type of testing, by whom it is done, and how much access is given to parties and citizens. The technology itself should be thoroughly tested prior to election day, but testing should also be conducted on the interaction of voters, election officials, and observers with the technology.

SEVEN PRINCIPLES GUIDING THE DEPLOYMENT OF E-VOTING SYSTEMS IN AN ELECTION PROCESS

OSCE/ODIHR (2013) identified seven principles that guide the observation of e-voting system usage in an election process:

1. *Secrecy of the Vote*: Secrecy of the vote means that it should not be possible to associate a vote with a specific voter. This secrecy permits the voter to exercise her or his choice freely, without the potential for coercion, intimidation, or vote buying. E-voting systems must be consistent with this requirement by not allowing voters to be able to prove to anyone how they voted, and the system itself must not allow identification of a voter with her or his vote. When e-voting systems provide voters with receipts or codes in order to verify whether the vote was recorded as cast, supplementary measures should be implemented in order to safeguard secrecy.

2. *Integrity of Results:* Similar to secrecy of the vote, e-voting systems must provide a guarantee of the integrity of results and there must be the possibility for meaningful verification of ballots cast electronically. E-voting systems that rely solely on public trust in the honesty of election officials, vendors, programmers, or technicians do not provide an effective means of verifying electoral integrity. The verification mechanism must also fully guarantee the integrity of the results without compromising the secrecy of the vote. In all cases, verification should be able to be performed by a body independent that conducts the election and verification of individual votes, and this should be performed for the entire number of votes counted. Systems that allow individual voters to verify that their own votes have been recorded correctly are

not necessarily effective in guaranteeing the integrity of the overall results, unless verification can also be performed on a broader basis.

3. *Equality of the Vote*: The principle of equality is that no voter will be able to cast more votes than another, nor will citizens be prevented from participating in voting. This means that e-voting systems must prevent any person from casting more votes than what is established by law, and must prevent any votes from being subtracted from the system. Some Internet voting systems allow voters to cast their vote more than once, with the condition that only the last cast vote counts. This helps to reduce the risk of voter coercion and vote buying. Also, the principle of equality means that voting should be accessible to all voters, especially for voters living within the country. Therefore, e-voting systems must not discriminate against certain groups of voters or discourage them from participating in the election process. E-voting systems should determine whether an invalid vote is cast intentionally or unintentionally. While intentional casting of invalid ballots could be possible, e-voting systems should advise voters on how to avoid casting an invalid vote if they do not intend to. If NVT systems are used together with traditional, paper-based voting channels, then all means of voting should be equivalent, and voters choosing either should receive equal treatment. Otherwise, the equality of the vote could be endangered.

4. *Universality of the Vote:* Universal suffrage means that all eligible adult citizens must have the opportunity to participate in an election, and effective means for their participation should be provided. If e-voting is used in polling stations, it should not be the exclusive method of voting, as less computer-literate voters may have problems operating NVT systems. In such cases, citizens should be provided with the option to use paper ballots if they wish. Internet voting has the potential to provide easier access and more options for participation in elections, especially for voters with barriers to accessing polling stations, including those living outside their home country or voters with disabilities. As with all forms of remote voting, including postal voting, this comes with a greater risk of voter coercion or vote buying.

5. *Transparency:* Observers need to have the opportunity to observe the work of election authorities at all levels, especially the voting, counting, and tabulation processes. Observers need to have additional access in order to be confident that the election is in full accordance with the law and with democratic principles. Observers should have full access to documentation about the system, including certification and testing reports, and they should not interfere in the process. Transparency also includes the obligation that all election stakeholders, including voters,

should be provided with sufficient means to learn in detail how e-voting systems function.

6. *Accountability:* In e-voting systems, those involved in an election process (i.e., election officials, vendors, certification bodies, and others involved in procurement, management, and utilization) must be accountable to the electorate. Election officials should be responsible for the overall conduct of elections, including the oversight of e-voting system. If an e-voting system involves technology supplied by private vendors, the roles and responsibilities of these vendors must be clearly defined. Similarly, certification agencies and other bodies must be held strictly accountable in order to ensure that they fulfill their respective responsibilities. Accountability also means that detailed minutes should be kept that describe the ways election administrations or other eligible personnel interact with the system, when this is done, and who actually performs the work.

7. *Public Confidence*: Public confidence in elections may be damaged by perceptions that elections are mismanaged or may not fully reflect the will of the people. Public confidence is a helpful building block for the use of e-voting systems. Where a significant level of distrust or dissatisfaction with the election administration exists, the introduction of the e-voting system may be problematic and may further diminish public confidence in elections. An incremental approach to introduction, together with thorough testing, verifiability, and full transparency, can help develop public confidence in the e-voting system.

ISSUES RELATING TO IMPLEMENTATION OF ELECTRONIC VOTING AND COUNTING IN THE ELECTION PROCESS

There are an increasing number of countries around the world that have implemented or piloted electronic voting and counting technologies. While each country's experience is different, there are some common themes that surface across these experiences (Goldsmith & Ruthrauff, 2013). This section provides a summary of thematic issues that often arise when electronic voting and counting technologies are used. Some of these issues, according to Goldsmith and Ruthrauff (2013) are:

1. *Legality of E-voting*: When considering the use of electronic voting and counting technologies, the compatibility of these technologies with a country's existing constitutional and legal framework needs to be considered very carefully. The use of these technologies may not only be contradictory to existing provisions in the legal framework, but may require that additional provisions be drafted to cover the ways in which

technologies impact electoral processes. For instance, the existing legal framework may make reference to physical ballot boxes and ballot-box seals, to actual ballot papers and the ways in which ballots are counted and adjudicated. All of these processes can occur with an electronic voting or counting machine, but in a different way. Therefore, the electoral legal framework needs to be reviewed to determine whether the use of electronic voting or counting technologies is in compliance with the law.

2. *Timeframe:* The timeframe for consideration and possible adoption of electronic voting and counting technologies is an issue that needs to be carefully considered. It is easy to underestimate the time that proper consideration and implementation can take, even for a pilot project. A full assessment of electoral requirements, availability of technologies, and identifying benefits and challenges of using such technologies can take many months. Once suitable technologies are identified, they must be procured—ideally and initially on a small scale—for a pilot. When pilots are held, a full and thorough evaluation of the process must be conducted before any plans or decisions are made for further implementation. Technology suppliers need adequate time to develop and deliver equipment and systems, including testing and certification of desired systems. Election officials need to be trained and voter-education needs to be conducted on use of the technologies. The complexity involved in implementation of such technology projects also means that even where comprehensive project plans and timelines are developed, there should be flexibility within the timeline to cope with unforeseen problems and challenges. Such complications often occur. Unlike other technology implementation projects, there is little room for delaying the completion date where elections are concerned. The election must take place on a certain date, and if the technology is not ready, it presents a serious problem.

3. *Sustainability:* Electronic voting and counting systems need to be sustainable for the long run. There are a number of contributing factors to the long-term sustainability of implementing electronic voting and counting, such as financial aspects, project management, and staffing arrangements. The implementation of electronic voting or counting systems is usually an expensive exercise. Estimating the full cost of implementing the systems is not as easy as it may first seem, and the costs involved go far beyond just the procurement of voting or counting machines. Such additional costs include ongoing supplier support for contracts; management facilities for central/local tabulation of results; special booths/stands for voting machines; securing environmentally controlled storage; maintenance and repair; replacement for expired equipment; consumables, such as ink cartridges and paper; testing and

certification; specialized staff/technicians required to configure; testing and support for the technology; and voter and stakeholder education costs. While a significant component of these costs is involved in the initial investment, there are many ongoing costs that need to be covered. A full appreciation of the costs involved over the life cycle of the electronic voting and counting machines needs to be factored into the estimate of financial sustainability for the technology. This is especially the case where a donor might be assisting a country in piloting or implementing a voting or counting system. The EAM needs to be confident that it can provide the finances to continue implementation of the technology in absence of donor support.

4. *Inclusiveness:* Elections should be as inclusive as possible, for voters and contestants alike. Inclusiveness is closely linked to the right to vote and the right to run for office, as well as the obligation of governments to facilitate these rights. There should be no discrimination toward any group in regard to voting rights or their implementation. An inclusive election process is also one that is based on open, broad consultation with stakeholders. Innovations offered by electronic voting and counting can create opportunities for a more inclusive election process. Increased accessibility is one of the arguments in favour of the adoption of such technologies. Certain groups of voters struggle to participate in traditional elections. For example, voters with disabilities may only be able to vote with assistance, which can violate their right to a secret ballot. Electronic voting machines must be designed with features to assist voters with disabilities to cast ballots unaided, enabling a country to better meet international electoral standards.

E- Voting machines must be designed with audio explanations to allow blind voters to vote unaided; font size must be adjusted for the visually impaired; and sip/puff solutions must be used for voters with limited or no motor capacity. Electronic voting machines must also facilitate the provision of ballots in other languages, with little additional cost, which may enfranchise linguistic minorities. Remote Internet voting may increase participation among military personnel and other voters living abroad. At the same time, implementation of new voting or counting technologies should not exclude any group of voters or inhibit their participation in any way. Certain groups of voters, such as the elderly, illiterate, rural, or low-income voters, may be unaccustomed to using computers or other electronic devices and may be initially reluctant to vote or cast their ballots electronically. Such considerations must be factored into both the design of the technology and related public outreach to ensure maximum usability of the equipment, particularly among groups that may be unfamiliar with electronic technologies.

5. *Transparency:* Transparency is a key principle for credible elections. A transparent election process is one in which each step is open to scrutiny by stakeholders (political parties, election observers, and voters alike) who are able to independently verify whether the process is conducted according to procedures and no irregularities have occurred. Providing transparency in an election helps establish trust and public confidence in the process. Electronic voting and counting technologies pose a challenge to ensuring transparency, since many visually-verifiable steps in a traditional election (such as how ballots were marked) are automated inside a machine, and therefore cannot be seen by the voter and others. In such circumstances, particular efforts must be made to provide transparency in each step of the process. A degree of transparency can be afforded through the design of the voting and counting technology. For instance, a VVPAT produces a paper record that can be checked by the voter to make sure the vote is accurately recorded. A paper record also provides the possibility of an auditable process. End-to-end verification systems allow a check to be conducted that all votes have been accurately recorded and tabulated. The procurement, development, testing, and certification of voting and counting equipment should be carried out transparently, so stakeholders are confident the machines meet relevant requirements, function properly, and have the necessary security features in place.

6. *Verifiability:* System verifiability or auditability is becoming an increasingly important feature for electronic voting systems. Electronic counting systems have a natural audit trail of the (often paper) ballot, so additional verifiability mechanisms are less important for such systems. With DRE voting machines, and also with remote electronic voting, there is no obvious way for the voter to be sure their ballot choices have been recorded or counted accurately. This lack of transparency was one of the main motivations for the development of the aforementioned VVPAT. Electronic voting machines with a VVPAT store the voter's ballot choices electronically, but also on a paper record, often within the voting machine. This allows the voter to check that their ballot choices have been recorded accurately on the paper record. Electronic results produced by the electronic voting machine can then be checked against paper records, and verified by the voter, to ensure the electronic result reflects the voter's choices. However, use of VVPAT solutions is not without complications, especially with respect to the internal printer. Other schemes have been developed to provide the voter with some form of receipt so they can individually check that the vote has been received and counted accurately. This transparency has to be accomplished without violating the secrecy of the vote, which is a challenge. End-to-end verifiable systems provide mechanisms for any oversight body to check that votes are received as cast, recorded as re-

ceived, and counted as recorded (i.e., all stages of the process function correctly and accurately). The voter will have some role in this verifiability, as only they know how they intended to cast their vote. Some end-to-end voting schemes provide the voter with a code they can use to check, after Election Day, that their vote has been included in the count with the correct value. Other schemes limit the role of the voter to checking that the vote was received and recorded accurately, and provide other independently verifiable proof that recorded votes are counted accurately.

7. *Integrity:* One of the fundamental principles elections must comply with is that they must accurately reflect the will of the voters. The integrity of the process when using electronic voting and counting technologies is somehow cumbersome and not really clear enough to both voters and observers because of the nature of these technologies. With traditional paper balloting and hand counting, the entire process is not only clearly visible to those observing it, but it is also easily understandable to the average voter. The ballot box can be shown to be empty at the start of voting by the polling staff, then sealed, observed in the polling station to ensure that only legitimate voters are putting in ballots, and at the end of voting the seal can be broken and the ballots counted in full view of observers. This overall transparency and simplicity of the process makes it relatively easy to observe the process and identify errors in the system if and when they occur. While political party and candidate agents, observers, and the media perform a monitoring function, they also carry out a verification function to ascertain whether the process leads to an accurate reflection of the will of the voters. This basic transparency is lacking for electronic voting and electronic counting, but especially for electronic voting. The complexity of electronic voting tends to be beyond the understanding of the vast majority of voters. The technologies have what are known as "black box" components that take input from voters and produce an output in a way that cannot be observed and verified by external observers, or easily checked by election administrators. This is a potential problem from a transparency, trust, and integrity perspective. Therefore, additional and varied measures are required to provide the same level of assurance that an electronic voting or counting process is actually delivering an election that reflects the will of the voters. Additional measures may include transparency mechanisms, testing and certification regimes, authentication mechanisms, and audit mechanisms.

ROLE OF ELECTION ADMINISTRATION MANAGEMENT (EAM) IN THE USE OF E-VOTING SYSTEMS IN AN ELECTION PROCESS

Since e-voting systems are interconnected with several aspects of the election process—including not only voting, but also party and candidate registration, tabulation of results, voter registration, and maintaining voter lists and information—the election administration should see the e-voting system as an integral part of the election process, rather than as a feature to be delegated to technicians or other institutions (OSCE/ODIHR, 2013). Some of the roles of the election administration in the use of the e-voting system in an election process, according to OSCE/ODIHR (2013), are:

1. *Re-structuring Voting Process*: Proper planning is a prerequisite for the successful conduct of an election, especially when using the e-voting system. In addition to technical specifications for the technology itself, the election administration should consider a restructuring of the voting process to explicitly take into account of the use of the e-voting system as an essential element, especially when it is being introduced for the first time. Changes may be required in the procedures for advance voting, printing voter material, setting up voting booths, identifying voters, and other elements. If the management of the voting process is not reviewed and redesigned, this may have unanticipated consequences for the electoral process. For example, insufficient numbers of e-voting devices or voters taking longer than anticipated to vote using the devices may result in long waits. Consolidation of polling stations in order to accommodate limited numbers of electronic voting devices may generate problems with voter lists or in voter confusion regarding their polling locations.

2. *Integration of Electronic and Paper-based Voting Processes in Multiple Voting Channels:* The complexity of the overall voting process will be increased when e-voting systems are used parallel to paper-voting systems. This is because the procurement and distribution of electoral materials, management of voter lists, instructions for polling officials, training, voter education, and tabulation of results will all be affected to some extent when using multiple methods of voting (or "channels"). Therefore, EAM must verify and ascertain that the availability of multiple channels does not disenfranchise voters, allow them to vote more than once, or force them to use an electronic system against their will. This requires communication between channels. For instance, there must be a system in place to prevent a voter from casting ballots by both Internet and paper ballot. In a system where voting by paper is legally canceled and replaced by Internet voting, the EAM should ensure that the canceling of electronic votes or duplicate electronic votes is done properly before votes are counted. This must be

done in such a way that the content of the vote cannot be associated with the voter. If this mechanism is implemented on election day, this should be carefully assessed by observers. For the tabulation and announcement of results in elections using multiple voting channels, the EAM must identify the method for transmitting the results in the paper-based system and in the e-voting system, and how the multiple sets of results will be aggregated. To ensure the transparency of the tabulation of results, political parties, candidates, and observers must verify that polling station results were tabulated correctly at higher levels of the election administration. This requires that the tabulation systems provide clear, detailed information that is readily and publicly available. The complexity of having multiple systems or any resulting delays in reporting should not be used as excuses for not providing adequate information.

3. *Oversight:* After identifying the management structure for the use of the e-voting system, the EAM should consider how management and oversight of the technology will be done in practice. The roles and responsibilities of each level of the election administration should be clear to the respective election officials, and the EAM should verify that each level receives the necessary materials, instructions, training, and financial resources in a timely manner. The EAM should also verify the extent to which in-house capacity could manage the e-voting system and whether effective oversight mechanisms are in place to ensure that each election administration body is carrying out its responsibilities appropriately. In addition, an assessment should be made of the degree to which election administration officials understand the technology in use and the potential risks. If officials believe that e-voting system issues are primarily technical in nature, and should therefore be left to technical experts, they may be less prepared to provide proper oversight or to take corrective action if problems arise. The EAM should also attempt to identify any concerns that election officials have about the e-voting system or its management.

4. *Risk Management:* The election administration management may plan for unexpected problems or even failure of the NVT system, due to either technological or human factors. The EAM should ensure that electronic data are preserved and recovered in the event of physical failure, such as loss of electricity; identify who is responsible for fixing the problem and the maximum response time; provide a manual to assist polling staff in addressing problems; and provide voters the opportunity to cast their ballots even if the system cannot be returned to working order. The voting period in Internet voting may be stopped several days before election day in order to give voters the opportunity to vote on paper, should major problems be detected during that period.

5. *Role of the Vendors*: Vendors often have a role to play in maintaining and updating the e-voting system due to their technical knowledge, but election officials are responsible for the conduct of elections and should have full authority, oversight, and accountability over technicians. The EAM should look into whether essential parts of the electoral process are outsourced to vendors and suppliers, and the vendors' liability and responsibility. The vendor should have a continuing responsibility to maintain and service the system. This includes addressing design errors, malfunctions, or other problems with the e-voting system. It should be clear that the role of the vendors and suppliers is to support the conduct of genuine and democratic elections. They should not replace any relevant functions of the electoral administration, which should remain in full control of the electoral process.

6. *Training of Polling Officials:* Considering the complexities and challenges of using the e-voting system, the EAM should conduct extended training for polling officials so as to enable them have a basic understanding of how the e-voting system works, in order to respond to minor and major technical problems associated with the technology, and respond accordingly to the questions that may be asked by the voters when using the systems.

7. *Voter Education:* Voters should generally be able to make their choices and cast ballots without assistance. Thus, voter education is critical for the implementation and use of e-voting. The EAM should assess the extent to which information about the system was made available to voters and the completeness of this information, particularly when a new system is being implemented or where significant modifications were made to an existing system. The EAM should ensure that detailed information on voting procedures was made available before election day, in different forms of media. Such information should also be available at polling stations on election day provided it is relevant. Voters should be informed about how the system works overall, how secrecy of the vote is ensured, and how the results can be meaningfully verified, in addition to the knowledge of how to use the system. Because voters themselves will often be the first to notice any problems with a given machine, voter-education materials should include information on how to deal with potential problems (normally, the appropriate course of action is to inform a polling official). Ideally, election day should not be the first occasion when a voter uses the electronic voting system. Apart from a gradual approach in introducing the e-voting system, hands-on testing by the public prior to election day, or mock elections can be an effective method of voter education.

BENEFITS AND CHALLENGES OF THE E-VOTING SYSTEM

The increasing adoption of the e-voting system in some countries comes in part from the recognition that technology may offer benefits over traditional methods of voting and counting (Goldsmith & Ruthrauff, 2013). Goldsmith and Ruthrauff (2013) identified the following benefits of e-voting systems:

1. Eliminating the cost and logistics involved with paper ballots; improved voter identification mechanisms
2. Improved accessibility to voting
3. Easy conduct of complex elections; increase in voter turnout
4. Eliminating invalid ballots
5. Faster, more accurate and standardized counting of ballots
6. Prevention of certain forms of fraud

However, the use of the e-voting system brings new challenges. Goldsmith and Ruthrauff (2013) identified the following challenges:

1. Lack of transparency
2. Negative impact on confidence in the process
3. Confusion for the illiterate or uneducated voters on process
4. Need to conduct widespread voter education, how to use it, and its impact on the process
5. Difficulties in auditing results
6. Secrecy of the ballot
7. Security of the voting and counting process
8. Cost of introducing and maintaining the technology over the life-cycle of the equipment
9. Potentially losing control over the process to outside technology vendors; recruitment of staff with specialized IT skills
10. Added complexity in the electoral process and the ability of the EMB to deal adequately with this complexity
11. Consequences in the event of equipment or system malfunction

CONCLUSION AND RECOMMENDATIONS

Election is a process that involves the total commitment of many stakeholders—government, the electoral committee, political parties, security agents, civil society, and the electorate—to their respective function at the right time. The e-voting system offers convenience to the voter and considerable ease to election administrators, as they can get election results out more quickly than conventional methods of manual voting. Even though e-voting systems have a number of advantages over manual systems, there a few challenges that must be overcome in order to fully realize its benefits (Ofori-Dwumfuo & Paatey, 2011).

To implement the e-voting system in an election process, certain procedures and guidelines must be understood, carefully studied, and followed properly.

This study discussed various types of e-voting system in existence and their benefits and challenges. The issues relating to the design of e-voting systems discussed in this study give insight to all stakeholders in the election process, in order to know what should be embedded in the e-voting system to meet the standard procedures. The issues relating to implementation of the e-voting and counting system give necessary information on the criteria that must be met when implemented the system.

It is my hope and belief that if all the procedures explained in this chapter are carefully taken into consideration when integrating the e-voting system into the election process, the system will really achieve all its benefits and be more appropriate than paper-ballot voting.

REFERENCES

Abu-Shanab, E., Knight, M., & Refai, H. (2010). E-voting systems: A tool for e-democracy. *Management Research and Practice*, 2, 264-274.

Ben Goldsmith & Holly Ruthrauff (2013). Implementing and Overseeing Election Voting and Counting Technologies. Retrieved on May 20, 2016 at: http://pdf.usaid.gov/pdf_docs/PBAAC136.pdf

Blair Labelle & City Clerk (2013), An Analysis of Alternative Voting Methods. Retrieved on May 22, 2016 at: http://guelph.ca/wp-content/uploads/AnalysisOf AlternativeVotingMethods.pdf

Bravenewballot (2008), Electronic Voting Technologies. Retrieved on May 21, 2016 at: http://www.bravenewballot.org/

Kozakova, P. (2011). Can "e-voting" increase turnout and restore faith In politics? Retrieved on May 21, 2016 at: http://www.eotwonline.net/2011/09/01/can-e-voting-increase-turnout-and-restore-faith-in-politics/

OSCE/ODIHR (2013). Handbook for the Observation of New Voting Technologies. Retrieved on May 22, 2016 at:https://www.osce.org/odihr/elections/104939?down load=true

Ofori-Dwumfuo, G.O. & Paatey, E. (2011). The Design of an Electronic Voting System, Research Journal of Information Technology, Vol. 3 No. 2, 91-98. Retrieved on May 19,2016 at: http://maxwellsci.com/print/rjit/v3-91-98.pdf

Sabo Ahmad, Siti Alida John Bt Abdullah & Rozita Bt Arshad (2015), Issues and Challenges of Transition to e-Voting Technology in Nigeria, Public Policy and Administration Research, Vol. 5, No. 4, 95-102. Retrieved on May 23, 2016 at: http://www.iiste.org/Journals/index.php/PPAR/issue/view/1659

The Quick Start Management Guide on Technology in Elections (2010). Retrieved on May 21, 2016 at: http://www.eac.gov/assets/1/AssetManager/Quick%20Start-Tech nology%20in%20Elections.pdf

CHAPTER 12
Impact of Technology Advancement on Election, Politics and Governance in Nigeria

Joseph Izang Azi — Ahmadu Bello University, Zaria
Siyanbola Afeez Babatunde — Adeyemi College of Education, Ondo
Ganiyu Sulayman Olubunmi — Adeyemi College of Education, Ondo

INTRODUCTION

The influence of technology on governance and politics in Africa has redefined the dynamics of development across the continent. Technological platforms are major drivers of growth and development, cascading to the grassroots level. Thus, this chapter examines the impact of technology on the democratic process with reference to African countries embracing technology as a strategic tool for engendering participatory politics and shaping perceptions. The technological platforms discussed in this paper are social media, electronic media, print media, and the Smart Card reader, with specific focus on the visual interaction and usability of the platforms.

The embracing of technology in Africa has dynamically influenced patterns of communication and living across the continent. Utilization of science and technology is imperative for African socio-economic transformation and the potential pathway to an inclusive economic prosperity. Countries in sub-Saharan Africa have amply integrated technology into governance, developmental strides, information management, elections, and electioneering. Kenya, Nigeria, Niger, Tanzania, and others are already harvesting the benefits of integrative technology. The narrowing digital divide has increasingly railroaded the inflow of investments into these countries. In addition, technology is pacing the African society with a group of innovative entrepreneurs who are redefining the essence of living. In Kenya, it was acknowledged that the success of the mobile banking system M-pesa has opened the door for tech startups, prompting some to refer to the country as the "Silicon Savannah" (Journalist's Resource, 2013).

Credible elections are a prelude to good governance and political development. However, technology is capable of fostering credible elections and robust electioneering. Participatory governance is essentially determined by easy accessibility to technological platforms and the ability to deploy its services for optimal use. Election does not guarantee good governance in isolation, but the active involvement of the citizenry in the decision-making process, and the consciousness in demanding accountability from the political office-holders, has done so. Technology provides an effective platform for focused interaction, which is benchmarked on measuring the impact of governance in the society. Thus, the mechanism for the effective dissemination of information and robustness of governance is largely influenced by the level of exposure to robust technological tools.

The Federal Government of Nigeria, through the Federal Ministry of Science and Technology, is engendering the utilization of technology for good governance by promoting the localization of technology for a seamless democratic process. This is captured in its policy statement on technology acquisition, localization, and diffusion of the Federal Ministry of Science and Technology in its 2015 Policy on ICT for Good Governance and Elections in Nigeria, as follows:

> In order to utilize ICT for good governance, Government shall encourage adaptation of appropriate and relevant technologies through reverse engineering for localization and diffusion in the management of our democratic processes.

Perhaps the success of the 2015 general elections in Nigeria can be attributed to the broad embrace of technology from the stages of electioneering to the elections. Electorates, contestants, and the umpire, which is the Nigeria Independent National Electoral Commission (INEC), leveraged on technologies during the 2015 elections more than what was obtainable in previous elections. Apparently, the Nigerian youthful populace is fast becoming tech savvy, especially due to the explosion of Smartphones and the high penetration of broadband Internet technology. According to Ehidiamen (2015), Nigeria is Africa's largest mobile market, with more than 125 million subscribers (statistics released by the independent national regulatory authority for telecommunications industry in the country, the Nigerian Communications Commission). Ehidiamen further disclosed that Nigeria also ranks as the 8th country in the world for high Internet usage. Election observers have employed technology to monitor elections and solicit feedback from citizens in African countries such as Tanzania, Ghana, Uganda, Kenya, and others.

Therefore, this chapter intends to focus on the technological drivers of governance in Africa, which include social media, electronic and print media, mobile telephony, and barometric machines vis-à-vis the visual interface of these platforms.

SOCIAL MEDIA

Liberalization of information and social interaction is largely driven by social media in modern times. Social media is creating a generation of Africans that previously seemed to not count in the political process, but whose voices aggressively resonate through social media platforms. Social media increasingly influences the political space and the shaping of political discourse. Social media disseminates information without hindrance, because it is not regulated. The information is transmitted in the form of broadcasts on social media platforms such as Facebook, WhatsApp, Twitter, BBM, and others. The unrestrained nature of social media allows users the limitless opportunity for posting and sourcing information. Social media users are not inactive, as with television, radio, and newspapers; rather, they are essential in the conception and exchange of information. Social media is the scaffolding allowing people to construct information and technologies that they never had access to before, function as information platforms that are not restrained by the state, and are revealing and definitive.

Mobile penetration in Nigeria has reached 65 percent of the population, accounting for the most users among African countries (Reid, 2016). According to We Are Social, a London-based social media communications agency, Facebook penetration in Nigeria was only at six percent as of January 2014, accounting for 11.2 million users. Reid (2006) also asserted the fact that the surge in mobile phone usage has been a catalyst for increased social media adoption, and in January of this year Nigeria was among the eight countries where Facebook Lite, a stripped-down version of the Facebook phone app designed for mobile users in emerging markets, was rolled out.

In an online monitoring of social media users during Nigerian Presidential and State elections conducted by DEMOS from March 18 to April 22, 2015, researchers collected 13.6 million tweets posted by 1.38 million unique users associated with the Nigerian presidential and state elections held in March – April 2015. It was noticed that Twitter was 10 times more active over the election period than at "normal" times. The researchers generated 12.4 million tweets about the elections over the period, and these tweets tended to be categorized into "reportage" (i.e., people describing events) and "comment" (i.e., people commenting on events). Their findings shows 1.38 million unique Twitter users posted content about the election on Twitter, and (in our data set) 216,000 Facebook users interacted with content on popular public Facebook pages (Bartlett, Krasodomski-Jones, Daniel, Fisher & Sasha Jesperson, 2015).

Content management on social media platforms was garnished with videos and visual images of candidates, logos of political parties, images of political rallies, developmental strides of the incumbent government at all levels, etc. Short documentaries and animations on YouTube, mini online conferences, the use of Twitter hashtags, and sponsored posts on political and lifestyle blogs expanded the online space (Owen & Usman, 2015). The opposition took advantage of government deficiencies in certain areas of development by trending pictures depicting the poor performance of the government to influence votes. Omojuwa (2015) noted that the main opposition party, the All Progressives Congress (APC), seemed to be the biggest beneficiary of the value social media brings to the table. According to him, APC's social media presence was effective, and the PDP's had the most inorganic, which seems to be comical. Mdigi (2016) acknowledged that the Kenyan-based crowdsourcing platform Ushahidi was instrumental in informing the ordinary Kenyan citizen of violent hotspots after 2007 elections. The managers of the platform extended its functionality to disaster monitoring and information dissemination. Ushahidi originally sent notifications through, but now also included email notifications. Kenyan politicians are also actively using social media to chart out their agenda. A search for the hashtag #kedebate 2013 demonstrates how African politicians use social media to clarify ideas.

Political content with visual imagery had a great number of shares, tags, and comments during the elections. Social media platforms were saturated with images and descriptive text captions. However, this is driven by the visual interactivity and learnability of the features on the social platforms. According to Partel (2015), 66 percent of all social media posts are solely or include images, and more than half of all Internet users have posted original video content or reposted visual content. Images get 94 percent more views than texts. Social media is influencing the development of visual content because it's a potent tool for shaping perceptions. Giroux (2009) also noted the impact of visual imagery on social platforms in the following statement:

> The Internet, YouTube, Twitter, and Facebook have re-constituted, especially among young people, how social relationships are constructed and how communication is produced, mediated, and received. They have also ushered in a new regime of visual imagery in which screen culture creates spectacular events just as much as they record them. Under such circumstances, state power becomes more porous and there is less control. Text messaging, Facebook, Twitter, YouTube and the Internet have given rise to a reservoir of political energy that posits a new relationship between the new media technologies, politics, and public life.

Visual content is expressive in conveying information and unmasking governance. Obviously, elections are not won and lost on social media, but the outcomes are shaped by the inclination of perceptions on the social platforms. Likewise, social media is capable of influencing the direction of governance in African societies. Therefore, it is incumbent on the government and the governed to advance on the dynamics of social media platforms by optimizing the usage of visual elements in their online content management.

ELECTRONIC MASS MEDIA

The media is critical to democracy, and a democratic election is unimaginable without media. A free and fair election is not only about the freedom to vote and the knowledge of how to cast a vote, but is also a participatory process where voters engage in public debate and have adequate information about parties, policies, candidates, and the election process itself in order to make informed choices. Furthermore, the media acts as a crucial watchdog to democratic elections, safeguarding the transparency of the process (aceproject.org). Democratic elections deprived of unhindered media coverage and media freedom are self-contradictory.

The media is simply an essential ingredient of good governance and the democratic process. Media diversity and the reach of television in Africa is growing at a high momentum, because African societies are fast becoming an integral part of the "global village." Access to quality information by the populace differs relative to the political contexts of political happenings. Issues such as politics (both contemporary and historical), media exposure, access to infrastructural development, economy, geographic location, and cultural difference all contribute to the inclination of the media landscape. The nature of political events and governance programs increasingly shapes the media's direction in an election. Trends of programming during elections are influenced by reach, political sympathy, and the need to set the focus of political discussion. This report by the Cairo Institute for Human Rights Studies captures the indispensable role of the media in the democratic process as follows:

> The media plays a major role in keeping the citizenry abreast of current events and raising awareness of various issues in any society. It also has an extremely significant impact on the public's views and way of thinking. The media is the primary means through which public opinion is shaped and at times manipulated. If this is the media's role then in normal course of events, it becomes even more vital in exceptional periods, one of which is electoral junctures, when the media becomes a primary player. Elections constitute a basic challenge to the media, putting its impartiality and objectivity to the test. The task of the media, especially national media outlets, is not and should not be to function as a mouthpiece for any government body or particular candidate. Its basic role is to enlighten and educate the public and act as a neutral, objective platform for the free debate of all points of view.

The electronic media consists mainly of television and radio platforms. Television is an effective means of cascading information to the grassroots level, and the reach is consistently expanding. In addition, terrestrial television broadcasts are being phased out to digitalization of broadcasting across Africa, and satellite programming is now available to viewers. Satellite transmission is anchored on high definition (HD), which enables viewers to watch crisp images of high quality. Satellite television is characterized by wide coverage. The digital switchover advanced existing technologies to connect remote communities that were previously unconnected in an effort to bridge the digital divide. For example, in 2009 in Egypt, satellite television penetration was 43 percent (by comparison, broadband penetration was 7.4 percent) (Ghannam, 2011). Viewers now have the opportunity to access non-state media, as well as freelance media that was not indirectly controlled by way of self-censorship and fright.

Television platforms are vital in galvanizing democracies for socio-economic growth via the broadcast of motion pictures to viewers, which informs them of events and happenings in their environment. Television programming focusing on governance can either be objective or distorted, depending on the ownership or sponsor of the content and the dynamics of the media landscape. The quality of visual content attracts public interest to the TV program. In Nigeria, Ghana, Tanzania, the Republic of Benin, and a few other African countries, candidates and political parties have the right to air their campaign on television stations, irrespective of ownership, through paid political advertisement, televised debates, documentaries, and the sponsored coverage of campaign activities that are also newsworthy. The visual identity of parties, colors, logos, text captions, and motion and still images of candidates constitute the TV advertisement campaigns. Animation is also embraced as a form of TV adverts by the political parties. The All Progressive Congress (APC) in Nigeria specifically employed appealing animated visuals in TV adverts communicating their electoral manifestos. This played a significant role in informing voters' opinions due to the explicit delivery of the visual content. This dramatically contributed in no small measure to the success of the party at the polls.

PRINT MEDIA

Print media includes daily to weekly newspapers, from news magazines to a range of special-interest publications. Print media is much cheaper and easier to manage. It represents a unique platform through which politicians attempt to launder their images and reach out to their teeming supporters. Furthermore, print media in a sense has more longevity, as it is exists for longer periods of time; however, the new information technologies put this into question, as the Internet accumulates old news from its initial spread. It has been detected that greater media exposure improves the degree of learning, without affecting the level of news forgetting (Meeter, Murre, & Janssen, 2005)

Print media is valuable in strengthening the democratic process. Information is easily circulated in print, inclusive of articulated government policy direction and achievements. The quality of a newspaper is benchmarked on the layout, design, overall color balance across the sheet, sharpness of images, content, and paper texture. All these factors determine the rate of readership and spread of the print publication. To buttress this, a survey carried out by the Rwanda Governance Board (RGB) on the state media sector in Rwanda, to understand the challenges throttling the growth of print media, showed poor content, inability to hire and retain experienced journalists, and lack of affordable printing services as factors. The survey also revealed that politics attract 73 percent of readers, followed by sports and education at 68.4 percent and 47.7 percent respectively. Seventy-four percent of interviewed news readers said the newspapers are affordable. Only 32 percent of them were willing to spend their money on a newspaper; others got them from offices, friends, and libraries. The delivery of value-oriented, quality newsprint and design is accentuated by the sophistication of the printing technologies. Digital technology embraced in all phases of printing has remarkably leapfrogged the print media into being, and in playing a crucial role in the governance.

SMART CARD READER

Elections in some African countries were alleged on several occasions to have been fraught. This electoral misconduct includes multiple voting, imposture, manipulation, and falsification of results, which eventually leads to chaos, un-ending litigations, and political instability. Hence, the electorate tends to pre-sume that their votes do not count, and this result of voter apathy has been wit-nessed in many elections across the continent. According to Alvarez and Hall (2008), electoral malpractices make the citizens lose confidence in the electoral process. A lack of confidence by the citizenry in the democratic process is an impediment in deepening electoral democracy, because if the citizenry does not believe in the fairness, accuracy, openness, and basic integrity of the election process, the very basis of any democratic society might be threatened. The con-flagration witnessed in democracies besieged by electoral malpractices insti-gated the global focus on ways of reducing fraud in elections across world, and enhancing the democratic process.

Innovative technology was explored as a means to curb the menace of elec-tion malpractices. The electronic Smart Card reader was developed and dep-loyed to restore the credibility of elections. Golden, Kramon and Ofosu (2014) noted that "these technological solutions, such as electronic voting machines, polling station webcams and biometric identification equipment, offer the prom-ise of rapid, accurate, and ostensibly tamper-proof innovations that are expected to reduce fraud in the processes of registration, voting or vote count aggrega-tion."

The Nigerian Independent National Electoral Commission (INEC) adopted the Smart Card reader machine to authenticate the Permanent Voter Cards (PVCs) for the 2015 general elections. The 2011 elections were perceived to have been marred by certain irregularities, and this led to the innovation of the Permanent Voters Card (PVC) to reduce the possibility of impersonation or us-ing of other people's cards to vote.

The more general use of biometrics in African elections is on the rise. No fewer than 25 sub-Saharan African countries (including Sierra Leone, Demo-cratic Republic of Congo, Zambia, Malawi, Rwanda, Senegal, Somaliland, Mali, Togo, and Ghana) have already held elections employing a biometric voter reg-ister (Piccolino, 2015). The Automated Fingerprint Identification System was used in the 2011 general elections in Nigeria as a digital register to eliminate doubles from the list, and was not capable of verifying the identity of voters at the polling stations (Piccolino, 2015). The Independent National Electoral Commission (INEC) noted that the Smart Card reader is a technological device that uses a cryptographic technology that has ultra-low power consumption, with a single core frequency of 1.2GHz and an Android 4.2.2. operating system. Barometrics are configured to certify the identity of an individual by recognizing fingerprints, which cannot be easily faked. The Engineering Network Team (2015) disclosed that the INEC card reader is designed to read information contained in the embedded chip of the permanent voter's card issued by the INEC to verify the authenticity of the Permanent Voters Card (PVC), and also carry out a verification of the intending voter by matching the biometrics obtained from the voter on the spot with the ones stored on the PVC.

Despite of the immense contribution of the Smart Card reader in engendering a free and fair election acceptable to all the stakeholders, the technological platform had its own challenges, which are quite peculiar to visual interactivity, user experience, and functionality. The inability of the device to capture the fingerprints of some voters was attributed to the greasy or dirty fingers of the voters. In most cases, people had to scrub their hands on the ground just to ensure that the device recognized their fingerprints (Okoro, 2015).

Some of the card readers were unable to function due to blank screens, non-activation of the Subscriber Identification Module (SIM) card in the device, or a low battery (Alebiosu, 2015). Vanguard (2015) acknowledged that some of the INEC officials attributed the failure of the card readers to INEC engineers who could not decode the inbuilt security installation in the card reader. Some attributed the failure to the incompetency of some of the INEC officials.

Significantly, the Smart Card reader was resourceful in restoring the needed credibility in the electoral process. The Nigerian electorates displayed a high level of enthusiasm in their participation in the 2015 polls because of the obvious openness, accuracy, and integrity in the elections. Thus, electoral litigations were reduced simply because the eventual outcome was satisfactory to all and sundry. Generally, the card reader has catapulted the democratic process in African societies to new heights. In essence, technology has been harnessed to protect the sanctity of the electoral process, thereby enhancing public participation, transparency, and accountability in governance and the electoral process. However, the use of the Smart Card reader can be improved upon by leveraging on the graphic user interface (GUI) through intuitive, interactive features which are user inclined.

CONCLUSION

Stable societies are reflections of good governance and a participatory democracy. Governments in Africa are yielding to the demands of their citizenry in embracing technology to safeguard and ensure transparency in their democratic processes. The quality of governance is being enhanced by revolutions in information and communication technologies (ICTs). Technology has strengthened the participation of citizens in governance in relation to the plurality of voices incensed by the diverse media channels' deepening democratic values. Indeed, Africa is evolving in a digital age of competitive economy anchored on good governance and sustainable, credible elections. However, the usability of these technological platforms can be enhanced with an enriched visual architecture. The developers have to consider the peculiarities of African societies in the design and integration of the interactive features in order to optimize usage. In addition, the managers and users of these platforms have to interact with expressive visual imagery that facilitates the seamless dissemination of information.

REFERENCES

ACE Project (n.d.). The Importance of the Media to Elections. Available at http://aceproject.org/ace-en/topics/et/et10. Accessed 16, May, 2016

Alebiosu, E. A. (2015). Smart Card Reader and the 2015 General Elections in Nigeria. Department of Political Science Federal University Wukari, Nigeria

Alvarez, R. M. and Hall, T. E. (2008) *Electronic Elections: The Perils and Promises of Digital Democracy*. Princeton; Princeton University Press

Bartlett, Krasodomski-Jones, Daniel, Fisher & Sasha Jesperson (2015). Social Media for Election Communication and Monitoring in Nigeria. Prepared by Demos for the Department for International Development

Cairo Institute for Human Rights Studies (2011). Media and Parliamentary Elections in Egypt: Evaluation of Media Performance in the Parliamentary Elections, *Human Rights Movement,* Issue 26, (Cairo, Egypt: Cairo Institute for Human Rights Studies, 2011): 27

Engineering Network Team (2015) Gains of the INEC Card Reader in the 2015 Elections. Accessed on 13, May 2016. Go.engineer-ng.net/m/blogpost?id=6404812%3 ABlogPost%3A103341.

Giroux, H. A. (2009). The Iranian Uprisings and the Challenge of the New Media: Rethinking the Politics of Representation. Fast Capitalism, 5(2).

Golden, M., Kramon, E. & Ofosu, G. (2014). Electoral fraud and biometric identification machine failure in a competitive democracy. Retrieved from on 16, May, 2016 http: //golden.polisci.ucla.edu/workinprogress/golden-kramon-ofosu.pdf.

http://www.ibtimes.com/nigeria-elections-2015-will-card-readers-work-electoral-commis sion-responds-concerns-1858622

Independent National Electoral Commission (2015). Frequently Asked Questions. Accessed 10, May 2016 from http://www.inecnigeria.org/?page_id=28

Jeffrey, G. (2011). Social Media in the Arab World: Leading up to the Uprisings of 2011, A Report to the Center for International Media Assistance, (Washington DC: National Endowment for Democracy, 2011), 26

Journalist's Resource (2013). Technology and collective action: Cell phones and violence in Africa. Retrieved on 10 May, 2016 from http://journalistsresource.org.

Mdingi P. (2016). The Impact of Technology in African Politics. Retrieved on 12 May, 2016 from CPAfrica.com

Meeter, M., Murre, J., and Janssen, S. 2005. Remembering the news: Modeling retention data from a study with 14,000 participants. *Memory & Cognition.* 33(5), pp: 793-810.

Okoro, E. (2015) Card Reader: Clash of Technology and Politics. Retrieved on 13 May, 2016 from http://dailyindependentnig.com/2015/03/card-reader-clash-technology-po litics/.

Omojuwa, J. (2015). Social Media and 2015 Elections: Beyond APC vs PDP retrieved on 15 May 2016 from NAIJ.COM.

Owen, O. and Usman, Z. (2015). Why Goodluck Jonathan lost the Nigerian Presidential Election of 2015. African Affairs, June, 1–17. doi: 10.1093/afraf/adv037

Patel, N. (2015). Visual Content Strategy: The New 'Black' for Content Marketers. Retrieved on 9 May, 2016 from contentmarketinginstitute.org

Piccolino, G. (2015). What other African Elections tell us about Nigeria's Bet on Biometrics. Accessed 13, May, 2016 on www.washingtonpost.com/blogs/monkey-cage/wp/2015/03/10/what-other-african-elections-tell-us-about-nigerias-bet-on-bio metrics/.

Reid, S. (2015). Nigerians look to social media amid information scarcity ahead of election. Aljazeerah America (2016). Retrieved on 8 May, 2016 from America. Aljazee ra.org

Rwandan Governance Board (2016) Rwanda Governance Board Launches maiden Print Media Survey. Retrieved on 14/05/2016 from www.rgb.rw

Vanguard (2015). After Initial Card Reader Failure: Nigerians Persevere, Vote in Peaceful Elections. Available at: http://www.vanguardngr.com/2015/03/after-initial-card-reader-failure-Nigerians-persevere-vote-in-peaceful-elections. Accessed 12 May 2016

CHAPTER 13
The Impact of Technology Integration in Electoral Processes: A Review of Corrupt Practices in Elections in Africa

Loubna Dali
Bowie State University

INTRODUCTION

Nowadays, corruption affects different levels of society, which has negative implications on its development. In order to identify the corruption problem in Africa and find out the difficulties that led to this plague, an in-depth study of the historical context of the political and social systems is necessary to categorize the basic features of replacement. Therefore, collective support of all components of society is mandatory to study it. The foundation of an effective framework for consultation and coordination between the government, civil society, and private sector is more than necessary. Mobilization to enhance transparency, ethics, and integrity should not be weak in the face of the difficulties and the heritage subsequent to decades of mismanagement. The fight against this scourge requires the implementation of a fair law, applied on an equal basis by an effective judiciary that is independent from the political authorities and the power of money. High awareness of public opinion about the consequences and the mobilization of all living vectors of society is also of paramount importance.

Corruption affects everyone, especially minorities and vulnerable populations. Where the number-one obstacle is in economic and social development, it ruins society in many ways. It undermines democracy and human rights by undermining governments. It also diverts funds that should have been allocated to public services, such as health care, education, and sanitation. And last but not least, it is a deterrent on foreign investment, resulting in reduced job opportunities.

The world of information technology (IT) has been growing rapidly, and is now fully integrated into our lifestyle. The interconnection of networks and the rapid expansion of the web have enabled the development of a large number of applications that users can run remotely without moving physically. One application that should take advantage of these technological advances is voting. Indeed, elections and referendums traditionally require moving all participants, and it is difficult to convince every voter to make a trip when it would be easier to vote from home or electronically. There would be several benefits if this approach were to be used. Its implementation will yield a greater number of participants, simplicity of the process, and automation for faster recount. It is also cost-effective by eliminating costs associated with the establishment of polling stations and staff required, etc. Nevertheless, the realization of an electronic voting system is not an easy task; it poses a dual problems: anonymity and confidentiality. For this reason, in this chapter we will introduce the newest technology called "Cloud computing" to help reduce this vulnerable phenomenon by using the most recent security system, TPM (Trusted Platform Module), via fingerprint. This solution not only solves the anonymity and confidentiality problems, but also is cost-effective in the long run.

THE ELECTORAL CORRUPTION ISSUE IN AFRICA

Several countries in Africa have experienced a constitutional amendment that requires immediate engagement in the process of the moralization of citizens and the fight against political and electoral corruption. In addition, representativeness and legitimacy of the forthcoming elections undoubtedly rely on integrity and transparency; hence, there is a need for a collective and participatory approach involving all political parties. For this reason, we will proceed with a summary on this issue based on an objective analysis of the problem and an assessment of control tools. This will lead us to identify and develop proposals that can promote integrity, transparency, and accountability.

DIAGNOSIS OF THE PHENOMENON OF POLITICAL CORRUPTION IN AFRICA

In the last decade, political parties have occupied privileged seats for extended terms, which led to the phenomenon of corruption. Corruption can be manifested and categorized into four levels:

1. In terms of governance of parties: Limited impact of political education and guidance to citizens. Also, nonconformity between platforms of the parties and the ethical and professional qualifications of the candidates.
2. In terms of electoral governance: Different forms of bribery, such as the handling of registration cards and unjustified intervention of the authority.
3. At the municipal governance: Violation of ethical provisions, regulatory and legal provisions, and rules of good governance.
4. At the parliamentary governance: Parliament occupied fourth place in the global barometer of 2011. Corruption at this level is reflected in

particular by the parliamentary transhumance phenomenon, which is the improper use of the devices associated with parliamentary immunity and the absence of the elected candidates.

EVALUATION OF THE FIGHT AGAINST POLITICAL CORRUPTION POLICY

The assessment of the current legal system relating to political corruption reveals a set of achievements: the criminalization of all acts of bribery, the establishment of a transparent mechanism to monitor financing, the identification and clarification of cases of incompatibility, and allowing the parliament to manage several constitutional and legal mechanisms, specifically the ratification of the budget law, the payment of expenditure, and the establishment of commissions. However, major failures can be reported, including the heterogeneity of existing laws related to the duration of sanctions and the amounts of bribery penalties; the lack of legal protection for whistleblowers' electoral corruption crimes; the possible accumulation of local, regional, and legislative mandates; and the limited effectiveness of inspection operations and administrative control, which does not necessarily lead to prosecution. On the other hand, the bills presented in the dynamic framework of constitutional innovations and evaluation have led to some achievements, including measures to extend the participation of women and youth; the prohibition of transhumance parliamentary mandate under penalty of election cancellation; identification of criteria that need to be observed in the selection of candidates for different elections; strengthening the resources of political parties; and making the imprisonment sanctions and financial penalties against perpetrators of electoral crimes heavier.

Despite the achievements previously presented, these projects have several shortcomings, specifically: the absence of civil responsibility of political parties regarding the various acts of corruption committed by their members; non-applying bans for parliament members subject to final judgments, or decisions of cancellation due to corruption during elections; and the inconsideration of parties as legal persons subject to the jurisdiction of the Auditors Court relating to fiscal discipline.

The rehabilitation of the legal and institutional system on good governance and the moralization of politics involve the following:

- The governance parties: The following provisions are the rehabilitation of the legal and institutional system:
  — Stipulate the liability of parties in respect of all acts of corruption committed by candidates.
  — Mandating and auditing the accounts of political parties by the court of auditors.
- The integrity and transparency of elections: To enhance this property, the government offers the following recommendations:
  — Criminalizing offenses for exceeding the limit and breaching of

the deadline for election campaign expenditure.
— Unifying the prison sentences and fines for electoral corruption, such as the use of public property in election campaigns for all legislative, communal, and professional elections.
— Ensuring legal protection for whistleblowers of acts of bribery, like those of other crimes.
— Making the lodging inventory of expenses incurred during any kind of election campaign to the Committee.
— Provide the report to the supervisory committee.
— Extend the scope of observation to include referendums in most of the elections.

- Representative governance: To advance in this component, the Bureau of Corruption Prevention recommends:
  — Cancellation of electoral decisions that have acts of proven corruption
  — Ban the accumulation of electoral mandates.
  — Create a commission in parliament to assess and monitor the budget with the possibility of using external expertise.
  — Stipulate the competence of parliament in approving public supply of goods and direct control of public institutions.
  — Provide the obligation of approval by the parliament defining the State's obligations vs. public institutions, in addition to the supervision of financial commitments of the state and large loans.
  — Plan as part of the budget law the adoption of a multiannual program of public finances and reduce the deadline for settlement of law of two years to one year.
  — Create a committee with the task of evaluating the implementation of laws and public policies, with the possibility of using external expertise for the legislative institution.
  — Plan to assign the chairmanship of the Committee on Economic Affairs and Financial parliament to the opposition party.
  — Submit the members of parliament to the jurisdiction of the Court of Auditors, in fiscal discipline.
  — At local levels, adopt a modern system of human resource management, based on objective and transparent criteria using Information technology.
  — Unify the principles and rules of management regarding procurement of the state, public institutions and local communities.
  — Strengthen transparency of local government, ensuring respect for the right access to information and simplifying administrative procedures.
  — Improve the effectiveness of Regional Accounts Courts.
  — Strengthen the institutional framework for the fight against corruption.

— Improve coordination and cooperation between supervisory, mediation, and monitoring.

PROMOTING THE ETHICS OF POLITICS

In order to strengthen the new legal and institutional arrangements under the new constitution by an ethical approach to the promotion of political life with all its components, we are proposing a national charter on political ethics whose main objectives are:

- The establishment of a new Cloud-based management mechanism to limit the excesses of behavior through legislation and regulations.
- Improve self-monitoring of various political mechanisms.

To overcome this phenomenon and solve the corruption problem, we propose here the design and implementation of ISECVOTE. It is a Cloud-based, secured electronic voting system using fingerprinting prototype on the Internet. The prototype protocol encapsulates a vote based on the use of advanced cryptographic tools via Trusted Platform Module (TPM) to ensure the integrity and confidentiality of the vote, authentication, and anonymity of the other voters.

CLOUD COMPUTING

Definition

Cloud computing is a general term for the delivery of hosted services over the Internet. It is the consumption of computer resources as a utility—just like electricity—rather than having to build and maintain computing infrastructures in-house. The Cloud offers the following attractive benefits for businesses and end users:

- The term *Common* implies multitenancy, shared resources
- Location-independent: Anywhere and everywhere
- Online
- The term *Utility* implies pay-for-use pricing
- *Demand* implies infinite, immediate scalability, automatic provisioning/deprovisioning of resources.

Before going any further into the types of services, the following illustration (Figure 13.1) shows the three possible Cloud-based services offered and also outlines the companies that currently offer these technological solutions.

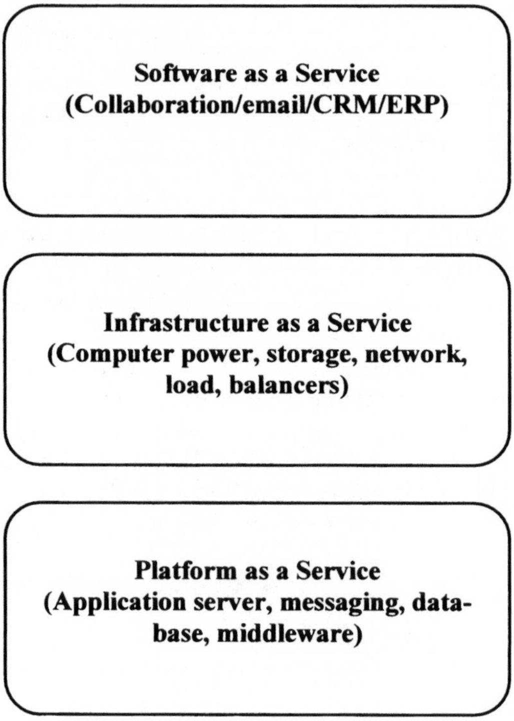

Figure 13.1: Technology capabilities of Cloud computing

TYPES OF CLOUD COMPUTING SERVICES

Infrastructure as a Service (IaaS) provides customers with infrastructure components. Components can include virtual machines, storage memories, networks, firewalls, and load balancers. With IaaS, customers have direct access to the lowest level in the software stack for the operating system on virtual machines, at the firewall management table, or balancing load. Amazon Web Services is one of the largest IaaS providers.

Platform as a Service PaaS (PaaS) offers a preintegrated platform according to customer needs. Customers have to build their own underlying infrastructure for their applications. On the back end, PaaS automatically resizes the necessary components and the provisions of infrastructure based on the application requirements. Typically, PaaS solutions provide an Application Program Interface (API) that includes a set of programmatic platform management functions and the development of the solution. Google AppEngine is a popular PaaS provider. Amazon WebServices also provides PaaS beside IaaS solutions.

Software as a Service (SaaS) provides software solutions such as online loans. SaaS software providers have complete control of their application software. Examples of SaaS applications include mail online, project management systems, Customer Relation Management (CRM), and social media platforms. The main difference between the two services SaaS and PaaS is that PaaS affords a platform for application development; however, SaaS delivers applications online that are already developed.

CLOUD COMPUTING MODELS

Public Clouds

A public cloud encompasses the traditional concept of Cloud computing, with the ability to use IT resources from anywhere in the world. The Cloud can be used as a pay-per-use service, which means that the customer will only pay for the resources used.

Private Clouds

Private Clouds are typically datacenters that are used in a private network, and can thus limit the adverse public from accessing data that is used by the company. It is obvious that this way has a safer substance than traditional public Clouds. However, managers still have to worry about the purchase, construction, and maintenance of the system.

Hybrid Clouds

As the name suggests, a hybrid Cloud is a mix of both private and public Clouds. This may involve the workload being processed by an enterprise datacenter, while other activities are provided by the public Cloud. Figure 13.2 is an illustrated insight into Cloud three.

Cloud Computing Deployment Models

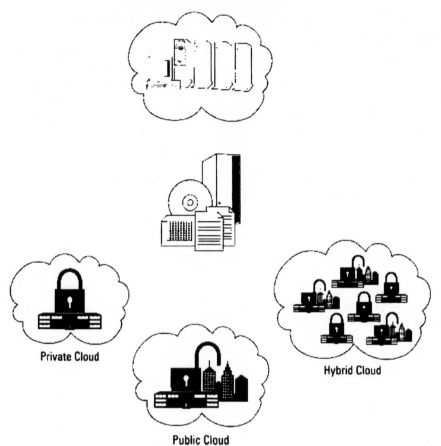

Figure 13.2 Cloud Computing Models

CHARACTERISTICS

Regarding the characteristics of Cloud computing, it is possible to distinguish three broad classes based on the particular case of the Amazon Cloud depending on the perspective of a Cloud supplier and a user.

Global Characteristics

The global characteristics are:

Quick and easy Elasticity: The Cloud allows the user to adjust upwards or downwards the resources it needs in a fine-time granularity (around the second or minute). This increase or decrease is easily realized through simple user interfaces.

1. On-demand service: Cloud provides that a user can control computer resources (bandwidth, computing power, storage space) without physical intervention.
2. Payment based on the resources used: Cloud also allows the emergence of a new economic model whose principle is to pay for what is used. Thus, the user will pay, for example, for the useful life of a computing resource, the duration of use of a storage space, etc.
3. Focus on the business: Cloud computing allows users to focus more on their strategic business area. Indeed, thanks to Cloud computing, the user no longer has to worry about managing the physical infrastructure and part of the architecture of their IT system. They can then allocate more efforts toward their business.
4. Economy of scale: The Cloud provider exploits the economies of scale, which means the "unit price" drops, depending on the quantity. Indeed, a Cloud provider has to have a large amount of equipment, such as servers (physical machines), cooling mechanisms, network equipment, etc. So with this large volume, it ensures you can get the best price.
5. Diversity of access: Thanks to the hosted mode services/applications within the Cloud system, and devices (Smartphone, PC or laptop, tablet PC, terminals, etc.) with the ability to connect to the Internet, the user will be to be able to potentially use its services/applications.

Financial and Organizational Characteristics
This section will show the financial and organizational features that includes six distinct characteristics:

1. Low-cost Investment: With the advent of the Cloud, it is no longer necessary for a user to invest in equipment to build a computer system. To start their activity, the user only needs to book the needed resources from the Cloud provider.
2. Fixed costs become variable: Investment in hardware to build or upgrade computer systems is no longer needed. For example, if the computers become slow and too old to meet the needs, and the user does not need to add /buy new machines. Heretofore, the user just needs to reserve its resources from the Cloud providers according to his needs.
3. Investments are becoming operational costs: Usually, investments are realized in the long term, and the user is engaged to use a given amount of resources for several years while operating costs represent actual usage of resources according to the needs.
4. Allocation: In the Cloud, it is possible to book/rent for a specific amount of time, a certain amount of computer resources, or storage space using the byte as the measuring unit.
5. Flexibility: Users can access to their computing resources anytime and anywhere, and their allocated resources can quickly respond to changes

in volume (hardware) or nature (software) according to the business's needs.

6. Cost optimization: Thanks to the quick and easy elasticity of the Cloud, the user can use and pay only for resources used at that moment. Similarly, it is simple for the Cloud to acquire and operate hundreds of servers for one hour than a single server for a hundred hours, which enables the development of diverse and varied strategies to minimize operating costs. And in order to offer services that are financially attractive for the user, the Cloud will tend to automate the maximum of its management processes to reduce the execution time and operating costs.

Technical Characteristics

This section will show the technical specifications, which includes seven distinct characteristics:

1. Quick adaptation: Adding additional hardware to the user's computer system in the Cloud takes a few minutes. Once the user releases the additional hardware, the supplier reassigns it to another user.
2. Resources (virtually) infinite: The user can consider the Cloud as a set of infinite resources that he can book/use anytime. He no longer has to manage the peaks, the growth of demand, and the execution. This issue will be handled by the supplier.
3. Management and administration: The user does not have to worry about the hardware, such as the type of physical servers to purchase or what new physical machine to replace. He does not need to know where and how to store and organize the physical infrastructure of the computer system. The user is only in charge of booking the resources according to need, and the entire material management is handled by the supplier.
4. Cloud cube model: A Cloud provides services in the form of individual cubes, billed separately. Therefore, it is possible for the user to use one or more of these services to build a computer system according to their actual needs.
5. Inexpensive experiment: With the ease of booking/releasing resources and payment for consumption, it is now much easier for a user to deploy a part of its infrastructure to make trials of a new service and test new applications, etc.
6. High and strong resources/services availability rates: The Cloud provider agrees on the availability of resources and services. This is achieved through the clustering of implementation of fault-tolerant servers with automatic failover capabilities.
7. Distributed computing: Applications are stored in a multitude of decentralized servers that the user accesses through an Internet connection and a web browser.

TRUSTED PLATFORM MODULE

The Trusted Platform Module (TPM) is used to enhance system security by offering ways of securely storing sensitive information and allowing verification of system integrity. TPM is a hardware device that is basically a secure microcontroller with added cryptographic functionality. It works with supporting software and firmware to prevent unauthorized access. The TPM contains a hardware engine to perform up to 2048-bit RSA encryption/decryption.

The TPM uses its built-in RSA engine during digital signing and key wrapping operations. Since Cloud-based systems mainly lie in virtualization, the extension of TPMs can be used with virtual machines (VMs). This is called TPM virtualization and it results in a virtual TPM (vTPM) design.

The TPM offers three main benefits: storage for secure content, secure specific reports by the platform requirements, and hardware authentication. Using a TPM module for secure content, the user has the advantage of storing files securely without relying on a software-based operating system. In the case of mobile devices, users can encrypt their entire hard drives using TPM, thus reducing the risk of losing sensitive data. It is possible for many users to connect to an unsecured storage device on an unsecure network and protect shared information without the need for a secure common operating system using TPM 1.2 technology. For example, many users today rely on secure storage servers hosted online so they can share data among multiple devices and access information everywhere. This requires the user confidence that their information hosted is set with administrators, server, and client OS, and additional security software, and the server BIOS and CPU.

The auditor also requires no contact with the transmitter, and should only rely on the TPM chip in the original machine. Significantly, the one-time certificates cannot be forged or falsified, even in a hacked machine, which could open their use for multiple applications offline.

A TPM can also collect, secure, and report information about the status of computer components, such as the BIOS, boot records and sectors, applications, and OS. The TPM can do so using the platform configuration registers (PCRs) to pass safely, measured by component information on the state of another component. During startup, the X component and Y component measuring status inserts the data into a PCR, where it is fixed and able to provide the state of the platform from the moment. In order to pass this information, known as the configuration of the platform to another entity, the TPM encrypts the configuration using a trusted signing key that can be decrypted by a remote TPM key with the required credentials.

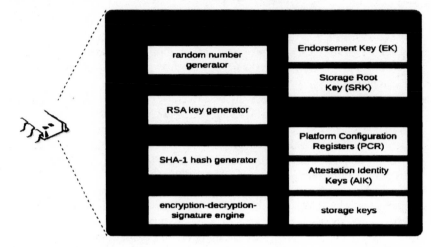

Figure 13.3: Trusted Platform Module

The TPM has the following capabilities:

- performing public key cryptographic operations
- computing hash functions
- key management and generation
- secure storage of keys and other secret data
- random number generation
- integrity measurement
- attestation

PROPOSAL ISECVOTE

Definition and Characteristics

ISECVOTE is electronic voting and an example of a distributed application that allows elections to take place on open computer networks. In this application, a set of voters sends their ballots through the network to a virtual counting center responsible for the receipt, validation, classification, and newsletters.

In general, participants involved in an electronic election are a group of voters and a set of voting authorities. The number and value of these authorities is a variable, as it depends on the voting pattern considered. The scenario of an electronic election can be divided into three phases:

1. *Registration phase*: During this first stage, the voting authority creates the electoral list of eligible persons who are registered for this operation to vote, and sends it through the network.

2. *Voting phase:* This phase allows voters to send their ballots using the communication facilities provided by the network.
3. *Countdown phase:* At the end of the voting phase, the authority stops receiving newsletters and triggers the results counting process. Finally, the results are published and available to voters across the network.

Several inquiries are required to ensure the proper functioning of the voting application:

1. Precision:
   - It is impossible to change a vote.
   - It is impossible to eliminate a valid vote.
   - It is impossible that an invalid vote will be counted.
2. Democracy:
   - Only eligible persons may participate in the vote.
   - The eligible person votes only once.
3. Confidentiality:
   - Neither the authority nor the vote should be able to make the link between a voter and his vote (anonymous). Anonymity is probably the keystone of any electronic voting system.
   - No one can prove that he voted in a particular way. Confidentiality is also important to prevent the purchase of voting. In fact, voters cannot sell their votes if they are not able to prove to the buyer that they actually voted according to their wishes.
4. Verifiability:
   - This property has two definitions, *universal verifiability* and *individual verifiability*. A voting system is *universally verifiable* if anyone can independently verify that all votes were counted correctly. A voting system is *individually verifiable* (lower resolution) if each voter can independently verify that his or her own vote has been properly counted.

Before explaining the proposed scheme of voting and how it will partially fulfill the safety requirements mentioned previously, we will briefly provide a literature review discussing the main types of voting protocols.

SYNTHESIS AND CRITICS OF ELECTRONIC VOTING PROTOCOLS

The first electronic voting protocols did not use cryptographic techniques. These protocols are generally based on two polling authorities; the first is used for the authentication of registered voters, and the second is in charge of the collection of ballots and the count of results. Despite their simplicity, these protocols have major drawbacks. Accordingly, protocols using cryptographic mechanisms have been proposed. These protocols introduce encryption to guarantee the confidentiality of the vote, in addition to the digital signature/attestation for authentication of voters to make sure that the voters cannot vote more than once.

To ensure the anonymity of voters, some of these protocols use two authorities to separate the authentication tasks of the voting and counting of the ballots. However, the anonymity problem has always been there because of the likelihood of collusion between the authorities, who may not well determine who voted for whom. Therefore, the blind-signature technique was introduced to dissociate the voter. This technique allows the authentication authority of the voters to sign their ballots without having a clue about the content or information about the ballots they have validated. In this way, the risk of collusion between the two authorities is removed. This is similar to placing a document with carbon paper in an envelope. Among the voting protocols that are blind-signature based, we distinguish the work of Fujioka, Okamoto, and Ohta, which defined a voting protocol using two central authorities.

OUR APPROACH

In order to implement our approach, we chose to adopt the Sensus protocol using the Trusted Platform Module over the Cloud environment. Our choice is mainly due to ensuring the maximum desired security and confidentiality, in addition to the two properties previously discussed: anonymity and auditability. Furthermore, compared to the protocol of Fujioka, Okamoto, and Ohta, Sensus allows a vote transaction in one session.

SCENARIO OF OUR PROPOSAL

Note that the protocol that we are employing uses two central authorities:

1. A central legitimating authority (CLA) that is responsible for authentication of voters and validation of their newsletters.

2. A counter central authority count (CCA) that collects the ballots and counts votes.

The Trusted Platform Module includes the following steps:

1. The voter prepares the ballot containing his vote.

2. The TPM encrypts the voter newsletter with a secret key using a key generator.

3. The TPM uses a hash function to encrypt the secret key using RSA key generator.

4. The TPM encrypts the resulted keys using a random number generator to enable the blind signature/attestation to the CLA.

5. The voter signs the condensate with the private signature key.

6. The voter confirms all these previous actions using his fingerprint if he is using Smart touch phone or computer (optional)

7. It sends the resulting message on the CLA.

8. The CLA verifies the signature of the voter with his public key.

9. The monitor verifies whether the voter has not submitted a report for validation.

10. If the voter is legitimate and has not validated a ballot earlier, the CLA validates his ballot by blind signing with his private key.

11. The CLA indicates if the voter has already validated his ballot.

12. The voter removes the camouflage factor to have the original encrypted form, hashed and signed by the CLA.

13. The voter sends to the CCA Bulletin (resulting from the previous step), and a copy of the encrypted vote produced during the second stage.

14. The CCA checks the signature on the form signed by the CLA.

15. The CCA uses the same hash function used in the early voting to calculate the condensate of the encrypted vote received in Step 12 and then compares it with the message from step No. 11.

16. The CCA checks that the CLA signature is valid and the newsletter was not changed during the previous steps, then places it within the list of valid ballots that will be published at the end of voting.

17. The CCA signs the ballot with its private key, and returns it to the voter as proof of reception.

18. After receiving the acknowledgment, the voter sends the secret key to the CCA.

19. At this time, the CCA uses this private key to decrypt the newsletter and adds it to the vote count.

In this proposal, we try to ensure the confidentiality of the vote and that the voter uses symmetric encryption with a secret key. Therefore, no one can know the contents of the ballot other than the voter and the CCA (after receiving the secret key decryption).The digital signature is used several times to allow the authentication of individual entities participating in the vote (voting, CCA, CLA). Therefore, any intruder can manifest as one of these entities. This protocol also uses the blind-signature technique to make sure that the validator (CLA) has no information of the ballots signed, and avoid the risk of collusion between the CLA and the CCA and the correlation of their databases, ensuring the anonymity of the vote. The concept of acknowledgment is the main difference noted between the protocol of Fujioka, Okamoto, Ohta, and Sensus. The latter does not require the voter to wait until the end of the voting phase to give the decryption key to the CCA, but uses the acknowledgment to allow the voter to verify whether the ballot has been received correctly by the CCA, and sends it right after the decryption key, which finishes the operation of the vote in a single session and makes it faster.

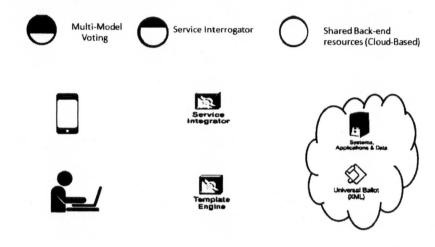

Figure 13.4: Steps of voting

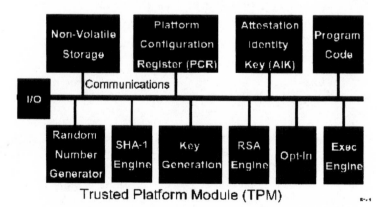

Figure 13.5 Trusted Platform Module (TPM)

THE VOTING PROCEDURE

The voting protocol that we have adopted in the previous section is the platform on which is built the architecture of ISECVOTE. We will explain the voting scheme detailing the exchanges of messages between the different authorities involved in the various stages of the voting process.

Voters Registration Phase

Before the actual voting process, this phase consists of the establishment and publication of the list of eligible voters wishing to participate in the vote operation. For this, the authority must have the list of persons authorized to sign (population list) beforehand. This phase in our voting system occurred because of two factors:

1. To strengthen the mobility in our system, no prior contact is required between the voter and the voting body (as part of the election process). Therefore, this phase should provide authentication of voters with the information available, such as an identification number and a password, so that information can be delivered to the voter from the institution organizing the vote.
2. The registration step also helps discern the number of voters abstaining, therefore reducing the ability of sending fraudulent votes.

The main difficulty faced during the implementation of this phase is how to authenticate persons authorized to register. To ensure this important service, we chose to use challenge-response authentication mechanism for the following reasons:

- A challenge-response authentication mechanism is based on the use of keyword expansion enhanced password. Signature mechanisms based on the keys cannot be used because these keys were not available before the creation of the voting process.
- Challenge-response faces the major attacks that may occur during a session authentication, such as the replay attack, with a minimum number of constraints (e.g., synchronization), and an acceptable degree of complexity, and it is feasible to implement.

To complete the registration step, each voter authenticated uses a password and identification number to generate a pair of private keys/public keys, then sends the public key to the registration authority where they verify the signature at the time of the vote.

Voting Phase
This phase includes two important steps:

1. The validation step of the ballot that includes symmetric encryption, hashing, camouflage, and signature of the vote, then sends it to the authority responsible for the validation (blind signature). The latter returns the validated voter to the vote.
2. The collection stage: during this stage, the voting begins by removing the camouflage factor from the validated newsletter. Then, it has to be sent to the collection authority to verify its validity and integrity before decrypting it using the secret key of the voter, which has been received through a secure channel.

Count Phase
This is the last phase of the voting process. It includes the decryption of the vote, then storing it with the corresponding decryption key in the Cloud database.

CONCLUSION

In this chapter, we presented ISECVOTE, a prototype of a secure electronic voting system. This prototype encapsulates a voting protocol based on the combination of TPM and Sensus over the Cloud environment. Throughout this research, we had to ensure the essential characteristics of a good electronic voting system. We can evaluate our system depending on each of the properties listed below:

1. Precision: Our proposed voting system satisfies this property. Indeed, any change in behavior, deletion, or addition of votes is detectable by examining the list published by the CCA at the end of the elections.
2. Democracy: This property is completely satisfied if all registered voters submit their votes. However, if voters abstain, it becomes possible for the CLA to validate and submit papers on their behalf. A third-party authority must take place to verify the signature of voters.
3. Privacy: By using the blind-signature technique in addition to the optional fingerprint option, we guarantee the anonymity property.
4. Verifiability: Verifiability property is also satisfied. Indeed, each voter can easily check if his or her vote corresponds to the number he received in the voting phase, through a list published by the CCA. This list also contains the decryption key of every ballot, which allows any independent party to verify the validity of the overall result of the voting operation, and correct any errors without sacrificing privacy votes (universal verifiability).

In addition to the properties discussed previously, ISECVOTE guarantees other properties related to its implementation:

1. Convenience: ISECVOTE allows voters to send their votes quickly, in one session and with minimal equipment and skills.
2. Flexibility: Our Cloud-based database accepts a variety of ballot formats, which allows the possibility to organize several types of voting.
3. Mobility: ISECVOTE can be used from any computer or mobile device that is connected to the network (Internet) and the Cloud servers (voting authority) can be run on any platform.

REFERENCES

Abouelmehdi, K. (2015). "Classification of Attacks Over Cloud Environment," World Academy of Science, Engineering and Technology vol: 9 no:5.

Abouelmehdi, K., Dali, L., El-Sayed, H., and Fatiha Eladnani, F. (2015). "Comparison Study of intrusion detection systems," *The International Journal of Information Security* (IJIS) Volume 4, October 30.

Attoh, A., Daniel, E. Gyimah-Boadi, D. E., and Annie Barbara Chikwanha, A. B. (2007). "Corruption and Institutional Trust In Africa: Implications For Democratic Development."

Bouzida Y., Cuppens F., Gombault S., (2006), "Detecting and Reacting against Distributed Denial of Service Attacks," IEEE International Conference on Communication, Volume 5.

Banerjee, P., Friedrich, R., Bash, C., Goldsack, P., Huberman, B., Manley, J., Patel, C., Ranganathan, P., Veitch, A.: Everything as a service: powering the new information economy. *Computer* 44(3),36–43 (2011). doi:10.1109/MC.2011.67.

Boampong, P.A., Wahsheh, L.A. (2012). Different facets of security in the cloud. In: Proceedings of the 15th Communications and Networking Simulation Symposium, pp. 5:1–5:7. Society for Computer Simulation International, San Diego, CA, USA.

Bentajer, A., Abouelmehdi, K., Dali, L. (2015). "An Assessing Approach based on FMECA Methodology to evaluate security of a third party cloud provider." *Journal of Theoretical and Applied Information Technology,* 30 April 2015, Vol.74 No.3.

Callen, M. and Long, J. D. (2012). "Institutional Corruption and Election Fraud: Evidence from a Field Experiment in Afghanistan," Working Paper UCSD, September.

Chen, S., Wang, R., Wang, X; Chen, K. Z. (2010). Side-Channel Leaks In Web Application: A Reality Today, A Challenge Tomorrow. *Security and Privacy*, IEEE Symposium, pp. 191-208.

Dali, L., El-Sayed, H., Abouelmehdi, K., and Fatiha Eladnani, F. (2015). "A Survey of Intrusion Detection System." The 2nd World Symposium on Web Applications and Networking (WSWAN'2015) IEEE Xplore, Tunisia, March.

Dali, L., El-Sayed, H., Abouelmehdi, K., and Fatiha Eladnani (2015). "The Benefits of The Duo IPv6 and TPM to Enhance the Cloud Security." The 2nd World Symposium on Computer Networks and Information Security 2015, WSCNIS'2015, IEEE Xplore, Tunisia, Sept. 2015.

Gong, C., Liu, J., Zhang, Q., Chen, H., Gong, Z. (2010). The characteristics of cloud computing. In: 39th International Conference on Parallel Processing Workshop, pp. 275–279. IEEE Computer Society

Gray, A. (2013). Conflict Of Laws and The Cloud Computer Law & Security Review Volume 29, Issue 1, February. p. 58–65, Washington, DC, USA. doi:10.1109/ICP PW.2010.45.

Hinden, R., and Deering, S. (2006). IP version 6 Addressing Arcitechture, RFC 4291, IETF, 2006, p.25.

Hoffman, B. and J. D. Long, J. D. (2012). "Party Attributes, Performance, and Voting in Africa," Comparative Politics.

Höglund, K., (2006). Electoral violence in war-ravaged societies: The case of Sri Lanka. Paper prepared for the Workshop on Power-Sharing and Democratic Governance in Divided Societies, Centre for the Study of Civil Wars, PRIO, 21–22 August.

Ijim-Agbo, U., (2007). The Independent National Electoral Commission as an (im) partial umpire in the conduct of the 2007 elections. *Journal of African Elections*, 6 (2), pp. 79–94.

Lenk, A., Klems, M., Nimis, J., Tai, S., Sandholm, T (2009). What's inside the cloud? An architectural map of the cloud landscape. In: Proceedings of the ICSE Workshop on Software Engineering Challenges of Cloud Computing, pp. 23–31. IEEE Computer Society, Washington, DC, USA. doi:10.1109/CLOUD. 2009.5071529.

Lizhe W. and Gregor V. L.,(2008), "Cloud Computing: A Perspective Study," *New Generation Computing* Volume 28, Number 2, 137-146, DOI: 10.1007/s00354-008-0081-5.

Mohamed, E., Abdelkader, H., and El-Etriby, S. (2012). Enhanced data security model for cloud computing. In: 8th International Conference on Informatics and Systems, pp. CC-12–CC-17. IEEE.

Pasman, H. J. Jung, S., Prem, K., Rogers, W. J. and Yang, X. (2009). Is Risk Analysis A Useful Tool For Improving Process Safety? *Journal of Loss Prevention in the Process Industries,* 22, p. 769–777

Patidar, S., Rane, D., Jain, P.: A survey paper on cloud computing. In: 2nd International Conference on Advanced Computing Communication Technologies, pp. 394–398. IEEE (2012). doi:10. 1109/ACCT.2012.15 [9].

Sadashiv, N., Kumar, S.: Cluster, grid and cloud computing: a detailed comparison. In: 6th International Conference on Computer Science Education, pp. 477–482. IEEE (2011). doi:10.1109/ICCSE.2011.6028683

Chapter 14
Democracy, Technology Integration in Elections, and the Transformation of Politics in Nigeria

Benjamin Arah
Bowie State University

INTRODUCTION

Technology has continued to radically revolutionize and transform the way most people live, do things, and interact with others across cultures without regard to geography or distance. People often engage in productive activities to express their humanity and give life its symbolic meaning. And things have changed significantly and will continue to change as a result of the use of information communication technologies, which have become intertwined with all aspects of human existence. This particular truth is evident when we look at how people work and produce goods, reproduce themselves, provide services, engage in various Internet business endeavors or financial transactions, construct new knowledge and facilitate the exchange of ideas, and participate in the electoral process to influence the political landscape and destiny of their nation. We experience some of these technology-driven changes with online banking or Internet shopping, the use of "Airbnb" to book accommodations in distant places, and we observe how family members, neighbors, and colleagues use assorted mobile devices (Smartphones or other tablets) with Internet connectivity to do marvelous things. Soon greeting or invitation cards will be a relic of the past, as young people prefer to use electronic invitations and send e-cards without incurring additional cost in postage stamps (although many of them resort to "e-vite" to give events that personal touch and show that they really care).

Schechter and DeLevie-Orey acknowledged how technology has impacted modern society, how it has both disrupted and revolutionized business or civil society, and noted how daily behaviors have been infiltrated to the point that a good number of people now expect the whole world to keep pace with technology (2016). So, the use of modern "innovative" technology has made life worth living with relative convenience and comfort, resulting in quality improvement and a higher standard of living. Not only has the use of modern technology helped to increase human capabilities, social progress, and economic development with easy access and spontaneous communication of sorts, but it has (directly or indirectly) allowed people in many parts of the world to do things in a more efficient and cost-effective manner than ever before. Technology can be put to good use in Nigeria, and should be integrated in the electoral practices for both transparency and accountability in the advancement of democracy and promotion of political development in that part of the world.

Technology has transformed the healthcare system with informatics and the careful use of electronic medical/health records (which is part of the health information technology), and has affected how academic leaders and school administrators now run educational institutions of higher learning in ways that enable instructors and students to meaningfully engage in online learning. We must agree with Kwache, that just as information communication technology has an impact on the quality and quantity of teaching, learning, and research in the traditional and/or distance education institutions using it (2007), it is reasonable to believe and hope that election technology can be used in Nigeria, by Nigerians, to enhance the electoral process and thereby improve how the citizens choose or elect their political leaders.

Nigerians have held elections since the country's independence in 1960, and since becoming a multiparty democracy in 1999. But the post-1999 elections (in 2003, 2007, and 2011) were flawed and fraudulent with rigging, ballot-box stuffing, abuse of human rights, manipulation of the election results, intimidation of voters, and plagued with threats of political violence and unrest that led to political instability. Takirambudde, the African Director at Human Rights Watch, acknowledged that "these elections were a true milestone for Nigeria, but they have signaled regression rather than progress ... Eight years after the end of military rule, Nigeria has yet to hold a credible election raising concerns of four more years of poor governance and human rights abuse" (2007). The elections were "the most disorganized and fraudulent ... during which people's votes were blatantly stolen, rigged and the mandate of the people hijacked by political elites belonging variously to different political parties" (Casimir, Omeh & Ike, 2013, p. 167). In his speech titled "Democracy and Governance in Africa," then President Olusegun Obasanjo noted that "denial of fundamental human rights, arbitrariness, absence of the basic freedoms of and for the individual have remained familiar traits of the majority of the governments in Africa" and as a result "Africans are now clamoring for greater responsiveness of their political leaderships, respect for human rights, accountability and a two-way channel of information between the people and their leadership" (1991, p. 22).

Democratic elections are when the citizens exercise their right to be heard; when the people have the opportunity to make important choices between competing party candidates and decide the nature of their representative government and its leadership; and when citizens will have to elect new leaders they can trust and hold responsible/accountable for their decisions, policies, and activities. Emphasizing the importance of elections for political accountability and good governance, President Obasanjo was unambiguous in adding that "the existence of choice in selecting those who will lead them, and the corollary existence of the chance to periodically review and renew or terminate the mandate given to the political leadership should provide the basis for good government."

Democratic elections give the people that rare opportunity to both actively and directly participate in politics (as it deals with the affairs of the public or people), and to make a critical choice in electing their leaders. Technology integration in elections can enhance this experience by helping the eligible Nigerian citizens (including those abroad, the disabled, and other minority groups) to have a say in the process through electronic voting. It allows people to vote with ease and comfort by either touch screen or a click on a computer or other technology-driven devices. To give people such an opportunity would, hopefully, help them develop interest, trust, and confidence in the political system; make Nigerians become engaged in the political/electoral process; and thereby increase the number of voters. Technology integration in elections could be a creative way to begin to organize and hold credible elections in the country. The basic features to look for in any credible election are whether it is open, safe, secure, free, and fair in the best interests of all citizens.

Election technology, in a way, is a form of technology integration in politics to transform the way people become engaged in public affairs and more active in the choice or election of their future political leaders or government officials. Election technology refers to the information communication technologies that are used to administer and manage political elections. In narrow terms, it means the various technologies that election officials are willing to adopt and implement to enable the citizens vote in credible elections. Using election technology can enable the people to achieve the desired justice in manners consistent with electoral integrity. Using certain specific election technology (voter registration, e-voting systems, biometric voter's card, electronic card reader) to conduct political elections (at the local, state and national or federal levels) and for voting will help to (a) improve the electoral process and achieve electoral justice with electoral integrity; (b) promote transparency and efficiency in the spread of democracy; and (c) establish legitimacy in the new government in ways that could enhance good democratic governance.

In essence, using the various election technologies has the potential of creating an efficient system for better voter identification, encourages voter turnout, promotes faster/easier voting with a reliable and accurate counting of the votes, and saves citizens the time and energy of going to voting stations and standing in long lines, all of which could lead to having a transparent electoral process in the country.

It is hoped that the Independent National Election Commission (INEC), the Nigerian electoral administration or management body, would explore and seriously consider the use of innovative information communication technologies (election technologies) to enhance electoral processes and in conducting elections in Nigeria at the various levels. Technology integration in elections would be a good national priority and an investment aimed to strengthen the electoral processes, would make and facilitate easier voting, and would ensure that elections are free to the aspiring party candidates as the country continues to evolve and transition from the post-colonial and post-military experiences toward a consolidated democratic outlook.

This study explores and highlights how Nigerians can embrace the use of election technology to achieve the desired electoral justice with integrity, after several years of fraudulent electoral activities and generations of ruinous military dictatorships in the country. The argument is that technology integration in elections would be good for Nigeria and should be encouraged, because it will transform politics and make leaders accountable to the people, as well as help to improve the electoral process. If the electoral process is open, free, and fair or transparent, then people will be able develop or build trust and confidence in their political system in ways that could result in reducing the proclivity of human error, intentional fraud, and unintended electoral malpractice.

Nigerians urgently need a transparent and accountable electoral process that enables citizens to have trust in their political system and respect for their political leaders. It is important for the people to be cognizant of the fact that, without honest, safe, secure[1], and credible elections, "the center would not hold," and as a consequence, everything in the country will continue to fall apart, which will retard national progress. Election is the heart of democracy, and democratic societies do well and flourish when eligible citizens are free to exercise their rights by participating in credible political elections and vote for their representatives in government. It is the responsibility of legitimate governments everywhere to ensure that the citizens participate in open, free, and fair political elections that are not subject to intimidation, harassment, violence, tampering with the voting machines, deliberate misinformation or misleading of voters, ballot stuffing and/or destruction of ballots, fraudulent tabulation of votes, or the willful announcement or pronouncement of the wrong election results to favor selected or particular party candidates, etc. So, political elections matter in Nigeria and for Africa, and it is in everybody's best interests to ensure that we conduct credible, safe, and secure elections for a resilient and most rewarding democratic experience.

Achieving electoral security is first, because the Nigerian government (via the Independent National Election Committee) must endeavor to ensure the safety of all stakeholders in the process (the party candidates, voters, party officials and members, and everyone else). The second thing is to protect the integrity of the electoral process itself, so that no official will be corrupted. Safe and secure elections are when there is no interference with the election materials; when the eligible citizens and voters are well-informed and understand the issues, and also know their rights and responsibilities in using their votes to elect qualified leaders; and when the election results are not manipulated or compromised after the votes have been cast, counted, and tallied. Political elections matter, and citizens and party candidates must be made to believe or have confidence in the electoral process in ways that give credence to the integrity of the electoral process. And electronic voting (or e-voting) is an innovative way of getting citizens to partici- pate in the electoral process and have them vote in elections for their candidates or on issues electronically via the Internet. Electronic voting (as an aspect of electronic technology), if carefully planned and well implemented, could result in an electoral efficacy and justice based on an impartial, safe, free, secure, and fair elections for all involved. Thus, using an electronic voting system in Nigeria would seem to be a good step toward increasing voter participation, reducing the possibilities for electoral fraud, building trust and confidence in the electoral system, and promoting transparency and integrity.

DEMOCRACY, ELECTIONS IN NIGERIA, AND ELECTORAL JUSTICE

Democracy and development go together, or are mutually reinforcing, and the advances in one presuppose or may produce advances in the other in a process of mutual interaction and reinforcement (Tommasoli, 2013, p. 7). Tommasoli also noted that the term "democracy" entails "citizens' voice, participation, in- clusion and nurturing a democratic culture." The author added that what makes democracy most unique (as "a government of, by, and for the people") are some of its core attributes, which include responsiveness to citizen demands, accoun- tability, safety and security, rule of law, and access to justice with a professional public administration and basic service delivery in areas such as education and health care (p. 7). In a democracy, it is important for the people to be able to have a voice and be heard, or participate in the deliberative decision-making process through which they can elect their political leaders as public servants to pilot and manage the affairs of the state by providing both leadership and ser- vice. Political election is that moment in time when citizens naturally come to- gether to have their voices heard as they participate to reach an important politi- cal decision, for better or worse, through which they shape and affect the politi- cal destiny of nations for years. It is not sufficient to hold political elections for the sake of electing qualified citizens to serve political offices; what matters in a democracy is that the elections must be "credible" and transparent, open, safe, secure, fair among the competing party candidates, and that citizens will be free to cast their ballots in secret without fear, intimidation, or duress. While democ- racy is a system of rules and processes, election constitutes an important miles- tone in which the people assume political responsibility for themselves. Kofi Annan, the former U.N. Secretary General and Chair of the Global Commission of Elections, Democracy and Security, remarked that "elections are the indis- pensable root of democracy ... to be credible, we need to see high standards before, during and after votes are cast ...When the electorate believes that elec- tions have been free and fair, they can be a powerful catalyst for better gover- nance, greater security and human development" (2012, p. 3-4).

Since elections do matter greatly in a representative democracy, it must be acknowledged that the development of an equitable, transparent, and fair elec- toral process is the foundation for the deepening and strengthening of a healthy democracy (Carrillo, 2014). The question is, how can this be achieved? Carrillo replied that "to meet these needs, the electoral process must be undergirded by two fundamental standards: credibility and integrity" (p. 4). To ensure electoral justice with both credibility and integrity, Carrillo concluded that, "other features, such as respect for the rule of law, political plurality, transparency, accountability and the professionalization of electoral management bodies, among others, are necessary."

Election is very important to and at the root of democracy (as a system of government), because it is via credible (free, safe, secure, and fair) elections that the people participate meaningfully in the political process to elect only those few people who are "fit to lead," and thereby "further democracy, development, human rights and security" (Cordenillo & Ellis, 2012, p. 5). So what is important or special about democracy and political elections? Cordenillo provided a thoughtful answer, as follows:

> Holding regular elections is an integral part of any functioning democracy. Elections give citizens the opportunity to participate in the political process by allowing them to identify and select their political representatives. These representatives, in turn, consult citizens, aggregate their political preferences and ensure that they are heard in democratic institutions and processes. In anticipation of elections, citizens—through various forums, including their respective political parties—acquaint themselves with the candidates for election and discuss and debate the burgeoning issues related to governance, the economy and the overall state of their country. After elections, citizens hold their elected representatives accountable to ensure that their political interests are heard and appropriately addressed. Failing to do so might make citizens rethink their choice of representatives for the next elections (2014, p. 17).

The relationship between democracy and the need for credible elections is eloquently summarized. It explains why people have to hold political elections and why elections must be credible to have integrity. Credible elections deepen and strengthen democracy, and should be organized and conducted in a manner that would give citizens full faith and trust, as well as confidence in their political system. When this is done, it would not be a surprise to anyone to see how citizens develop respect for their political leaders, and might even be inspired by some of them. The nation's leaders are supposed to be responsible and accountable to their citizens, and one sure way for the people to trust their leaders is when political elections are credible and both the process and results appear transparent. Cordenillo remarked that "elections that are conducted with integrity uphold human rights and democratic principles, and are more likely to produce elected officials who represent their citizens' interests" and "as such, democratic governments serve their strategic interests by supporting elections with integrity" (2014, pp. 17-18). Nigerians, since their political independence from Britain in 1960, have been attracted to a democratic form of government with the expressed aspiration of having a responsible/responsive government that will successfully meet the needs of the diverse (ethnic) population, and improving the standard of living for all of the people (regardless of tribe, tongue or religion). After the nationalist struggles and political independence, Nigerians were hopeful in their aspiration to live a life of dignity and freedom, as well as peace "with a fair share in their country's resources and an equal say in how they are governed" (Beetham et al., 2008, p. 17).

Nigeria has been in the news and has been notoriously known for years for electoral fraud or malpractice with relative political violence that marked her 50-plus years of political history and independence (Olaniyan & Amao, 2015; Lawal, 2015; Casimir et al., 2013; Bariledum, 2013; and Awopeju, 2011). In a joint Foreword to their *Final Report*, President Carter and Mr. Wollack (of the National Democratic Institute for International Affairs) were in agreement that:

> Nigeria is a nation of vast natural and human resources. It is also a nation of greatly unrealized potential, plagued for decades of financial mismanagement, widespread corruption, and explosive ethnic tensions. Successive military and civilian governments have plundered the public coffers and allowed the nation's infrastructure and productive capacity to fall apart (1999, p. 8).

But, by 1998, following the death of General Sani Abacha, which has been dogged "a coup from heaven," we learned that Nigerians deeply "hungered for change" with "a fervent desire to elect a civilian president and live under a new democratic system of government dominated the aspirations of nearly all Nigerians" (Carter & Wollack, 1999, p. 8). On Feb. 27, 1999, Nigerians held their first post-military presidential election in which the retired General Olusegun Obasanjo was elected. His successful election would signify "the culmination of a political transition to install democratically elected civilian officials at all levels of government." It also "represents a landmark opportunity for Nigeria. The transition from military to civilian rule was conducted generally without violence … However, the registration process and all four election rounds were marred, to varying degrees, by electoral irregularities, and sometimes, outright fraud" (pp. 8-9). The use of innovative election technology via the Internet, Smartphones, or electronic voting (to help verify the voter identification and eligibility, compile voter lists, cast and record votes, count votes, and announce/publish the election results) in Nigeria or anywhere else in Africa, would increase voter participation and make it easier and more convenient for people to vote without having to go to the polling stations or stand in long lines for hours to cast their votes. It would help to improve the electoral process and reduce the possibility of fraud and rigging. The use of new and innovative technology in the conduct of political elections (particularly for casting, recording, and counting votes) in Nigeria, I would like to say would:

> … have the potential to increase voter turnout, make it easier to involve citizens living abroad, lower election administration costs, facilitate the conduct of simultaneous elections, reduce human error (including invalid ballots), improve the accuracy of counting, and increase the speed of tabulation and publication

of results ... may also have the potential to increase access for voters with disabilities and voters who speak minority languages (Handbook, 2013, p. 5).

In the long run, it may create the necessary condition that ensures electoral justice with both transparency and integrity. Electoral integrity is simply about having and conducting a transparent election that meets international democratic principles or standards in conformity with the best practices for credible, open, safe, secure, and free elections. The new election technology should be a form of paperless election that could be done with the use of a touch screen or push-button device, or by Internet voting that allows the eligible citizen-voter to vote electronically at anytime and from anywhere with the right access code or password.

POST-INDEPENDENCE MILITARY POLITICS AND DICTATORSHIPS IN NIGERIA (1966-1999)

Democracy is a system of values, rules and principles. It is a certain kind of government that is constituted of, by, and for the people. Democratic government is a unique political system where the people (as responsible citizens and eligible voters) are indirectly involved in the affairs of their own government, and periodically vote in elections to elect new leaders who will serve as their official representatives. The unique aspects of modern democratic and representative governments are the values of individual liberty or freedom, equality of opportunities under the law, political order and justice, and deliberation and consent of the governed for their collective good and general well-being.

Nigeria, as a political entity, was created or designed by the British administrators in 1914, for all kinds of reasons. But since then to probably 1999, Nigerians have yet to enjoy the basic rights of freedom and equality. The people were never consulted, nor did they have any voice in, or consent to, the political creation that became Nigeria, by Lord Frederick Lugard. It was Ms. Flora Louise Shaw (his mistress and later Lady Lugard) who was credited for giving the country a name ("Nigeria" to signify the diverse ethnic groups living around the great River Niger area). So from Nigeria's political birth in 1914, Nigerians have lived under undemocratic and authoritarian administration, and the colonial British government and administrators found creative ways to both repress and oppress the people until independence in October of 1960.

Within three years after her political independence, Nigeria became a federal republic with President Benjamin Nnamdi Azikiwe (the country's first elected president) and Prime Minister Abubakar Tafawa Balewa. Both men were two great national political leaders and they served from October 1, 1963 until January 16, 1966. But before the people could begin to enjoy the fruits of their new democratic government, which was founded on the principle of self-rule or self-determination, their country suffered its bloody military coup d'état on January 15, 1966, led by Major Chukwuma K. Njeogwu, Major Emmanuel Ifeajuna, and others. Sadly, this tragic experience became an unfortunate beginning of military intervention in Nigerian politics, and the late Major General Aguiyi-Ironsi be-came the first military Head of State. This was followed by yet another bloody military coup that brought the young General Yakubu Gown to power at the national level, followed immediately by the bloody Nigerian-Biafran Civil War (of 1967-1970) in which innocent Nigerian citizens (mostly children and wom-en) lost their precious lives for no just cause. With that unnecessary, most ill-advised, unfortunate, and inexcusable civil war, the Nigerian military officers (consisting of the regular Army, Navy, and the Air Force) found themselves in politics without the consent of the people nor their general will. They ruled the country with an iron fist and autocratic decrees for their "immediate effect" until May 1999, when General Abdulsalam Abubakar, as the last military leader who succeeded the late General Sani Abacha in 1998, transferred national political power to President Olusegun Obasanjo, the former military dictator who ran under the Peoples' Democratic Party. President Obasanjo, as a democratically elected leader, was duly sworn in on May 29, 1999 as both the president and head of state of the Federal Republic of Nigeria (since the military, under Gen-eral Muhammadu Buhari, overthrew President Shehu Shagari, on December 31, 1983).

In all of these years of military rule and dictatorship, democracy remained elusive to Nigerians in that rich and prosperous African country. And all these years, Nigerians wanted to be free and hungered for the opportunity to embrace democracy and hold elections through which they could begin to build on and consolidate their democratic gains.

In 1979, Nigerians elected Alhaji Shehu Usman Alihu Shagari (of the Na-tional Party of Nigeria, NPP) as the president with Chief Dr. Alex Ifeanyichuk-wu Ekwueme as vice president, and they succeeded General Olusegun Obasanjo (who ruled after the assassination of General Murtala Ramat Muhammed, from 1976 to 1979). After the re-election of President Shagari in August 1983, in an election that was considered to be plagued with widespread vote rigging and political violence (Falola & Ihonvbere, 1985), Major General Muhammadu Bu-hari took over power as the leader of the new military government following a military coup, with Major General Tunde Idiagbon as the second-in-command. President Buhari served as the Nigerian head of state from December 31, 1983 to August 27, 1985. He was overthrown in a somewhat bloodless military coup led by General Ibrahim Badamasi Babangida (also known as "IBB") on August 27, 1985, who thereafter ruled Nigeria until August 27, 1993). It will be ac-knowledged that President Babangida's administration was corrupt and respon-sible for the creation of the country's endemic culture of political corruption (Diamond, Kirk-Green & Oydeiran, 1997).

President Babangida was succeeded by Chief Ernest Adegunle Oladeinde Shonekan, who served as a transitional interim president of Nigeria (from Au-gust 26 to November 17, 1993), and it was he who was overthrown or undemo-cratically replaced by General Sani Abacha on November 17, 1993. He ruled with sheer force of brute power until June 8, 1998. Although Abacha's adminis-tration was remarkable for its economic achievements, it was notorious for human rights violations and abuses (an example is the execution of Ken Saro Wi-wa, on November 10, 1995), coupled with high-tech political corruption and looting (Lewis, 2007; Pieth, 2008). Falola stated that "Abacha was to become the country's worst dictator yet and the most brazenly corrupt and cruel. Under his regime, Nigeria's foreign policy was in shambles, the country became a pariah state, and living standards reached their lowest level during the twentieth century" (1999, p. 196).

In comparison, Abacha's political administration was worse than that of President Ibrahim Babangida, because all throughout his term he displayed a "reign of terror" and injudiciously "concentrated power in himself ... and successfully turned the government into a repressive machine" (pp. 196-197). Interestingly, he died of an unexplained circumstance, which was celebrated by people all over the world as a moment for new leadership and political change in Nigeria. Since his death (which was God's divine coup against poverty of leadership and human callousness), the Nigerian government has been making efforts to recover the billions or millions of funds (in different currencies) stolen, and national assets looted from the Nigerian treasury under Abacha's administration.

General Abdulsalami Abubakar, who succeeded General Sani Abacha, served as the interim or transitional president of Nigeria from June 9, 1998 to May 29, 1999. If nothing else, it should be a matter of historic record that some good things happened under his brief presidency. President Abubakar was gracious in releasing many political prisoners and dropped their charges, dismantled the Abacha's Presidential Task Force, and demonstrated keen interest in the effort to embrace the transition toward democratization in Nigeria (from years of military dictatorship to a more democratic political system where citizens would have the right to participate in politics and vote in elections). It seemed that "Abacha's death provided the West with the opportunity to help rebuild relations with Nigeria" and immediately "Britain, the United States, and other countries called for a stable transition to democracy and a government that would restore and respect human rights" (Falola, 1999, pp. 212-213). There was a coordinated international effort, led by the United Nations, to reintegrate Nigeria into the family and community of nations working to promote global peace, political stability, and real economic development. In addition, President Abubakar (somewhat to his credit) laid the foundation to end military politics in Nigeria, and he fully "accepted the nation's desire for democracy and acknowledged that previous efforts had been marred by the manipulation of political institutions, actors, and structures" (p. 215). He, unlike other military leaders before him, appeared to have been committed to holding political elections and for the transfer of political power to a democratically elected president. To achieve this particular goal for Nigeria, and move the country in the right direction in preparation for this historic transition and democratization, President Abubakar did the following: (a) re-established the Independent National Electoral Commission (INEC) with the immediate appointment of the former Supreme Court Justice Ephraim Akpata (to serve as chair); and (b) pushed for adopting the Nigerian

Constitution on May 5, 1999, which would enable President Olusegun Obasanjo to assume the presidency and govern in earnest. History will have its favorable judgment on him because of his historic effort and leadership to push for democratic transition and an end to military politics in Nigeria. President Abubakar was remarkable in his singular effort and bold leadership in discouraging the military from active political life because, according to Falola, "the military was not good for Nigeria" and he challenged future Nigerian "aspiring politicians to govern well and resolve not to involve the army in settling their disputes" (p. 215).

The Independent National Election Commission (INEC) hit the ground running by quickly organizing and coordinating several democratic political elections (at the local, state, and national levels) in 1998, with that of the president held on February 27, 1999. The retired General Olusegun Obasanjo won, and became the first elected two-term civilian president of Nigeria (from May 29, 1999 through May 29, 2007). President Obasanjo was succeeded by President Umaru Yar'Adua of the Peoples' Democratic Party on May 29, 2007 through May 5, 2010; he too was succeeded by his vice president, President Goodluck Jonathan (on May 6, 2010) who ruled Nigeria until May 29, 2015. Then the current President Muhammadu Buhari (of the All Progressive Congress) defeated President Jonathan in the 2015 general elections and took over political power on May 29, 2015. The election of 2015, between President Muhammadu Buhari and the former President Goodluck Jonathan, was the fifth of such national elections since the end of military politics in 1999 in which eligible Nigerians had the opportunity to participate in what has been considered a "credible" election, and in which (for the first time in Nigeria's political history) an opposition party candidate was able to defeat and unseat an incumbent president with over 2.5 million votes.

This general election was initially scheduled for February 14, 2015, but the INEC later changed the date to March 28, 2015 (which was six weeks after). The reasons were the poor distribution of the new national Permanent Voter ID Cards and also to enable the military (under President Jonathan) to contain the Boko Haram insurgency in some parts of the North (Buchanan, February 2015). But prior to the 1999 democratic transition, the military had been active and involved in Nigerian politics since 1966, and the country has since these number of years been subjected to military dictatorship as follows: 1966-1979 (from the first bloody coup through the Nigerian-Biafran Civil War to a period of peace and the oil boom), 1983-1989, 1989-1993 (with restricted democratic activities), 1993-1998, and 1998-1999 (which was itself a short period of transition that witnessed the formation of nine new political parties and many local elections).

Since 1999, Nigerians have been taking steps to build a united and democratic government with a free market system and sustainable development that will be rooted on both political and economic freedom, while instituting a new democratic government of, by, and for the people, that will respect the peoples' freedom in its exercise of political power and authority.

TRANSITION TO REPRESENTATIVE DEMOCRACY
VIA CREDIBLE ELECTIONS

From 1999 to the present, Nigerians have been learning how best to build a representative democratic government under democratically elected civilian leaders. Democracy is a unique system of government based on majority consensus (simple majority) and the rule of law, and it is such a political system that allows the people (as citizens) to periodically call for and hold open, free, credible, and fair elections. It is only during elections, rather than with bloody military coups or violent political revolutions, that people (as citizens who are eligible to vote) exercise their fundamental right by participating in political elections and vote to elect the leaders from the poll of competing individuals or opposing political parties.

The general election of 1999 was filled with unspeakable fraudulent tactics and irregularities to the degree that most "international observers concluded that the election in fact had been tainted," but "since both parties engaged in electoral fraud, it is hard to know the extent to which the outcome reflects a popular mandate or whether the outcome would have been substantially different" (Falola, 1999, p. 221). Nigerians have a serious problem with conducting the kind of elections that will meet international standards, and not just holding elections for sake of appearance and empty optics. Election is a serious national business for the sake of seeking and obtaining political power by leaders, and should be designed and managed by responsible professionals and caring Nigerians to enable eligible citizens to elect their leaders with the goal of promoting national progress and political development. Elections give the citizens the power to elect or un-elect leaders, to create viable political institutions, and elect leaders who will lead and serve them. In order for elections to have integrity and bring about the desired positive results in the collective interest, leaders and INEC officials must be credible and accountable, as well as be disciplined enough to manage every electoral process with honesty and professionalism for people to have trust and faith in their political system. In one essay it is stated that holding credible elections with integrity and justice, as Stedman et al. would have it, can yield other tangible benefits for citizens, such as "... empowering women, fighting corrupting, delivering services to the poor, improving governance, and ... develop economies, create good governance, or make peace ... be a catalytic step towards realizing democracy's transformative potential" (September 2012, p. 5). In this regard, Larry Diamond (2004) gave a concise overview of the basic elements that underlie a democracy and which, for him, makes democracy a unique form of government through which the people deliberate in the public square and reach important decisions that shape their political destiny. These are based on:

   a. choosing and replacing the government through free and fair elections
   b. the active participation of the people, as citizens, in politics and civic life

c.   the protection of the human rights of all citizens
d.   a rule of law, in which the laws and procedures apply equally to all citizens

Two things stand out in his explication of democracy, and these are that democracy is a political system for choosing and replacing the government through free and fair elections, and active participation of the people in the political/electoral processes is required. Democracy is a system that encourages the citizens to become actively engaged and participate in the political processes as a matter of both moral obligation and civic responsibility, and one way that they can do this, short of military coup or political revolution, is by credible, safe, secure, free, and fair elections. It is explicit that democracy, which at times may be messy and disorderly, is a system of competing ideas and interests in the quest for power and legitimacy. Since the people are the ultimate authority with sovereign political power, interested political candidates must subject themselves to the rigors of free, open, credible, and fair elections through which, as Diamond added, the people can be allowed to make critical decisions in "choosing and replacing the government" as part of the requirements in that type of constitutional or representative democracy.

Nigeria, which is Africa's most populous country, with close to 183 million people, has become the continent's largest market economy (in 2014), and has recently conducted a nonviolent, national, political election (March 29 – 31, 2015) that was followed by an equally peaceful transition and transfer of power from the outgoing President Goodluck Ebele Jonathan to the incoming President Muhammad Buhari. President Buhari (at 72 years) assumed the office on May 29, 2015, and this will be his second after the tradition set by President Obasanjo (the first time was as military dictator, the 7th Head of State). It is interesting to note that President Buhari, who described himself as a "converted democrat" and the shining hope for the country (as an authentic and incorruptible leader that Nigeria never had), will not falter in the collective effort to make a radical change in the way that African leaders behave and/or serve their various constituents. Hopefully, he will help the country solve some of the nagging problems that emanate from political corruption, gross mismanagement of national resources, misplacement of priorities, dishonesty and poverty of political leadership, to abuse of power and fraudulent electoral practices, and now the ongoing violence and mayhem from the extremist Boko Haram's Islamist insurgency.

The transition from military politics and dictatorship to the democratization that began in 1999 with the successful democratic election of President Olusegun Obasanjo, is gainfully visible and still ongoing to the point that Nigeria can be regarded as an "emerging democracy" in Africa. As a young and growing democracy, Nigerians have begun to experience and enjoy some features inherent in a thriving democratic political system, and these are: (a) effective participation; (b) equality in voting; (c) gaining enlightened understanding; (d) exercising final control over their national agenda; and (e) inclusion of adults in the processes (Dahl, 1998, p. 38). As an emerging democracy, it is important for

Nigerians to bear in mind that democracy is the necessary condition or ingredient for development in which all those elected officials shall remain accountable to the ruled, and rule in the best interests of all the citizens. A representative form of democratic government allows and encourages citizen participation in elections and other political or electoral processes through which the qualified and able citizens of Nigeria elect their leaders via credible, safe, secure, free, and fair elections. Elections are good and help the citizens to hold their leaders in check, accountable, and to either punish or reward those who contribute to "good governance" in the service and uplifting of the people. A representative democracy is an open, public, and participatory system that encourages the elected leaders to be as responsible and responsive as they can be, and challenges the citizens to participate in the electoral processes in order to be heard and vote to elect future political leaders who are "fit to lead" and advance public interest or good. Democracy is not a blame game, but a politics of mass participation where citizens use the power of their "one vote" to make an important change for the common good. So how can citizens do that or make that change? By simply participating in politics and voting for the right or best party candidates during elections. Elections matter greatly in our modern representative government, because they allows citizens to make their choices and decisions that can transform politics and the lives of people.

TECHNOLOGY INTEGRATION IN ELECTIONS (E-VOTING) AND TRANSFORMING POLITICS IN NIGERIA

People are accomplishing all kinds of good things with media technology, and there is no justifiable reason why the INEC should not aggressively and proactively consider the adoption and implementation of appropriate innovative technologies to improve the electoral process and enhance or transform politics in Nigeria. The goal of elections, as in a democracy, is to give the citizens the opportunity to participate in politics and exercise their fundamental right in making a choice, or having a preference regarding certain issues, or electing who their leaders should be. There are election technologies that citizens in Nigeria can effectively use in making those political choices and decisions, and essentially use to cast and count their votes with great ease and convenience. Some of the election or voting technologies to be considered, which are relatively innovative and effective tools designed to improve how people (in Africa or in other parts of the world) elect their future leaders, are the electronic voting systems, which include the following: voter registration identification cards, electronic voters' list, electronic recording of votes cast, electronic counting machine, and the electronic publication or announcement of the overall election results.

Electronic voting, or simply e-voting[3] can help the people solve many of the election problems, because it is an innovative and convenient way for the people to cast their votes electronically with the use or mediation of specific technologies. It has been introduced and used in many different countries such as Belgium, Brazil, Estonia, France, India, some parts of the United States, and Venezuela. Discussion has focused on the different electronic voting areas: casting votes, recording the votes, and counting the votes cast by the citizens. The electronic type of voting can ensure that more people will have the opportunity to participate in elections, be able to cast their votes for their own party candidates, and enables the INEC to electronically record and count the votes cast by eligible citizens (with the proper access code), with the election results published or announced electronically with a minimum of human interaction and/or error.

This is both an information age and the era of digital revolution, with most people all over the world doing significant and wonderful things electronically via the use of computers (or mobile devices) and Internet technology. Nigerians, because of their long history of election fraud and electoral irregularities, should be encouraged to explore the possibility of using electronic voting as a way to hold elections that have justice and integrity. Depending on the particular electronic voting system to be considered and adopted, the INEC can opt for and implement (with certain specifications) the: (a) Direct Recording Electronic voting system (DRE); (b) Optical Mark Recognition (OMR); (c) Electronic Ballot Printer (EBP); or (d) the Internet Voting System (IVS) (Wolf, 2011, pp. 10-11). With such systems, Nigerians can be trained to alternate by voting in either a controlled environment (by voting at the polling places) and using any of the electronic voting systems: punch card, optical scanning, or direct recording. But they can also vote in an uncontrolled environment by casting their votes, from anywhere (from the convenience of their offices, homes or while in transit) and at any possible time within the day, on the slated election day, with the Internet technology.

Some countries (Belgium, Brazil, Germany, India, Netherlands, Venezuela, Switzerland, and the United States of America), since the 1960s, have in some ways used or tried the various electronic voting models. It is urgent that the Independent National Election Commission (INEC) explores and conducts the feasibility studies to determine the possibility of adopting and implementing appropriate electronic voting technology that will be relevant, functional, and easy for most Nigerians to use for the purpose of enhancing elections, achieving electoral integrity, and transforming politics.

Before recommending and adopting any type of electronic voting system, it is advisable that the INEC officials should carefully review and consider certain basic requirements for each system. People vote in democratic elections to elect qualified leaders and representatives, and any election technology adopted and used must be geared toward that one goal and to make it possible, or even easier, to do so. They do so to exercise their right to vote, knowing that they have the freedom and secrecy to vote without duress via secret ballot, and that any new election or voting technology would not be used to undermine that basic right. So in recommending and designing any new, innovative electronic voting technology, it will be prudent and highly expected that the INEC officials endeavor to conduct trials and educate the Nigerian public about how they can effectively use such an election tools to cast their votes with ease and deliberate speed. Developing and instituting a dysfunctional election technology should not be advised and encouraged, because it could have a disastrous political outcome. The goal of using the INEC's approved and adopted PVC technology (Chinese-made) was to help reduce electoral fraud. Some Nigerians believed or suggested that it was helpful and easy for them, and thus it made the difference in that election, although some eligible voters were prevented from casting their votes. However, the use of the Permanent Voter Card (with its ancillary biometric reader), which the INEC began to roll out in 2012, worked.

Any introduction and adoption of any new, innovative election or voting technology in Nigeria would need careful planning and gradual implementation, with a massive voter-education campaign, in order for it to be successful and efficient. The PVC and its biometric component helps to read voters' names or identify pictures, and also authenticates their fingerprints. The use of such new election technology will not only be made lawful, useful, and transparent, but will create the necessary conditions for the voters to begin to develop trust that no one will doctor or manipulate the results.

For new election or voting technology to be accepted and successful, there is also the need for the INEC to work with the masses of the Nigerian public or the electorate many months before the particular election, to educate and inform the people about the technology and its functions or operations in order to assure and sustain public satisfaction. Nigerians, following the outcome of the peaceful 2015 general election in Nigeria that brought the All Progress Congress (APC) and President Buhari to power, seemed overwhelmed with joy and hope for a better Nigeria; and most of them were satisfied with the PVC and expressed relief or positive responses that the election was relatively better than those held in the past, and was somewhat fair with the desired justice and integrity. Future elections in Nigeria will be even better and more promising, when the citizens will have to use election or voting technology to cast their votes. Then the INEC will automatically and electronically count their votes and also announce/publish the election results without human inference, deliberate rigging of the electoral process, and manipulation of results for narrow personal or party goals. Incidents of vote buying, stuffing of the ballot boxes, going to and standing in long lines at the voting stations (for long hours), intimidation by some election staff members at the polling places, etc., could be minimized or become non-existent when qualified citizens vote electronically (with their Smartphones, etc.).

Political elections would need to be carefully managed by competent professionals who, as a matter of urgency and requirement, must ensure that the elections are credible, fair, and transparent. They must also equally support the competing political party candidates, and demonstrate keen interest in what it is that they do for the nation to ensure electoral justice and integrity. The INEC officials must display competence and professionalism in managing elections, assure the citizens that political elections meet the international standards/principles, and show commitment in monitoring the electoral activities of everyone without favor or malice in their willingness to count and publish/announce the election outcomes without doctoring the results.

Wolf et al. hinted that many countries are currently considering introducing e-voting systems with the aim of improving various aspects of the electoral process, and e-voting has become a necessary tool for advancing democracy, building trust in electoral management, adding credibility to election results, and increasing the overall efficiency of the electoral process (2010, p. 6). One advantage of electronic voting is "to eliminate certain avenues of fraud, speed up the processing of results, increase accessibility and make voting more convenient for citizens" (p. 6).

In most places, citizens who vote must register based on meeting certain requirements with their identification to establish and authenticate their identities and eligibility. Countries have voter requirements that each citizen, in order to vote, must meet in terms of place or country of birth and age (18 years of age or above). Therefore, the voter must be able to establish the basic voter requirement and obtain voter identification. To vote in elections, the potential voters must have the proper identifications and register to vote. When applying for voter registration, the voter must complete the necessary form with proof of eligibility and provide authentic documents. This personal information is stored in a national database and should be readily available to election officials whenever needed. Scanning technology and digitized voter photographs can be used to capture and store the images (as signatures and photographs) of the voter, which the election officials will easily access for visual comparison or to help in determining any possibility of error and/or fraud. Voter identification can be gathered and stored via a bio-identification system by either visual or electronic models. The bio-identification type uses photographs, signatures and/or finger/thumbprints on voter identity cards. Electronic bio-identification may include digitized voice, finger/thumb/handprint, and retinal images.

For every election, voter identification is crucial and will always be required. People need the voter identification to establish clearly that they are eligible to participate in the process, meet the requirements, and have the right to vote. It will make sense if, at the time of or during the election period, the voter will be able to authenticate his/her identification electronically and can vote from anywhere, such as with Internet technology. So the INEC would need to design an automated system where the citizens' data is digitized or computerized and can be accessed or verified electronically. With this electronic type of voting, eligible citizens should be able to cast their votes, have the votes recorded and counted, and the voting/election results published/announced, all electronically.

What are some of the strengths and advantages of resorting to electronic voting? According to Wolf, countries opt for the e-voting system for the following reasons:

a. faster vote count and tabulation
b. more accurate results, as human error is excluded
c. efficient handling of complicated electoral systems formulae that require laborious procedures

d.   improved presentation of complicated ballot papers
e.   increased convenience for voters
f.   potentially increased participation and turnout, particularly with the use of Internet voting
g.   more attuned to the needs of an increasingly mobile society
h.   prevention of fraud in polling stations, and during the transmission and tabulation of results by reducing human intervention
i.   increased accessibility, for example, by audio ballot papers for blind voters, with Internet voting as well for housebound voters and voters from abroad
j.   possibility of multilingual user interfaces that can serve a multilingual electorate better than paper ballots; potential long-term cost savings through savings in poll worker time, and reduced costs for the production and distribution of ballot papers
k.   cost savings by using Internet voting; no shipment costs, no delays in sending out material and receiving it back…(2010, p. 8).

These are important highlights pointing out why electronic voting is advised and encouraged in countries like Nigeria, if her rich political history and years of fraudulent electoral irregularities and other election malpractices serve as a lesson. Most people now do online banking and transact businesses worth millions of naira or dollars via their computers, Smartphones, and the Internet. Nigerians can, in this day and age, engage in politics by participating in political elections, and use the designated election or voting technology to cast their votes. Doing so will obviously, and with the best of intentions, minimize the tendency of bribing people and buying votes, and will cut down on ballot stuffing and blatant rigging of the elections through fraudulent practices or mere human error. Everyone agrees with Wolf et al., that "the advantages of e-voting listed may only be among the reasons why an EMB considers the introduction of this technology" and "considerations such as the faster processing of results, the prevention of fraud and the provisions of a better service to voters are often high priorities" (2010, p. 15).

In adopting and implementing electronic voting technology, it is advised that the INEC (as the election management board) should pay careful attention to the established international "guiding principles" with focus on achieving the set desired goals based on building trust and confidence, transparency, and efficiency, and increasing voter turnout in the spread of democracy in Nigeria or in Africa.

Election is one of the most important ways that individuals, in normal circumstances, who happen to be citizens, from time to time endeavor to come together in order to participate in representative democratic politics. In or during elections, individuals vote for candidates of their choice in terms of who can truly represent, advance their common interests, and serve them with integrity and commitment. So "the most common act of individual participation in politics is to vote" (Lawson, 2003, p. 139). And the use of election and voting technology in elections (like the one that Nigerians had in 2015 between President Jonathan and President Buhari) will enhance this process and promote the experience of Nigerians becoming more active in politics in ways that would enable them to own that process.

Jahan et al., in the *Human Development Report 2015*, noted that the technological revolution has transformed the types of work that people do and the way they carry out tasks to foster positive outcomes for people's well-being (2015, p. 80). Technology, in its various forms and at different stages, has continued to evolve from steam, to electricity, and now to the widespread use of computers and Internet connectivity. Upon close examination, reasonable or intelligent people can agree that there is something to cherish about this ongoing technological revolution. What's more, it has this inherent potential "to vastly improve people's lives" and thereby "reshape the fabric of societies and revolutionize work" (Jahan, p. 80). So this is a moment in time for Nigerians (and Africans) to embrace the use of new and innovative election or voting technology, and also to quickly learn how to use it to: (a) build the necessary infrastructure and human capabilities; and (b) take advantage of the ample opportunities that it presents in order to improve not only how people now work, but how to effectively use it to elect credible or more qualified future political leaders in ways destined to transform politics and increase participation in the political/electoral processes.

Within the state, as a necessary political association or moral community, there are the underlying forces that conspire to make for a political life, and these are social and religious institutions, cultural norms and values, prevailing attitudes and ideologies, and economic conditions. Ethridge and Handelman noted that political decisions within and among nations will largely determine whether the future is one of expanding progress, prosperity, peace, and an improved quality of life, or one of escalating war, worsening economic conditions, and tyranny (2015). They added, somewhat in passing, that "the way governments work, or fail to work, has tremendous effects on all of us" (p. 3).

Government affects everything that people do, from the point of birth to death, for good or bad, and that is why politics has been considered to be the master science that informs, shapes, and influences the meaningful allocation of limited or scarce resources and the distribution of wealth in most communities. People, as responsible citizens and political participants, have the urgent need to participate fully in politics in order to help their elected officials, representatives, and leaders deliberate on issues of great consequence in their lives. They must join them in reaching very important decisions that will forever have a pancosmic effect on everyone within that given political community, state, or nation. In this regard, politics has been defined as "the process of making collective decisions in a community, society, or group through the application of influence and power" (p. 7). What that means is that government, despite its various political forms with interrelated institutions and functions, "consists of the people or organizations that make, enforce, and implement political decisions for a society" (p. 8). One sure way that people, as informed and eligible citizens, participate in politics or in the political process to shape and influence the destiny of their nation is through credible elections.

One sure way to transform politics in Africa, mobilize and encourage citizens to participate in democrat politics, and for the people to take an active part in deciding on the issues of great social and moral consequence to them and their families (or communities) is through civic engagement and participation in political elections. Elections must be open, free, and fair to allow the people (as citizens) to exercise their basic rights and be heard. Voting in elections is both a civic duty and political responsibility, and it appears to be a simple political act that is in fact not all that easy or simple. What happens during most elections is that, for all kinds of personal or political reasons, people do not vote; or those who vote may not vote correctly. High voter participation is critical in order for a democracy to thrive, because "democracies offer citizens opportunities to participate in their own governance" and "in democracies, the people elect their own leaders" (Rosenstone & Hansen, 1993, p. 1). In most democracies, the people do not vote and the voter turnout is always very low, as many eligible citizens do not register to vote or fail to go to the polling stations to stand in lines for long hours.

There may be justifiable reasons to explain the factors for low voter turnout during elections, but having the right election or voting technology for people to use seems to be the panacea to increase active participation and voter turnout in political elections. The problem is not with elections, particularly in Nigeria, and is not that the citizens do not vote, because they do; the problem has do with the almost acceptable attitude of widespread electoral fraud and rigging, which technology can help stop. Ibukun reported that "Nigeria's electoral commission says that it has found a means to fight fraud that has marred votes repeatedly in Africa's most populous nation: technology... all of the previous elections were marred by ballot stuffing, multiple and underage voting, and falsification of figures—according to local and international monitors" (March 2015, p. 1). This is why this essay calls for the introduction and use of a targeted new and innovating election or voting technology (in the form of the electronic voting or e-voting) that the people can use as a necessary tool for voting in their elections, and which should, for all intents and purposes, be aimed at making the electoral process more efficient, transparent, and time-saving.

Teich informed us that technology is more than just machines, and would approach it as something that is a pervasive, complex system whose cultural, social, political, and intellectual elements are manifest in virtually every aspect of our lives (2009). We must be cognizant of any counterargument that technology is possibly dangerous, and as such is antithetical to human good. Postman, in his *Technopoly: The Surrender of Culture to Technology*, remarked that "there is a dark side to this friend. Its gifts are not without a heavy cost." He noted that "an accusation can be made that the uncontrolled growth of technology destroys the vital sources of our humanity" (1993, p. xii). And he added that technology enables people to create a culture that undermines human attainment of the good life worthy of our existence, and consequently is "a particularly dangerous enemy."

Postman's forceful argument notwithstanding, we have to come to terms with the fact that technology is something medicinal (that is both good and bad) and have to agree with Arthur that it should be used carefully and creatively as a necessary tool or unique "means to fulfill a human purpose" (2009, p. 28). By advocating for electronic voting technology and/or systems, the author is aware that such a technology can be used by eligible citizens to cast their votes, record those votes, and in counting votes by the INEC; and that the voters can have the option of using it at the polling places or via the Internet or with their Smartphones outside of the voting stations. It is interesting that it offers voters many options, but the good thing is:

> These technologies have the potential to facilitate and improve electoral processes and are adopted for a number of reasons. These include the perceived advantages in increased voter access, the possibility of decreased costs... facilitation of the conduct of simultaneous or complex elections, earlier announcement of results, potentially fewer opportunities for retail fraud, and fewer errors by voters and poll workers (Carter Center Handbook on Observing E-Voting, January 2012, p. 1).

Nigerians, like people everywhere in the world, should not surrender nor succumb to technology, but must learn how to adapt and use it as an important device designed to enable them improve the quality of their human condition and with which to achieve some level of efficiency and trust in the electoral system. Nigerians have great mistrust and misgiving about the corrupt political system and their "unelected" selected leaders, and this was partly because of their years of having dishonest and untrustworthy politicians and ruthless military dictators (once known as "harvest of thieves") which they inherited from rigged elections and/or military coups. It is hoped that in selecting and adopting a new and innovative election or voting technology (to improve electoral outcomes and bring about electoral justice with electoral integrity), that careful and well-thought-out consideration by the INEC officials will be in order and most expected, for any effort to secure and implement the wrong or inappropriate technology for the country may have serious risks and consequences that could certainly undermine the basic rights of the people—and by so doing, subvert their will to elect competent political leaders of their own preference.

Human existence has evolved to the point that it has become intertwined with various aspects of innovative technologies, and what is true now is that one cannot lead a good and quality life without the mediation of technology. But this does not mean nor imply that human beings have surrendered to the control of technology, as Postman would put it. Instead, Bain rightly noted that technology is the most important single factor that affects everything, and is so pervasive that everything else (values, morals, manners, wishes, hopes, fears, and attitudes) seems directly or indirectly dependent upon it and is being mediated by it (1937, p. 860).

Technology has enabled us to re-create ourselves or manipulate our lives, and its use has enhanced the quality of human life. Moving on, we have to ask whether electronic voting is possible in Nigeria, and also if the INEC can effectively manage to use it to reduce fraudulent electoral activities.

The author, in this chapter, has tried to argue that Nigerians can do well in politics (elect credible and qualified as competent candidates) and in elections, if the INEC and national leaders can decide to integrate new and innovative technology (particularly election, or more specifically, voting) in the elections (national, state, and local), and if Nigerians could resort to electronic voting or e-voting (Wu et al., 2014) for its inherent benefits. Election or voting technology will surely have an impact when used to facilitate and improve electoral processes and politics in Nigeria, and the INEC would need to conduct a clear, thorough, need-based evaluation to determine the path forward to ensure that future political elections are transparent, credible, inclusive (of those with mental disabilities and/or physical challenges), efficient, and that electoral justice is achieved with integrity.

Election or voting technology, as one aspect of this emerging technology, may not be the answer to the nation's political and economic problems, as well as its leadership challenges, but it is something that can reduce the tendency of widespread, fraudulent election practices with careful planning and steady implementation. This means that the INEC officials must be ready to lead the way for change and manage its impact, be willing to help Nigerians stop rigging and buying votes during political elections, act as true election professionals, and work with all the stakeholders in the country to ensure a successful transition. The INEC officials also must be able to develop strategies for the education of the masses of ordinary citizens, allow ample time for people to learn the new election system, and not start too late to engage in public campaigns to ensure that people have a reasonable expectation of what they need to do, and provide the staff members and field personnel with sufficient training and information to be both responsible and responsive to the people during the election period.

Electronic voting (as an innovative information communication technology), in the final analysis, should be considered and adopted as a way to improve political elections in Nigeria with the hope that, if adopted and implemented by the INEC, it will foster the necessary condition for public trust, promote the spread of participatory democracy, and minimize electoral fraudulent activities and associated political violence that may threaten national unity and political stability.

One critical element in elections is the importance of "accuracy." Accuracy, in political elections, has to do with the credibility of the particular election with respect to having an updated electronic voters' list, record of accurate votes cast, that the votes were counted and recorded with precision and clarity without doctoring of numbers or figures, and also that the election outcome (in the form of total results) was published and/or announced without ambiguity or confusion. If voters voted free and without duress, and there is accuracy in everything else, then the election could be considered fair and transparent, and that is what the adoption and specific use of any election or voting technology could help to achieve. Therefore, this essay favors electronic technology for e-voting operations via technology integration in political elections, to modernize and strengthen the electoral processes, transform the nature of democratic elections and politics in Nigeria, and ensure more transparent and credible elections, which will be reduce widespread electoral fraud and political violence of the past.

CONCLUSION

Some of the benefits or advantages of electronic voting, if considered and adopted by the Independent National Election Commission (INEC), clearly outweigh the demerits. People do all kinds of things with technology, and such innovative technology can also be applied to elections and voting to help create trust and confidence in the system, as well as reduce the tendency of election fraud or human error. The use of election technology notwithstanding, to have credible elections in Nigeria and overcome fraudulent activities, the INEC (as a trusted national electoral management body) has to remain totally independent and be able to demonstrate the features of "impartiality, integrity, transparency, efficiency, professionalism and service-mindedness as guiding principles" (Wolf et al, 2010, p. 17). In the final analysis, it is imperative to choose the right election and/or voting technology that will help the country and the INEC address certain problems associated with lack of voter turnout, rigging of elections, counting and announcing election results or outcomes accurately, and how to be cost-effective in the conduct of elections.

Nigeria remains a prosperous African country with ample human capacity endowment and a wealth of natural resources. It is the largest market-driven capitalist economy in Africa, with the largest population, but has, since her political independence, always been a nation in search of her destiny. She is also in transition toward a democratic consolidation. The country has—since 1960 to 1999, and from 1999 to probably May of 2015—not yet arrived at her political destination for the citizens to begin to fully enjoy the blessings inherent in a democratic disposition and the rule of law. This is so because the "sufficient condition for the completion of a democratic transition is the holding of free and contested elections (on the basis of broadly inclusive voter eligibility)" and "no regime should be called a democracy unless its rulers govern democratically" (Linz & Stepan, 1997, p. 14).

Technology integration in political elections has to do with the use of relevant and appropriate election and/or voting technology as a means to enable Nigerians to participate in the electoral process and to vote for candidates of their own choice. Electronic voting is a new, innovative tool for elections that the people can use to elect leaders in ways that will help them manage elections effectively and minimize the possibility of human error or fraud. They can also use election technologies to build trust and confidence in the political system in their spread of democracy in the country (and in Africa). The INEC will better serve the country and advance political development if the officials and law makers give serious consideration to the idea of exploring, adopting, and implementing the use of technology (in particular, election or voting technology for e-voting) in Nigeria to deepen and strengthen democracy.

REFERENCES

Adamiak, Jacek. (2013). Handbook: For the Observation of New Voting Technologies. Warsaw, Poland: OSCE Office for Democratic Institutions and Human Rights (ODIHR), 2013.

Annan, Kofi A. (2012). Foreword (pp. 3-4). Foreword (pp. 3-4). In Stephen Stedman, Zachary Alpern, et al., Deeping Democracy: A Strategy for Improving the Integrity of Elections Worldwide- The Report of the Global Commission on Elections, Democracy and Security. Sweden: International IDEA.

Arthur, Brian W. (2009). *The Nature of Technology*. New York: Free Press.

Awopeju, Ayo. (2011). Election Rigging and the Problems of Electoral Act in Nigeria. *Afro Asian Journal of Social Science*, 2(2.4-4), 1-17.

Bain, Read (December 1937). Technology and State Government. American Sociological Review, 2(6), 860-874. Retrieved from http://www.jstor.org/stable/2084365

Bariledum, Kia. (2013). Electoral Corruption and Democratic Sustainability in Nigeria. *Journal of Humanities and Social Science,* 17(5), 42-48.

Beetham, David, Carvalho, Edzia, Landman, Todd, & Weir, Stuart. (2008). Assessing the Quality of Democracy: A Practical Guide. Sweden: International IDEA.

Buchanan, Rose Troup. (February 2015). Nigeria Delays Elections over Boko Haram Threat. *The Independent* (Saturday Online Newspaper). Retrieved from http: www. independent.co.uk/news/world/africa/nigeria-delays-elections-over-boko-hara

Carrillo, Manuel. (2014). Foreword (pp. 4-5). In Raul Cordenillo (ed.), *Improving Electoral Practices: Case Studies and Practical Approaches*. Sweden: International IDEA.

Carter, Jimmy & Wollack, Kenneth. (1991). Observing the 1998-1999 Nigerian Elections —Final Report: Special Report Series. Atlanta, Georgia & Washington, D.C.: Joint Report by the Carter Center & National Democratic Institute

Casimir, Ani, Omeh, Emma, & Ike, Chinedu. (2013). Electoral Fraud in Nigeria: A Philosophical Evaluation of the Framework of Electoral Violence. Open *Journal of Political Sciences*, 3(4), 167-174.

Cordenillo, Raul. (2014). Introduction (pp. 17-22). In Raul Cordenillo (ed.), *Improving Electoral Practices: Case Studies and Practical Approaches*. Sweden: International IDEA.

Cordenillo, Raul & Ellis, Andrew (eds.). (2012). *The Integrity of Elections: The Role of Regional Organizations*. Sweden: International Institute for Democracy & Electoral Assistance (International IDEA)

Cowen, Michael & Laakso, Liisa. (1997). An Overview of Election Studies in Africa. *The Journal of Modern African Studies* (by Cambridge University Press), 35(4), 717-744.

Dahl, Robert. (1998). *On Democracy*. New Haven, Conn.: Yale University Press.

Diamond, Larry. (2004). "What is Democracy?" This was a lecture delivered at Hilla University for Humanistic Studies, on January 21). Retrieved from http://web.Stan ford.edu/-ldiamond/irq/WhaIsDemocracy012004.htm

Diamond, Larry. (2008). *The Spirit of Democracy: The Struggle to Build Free Societies Throughout the World.* New York: Henry Holt and Company.

Diamond, Larry; Kirk-Green, Anthony & Oyediran, Oyeleye (eds.). (1997). *Transition without End: Nigerian Politics and Civil Society under Babangida.* Vintage Publishers.

Easton, David. (1965). *A Framework for Political Analysis.* Englewood Cliffs, New Jersey: Prentice Hall.

Ethridge, Marcus E. & Handelman, Howard. (2015). *Politics in a Changing World: A Comparative Introduction to Political Science.* Stamford, CT: Cengage Learning.

Falola, Toyin. (1999). *The History of Nigeria.* Westport, Conn: Greenwood Press.

Falola, Toyin & Ihonvbere, Julius O. (1985). *The Rise and Fall of Nigeria's Second Republic,* 1979-1983. Zed Books.

Fischer, Jeff. (2002). Electoral Conflict and Violence: A Strategy for Study and Prevention. IFES White Paper 2002-01. Washington, D.C.: International Foundation for Electoral Systems.

Ibukun, Yinka. (March 25, 2015). Nigeria turns to Tech to Battle Legacy of Electoral Fraud. Bloomberg News. Retrieved from http://www.bloomberg.com/news/articles /2015-03-25/nigeriagy-to-battle-legacy-of-electoral-fraud.

Jahan, Selim et al. (2015). Human Development Report 2015: Work for Human Development. New York: United Nations Development Programme (UNDP).

Kwache, Peter Zakawa. (2007). The Imperatives of Information and Communication Technology for Teachers in Nigeria Higher Education. Merlot-Journal of Online Learning & Teaching, 3(4), 395-399.

Lasswell, Harold Dwight. (1936). *Politics: Who Gets What, When, How.* New York: Whittlesey House/McGraw-Hill Co.

Lawal, Salahu Mohammed. (2015). An Appraisal of Corruption in the Nigerian Electoral System. *European Scientific Journal,* 11(25), pp. 256-273.

Lawson, Kay. (2003). *The Human Policy:A Comparative Introduction to Political Science* (5th ed.). New York: Houghton Mifflin Company.

Lewis, Peter. (2007). *Growing Apart: Oil, Politics, and Economic Change in Indonesia and Nigeria.* Michigan: University of Michigan Press (p. 178).

Linz, Juan J. & Stepan, Alfred. (1997). Toward Consolidated Democracies (pp. 14-33). In Larry Diamond, Marc F. Plattner, Yun-han Chu & Hung-mao Tien's ed., *Consolidating the Third Wave Democracies: Themes and Perspectives.* Baltimore, MD: The John Hopkins University Press.

Obasanjo, Olusegun. (1991). "Opening Remarks: Democracy and Governance in Africa" (pp. 21-31). In Ayodele Aderinwale & Felix G. N. Mosha (eds.), Democracy and Governance in Africa, Conclusions and Papers Presented at a Conference of the Africa Leadership Forum (November 29-December 1).

Olaniyan, Azeez & Amao, Olumuyiwa Babatunde. (2015). International Affairs Forum, pp. 70-81.

Orozco-Henriquez, Jesus et al. (2010). Electoral Justice: The International IDEA Handbook. Sweden: International IDEA Pub.

Osabiya, Babatunde Joseph. (2014). Nigeria and Democratic Elections. Journal of Good Governance and Sustainable Development, 2(3), 53-64.

Pieth, Mark. (2008). Recovering Stolen Assets. New York: Peter Lang Publisher, pp. 43-44.

Postman, Neil. (1993). Technopoly: The Surrender of Culture to Technology. New York: Vintage Books-A Division of Random House, Inc.

Rosenstone, Steven J. & Hansen, John Mark. (1993). *Mobilization, Participation, and Democracy in America.* New York: MacMillan Publishing Company.

Schechter, Peter & DeLevie-Orey, Rachel. (2016, March). Foreword. In Conny B. McCormack, *Democracy Rebooted: The Future of Technology in Elections.* Washington, D.C.: Atlantic Council.

Stedman, Stephen. (2012). Executive Summary and Recommendations (pp. 5-9).

Stephen Stedman, Zachary Alpern, et al., *Deeping Democracy: A Strategy for Improving the Integrity of Elections Worldwide — The Report of the Global Commission on Elections, Democracy and Security.* Sweden: International IDEA.

Takirambudde, Peter. (2007). Nigeria: Presidential Election Marred by Fraud, Violence. New York: Human Rights Watch. Retrieved from https://www.hrw.org/news/2007/04/25/nigeria/-presidential-election

Teich, Albert H. (2009). *Technology and the Future* (11th ed.). Boston, MA: Wadsworth Cengage Learning.

Tommasoli, Massimo (ed.). (2013, September). Democracy and Development: The Role of the U.N. Discussion Paper. New York: United Nations & International Institute for Democratic & Electoral Assistance (IDEA).

Wolf, Peter, Nackerdien, Rushdi, & Tuccinardi, Domenico. (2010). Introducing Electronic Voting: Essential Considerations. Policy Paper. Sweden: International IDEA.

Wu, Zhen-Yu, Ju-Chuan Wu, Sung-Chiang Lin, & Charlotte Wang. (2014). An electronic voting mechanism for fighting bribery and coercion. *Journal of Network and Computer Applications,* 40, pp. 139-150.

ENDNOTES

1. The word here is about "security," which is fundamental to any credible and successful election. Election is an important democratic event, and governments need to assure the safety and well-being of the citizens. A secured election is having a conducive environment to enable individuals exercise their basic rights freely and where each citizen is treated fairly, respectfully, and without coercion or duress under the rule of law. Jeff Fischer defined election security as the process of protecting electoral stakeholders, information, facilities, and events (2002).

2. In Nigeria, the Independent National Electoral Commission (INEC, based on the 1999 Constitution of the Federal Republic of Nigeria) was established (in 1998, under General Abdulsalam Abubakar) to serve, organize and conduct or supervise elections to political offices in the country of all the various political parties to ensure that the processes are open, free, fair and credible at every level. The key responsibilities of INEC, as a national/permanent Election Management Body (EMB) for the country, are stated and enshrined in the 1999 Constitution (Section 15, Part 1 of the Third Schedule and also in the Electoral Act of 2010 Section 2). This information can be retrieved from the following website: http?www.inecnigeria.org/?page_id=14.

3. Electronic voting (or e-voting) is clearly one aspect of technology integration in the electoral process to increase voter turnout and participation, and even more so to make the electoral process more transparent and efficient as well as enable citizens to develop both trust and confidence in their political system. Please see Peter Wolf, Rushdi Nackerdien, and Domenico Tuccinardi (2011), *Introducing Electronic Voting: Essential Consideration Policy Paper.* Stockholm, Sweden: International IDEA. Retrieved from http://idea.int/publications/introducting-electronic-voting

Chapter 15
Transformation of Elections in Africa: A Content Analysis of Election Misconduct in Selected African Countries

Cosmas Uchenna Nwokeafor
Bowie State University

INTRODUCTION

Corruption as an election malpractice could be likened to as dishonest, illegal behavior or fraudulent conduct by those in powerful positions in government agencies and organizations, typically involving bribery. The synonyms associated with the word "corruption" include, but are not limited to, *dishonesty, unscrupulousness, double-dealing, fraud, misconduct, crime, criminality, and wrongdoing* (https://www.merriam-webster.com/dictionary). Corruption could also be defined as the process by which something, typically a word or expression, is changed from its original use or meaning to one that is regarded as erroneous or debased. Alteration, bastardization, debasement, and adulteration are typical of corruption. Corruption is an action that destroys people's trust of a system, an organization, a government or a group/individual (https://www.vocabulary.com/dictionary).

The noun *corruption* comes from the Latin word *com*, meaning "with, together" and *rumpere*, meaning "to break." Engaging in corruption can "break" or destroy someone's trustworthiness and good reputation with others. For example, news of corruption in the office of an elected officer or a high-profile staff member in an organization might result to a replacement of such an officer or staff. When you corrupt something that is pure or honest, you take away those qualities. That's why "corruption of minors" is a serious offense in our legal system (https://www.vocabulary.com/dictionary). It is the act of corrupting someone or something that has been changed from its original form, impairment of integrity, virtue, or moral principle. It is the inducement to wrong by improper or unlawful means (such as bribery), or a departure from the original or from what is pure or correct.

Malpractice, one of the constructs identified in the title of this chapter, is an improper, illegal, or negligent professional activity or treatment, especially by a medical practitioner, lawyer, or public official. Birch (2011) defined electoral malpractice as the manipulation of electoral processes and outcomes so as to substitute personal or partisan benefit for the public interest. The Merriam-Webster dictionary defines election malpractice as a dereliction of professional duty, or a failure to exercise an ordinary degree of professional skill or learning by someone rendering professional services which results in injury, loss, or damage. Malpractice could as well be likened to an injurious, negligent, or improper practice by an entrusted vendor or public servant, such as an elected official, which generally damages the credibility of the principle rules and regulations.

Birch (2011), in her Oxford Scholarship Online publication titled "Electoral Malpractice," postulates that elections ought to go a long way, in theory, toward making democracy "work," but in many contexts, they fail to embody democratic ideals because they are affected by electoral manipulation and misconduct. Focusing on the stipulations of the electoral process, Birch (2011) provides an analytic and explanatory investigation of electoral malpractice, which is understood as taking three principal forms, namely: (1) manipulation of the rules governing elections; (2) manipulation of vote preference formation and expression; and (3) manipulation of the voting process. Among these forms of electoral malpractice, Birch (2011) argues that the manipulation of electoral rules is most common, whereas the highly risky manipulation of administration is least common, and both considerably impact the process of credible elections. The manipulation of vote choice, campaign tactics and strategies, vote buying, and voter intimidation from both a theoretical and empirical perspective are considered election misconducts that almost always destabilize the way the electoral process is conducted.

FORMS OF ELECTORAL MISCONDUCT

In any democracy, apart from death and taxes, the next logical, sure phenomena are elections. Nigeria, a 1914 amalgamated entity, gained independence in 1960, became a republic in 1963, fought a civil war from 1966 to 1970, experienced coups and countercoups, returned to civil rule in 1999, but was still plagued by electoral malpractices. The amalgamation of Nigeria was a spirited attempt by British overlords to achieve administrative convenience, economic maximization, and political cohesion. The first election in Nigeria was held in September of 1922, and was a product of the Clifford Constitution, which introduced the elective principle. Political scientists and students of history, in their documentations and scholarly presentations, opined that since this first election, Nigeria has not failed to run short of electoral malpractices, as was the case with the other sampled African countries in this chapter. The ultimate question is, why are election results and census outcomes subject to great controversy in Africa? The answer is simple, as Ugwuanyi (2015) puts it: "It is all about malpractices."

Politics (Ugwuanyi, 2015) can be defined as the sum total of activities associated with the governance of a country. It is the art or science of governing an entity or a nation. An election is a formal decision-making process by which a population, people, or electorate chooses an individual or persons to hold office, and to represent them in governance. It is the single most potent opportunity provided by law for electorates to have a say in governance. In Nigeria, for instance, electoral malpractices have been a cog in the wheel of good governance. It includes but is not limited to any act by omission or commission that attempts to or in essence circumvents the electoral process to favor a person, a candidate, or party. It is any wrongdoing affecting electoral procedures, electorates, and electoral materials. According to Ugwuanyi (2015), electoral malpractices constitute of the following: (1) intimidation of voters; (2) partisanship by electoral officers; (3) underage voting and impersonation; (4) diversion of electoral materials; and (5) theft of ballot boxes.

PRIMARY MEANING OF CORRUPTION

According to the Vocabulary Dictionary, the primary meaning of corruption is the lack of integrity or honesty (especially the susceptibility to bribery); use of a position of trust for dishonest gain or moral perversion; impairment of virtue and moral principles which destroys someone's (or some group's) honesty or loyalty; undermining moral integrity; and induces such an individual (e.g., a public official) by improper means (such as bribery) to violate duty by committing a felony. Also, the action of making someone or something morally depraved.

Generally speaking, Transparency International discussed the primary meaning of corruption as "the abuse of entrusted power for private gain." Corruption can be classified as grand, petty, and political, depending on the amounts of money lost and the sector where it occurs. Grand corruption consists of acts committed at a high level of government that distort policies or the central functioning of the state, enabling leaders to benefit at the expense of the public's good. Petty corruption refers to everyday abuse of entrusted power by low- and mid-level public officials in their interactions with ordinary citizens, who often are trying to access basic goods or services in places like hospitals, schools, police departments, and other agencies. Political corruption is a manipulation of policies, institutions, rules, and procedures in the allocation of resources and finances by political decision makers who abuse their position to sustain their power, status, and wealth.

Corruption simply means the art of jeopardizing the status quo in which a person of a particular function, public or private, accepts gift offers and promises to perform, delay, or omit to do an act, directly or indirectly, as part of his/her duty. Today, corruption is a social evil that is spreading increasingly across the world—most importantly throughout the continent of Africa, where it has persistently been prevalent. In various African countries, the policy makers and the public officials are always accused of being the prime movers of corruption and corrupt practices. However, insightful analysis shows that the politicians are far more than being the primary culprits of corruption, and that the poor citizens themselves are reprehensible. Therefore, in seeking to prescribe an antidote to the evil, which is itself a component of the economic tyranny in society, we must first tackle poverty, which is considered to be a major cause of corruption—especially in the continental African nations, the second largest in the world.

PURPOSE OF STUDY

The outcome of this empirical discourse will present a scholarly position to point individuals, as well as government agencies and organizational leaders, to the appropriate framework as to the dangers of corruption. As it pertains to the political system across the world (mostly continental Africa), this research will direct attention to the corrupt practices during elections. The purpose of this chapter is to review and present strong discussions relative to the theme of the research on the transformation of elections in continental Africa, with strong argument as to how corruption and corrupt practices have hampered credible elections. In order to achieve its purpose, the chapter will discuss corruption and corrupt practices in elections in detail, and use five African countries (Nigeria, Ghana, South Africa, Kenya, and Uganda) as examples of where corrupt practices have significantly affected election campaigns, and the subsequent results. It will also show how a transformation agenda through technology could curb the corrupt practices consistently observed during elections in Africa.

SIGNIFICANCE OF THE STUDY

Treisman (1998) defined corruption as the misuse of public office for private gain. Corruption is perceived to be more widespread in some countries than others. It has been blamed for the failures of certain "developing" countries to develop, and recent empirical research has confirmed a link between higher perceived corruption and lower investment and growth. Treisman (1998) in Mauro (1995) (reported initially by World Bank 1997) noted that political scandals have sparked public outrage against political corruption in countries across the globe during the last few years, most importantly on the continent of Africa where at least one incumbent regime has been forced out of office under one corrupt election practice or the other. At the same time, corruption is viewed as one of the main obstacles that post-communist countries face in attempting to consolidate democratic institutions and open market economies (Treisman, 1998).

Looking at the purpose of this study, which is the transformation of elections in continental Africa with stronger argument as to how corruption and corrupt practices have hampered credible elections, five African countries will be showcased where corruption and corrupt practices have led to inaccurate mathematical numbers and skewed election results, which most of the time are shoved down the throats of the electorate. This study, therefore, will present a thorough empirical discourse that shows the definition of corruption and the adverse effect of corrupt practices during election campaigns in Africa. It will also provide considerable insight as to how the integration of modern technological infrastructures will bring resolution to the election malpractices that have continued to mar elections not only in those selected African nations, but the entire African continent as well.

REVIEW OF LITERATURE

This chapter examines how elections could be transformed in Africa with a review and content discussion on how technology would advance a process of minimizing corruption and all forms of malpractice during elections. The literature extrapolated supporting data and relevant publications and viewpoints of scholars of political science, politicians, and government agencies to support the claim of this study, which is: "In order to transform elections in Africa, there should be a tendency to rid corruption in the process by integrating technology."

Many chapters in this book have discussed the various impact of technology in elections, but the main focus of this chapter hinges on the transformation of elections in continental Africa with a robust discussion on technology, corruption, and corrupt practices during and after election campaigns. The literature review includes: (1) causes of election malpractices in Africa; (2) the impact of corruption and corrupt practices on the electorates (citizens); (3) how corruption affects the system (society); (4) the effect of corruption and corrupt practices on the economic well-being of a nation; and (5) efforts to combat corruption and election malpractices in Africa.

The study sampled 100 African residents ranging from professional adult males and females, and graduate students resident in the United States who are citizens of the five selected African countries (Nigeria, Ghana, South Africa, Kenya, and Uganda).

CAUSES OF ELECTION MALPRACTICES IN AFRICAN COUNTRIES

African countries with poor economies are generally associated with countless corrupt practices that have deep anchorage in the socio-political and cultural psyche and existence in the various nations (Samura, 2009). These corrupt practices are particularly so in those African nations where the vast majority of the people—most importantly those in the rural areas—suffer untold hardship as a result of organized or systematized corruption. The causes of corruption are numerous, and the situation is often similar in many ways among continental African countries.

As Samura (2009) rightly opined, patronage ties between political elites and those they represent often place heavy, informal obligations and demands on the former. Typically, elected representatives are not only overwhelmed with financial pressure from their families, but also from kith and kin, clan, hometown, and tribal or ethnic constituents. Such obligations are almost always fulfilled through corrupt means. Thus, the participants in corruption are many, besides the politician or elite who actually engage in the act. Because of the absence of state welfare institutions in most of the African countries, political constituents expect politicians representing them to cater to their immediate, long-term and small-scale infrastructural needs (Samura, 2009). In other words, Samura (2009) in his article titled "The Negative Effects of Corruption on Developing Nations," argued that neopatrimonialism regimes become the rule, and the state emerges as an extension of the ruler's household, patronage, ethnic and kinship ties, and therefore bribes become major modes for governance. Corruption-funded patronage to kinsman and crimes have exacerbated regional, tribal, religious, and ethnic divisions. This impression is a clear indication of what is obtainable in every nation in Africa, which has tremendously frustrated every effort to strategically organize a fraudulent-free election.

Samura (2009) identified psychological reasons as another cause of corruption, when he referenced numerous psychological factors that can help to explain some types of corruption. He argued that some people are "naturally evil" and will commit criminal acts, including corrupt ones, in any type of system, including political systems and elections. Pressure and unhealthy peer comparison can contribute greatly to acts of corruption, especially where the socially revered are the corrupt ones. In view of the psychological reasons, Samura (2009) presupposes that in an environment where an individual sees others around him/her benefiting from corruption, they may well choose to indulge too. Nepotism—that is, helping others because they are closely related to you—can also be related in psychological term as a corrupt practice. The cliché "blood is thicker than water" is a common saying among Africans. This can also be explained in terms of people wanting to entrench themselves or maximize their hold on power (Samura, 2009).

Monopoly of power can also be attributed to another cause of corruption in Africa, mostly as it pertains to political elections. This could often exist for the simple reason that people in power are the ones mainly charged with the responsibility of governance. Thus, out of discretion they can expend such powers to perform acts of corruption as may be dictated by their circumstances (Samura, 2009).

Furthermore, a weak judicial system could also be identified as a serious cause of corruption in Africa. Most often, judicial systems are weak as a result of poor conditions of service. In such situations, it is the poor people that suffer the brunt of injustices as the rich always stand a better chance of getting justice over the poor through their deep pockets. In Africa, the bedrock to a fair hearing and/or winning a case lies on the ability to "grease the palm" of the judiciary— in other words, bribing them. Furthermore, the absence of a clear-cut separation of power between the judiciary and executive arms often results in the latter exercising undue influence over the former. Such undue influence Samura (2009) discussed as the most pervasive in situations where there is no guarantee of security of tenure for the judicial officers. In Nigeria, Ghana, South Africa, Kenya, and Uganda, for example, the president has the power to appoint judges on contractual basis after their retirement, without security of tenure of office. This opportunity creates yet another loophole for corruption.

THE IMPACT OF CORRUPTION AND CORRUPT PRACTICES ON THE CITIZENS

The impact of corruption is very hard on public life because people have developed an opinion that it is the only way to get their work done; otherwise the work will be pending for long periods of time, or might not be done at all. A corrupt system lacks quality of services in areas like a city or town that has corporate status and local government (municipality), distribution of electricity, and relief funds that require a price for quality work to be dispensed. If a prospective medical student has to obtain a medical degree, due to corruption in education, the student, after completion of his coursework, will not want to provide quality health services if there is not enough remuneration for the profession in which he obtained a degree. Furthermore, students who may not have the ability to study medicine, but have parents and family members who can buy their way through the matriculation process, could easily be admitted and work through the curricula and earn a medical degree with little or no competency to practice. This is very common in various African nations, and the productivity level of these incompetent, certified quacks has tremendously impacted the citizens.

The lack of proper justice could be regarded as another reason or impact of corruption on the people. Corruption in the judiciary system leads to improper justice, where the victims of an offense might suffer, and a crime may be proved by the benefit of the doubt due to a lack of evidence, or the evidence being erased. Due to corruption in the police system, the investigation process goes on for decades, which allows the culprits to roam the streets free, and likely to perform further crimes. There is even the chance that the prosecution of those criminals, due to old age and delayed investigation, may result in a delay in bringing about justice ("Justice delayed is justice denied"; www.mindcontroversy.com/impact-effects-corruption).

Chances of unemployment have been identified as a major reason why people and government agencies engage in corruption and corrupt practices. For example, in the private education and training institutes where permits are given to start providing education, the permits are given based on the infrastructure and sufficient recruitment of eligible staff. Here there are good chances of corruption. The institute or college management tries to bribe the quality inspectors so as to get permits. Though there are no sufficient eligible staff, these institutes get permission by the inspectors, thereby leading to unemployment. Instead of 10 faculty members, a college is run by five. Therefore, even if well-qualified persons wish to get a job there, it will not be offered to them. If there was no corruption by inspectors, then there would be a chance for more employment (www.mindcontroversy.com/impact-effects-corruption).

This same example applies to the political system, where electoral commissioners are bribed to influence voting results and announce candidates based on the amount of money they paid. In Nigeria, for instance, INEC commissioners were receiving hundreds of millions of naira from candidates to announce false results, even when those winners had no votes to justify their victory. Considerable amounts of funds, in the hundreds of millions, are offered to high-profile electoral officers as bribes to breed a high class of election malpractice to get a candidate elected. A vivid example from the Nigerian perspective is very evident, where a minister hauled funds in the hundreds of millions of dollars for bribes to pave the way to get an incumbent president re-elected.

Poor health and hygiene, pollution, accidents, and failure of genuine research results are other forms that could impact corruption and practices on the citizens of a country. In countries with more corruption, one can notice more health problems among the people. There will be no fresh drinking water, proper roads, quality food grain supplies, and milk adulteration. These low-quality services are all done to save money by the contractors and officials who are involved. Even the medicine provided in hospitals is of substandard quality. All of this can contribute to ill health of the common man (www.mindcontroversy. com/impact-effects-corruption).

THE IMPACT OF CORRUPTION ON SOCIETY

When citizens find that an electoral officer is corrupt or engages in various corrupt practices, such an officer is disregarded and disrespected. He will lack the deserved respect and will be a talking point in a negative manner across the city and state. This disregard, or sense of disrespect toward such an official, builds distrust. The lack of respect for rulers shows another way by which corruption impacts society. Rulers of a nation, like presidents or prime ministers, lose respect among the public when they are found wanting. In most instances, they are associated with corrupt practices and all sorts of fraudulent election malpractices, as well as stacking their nation's money in foreign accounts, which adversely affects their society. Respect is the main criteria in the understanding of a social system, and for the people existing within such a system. People go to vote during elections not only with the desire to improve their living standards by the candidate who wins, but also with respect for the leader. Most Africa politicians involved in corrupt practices (ranging from election fraud, paying minors to vote, and stealing of public funds) lose respect and most of the time are denied their re-election bid. (www.mindcontroversy.com/impact-effects-corruption).

Lastly, the lack of faith and trust in the government weighs in as a strong impact of corruption on society. People vote for a candidate who is aspiring for a position based on their faith in them. However, if such candidate is found to be involved in corruption, the people will lose faith and may not support their re-election bid by not voting for them.

THE IMPACT OF ELECTION MALPRACTICES/ CORRUPTION ON THE ECONOMY

Corruption could adversely affect the economy of a country by the rate of decrease in such a nation's foreign investment. There are many incidents where foreign investments have been willing to come to Nigeria—for instance, during the late 1980s and early 1990s when the country was labeled a corrupt country. During this period, the Nigerian economy was in a tailspin and suffered tremendous setbacks because of the government's and private sector's engagement in all sorts of corrupt practices, including the then-popular 419 scam. The situation in Nigeria—as well as in other identified African nations such as Ghana, South Africa, Kenya, and Uganda—caused a tremendous delay in growth and infrastructural development. Foreign investors were not interested in any development deals with the mentioned African nations. During this time in question, industrial growth, proper road networks, clean water, and steady power supplies were in a comatose state due to unsuitable economic infrastructure that adversely hindered the economic progress of the nations.

The differences in trade ratios is considered another impact that corruption has had on the economy of the country, mostly as it impacts the five identified African nations sampled in this study. Some countries have inefficient standard control institutes—in other words, these standard control institutes are corrupt in that they can approve low-quality products for sale in their country. Hence, you can see foreign countries dumping their cheaply manufactured products in the markets of these nations. These foreign countries, on the other end of the spectrum, will find it very difficult to dump any of their substandard products on countries with strict standard control institutes. They can do so only in countries with chances of corrupt officials in standard control who can accept bribes to allow their countries to become a dumping ground for such substandard products. One example is China, whose products can't just be dumped into Europe and US markets due to their strict standard control institutes. However, African markets are fertile ground for Chinese substandard products due to non-existent standard control. Even in cases where there are standard control officers, they are susceptible to fraudulent practices, thereby compromising the integrity of the nation. This situation could lead to trade deficits whereby these countries cannot manufacture their own products at cheaper prices than those exporting to them. If corruption is minimized in these nations, it will enable them to have fewer trade deficits in terms of exports and imports with other countries, and their economies can prosper (www.mindcontroversy.com/impact-effects-corruption).

EFFORTS TO COMBAT ELECTION MALPRACTICES IN SELECTED AFRICAN COUNTRIES

The statement that corruption damages the social and institutional fabric of any nation is not an overstatement. As has been found in various nations and organizations where people entrusted with power become dishonest and susceptible to bribery, and use their position of trust for personal gain, they tend to establish a moral pervasion and an impairment of virtue that almost always sets a deplorable and abusive standard that debases the entire nation—and in the case of an organization, the staff. Corruption undermines moral integrity, and in most cases has been fought by leaders to help in the establishment of a moral standard.

In order to curb corruption and establish a morally driven system in Africa—most importantly in the five sampled countries for this study—the leaders should turn to reform options open to governments to reduce corruption and mitigate its effects. Rose-Ackerman (1998) recommends a two-pronged strategy aimed at increasing the benefits of being honest, and the costs of being corrupt; a sensible combination of reward and punishment as the driving force of reforms. In Nigeria, for instance, the tenure of every democratic elected government has made efforts to fight and reduce corruption, but the efforts, no matter how intensive, have failed to yield favorable results. Most of those past and even present leaders who may have been involved in one corrupt practice or another are still free, parading around regardless of the severity of their offenses. The lack of accountability and punishment of offenders, regardless of their status in society, has made it very difficult to curb corruption in Nigeria. This is the same in other parts of Africa. The current president of Nigeria is saying the right things about tackling corruption. Unlike most other presidents before him, he has launched wide-range headline-making corruption probes.

> The poster-persons for these investigations have been Nigerian Petroleum Minister between 2010 and 2015 and the national security adviser between 2012 and 2015, under whose watch, billions of dollars of oil earnings are alleged to have been diverted to private pockets, while he is in detention since December 1, 2015 and is being probed over the alleged mismanagement of $2.1 billion in funds allocated to his office. (Several other high-profile persons have either been arrested or are being investigated, including former ministers, media owners, and businesspersons). The opposition, People's Democratic Party (PDP), with whom most of the arrested persons are affiliated, has been strident in its criticism, alleging that the President is an unrepentant dictator pursuing a purge that disproportionately targets the PDP while ignoring credible corruption allegations against presidential allies in the ruling party (Ogunlesi, 2016).

The present government, despite a series of distractions, has designed systems that make it as difficult as possible to steal government funds on the wholesale scale, which has become the tradition in Nigeria. The full implementation, in September 2015, of the Treasury Single Account, which consolidated hundreds of disparate government accounts in commercial banks into a single accounting system overseen by the Central Bank, has made it easier for revenues and spending to be more easily tracked. On top of this, the government ought to ensure that all budgets and contract details are speedily and routinely made public on the Internet (Ogunlesi, 2016).

> Punitive regulation is also critical. The Central Bank needs to impose more stringent sanctions on banks implicated in money laundering. It is only by tar-

geting and severely penalizing senior banking executives that Nigeria can finally hope to break entrenched patterns of fraudulent conspiring between banks
and corrupt government officials. Finally, judicial reform. While the Economic
and Financial Crimes Commission, the country's main anti-graft agency, has a
decent record with small-scale crimes, especially fraud cases, its record in dealing with political corruption, especially that carried out by those described by
Human Rights Watch as "nationally prominent political figures," is uninspir-
ing. Part of the reason lies in the ease with which the legal system is often manipulated. In a speech to the lawyers' association in August 2015, President
Buhari noted that the ability to manipulate and frustrate the legal system is the
crowning glory of the corrupt and, as may be expected, this has left many legal
practitioners and law courts tainted in an ugly way (Ogunlesi, 2016).

The Nigerian president's anticorruption drive has since set up a Presidential Advisory Committee Against Corruption to advise him on a comprehensive reform
of Nigeria's criminal justice system. Two important bills, establishing protection
for whistleblowers and witnesses, are currently awaiting presidential assent.
Government insiders have also hinted of plans to establish dedicated courts for
corruption cases. The Nigerian government's commitment to fighting corruption
is sincere, but it will take a lot more than sincerity or good intentions to help
Nigeria break free from the debilitating grip of corruption. They will, sooner
than later, have to show demonstrable proof that this aggressive reform can go
beyond the familiar melodrama of cycles of arrests, trials, and shocking revela-
tions, and succeed in setting Nigeria in a radically different direction (Ogunlesi,
2016).

In his annual December 31st message to Ghanaians, former president Rawlings said, "Ghana is saddled with some very negative images about corruption,
some wrongly perceived, but some convincingly accurate," while the king of
Akyem Abuakwa describes the level of corruption in Ghana as "madness." In
their New Year message, Ghana's Catholic bishops noted that the
"twin evils of bribery and corruption" are ravaging every fabric of the Ghanaian
society—a situation the deputy speaker of parliament and New Patriotic Party
Member of Parliament for Essikado argue could make Ghana a failed state (Alidu, 2015). To take the corruption fight head-on in Ghana, as was discussed in
previous paragraphs pertaining to other countries, requires a general increase in
moral values resulting in a collective resolve of the general population to eschew
corruption. Alidu (2015) suggested that even when moral values are increased,
there must be the tendency for the government to follow up. He opined therefore
that:

> While such an occurrence will be wonderful, it will forever remain a fantasy.
> There is no evidence anywhere in the world where morality has been used to
> successfully tackle corruption. On the contrary, the evidence suggests that
> countries that have been successful in fighting corruption attained success by
> increasing the punishment and removing the opportunities for corruption; noth-
> ing to do with a general increase in the level of morality or integrity.

There is also the view that the cause of corruption in Ghana is low salaries paid to workers, and to fight corruption the government should pay people in the public service well. A final viewpoint is that the government needs strong laws to fight corruption. For instance, in Ghana laws can only be proposed by government, and the authority responsible for prosecution, the attorney general, is appointed and completely answerable to the president. It will therefore take a certain political will to enact laws that make the anticorruption bodies truly independent, and make the enforcement of laws impartial and effective. In the end, to have strong and effective laws, you need political commitment (Alidu, 2015).

In Sierra Leone, efforts to curb corruption can be traced to its recent past. In 2000, the former government established the Anti-Corruption Commission in a bid to minimize corruption. Former President Kabbah regarded this move as the primary reason for the country's slow pace in terms of economic advancement. The ACC Act 2000 was, however, marred with several defects, primary amongst which was the lack of independence of the Commission in prosecuting alleged corrupt officers. Secondly, the mandate of the Commission was severely limited to investigation and sensitization. Discretion for prosecution of cases was dependent on the discretion of the attorney general. Upon succession to power, the current government went a step further by assenting to an amendment made on the 2000 Act in September 2008 (Samura, 2009).

In Cameroon, the President of the National Anti-Corruption Commission (CONAC), Dieudonne Massi Gams, emphasized the consequences of corruption in Cameroon, which have had a considerable damaging and retrogressive effect on the nation's forestry sector and the promotion of the illegal sale of drugs. The CONAC president, alongside the citizens in collaboration with the international community, observed the 12th edition of the International Day for the Fight against Corruption on December 9, 2015 (Ayuketah, 2015). The day was observed by Transparency International, who released its 2015 Barometer on Corruption. Records indicate that despite the creation of avenues to fight corruption in Cameroon, the vice still has a firm grip on the country. According to the results of a survey conducted, the police, the judiciary, and tax agents were identified as the most corrupt circles (Ayuketah, 2015).

In order to destroy corruption in Cameroon, Transparency International has recommended the following: (1) the enactment of anticorruption law; (2) a truly independent judiciary; and (3) the protection of whistleblowers. In the meantime, Cameroonians have hailed the efforts of CONAC since its creation in March 2006, and have called for more stringent measures on perpetrators of corrupt acts (Ayuketah, 2015).

Claros (2014), in his article "Future Development: Economics to End Poverty," identified six considerable strategies to fight corruption, which are: (1) the idea of paying civil servants well; (2) creating transparency and openness in government spending; (3) cutting red tape; (4) replacing regressive and distorting subsidies with targeted cash transfers; (5) establishing international conventions; and (6) deploying smart technology. These stated strategies could become a panacea to corruption and corrupt practices from a global perspective; however, each country may have a designed strategy that works for their system, as clearly discussed in the literature of this chapter.

DEMOCRACY IN AFRICA—ELECTORAL MALPRACTICES AND CORRUPTION

Political elections and democracy in Africa have been volatile in the past, and this has raised concerns for a considerable amount of time due to various factors, including economic, social, cultural, incessant malpractice, and corruption. These reasons have left democracy under the tutelage of corrupt leaders who design strategies to maneuver the system to benefit their personal interests, thereby leaving the practice of democracy in Africa under a fragile platform. It is not a gainsaying that Africa has long been considered politically unstable and fragile due to the predominance of unconstitutional regimes, such as through consistent military coups, since the early 1960s.

Africa has experienced about 200 coups d'état over a period of about 56 years. However, recent years have raised hopes for improved political transition and stability across the continent. Free and transparent political elections constitute an important and essential step toward successful leadership and democracy. The failure or absence of free political elections may impede social and economic development of a country or region, as it may lead to social upheaval. Political stability is of primary importance in fostering economic and social development and in attracting foreign direct investment to the continent (www. afdb.org/...Africa.Politcal elections and democracy). However, elections and democratic fragility in Africa have continued to hamper economic and democratic governance, because by looking at democratic elections that have been held in the past two years in countries such as Senegal, Tunisia, and Zambia, it has been demonstrated that African countries can succeed in organizing free and fair elections. Nevertheless, recent events, including the re-emergence of military coups in Guinea-Bissau and Mali, have once again highlighted the political fragility and risks in some African countries. These events turn back the continent's efforts toward strengthening democracy (www.afdb.org/...Africa.Politcal elections and democracy). The erosion of well-established democratic standards in countries such as Mali is a major threat to the ongoing political, economic, and social development on the African continent. However, overall democracy in Africa is still fragile, mainly due to adverse social and economic conditions.

Persistent and high levels of poverty and corruption in Africa, when compared with other regions of the world, represent a threat to the sustainability of democracy. In addition, due to domestic manipulation, political elections in Africa have not led to the election of representative governments in all of its 49 countries (www.afdb.org/...Africa.Politcal elections and democracy). A few important elections took place in Africa in 2015. Nigeria, Tanzania, Zambia, and Burkina Faso (despite some stops and starts) all saw democratic transitions of power. No wonder, then, that more than half of the continent believes that they live in democracies.

Elsewhere, things weren't quite so straightforward. In Burundi, for instance, a controversial amendment of the constitution paved the way for the incumbent Pierre Nkurunziza to seek and win a controversial third term that has led the country into untold crisis ever since. Meanwhile, in Ethiopia the prime minister managed to return to power with a remarkable 100 percent of the vote. So, despite some movement toward electoral democracy, challenges still remain. And in 2016, there will be more elections to measure the continent's progress in its pursuit toward a more democratic future (www.afdb.org/...Africa elections and democracy).

There are six African countries that are worth watching more closely as they continue to wiggle themselves through corrupt practices to win elections at all costs. Uganda's most recent election, which retained the incumbent president, Yoweri Museveni, for a third term of five years (having already led the country for about 30 years) is a travesty and a complete rape of democracy. His supposed cruise to victory welcomes the position of this chapter regarding malpractice and corruption associated with elections in Africa. Despite lagging its neighbors Kenya and Tanzania economically, Uganda plays a significant role in the region, especially on security issues. The country has contributed forces to the African Union's (AU) efforts to fight al-Shabab and provide security in Somalia. Recently, Museveni hosted talks in Burundi to try to find a solution to the crisis that some fear could descend to a civil war (Mohammed, 2016).

In Niger, the incumbent president, Mahamadou Issoufou, has used his power to intimidate his opponents. The one most prominent opposition he would have had is the former prime minister, Hama Amadou (who was arrested for child trafficking charges) and former president of Niger, Mahamane Ousmane, along with Seyin Oumarou, who were also accused. The intent was to silence them through intimidation and weaken their efforts to vie for the presidency. He also arrested senior military officers for allegedly plotting to overthrow his government. All of these are cheap and corrupt practices used with the intention of remaining visible and running without stronger opposition. He was placed under tremendous pressure from the opposition and civil society to make changes to the voters' roll and election processes. He would rather use the pretext of a destabilization plot to avoid making changes that could be to his disadvantage in the election (Mohammed, 2016).

President Edgar Lungu of Zambia won power earlier this year to serve out the remainder of Michael Sata's term, after Sata died in office. To secure a full five-year term as president, Lungu convinced the electorate that he would be better placed than the man he defeated in 2015, Hakainde Hichilema, to fix the country's huge challenges. These challenges include chronic electricity problems and a struggling economy that is not helped by one of the worst performing currencies in the world. The continent's second largest copper producer will also need to overcome a global commodities market that is markedly slowing down (Mohammed, 2016).

The Democratic Republic of Congo (DRC) will be conducting a presidential election on November 27, 2016. The incumbent president, Joseph Kabila, will do everything to get back to the ballot to run after 15 years in office as the president. However, the country's constitution limits him from seeking another term. There has been careful attention toward how the Democratic Republic of Congo, one of the most affluent countries in natural resources in the world, will conduct a free and fair election without the malpractice that has continued to wreck the prospect of true democracy in Africa.

Ghana has been positioned on continental Africa as a model of political stability in a region that has most of the time struggled to sustain the posture of democracy. The incumbent president, John Mahama, was elected with overwhelming expectations, among which were the economy, infrastructural development, and the creation of jobs for the citizens. However, since his tenure, Ghana has been beset by a series of corrupt practices and mountainous problems ranging from electricity blackouts, budget deficits, high inflation, declining growth, and most of all, a weakening economy that has resulted in him seeking one billion dollars in IMF loans. These identified national problems have no doubt resulted in a tough re-election bid with his 2012 rival, whom he defeated. Mahama may have re-election strategies that meet tough competitors considering the economic and social status of the nation (Mohammed, 2016).

The political instability in Somalia that has characterized the last two decades, spawning militant groups such as al-Shabaab, may be about to end. This comes after the incumbent government of President Hassan Sheikh Mohamud earlier this year suggested his government is not yet ready to preside over a general election due to security reasons (Mohammed, 2016). Different political factions in the country came together and formed a National Consultative Forum (NCF) to decide on what format the polls will take. The challenge now is whether the agreed-upon format will be decided in time for the elections to be held before the end of 2016 (Mohammed, 2016). According to the outgoing representative for the United Nations Secretary General in Somalia, Nicholas Kay, "Somalia in the past two-three years has come together quite significantly. It is both politically stable and developed as well."

RESEARCH QUESTIONS

Political scientists, Transparency International, and scholars of government affairs, in their various attempts to disseminate factual information pertaining to politics, elections, and corruption, came up with issues as to what causes corruption and how corrupt practices hamper progressive attempts by the government to accomplish set goals for the people. In the developing countries, for instance, corruption has eaten so deep into the fabric of the various African societies such that it has become a part of their way of life. During election campaigns and the period of actual voting, many atrocities and heinous crimes are perpetrated just to win an elected office. The engagement in such corrupt misconduct has tremendous consequences for democratic governance in various African countries. In most situations, electoral corruption results in the wrong and unqualified people being elected, and can therefore subvert the democratic will. Birch

(2011) referred to electoral corruption as the resulting government being less representative and less accountable than it would be otherwise. Those who are elected in corrupt elections will obviously have less of an incentive to do as their constituents would want them to do. Poor-quality elections can also have an adverse impact on popular perceptions of the legitimacy of political leaders, and it can undermine the bonds of trust that must link the people with their rulers, as well as individual members of the political elite with each other (Birch, 2011). In order to weigh the atrocities resulting from corrupt practices during elections, this study will seek to answer the following questions:

1. To what extent do government agencies support the transparency and the rule of law of the land that is entrusted under their watch?
2. Are there any significant differences between corruption as a major obstacle to democracy as opposed to corruption as a depletory of national wealth?
3. To what extent does corruption breed obstacles to democracy and the rule of law?
4. To what extent do corrupt practices challenge the development of accountable political leadership in a country?

RESEARCH METHODOLOGY

This study, looking at technology integration in elections, reviewed the transformation of elections in Africa with a content analysis of five selected African countries: Nigeria, Ghana, South Africa, Kenya, and Uganda. The choice of the five selected African countries were based on: (1) their recent general elections and the attempt to use technology to change the status quo; and (2) the current democratic system that existed in the five selected countries and how such democracy has changed in the recent past. The identified two reasons informed the choice of the selected African countries. A research instrument with five survey questions was administered to a randomly selected 100 Africans adults, 20 from each country, who have traveled back to their respective countries within the past five years.

The survey also looked at political interest, and knowledge of the transformation implications in elections when using technology to curb corruption and corrupt practices. The questions were analyzed by a simple percentage calculation after the completion of the survey to determine the extent to which the government and its agencies support election transparencies and the rule of law. The analysis also looked at the significant differences between corruption as a major obstacle to democracy and the depletion of national wealth. In addition, the survey had two other questions that ranged from the extent to which corruption bred obstacles to democracy and the rule of law, and how it challenges the development of accountable political leadership in Africa—most importantly, in the five selected nations. The study used the findings to make considerable inference that, based on the content analyzed, there are tendencies for election malpractice in the selected African countries. However, the analyzed data shows that with the integration of technology to elections, there are reasonable transformation tendencies that have significantly improved elections when compared to the past practices fraught with election malpractices.

RESEARCH DESIGN

Research design is the framework that has been created to seek answers to research questions, which shows that the researcher is able to tackle the research problem in a coherent and explicit way. It refers to the overall strategy that an investigator (in this case, the researcher) chose to integrate the different components of the study in a coherent and logical way, thereby ensuring effectively how the research problem will be addressed. Research design, therefore, constitutes the blueprint for the collection, measurement, and analysis of data. Research design could be compared to an outline of how an investigation will take place. A research design will typically include how data is to be collected, what instruments will be employed, how the instruments will be used, and the intended means for analyzing the data collected (www.businessdictionary.com/definition/research-design.html).

In an attempt to analyze the data collected for this study, we used a stratified sampling method to achieve a conceptual base for the validation of the instrument (survey), which characteristically places the population selected for this study in a more logical and empirical perspective. The outcome of the stratified sampling shows that all the various populations sampled have an equal chance of being selected as part of the survey. For the purpose of this study, approximately 100 respondents were drawn from the five African countries that participated in the survey. The respondents chosen for the survey were classified as the population of interest, a sampling frame that helped in making assumption as to how the integration of technology in elections in Nigeria, Ghana, South Africa, Kenya, and Uganda would, to a larger extent, result in cutting down election malpractices that have marred previous elections (during which time technology was not even factored into the process of conducting elections) in the identified selected African countries. In furtherance of the research design applicable to this study, the researcher utilized a quantitative approach with a view toward employing a causal comparative investigation of how elections are conducted in the five selected African countries prior to the present time, when technology tends to be integrated into election processes. The research design and the survey were meant to show whether the integration of technology in elections in the selected African countries may have had some causal effect in the outcome of the election.

REASON FOR SELECTING A SAMPLE FOR THIS STUDY

The idea behind the selection of a sample for this research endeavor is to be able to generalize the findings to the whole population, which means that the selected sample must be: (1) representative of the population. In other words, it should contain similar proportions of subgroups as the whole population, and not exclude any particular groups, either by method of sampling or by design, or by who chooses to respond. The five African countries selected for this study are representative of the African nations that have factored technology into their current national general elections; and (2), the sample is large enough to show evidence of enough information to avoid errors. It does not need to be a specific proportion of the population, which should, by its measurement standards, be at least a certain size so that the results will give an adequate and reasonable outcome likely to be broadly correct. A sample that is not representative and lacks the expected size may result in a bias and imprecise outcome. However, when the relationship between sample and population is right, the study will draw strong conclusions about the nature of the population.

ANALYSIS OF DATA

The sample size for this study was drawn from 100 respondents from the five selected African countries who participated in the survey, as discussed in previous sections of this chapter. This chapter, in an attempt to evaluate the transformation of elections in Africa with the impact of integrating technological apparatus, analyzed why elections in Africa record a higher propensity of malpractice, corruption, and sometimes vague election results, all of which have consistently marred the political system and governance. The study reviewed the causes of corruption and corrupt practices, efforts to combat corruption in elections in the selected African countries, and the impact of corruption on the economy, society, and the citizens. Data collected from the sampled questionnaire addressed to the respondents generally looked at the transformation of elections in Africa with a content analysis of election malpractices in the selected five African countries. The study also attempted to prove that corrupt practices during subsequent elections in the selected African countries (Nigeria, Ghana, South Africa, Kenya, and Uganda) may have been the reason why the outcomes of those elections were skewed.

A total of 10 questions were asked of the respondents. These questions, all related to the five primary research questions, had the objective of providing results to assist the researcher in making inferences as to whether the lack of the use of technology plays a causative role in election malpractice. Percentage results were calculated to determine the extent to which government agencies support transparency in elections and the rule of law. It also weighed into the significant differences between corruption as a major obstacle to democracy. The study looked at other relevant questions as well, such as the extent to which corruption breeds obstacles to democracy and the rule of law, and how corrupt practices challenge the development of accountable political leadership.

Table 15.1
To what extent do government agencies in the five selected African countries support transparency during elections?

Options	Frequency	Percentage
to greater extent	20	20%
to lesser extent	70	70%
non-applicable	10	10%
Total	100	100%

Discussing the outcome of the data as shown on Table 15.1, we see that 70 percent of the population sampled was not in agreement that government agencies support transparency during elections. However, 20 respondents, or 20 percent of the total respondents, indicated in clear terms that government agencies support transparency during elections, while a very small number of 10 respondents, or 10 percent, chose the nonapplicable option. The overall outcome of the respondents to question number one shows that government agencies—which includes the independent electoral body in the respective selected countries—show to a lesser extent that government agencies in the five sampled African countries support election transparency.

Table 15.2
To what extent do corrupt practices disrupt election campaigns and governance in the selected African countries?

Options	Frequency	Percentage
to greater extent	90	90%
to lesser extent	8	8%
nonapplicable	2	2%
Total	100	100%

The data recorded in Table 15.2 shows that 90 percent of the respondents agreed significantly that corrupt practices, to a very high extent, contribute in the disruption of election campaigns and make governance very difficult in the selected five African countries; 8 and 2 percent respectively answered "to a lesser extent" and "nonapplicable" that corrupt practices disrupt election campaigns in the selected five African countries. It also indicates that corrupt practices—including election malpractice associated with party affiliates during and after the campaigns—as well as the designated voting periods most of the time produce an outcome that makes governance very difficult for the winners of the election.

Table 15.3
To what extent do significant differences exist between election malpractices and the lack of rule of law during the conduct of elections in the selected five African countries?

Options	Frequency	Percentage
to greater extent	45	45%
to lesser extent	50	50%
nonapplicable	5	5%
Total	100	100%

The percentage of respondents in table 15.3 present a very different argument, and also shows that 45 respondents, or 45 percent, strongly believe that there is a significant difference between election malpractice and the lack of rule of law. On the contrary, 50 percent of the population sampled agreed that there is a significant difference between corrupt practices and the rule of law, while 5 percent failed to identify with the question and rather indicated nonapplicable. "Rule of law" refers to a principle of governance in which all persons, institutions, and entities, including the State itself, are accountable to laws that are publicly broadcasted, equally enforced, and independently adjudicated, and which are consistent with international human rights, norms, and standards. Fedotov (2013) argued that weak rule of law and lack of good governance pose a major threat to social and economic development the world over, and they have hindered progress in attaining the Millennium Development Goals. "Effective and humane justice systems and institutions are fundamental to building societies that facilitate growth and development."

The percentage of respondents on this question shows that there is no significant difference between election malpractice and the lack of rule of law. The electorates' involvement in corrupt practices during elections significantly shows the lack of the rule of law among the citizens. Strong evidence has shown that there is considerable election malpractice and corruption during elections in various African countries, most importantly in the five sampled African countries, which is a result of weak rule of law, and in most instances, the lack of it.

Table 15.4
To what extent does election malpractice challenge the development of an accountable political leadership in a country?

Options	Frequency	Percentage
to greater extent	75	75%
to lesser extent	10	10%
non-applicable	15	15%
Total	100	100%

Table 15.4 resulted in the following answers: A total number of 75 respondents out of the 100 sampled population, or 75 percent, answered in affirmation that election malpractices do challenge the development of an accountable political leadership, whereas 10 out of the total sampled respondents, or 10 percent, did not think that election malpractices challenged the development of an accountable leadership. Fifteen respondents, or 15 percent, on the other hand, felt that it did not matter to them whether election malpractice challenged the development of an accountable political leadership.

Looking at the four different research questions posed for this study, and clearly represented in Tables 15.1 through 15.4, the results were representative of the expected outcomes. For instance, in Table 15.1, the African government's support of transparency during elections received a considerable negative percentage of 70, showing that corrupt campaigns and electoral malpractice abound, regardless of how they may attempt to cover up the processes with their clandestine strategies. In Table 15.2, 90 percent of the respondents clearly state that in African nations, corrupt practices disrupt election campaigns, which significantly impacts governance. The question on the rule of law and election malpractice in Table 15.3 shows a 50/50 percentage split, which goes a long way to establishing the fact that there is no significant difference between election malpractice and the lack of the rule of law. It also clearly indicates that the existence of malpractice during elections connotes the lack of the rule of law. Table 15.4 shows that election malpractices challenge the political leadership in Africa, as a considerable 70 percent of the population surveyed answered in affirmation that election malpractice during elections challenges the development of an accountable political leadership in Africa, most importantly in the five sampled African countries.

Election malpractice in Africa could be summarized under malpractice and manipulation prior to and after the results have been announced, where the electoral body creates room for the falsification of results. Other election malpractices could include allowing violence to take charge of the responsibilities of the body that was charged to conduct the elections, snatching and illegal stuffing of the ballot boxes from the hired thugs, multiple voting, impersonation, illegal voters registration lists, and mostly the switching of votes among the winners and losers by the resident electoral officers, where in most instances a loser has been announced as a winner and vice versa. Electoral officers in various African countries (most importantly the sampled five African countries for this research) usually use electoral regulations to some extent to disenfranchise candidates or groups, as well as disqualifying candidates by setting up unnecessary rules and regulations that sometimes are designed to favor their candidate of choice. In most of the selected African countries (as representative of what occurs in other African nations), cultural, religious, and ethnic manipulations—including outright and deliberate attempts to prevent an independent candidate from participating in the elections, as well as even contesting for any elected position—sometimes go a long way to speaking to the existing election malpractices that pose a huge challenge to election processes in Africa.

The issue of monetization of the electoral processes could be a global problem, because the process of running an election could run into hundreds of millions, as shown with the current 2016 presidential election in the United States, where spending by both the Democratic and Republican parties must have run into the billions of dollars. The same result presents itself in Africa, because politicians throw bags of money and material things around to entice the electorates to vote for them. The snatching and stealing of ballot boxes puts African elections on a very negative pedestal, which seems to have been checked by the integration of technology that seems to have presented a safe haven for the voters to be disenfranchised.

According to Olawole (2013), there are other election manipulations and frauds that adversely impact the election outcomes, such as stuffing of ballot boxes with legal and illegal ballot papers, starving opposition strongholds of electoral material with a view to disenfranchise them, encouraging minors to vote, deliberate omission of candidates' photographs and names on the ballot papers, deliberate refusal to count ballot boxes and voters' papers from the opposition strongholds, doctoring of results between the voting centers and the collation centers, declaration of results before the arrival of ballot boxes from the polling centers, and outright cancellation of election results or total annulment of election results (as was the case in Nigeria on June 12, 1993, where the projected winner was denied his opportunity because a military leader took such a rash, undemocratic decision to annul the election, which was projected to be the fairest of all the elections ever held in Nigeria). Other forms of electoral malpractice and/or fraud, as documented by Olawole (2013), include but are not limited to: appointment or selection of partisan electoral officials; declaration of a winner where no candidate was fielded; inflation of the electoral register; disqualification of candidates envisaged to be a threat to a favored candidate; using of the apparatus of state media, logistics, and personnel in favor of the incumbent, particularly at re-election periods; and finally, intimidation and harassment of voters by thugs and police to discourage people from exercising their voting rights.

CONCLUSION

Fighting corruption effectively is a Herculean task, and depends greatly on both the political will and financial resources. Amongst the challenges faced by the Anti-Corruption Commission are finance, and logistics in the form of vehicles, computers, printers, tape recorders, and a host of other equipment required in order for staff to perform their work effectively. The Commission also needs trained and qualified staff with modern investigative and systems-review techniques. The Commission also needs a better building facility in order for it to function efficiently.

Corruption impacts societies in a multitude of ways. In the worst-case scenario, it costs lives. It also costs people their freedom, their health, as well as their money. The cost of corruption can be divided into four main categories: political, economic, social, and environmental.

On the political front, corruption is a major obstacle to democracy and the rule of law. In a democratic system, such as in the five sampled African countries (Nigeria, Ghana, South Africa, Kenya, and Uganda), offices and institutions lose their legitimacy when they are misused for private advantage. This is harmful in established democracies, but even more so in newly emerging ones. It is extremely challenging to develop accountable political leadership in a corrupt climate, as has been the case in most electoral processes in Africa.

Economically, corruption depletes national wealth. Corrupt politicians invest scarce public resources into projects that will enrich their pockets rather than benefit communities, and prioritize high-profile projects such as dams, power plants, pipelines, and refineries over less spectacular but more urgent infrastructural projects such as schools, hospitals, and roads.

Corruption also hinders the development of fair-market structures and distorts competition, which in turn deters investment. Corruption corrodes the social fabric of society. It undermines people's trust in the political system, in its institutions, and its leadership. A distrustful or apathetic public can then become yet another hurdle to challenging corruption.

Environmental degradation is another consequence of corrupt systems. The lack of, or non-enforcement of environmental regulations and legislation means that precious natural resources are carelessly exploited, and entire ecological systems are ravaged. From mining, to logging, to carbon offsets, companies across the globe continue to pay bribes in return for unrestricted destruction.

RECOMMENDATIONS

Many developing nations, including the five sampled African countries noted in this chapter, are miles away in achieving corruption-free societies, and as stated previously, the political will and financial support from central governments has to be sacrosanct for the fight against corruption to succeed. In Nigeria, Ghana, South Africa, Kenya, and Uganda, the fight against corrupt practices and the malpractices that are associated with elections are far from being over. The Independent National Electoral Body in each of these identified countries, as well as in other nations of Africa, has continued to battle the dangers of incessant election malpractice over a very long time. The attempt made by these countries to establish a rule of law that would guide against election malpractice seems not to be working; however, the integration of technological infrastructure seems to have cut down on the outright election malpractice and fraudulent methods that have continued to damage the move toward democratically elected leaders.

The issue of free and fair elections in continental Africa has remained unabated. This chapter, in its attempt to present a detailed content analysis of the dangers of election malpractices, showcased detailed consequences resulting from corruption and election malpractices. Scholars of history and political scientists have presented a series of convincing data to show how imperative it is to work toward a legitimate and fraudulent-free election. A strong effort was made by the author of this chapter to stress the importance of a corruption-free election, as he stated in clear terms that election malpractices overly undermine the electoral/citizens' trust in the political system, its institutions, and leadership. As a result of the challenges posed by the several efforts to achieve fraudulent-free elections in Africa, the author has arrived at numerous recommendations.

We should restructure the imposed imbalance of leadership in African countries by the European imperialists. The political structure that was created by the founding imperialists to better their situation has led to the creation of a hegemonic system that drives the political system, as well as empowers a section in a particular country to dominate its leadership. For instance, in Nigeria, Olawole, et al. (2013) argued that the creation of this imbalanced structure has led the North to believe and act as though leadership in Nigeria is their birthright. They seem to be empowered electorally and demographically more than the other two regions, which resulted in their alleged continued domination of Nigeria's political system. Hence, the alleged continued domination of Nigerian politics by the Northerners (Olawole et al. 2013).

As a result of this arrangement by the British in Nigeria, it becomes very difficult to wrestle the mantle of leadership away from the Northerners. They can manipulate the systems in all sorts of fashions to make sure that presidential elections are won by their candidates. This research, therefore, recommends restructuring the center such that it discourages political and ethnic hegemony, where all the existing ethnic units or geographical zones are assured of equal accessibility to power in Nigerian federation. Political power must not be seen as an exclusive preserve of a section, zone, or group. There must be a change for rotational arrangement in Nigerian politics similar to the federal character provision as contained in both 1979 and 1999 constitutions. In this regard, efforts at ensuring equitable distribution of power are to ensure that cooperative rigging and manipulations of elections are discouraged.

It is common knowledge that all tribes in Nigeria cooperate to manipulate electoral processes for one reason or another. But the moment these tribes are aware of genuine arrangements to assure them of their turn, then cooperative rigging will be discouraged. Elections will therefore become a yardstick to confer legitimacy on government and its leadership (Olawole, et al. 2013). In Cameroon for instance, the arrival of the French made it possible for the French-speaking Cameroonians to dominate the seat of political power over the Anglophone zone that is made up of the North and Southern regions of Bamunda, Nkambe, Woom (north), and Victoria, Kumba, and Mamfe (south). The point here is that the Francophone zone will do everything possible, including all sorts of election anomalies, to maintain the hegemonic principle that has kept them in power for so long.

The issue of the "political godfather" should be completely erased from elections and the choice of a candidate in the African political system. A leader should be groomed and sometimes allowed to present him/herself to the people that he or she plans to lead. The idea of forcing a candidate on the people by the so-called political "movers and shakers" must stop, because in various instances the choice of the people is sometimes overshadowed by a candidate of the godfather's choice. A godfather who has both money and political clout would use his position to buy votes, and in the process, utilize all forms of fraudulent strategies, including voting malpractices, to win the election for his candidate.

The African political system should maintain a very strategic and sustainable federalism where the center will have minimal authority over the state units. A federal system will allow the state units the authority to design a strategic way to develop their entity—a practice that will lead to a viable, positive competition among states and generate considerable growth and health development. It will also assist in the grooming of qualified political leaders, who can rise from the state level based on their development achievements and political credentials to vie for the office of the presidency regardless of their state of origin or zonal affiliation.

Time limits should be maintained in the African election landscape. It is imperative that African political leaders from the local, state, and national levels respect time limits and let go of the offices they occupy when they lose elections. In many African countries, including the five sampled for this study, leaders find it very hard to relinquish their position, and as a result they become so entrenched in leadership that they engage in various election malpractices to hold on to power. In Zimbabwe, and most recently Uganda, the respective presidents have held on to power for so long that they strategically manipulate the election outcome to continue to win. The odd part of this practice lies on the power of incumbency, which must be addressed by the various nations of Africa.

Electoral malpractice in Africa has been rampant because of copious engagement in stirring the minds of the poor electorates, mostly those at the grassroots level where poverty has created a fertile ground that encourages the buying and selling of votes to the electorates, the inability of the candidates and political parties to access media, and the media's inability to practice equal time due to who has the deepest pocket to pay their most exorbitant price.

Monetization of the electoral process in the African electoral landscape should be minimized, because the integration of money with regard to who gets elected has made it very difficult for a free and fair election to take place. Poverty of ideas and wealth has made many of the electoral manipulations easy. It has made it difficult for the creation of a level playing field politically (Olawole, et al., 2013).

According to Olawole et al., (2013), in Africa, an inexperienced candidate with impoverished ideas about governance may be rich, and his wealth may pave the way for him to have direct access to hungry and poor minds in the cities and villages. With the necessary election paraphernalia such as posters and electronic media campaigns, as well as abundant food materials and monetary bribes, there are enough resources to induce the poverty-stricken electorates with the intention of manipulating them to vote against their conscience. It is equally possible to buy over-hungry voters, polling and counting officials, and law enforcement agents. All these electoral officers can be induced to facilitate the rigging of elections by the wealthy politicians. Poverty has also paved the way for the emergence of the new, dangerous development in Africa's politics (Olawole, et al. 2013).

REFERENCES

Alidu, A. N. (2015). Defeating corruption in Ghana – Mahama is the key. Citifmonline. March

Ayuketah, E. (2015). Fighting corruption: Cameroon to device new strategies. *Journal National.* December.

Birch, S. (2011). Electoral malpractices. Oxford Scholarship online. May.

Claros, A. L. (2014). Six strategies to fight corruption. Future development –economies to end poverty. May 14.

Fedotov (2013). Weak rule of law and lack of good governance a major threat to development. United Nations Office on Drugs and Crime (UNODC).

Frederick, J. C. (1972). *The Pathology of Politics: Violence, Betrayal, Corruption, Secrecy and Propaganda.* New York: Harper & Row, pp. 127-141.

Merriam-Webster Online dictionary

Mohammed, O. (2016). Democracy Now: The six African elections to watch out for in 2016. *Quartz Africa Weekly Brief.* January, 4.

Ochonu, M. (2008). Corruption and poverty in Africa: A deconstruction. www.pamba zuka.org

Ogunlesi, T. (2016). Fighting corruption a different way in Nigeria. *Newsweek.*

Olawwole, O., Adewunmile, E. T., & Oluwole, E. (2013). Electoral malpractices and problems in Africa: A critical analysis. *Journal of Research and Development.* Vol. 1, No. 6.

Palmier, L. (1983). Bureaucratic corruption and its remedies. In Clark (1983a), pp. 207-16.

Samura, B. K. (2009). The negative effects of corruption on developing nations: A Perspective on Sierra Leone's Effort.

Treisman, (1998). *The Causes of Corruption: A Cross National Study.* University of California. Los Angeles.

Transparency International Global Corruption Barometer (2015/2016).

Ugwuanyi, M. (2015). Tackling electoral malpractices in Nigeria http://www. afdb.org/ ...Africa elections and democracy. African development Bank Group. January 2, 2013. http://www.mindcontroversy.com/impact-effects-corruption-public-life-india

Vocabulary.com http://www.vocabulary.com/dictionary

CHAPTER 16
Technology and the Electoral Process in Cameroon

Augustin Ntembe
Bowie State University

INTRODUCTION

Cameroon became a League of Nations-mandated territory after Germany lost all its territories in Africa, following their defeat during the First World War by the Allied Forces. The administration of the territory was handed to Britain and France. While Britain was given the stretch along the eastern Nigerian border, the French received nearly four-fifths of Cameroon. In 1945, Cameroon became a United Nations Trust Territory under French and British administrations respectively. On January 1, 1960, the territory under French administration was granted independence and became the Republic of Cameroon *(la Republique du Cameroun)* with Amadou Ahidjo as the first chief executive (Levine, 1964; Mbaku, 1985). Following the plebiscite organized in 1961 by the United Nations, British Southern Cameroon opted for reunification with *la Republique du Cameroun* while the British Northern Cameroon chose to join the independent Republic of Nigeria. Thus, the union between British Southern Cameroon and the independent Republic of Cameroon took place in 1961, and this union created the Federal Republic of Cameroon with Amadou Ahidjo as the first head of state (Lavine, 1964; Njeuma, 1989; Mbaku, 2004).

The Federal Republic of Cameroon was abrogated on May 20, 1972[1] at which time Ahidjo and was replaced with a unitary form of government, thus reinforcing the one-party rule which was adopted as far back as 1966 following the abolition of political parties and the creation of the Cameroon National Union (CNU) party. This change consolidated the country as a one-party dictatorship headed by Ahidjo and his Cameroon National Union. However, Ahidjo's long dictatorial rule ended on November 6, 1982, when he voluntarily resigned[2] as head of state, and handed power to the Prime Minister Paul Biya (Levine, 1986, p. 20-52; Mbaku, 1993 p. 29-39; Mbaku 2004, p. 31-63).

In an attempt to remedy the ills of the Ahidjo regime, Biya renewed the framework and structure of the single party with a change of the name of the party from the Cameroon National Union (CNU) to the Cameroon Peoples' Democratic Movement (CPDM), with himself as the party president. Even with this change, the functioning of the party remained the same.

Although being a one-party state, Cameroon had its first competitive election in 1988, with candidates drawn from the ruling Cameroon Peoples' Democratic Movement (CPDM), which replaced the CNU in 1985 following the CNU congress in Bamenda. In response to pressure mounted on the Biya regime— especially by West Cameroon intellectuals—Biya announced his intention and commitment to re-establish multiparty democracy, and claimed this would be a starting point for the commitment of his government to create a more democratic country (Mbaku, 2004). Despite the declaration of his intentions, Biya was unwilling to relinquish his grip and monopoly on political authority, as the national assembly and the media were still heavily controlled by the regime. The pressure mounted on the regime by the opposition, and political demonstrations and strikes in favor of a more pluralistic democracy, led to a compromise that lifted the ban on demonstrations and public meetings.

The breakthrough to multiparty politics in Cameroon came in 1990 with the launch of the Social Democratic Front (SDF). The government did not take this easily and thus responded with a series of crackdowns leading to the killing of civilians by military forces, arrests, and imprisonments. All political meetings were banned, the chairman of the newly launched SDF was put under house arrest, and a curfew was imposed on the city of Bamenda, where this new political party was launched. Political and social unrest soon spread across the country and the economic situation worsened. The National Assembly was convened in response to the stiff resistance from the population, and a series of laws were designed to control the creation of political parties.

The first multiparty elections were held in March of 1991, after almost 25 years. The new freedom for political activities led to the creation of a plurality of political parties, most of which were too tiny or insignificant to take part in elections with only 32 of the 60 political parties having participated in the 1991 legislative elections. Prominent among the opposing political parties were the Social Democratic Front, with much support from West Cameroon, the National Union for Democracy and Progress (UNDP), the Union des populations du Cameroun (UPC), the Mouvement pour la Defense de la Republique (MDR), and the Union Democratique du Cameroun (UDC). Although the Law of Association of December 19, 1990 was signed, authorizing multiparty democracy in Cameroon, the incumbent president and his supporters were not actually willing to accommodate this new political dispensation, and this explains why the basic foundation of multiparty democracy was never put in place (Konings, 2004; Acha, 2011). Furthermore, the incumbent's maneuvers to weaken and divide the opposition since the legalization of pluralistic democracy is glaring evidence that accepting multiparty democracy was not a matter of choice, but was due to political pressure that was being mounted on the regime.

The first post-independence pluralistic elections held in 1991, the municipal and parliamentary elections, were boycotted by the SDF, the main opposition party, because of the government's failure to meet the demands of the opposition, which included the creation of an independent electoral commission to organize the elections. The ruling CPDM failed to win a majority of the seats and the UNDP came out as the strongest opposition party, winning more seats than expected. The opposition had a majority of seats, but was soon corrupted by the ruling government so as not to form a coalition. Some were bought over by the government to give the ruling party the majority to control the national assembly. It is important to underscore here that the good performance of the opposition in the 1991 parliamentary elections was due to the ill-preparedness of the ruling party and its inability to engage in massive fraud following the sudden decision by the SDF (the leading opposition party) to boycott the elections. The opposition alleged widespread fraud and irregularities by the government, but international observers reported the absence of any evidence of widespread fraud, as claimed by the opposition.

The first pluralistic presidential elections in 1992 were marred by widespread fraud to give undue advantage to the incumbent. The National Democratic Institute, which monitored the elections, reported irregularities and manipulation of the electoral process beginning from voter registration to ballot tabulation. The opposition candidates scored a combined total of 60.024 percent as opposed to the 39 percent of the votes in favor of the incumbent president. This was a signal that the overwhelming majority of Cameroonians wanted change (NDI, 1992). This rigging machine that resulted after the elections in 1992 became perfected, which has been clearly seen in Cameroon elections. According to Wallechinsky (2006), the election process in Cameroon is creatively innovated to favor rigging, and gives credibility to a process that is heavily rigged. Wallechinsky further suggested that the international observers invited to the 2004 presidential election, made up of six U.S. congressmen, were paid to certify heavily flawed elections as free and fair.

It is important to underline that voting malpractice in Cameroon is not the only source of electoral malpractice. Corrupting international observers to give false claims and reports, creating new opposition parties by members of the regime to be camouflaged as opposition, destabilizing the opposition, and using administrative authorities as enablers of fraud are other sources of irregularity in the Cameroon electoral process. Most of these problems might not be solved by technology, but by commitment of the government to promote credible democratic processes.

CHALLENGES OF THE ELECTORAL PROCESS IN CAMEROON

The election begins with the registration of voters, the voting proper (which in Cameroon takes place on an officially selected date), the counting of the votes, and the proclamation of results. These processes are overseen by an election management body, which in principle is expected to be independent. Domestic and foreign observers are invited to observe the general conduct of the election, beginning from the preparations through the voting, the counting, and the proclamation of the results. The role of the observers is not to supervise, but to observe the process to assess whether it was conducted according to the standards set in the electoral law. We examine this process in the following subsections and explore the links between the outcome of the electoral process and the innovations and technology that have been applied during the past elections.

Voter Registration and Update of Voter Lists

Elections in Cameroon begin with voter registration, which is the most important stage of the electoral process. Elections in Cameroon shall be placed under the supervision of the electoral board, as clearly provided by Section 9 of the Electoral Code. Thus, it is this body that updates electoral registers on a yearly basis. Section 74 of the Electoral Code provides that electoral registers shall be permanent and shall be revised throughout the territory every year. This exercise will begin on January 1 and continue through August 31 of each year. The credibility of the election depends primarily on transparency, efficiency, and the credibility of the voter registration process.

The electoral law requires Cameroonian citizens of voting age to prove their identity before enrolling, and this often requires that they possess an identity card. Prior to the computerization of identity cards in Cameroon, voter registration was often fraught with multiple registrations, with some voters enrolling in multiple voting stations, which encouraged voters to vote multiple times in favor of their political parties. The electoral law requires that voter registration is accomplished well in advance of the elections so that voters can verify that they have been registered to vote. However, this process is flawed, as the publication of the electoral lists is not always done nationwide. Even if this is done, as is the case in some electoral districts, there is no mechanism to check for multiple registrations.

Innovations in the Voter Registration Process

The new biometric voter registration system is used in updating electoral registers between electoral events. Biometric voter registration is a process for enrolling voters using one or more digitally recognizable features, which may include fingerprints, facial recognition features, iris recognition, and hand geometry. The technology uses digital registration kits and computers to update voter registers. The mobile, self-powered biometric voter registration kit was first introduced in Cameroon in 2012. ELECAM deployed a total of 1,200 kits throughout the country for voter registration to match six fingerprints, photos, and additional registration information. The kits are used in mobile registration and the content is then updated to a central database. The new voter cards that are issued include photos, fingerprints, names, place of birth, occupation, residence, and parents' names.

While it is desirable to increase voter registration and use technology that renews trust in the electoral process, implementing the new tools brings significant challenges. First, the registration takes time to complete, and with only a few kits (as was the case in 2012), it is likely that many of the over 10 million eligible voters will not be able to register. Second, it takes about a day for the biometric cards to print and voters are required to return later in the day to collect their cards, which may be difficult for people with limited mobility (such as people with disabilities or older people). Also, people with limited means may tend to have limited access to registration.

Another concern is that a large number of voters—especially those living in remote areas—have limited means for the cost of obtaining an identity card, which is required for registration. Besides, voter apathy is exacerbated by the manipulation of the media in favor of the ruling party and allegations of electoral fraud in previous elections. Engaging the civil society in the registration process and providing assistance for those who are unable to afford the cost of obtaining national identity cards can be helpful in expanding voter registration. Campaigns to mobilize voter registration could also be extended to weekends, and registration offices opened to register all voters. The cost of obtaining an ID card was reduced in 2011, and it has become less expensive to get an ID card. Despite the reduction in cost, not all eligible voters are able to afford ID cards, which cost about five U.S. dollars. Identifying these individuals and waiving the fee associated with obtaining ID cards can encourage eligible voters to register for elections.

In addition to the privacy concerns related to the use the biometric systems that provide the advanced technology used to confirm voter eligibility at voting locations, the technology is also costly. Despite these concerns, the system seems to provide solutions to some of the most common sources of electoral malpractice in Cameroon.

Political Campaigns and the Voting Process

Although political parties can organize political activities all year long, the campaign period for most elections in Cameroon is two weeks prior to the election day. Political parties are expected to set out their policy platforms, which outline the policies and how they plan to govern if they were to win the elections. Various media, including radio, TV, newspapers, and rallies are often used as forums to lay out their programs to voters. In the past, when the major source of communication was national TV and radio run by the government, political parties were often cheated in the allocation of airtime for campaigns. The proliferation of private TV and radio, as well as modern technology, such as the use of SMS and Facebook, and other social media, has actually improved electoral campaigns recently.

Voting in Cameroon is often scheduled on a Sunday, and polling stations are open from 8:00 a.m. until 6:00 p.m. The political body controlling elections in Cameroon is ELECAM. This body is assumed to be independent, although its members are appointed by the President of the Republic, who doubles as the head of the ruling party. The opposition is not comfortable with this arrangement, as its members are often affiliated with the ruling party. The head of a polling station is appointed by ELECAM. This chairperson is assisted by representatives of political parties taking part in said elections. In principle, it is not possible for a voter to vote more than once, since the voter is registered only once following the introduction of the biometric system. On election day, the voter presents the voting card and the officials at the polling station verify that the voter is at the right voting station. After this verification, the officials proceed with the verification of the name of the voter on the electoral register, and whether the voter presenting the card is the actual person on the voter register. Once this is done, the voter casts his/her vote and signs the electoral register.

Although fraud is reduced with the use of biometric cards, multiple voting was still reported during the 2013 parliamentary elections. This is possible in polling stations where the opposition parties are not equally represented.

Although vote counting and tallying are done at the polling stations, at the close of the vote, as long as the votes cast are not transmitted electronically to the central database, the results of the election could still be manipulated. The members of the local polling station could be corrupted, intimidated, or cajoled to alter the results given that the Council branch of ELECAM has up to 48 hours to receive the report. In the absence of disorder in any form, representatives of political parties can watch out for fraud.

Malpractices and Fraud in Cameroon Elections

The most serious problems that tend to undermine the outcome of elections in Cameroon begin with the selective registration of voters who are biased in favor of members of the ruling party (Ndeh, 2011). This method of disenfranchising the electorate is undemocratic and is the root cause of the instability of the Cameroon political system. These anti-democratic maneuvers are in conflict with universally acceptable norms and standards. Article 21 of the Universal Declaration of Human Rights (UDHR) states: "The will of the people shall be the basis of the authority of government; this will shall be expressed in periodic and genuine elections which shall be by equal suffrage and shall be held by secret vote or by equivalent free voting procedures." Article 25 of ICCPR ensures further that "every citizen shall have the right and the opportunity, without any of the distinctions mentioned in article 2 and without unreasonable restrictions: to vote and to be elected at genuine periodic elections which shall be by universal and equal suffrage and shall be held by secret ballot, guaranteeing the free expression of the will of the electors." These two articles invite countries to take appropriate measures to ensure that all citizens have a right to vote and exercise that right. In order to protect the right to vote, Human Rights Advocates (HRA) (2014) urges states to: (1) reform their voting laws to ensure that any restrictions on voting are reasonable, objective, and proportional; and (2) develop effective mechanisms for challenging electoral irregularities.

Since the inception of multiparty democracy in Cameroon, there has not been any election that has not be contested. Electoral manipulation is common and usually takes three different forms, which include, inter alia: (1) manipulation of election rules; (2) manipulation of vote choice; and (3) manipulation of voting. What has been common in Cameroon elections in recent years is the manipulation of the boundaries of electoral constituencies in favor of the ruling party. Gerrymandering has been a common political ploy by the ruling CPDM party to outsmart the opposition in areas of the country where the opposition is a force to reckon with. This was the case when the government of Cameroon decided to make Balikumbat a special constituency to pave the way for the election of the late Fon of Balikumbat, a staunch supporter of the ruling CPDM as a member of parliament. In some polling districts, electoral officials are biased in favor of either a political party or a particular candidate, and this happens especially when the opposition has little or no representation in polling stations and electoral districts.

Besides other technical issues involved in the organization of elections in Cameroon, the manipulation of voter registers stands out as the most serious problem. Most often, certain categories of people are prevented from registering to vote or are deliberately refused issuance of voter cards. The opposition is the most disfavored, since the names of their supporters displace the lists, and some lists have names of underaged and even deceased individuals. These forms of malpractice tend to compromise the credibility of the election results, which are frequently contested by the opposition parties.

The manipulation of voter choice is also a serious problem in elections organized in Cameroon, whether at the local level or at the level of the parliament or the president. A basic tool used to manipulate voter choice is an imbalance in media coverage of elections. The media is often biased in their coverage of political activities of the people vying for elections, providing more coverage to a candidate they favor and less coverage to those they do not favor. Also, the circulation of false information and rumor has been used against other parties in order to turn voters away from the parties or candidates. When false information was first circulated that the leading opposition party had secret dealings with the ruling CPDM party, it led to voter apathy—especially for SDF supporters, who started to believe the outcome of the election would not bring any change since their party leaders were collaborating with the ruling party.

The use of ballot papers that are rather confusing to voters tends to result in voters giving their votes to candidates that are not their choice. Another way that fraud has been perpetrated in Cameroon elections is individuals pretending to be someone else in order to cast votes in place of others who are either absent or are deceased.

Other examples of vote manipulation include the recording of votes differently from votes cast, or the buying of votes by sharing out money, bags of salt, soap, drinks, and other items. Sometimes voters are paid to vote for a particular candidate or for a particular party. The use of intimidation and other forms of obstruction has been common in Cameroon elections. These intimidations lead to several types of violations of electoral standards. For example, the bosses at the voter's place of employment may request that everyone vote for a particular party or candidate, or the person will be fired if they refuse to comply. It is also common for people living in a certain area to be deprived of water, roads, and electricity if they fail to cast their votes for a given candidate or political party. This economic scare is fast changing election outcomes in Cameroon today. Once the community is aware that they might lose services by supporting a certain political party, they withdraw their support from that candidate or party simply because they do not want their services to be curtailed. The exercise of violence of various forms and unlawful disruption of political activities, such as the campaigns of certain candidates and parties, creates insecurity and fear during elections.

Elections organized under these circumstances cannot be fair or representative, and obviously, elections cannot be adequately run by aggrieved people to change the way the country is governed and to replace unpopular governments. Fraudulent elections also lead to the installation of incompetent leaders in power, and such leaders are accountable to no one other than themselves. We have witnessed the decay of political authority in Cameroon in recent years in situations where it is difficult for the government, local council, or political authority to complete projects that are helpful to the economy and to the alleviation of poverty.

ELECTION MANAGEMENT BODIES AND TRANSPARENCY OF THE ELECTORAL PROCESS

Cameroon functioned like an autocracy until the 1992 election, during which the incumbent President Paul Biya was narrowly re-elected amidst irregularities and fraud reported both by the opposition parties and the international observers (CCDHR 2009). The fear that the 1997 presidential elections would be marred by irregularities led to threats by the opposition to boycott the elections, along with demonstrations across the nation, which eventually led to the creation of the National Elections Observatory (NEO) in 2000. With the creation of this body, there was hope that the will of the people, as expressed in the election outcomes, would be respected, yet the election was again marred by widespread fraud and irregularities despite minor improvements as observed by the international election observers. The presidential elections in 2004 and the parliamentary elections in 2007 experienced several problems of fraud and election malpractice, ranging from widespread problems of voter disenfranchisement (resulting from inadequate management of voter registration lists), to the failure to utilize indelible ink to prevent fraud. This highlighted the need for an electoral body that was completely free of any interference by the Ministry of Territorial Administration and Decentralization (MINATD). The inability of the NEO to realize the presence of these inherent problems reinforced the belief that this body was not different from the MINATD's handling of the elections. The NEO's failure to organize free and fair elections was reinforced by the fact that the management body was a flip of the MINATD. External and internal pressure on the Cameroon government to reform the electoral system and revise the electoral law led to the creation of Election Cameroon (ELECAM).

The creation of ELECAM in December 2006 was seen as a new opportunity to give credibility to the democratic process in Cameroon. Despite this, the new body is not completely different from the previous one, and some of the problems of the previous bodies are inherent in the new body. Despite operational difficulties, ELECAM is still capable of having a positive impact on elections in Cameroon, if it were independent and if the members of this electoral board were neutral and impartial. Instead, the appointments of the members of the board showed widespread party bias, thus exposing a ploy by the government to weaken the election body. The appointment of ELECAM members by the President of the Republic, and the renewal of their term of office by the president, as well as the fact that most of the members are former surrogates of the ruling party, interferes with their neutrality (CCDHR, 2009). Besides, the law allows the president to fill any vacancy in ELECAM without consultation with political parties. Because of this interference by the president and the director general (who can reassign civil servants to the board), the neutrality of the management board can be compromised.

Technology in Election Monitoring

The use of new techniques in election monitoring and information management by nonpartisan domestic monitors, whose role is to provide an impartial assessment of the electoral process and deter electoral fraud, is key to any credible election. Election monitors should be able to utilize statistically based election monitoring techniques during elections to ensure that the electoral process is clearly understood, and know how to evaluate this process. Statistically based election monitoring was used in the 2008 elections in Ghana, during which the Coalition of Domestic Election Observers conducted a statistical analysis of the results. ELECAM can organize transparent elections free of agitation by allowing monitors to utilize the parallel vote tabulation monitors to forecast the results of the elections to be within a certain margin of those announced by ELECAM. This has the tendency of providing political parties the confidence to accept the outcome of the election, and to avoid conflict or violence that might result from such close margins. The domestic election observers can use the statistically based monitoring techniques to forestall election manipulation by election officials who are often sympathizers of the ruling party.

The announcement of the PVT results by neutral monitors can force the election commission to announce the actual results and avoid fraud. The use of the media and the Internet to make such announcements can pressure political participants to stick to acceptable standards for election behavior. Avoiding fraud also depends on the number of observers that are mobilized to monitor the election. Allowing these observers to cast their votes outside of their electoral districts can in turn encourage more monitors to cover elections outside of their districts. The use of statistically based monitoring techniques should not compete with the election commission, but should rather collaborate with them by providing additional support to the commission to ease tensions in elections. This technique was successfully used in Ghana during the 2008 election, and in

Malawi during the 2009 elections. The statistically based monitoring effort can only be credible if the monitors are able to identify all the polling stations, as well as their exact locations. The validity of this process also depends on the presence of effective communication tools to provide the results from the field.

TECHNOLOGY AND ELECTION OUTCOMES

How can elections in Cameroon be rendered free and fair? What are the mechanisms to guarantee hitch-free elections? Can the use of various technologies work even without the political will of the election control body? We examine what is working and what is not in the following sections in order to define a clear-cut strategy for improving election outcomes in Cameroon.

Based on the report of the Commonwealth Expert Team that observed the September 2013 Legislative and Municipal Elections in Cameroon—the third election organized by ELECAM since it became operational—the credibility of the election body was reported to have been enhanced. The newly introduced electoral code shows significant improvement in the transparency and credibility of the election process in Cameroon. The introduction of the new biometric registration process has substantially improved the management of voter registers (Commonwealth Expert Team, 2013). The improvement in the voter registration process—which by all standards was considered outdated—with the introduction of biometric verification of voter registration resulted in more voters being registered to vote, and the hope was that the new register would reduce irregularities in the voting process. (See Table 16.1 for voter turnout since 1960 for parliamentary election and 1988 for presidential elections.) Despite the increase in voter registration in both the 2011 presidential and the 2013 parliamentary elections, and the creation of the election management board ELECAM, the actual number of people who participated in the election declined, reflecting voter apathy with past elections compared to previous years and previous election management bodies. Voter apathy is mostly attributed to electoral fraud and government meddling in the electoral process in favor of the ruling party. The lack of trust in the electoral process and the general discontent among the voters—especially the youths, who find no incentive for participating in the political process—is another source of voter apathy. Tah (2014), after studying the strategy implemented by ELECAM to change attitudes toward voting, suggests that the strategy utilized by the election management body (such as the use of information dissemination via TV, radio, and billboards) was less effective than participatory methods of communication, such as traditional meetings, local tontines, and traditional authorities.

Table 16.1: Voter turnout data for Cameroon
Parliamentary

Year	Voter Turnout	Total Vote	Registration	VAP Turnout	Voting age Population	Population	Invalid Votes	Compulsory Voting
2013	76.79%	4,208,796	5,481,226	37.55%	11,207,373	22,534,532	4.40%	No
2007	62.01%	3,100,000	5,000,000	34.51%	8,982,601	18,060,382		No
2002	65.66%	2,882,164	4,389,572	36.89%	7,813,588	15,803,220		No
1997	75.60%	2,906,156	3,844,330	46.70%	6,222,978	13,829,000		No
1992	60.59%	2,435,443	4,019,562	44.42%	5,482,800	12,184,000	9.80%	No
1988	90.32%	3,282,884	3,634,568	67.03%	4,897,350	10,883,000	3.10%	No
1960	69.56%	1,349,739	1,940,438	57.44%	2,350,000	4,700,000		No

Table 16.1 continued
Presidential

Year	Voter Turnout	Total Vote	Registration	VAP Turnout	Voting age Population	Population	Invalid Votes	Compulsory Voting
2011	68.28%	4,951,434	7,251,651	50.25%	9,854,578	20,129,878	2.31%	No
2004	79.52%	3,738,759	4,701,953	45.28%	8,256,564	16,063,678	4.50%	No
1997	87.00%	3,377,833	3,882,725	53.67%	6,293,250	13,985,000		No
1992	71.87%	3,015,440	4,195,687	55.00%	5,482,800	12,184,000		No
1988	91.40%	3,321,872	3,634,568	67.83%	4,897,350	10,883,000		No

Source: International Institute for Democracy and Electoral Assistance (International IDEA)[3]

Prior to each election, voter registers are open six months before the election, and eligible persons can register to vote. Once the qualified individual's name is entered in the register, a permanent registration card is issued in his or her name. However, the cards are not immediately available for distribution, which is the responsibility of ELECAM. Each voter must provide a valid national identity card, mandatory in accordance with Law no. 90/042 of December 19, 1990, instituting the National Identity Card. A biometric voter card is issued to each voter whose name is on the voter register. The biometric card has the name of the voter, the occupation, the residence, a photo, and a fingerprint. ELECAM distributes these cards in various councils, and each individual is expected to pick up the card with the presentation of the National Identity Card or his or her receipt. This is an innovation that has substantially improved the registration process, and has reduced cases of irregularity in the elections in most recent years. During the elections of September 2013, despite the improvement in voter registration using the new registration method, some of the registration cards were not delivered to voters and such cards were brought to the polling stations to be collected on election day. Delays in distributing biometric voter cards could undermine the progress made so far if measures are not taken to address this shortcoming so as not to disenfranchise voters. What has been observed in recent elections—especially during the 2011 presidential election—was that some voters had their registration cards but could not find their names on the voter list, and thus were not allow to vote, which inherently affected the outcome of the elections. The use of indelible ink after elections has been ineffective. If the ink is not of good quality, and in consideration of where this ink has to be used, it has to be mandatory and the voter registration cards should be stamped or even perforated to avoid multiple voting.

Election Campaign, the Media, and Technology

The media plays a vital role in all election coverage, and increasing this role can have a significant impact on election outcomes in Cameroon. The role of the media in electoral campaigns in Cameroon has evolved significantly since the first multiparty elections in 1992. The new unified electoral code adopted in 2012 has provided guidelines for campaigns by political parties during municipal and legislative elections. In contrast to the past, when campaigns were supervised by the MINADT, it is ELECAM, the election management body, that has been entrusted with the authority to supervise elections in Cameroon.

One of the most common forms of the media used in Cameroon elections is the use of posters. The candidates, or their respective political parties, prepare the posters and electoral law requires that ELECAM endorses such material before it is posted. ELECAM would not endorse any document that might incite violence or hate, or that can undermine the sovereignty of the State or threaten national unity. The posters are expected to be withdrawn on election day to avoid conflict among supporters of various political parties.

The pattern of election campaigns in Cameroon is such that the State-run media has a wider geographical coverage than private media, which gives an undue advantage to the ruling party. Journalists working for the State-run media tend to favor the ruling party in coverage since their job security is inextricably related their loyalty to the ruling party, thus giving the ruling party an unfair advantage. Before the liberalization of the media, the state-run media, which includes television and radio, was the only source of information besides the print media. A fair election can only be guaranteed if the coverage of campaigns by both the electronic and print media is fair and equitable to all political parties and to all candidates, and this is only possible if the media is independent. An independent and fair media provides voters with information that is indispensable for making choices based on their assessment of the programs proposed by different candidates and political parties. The State-owned media should not be an exception, and should provide equal access to all candidates irrespective of their political affiliations.

The continuous intervention of the MINATD in elections, as portrayed in the Commonwealth Report on the 2011 presidential elections, is a call for concern. During the 2011 election, MINATD systematically allowed the ruling party to purchase all billboard space, leaving less room for competition among the candidates. Billboards are critical tools that are used in election campaigns, and they are highly effective in reaching out to voters, especially in areas where there is no television coverage or when people do not own TVs. The government owns and controls billboards, and tends to charge high prices for them. It even imposes restrictions on where to post the billboards, thus blocking opposition parties from campaigning freely. This kind of obstruction may discourage supporters of opposition parties from participating in elections.

The Ministry of Communication was in charge of granting accreditation to journalists who expressed the wish to cover the campaigns of the candidate for the ruling party, instead of allowing this role to an independent body like ELE-CAM. The absence of any independent body to ensure that certain standards are maintained renders the work of journalists insecure, as some of them face threats of incarceration and other forms of intimidation for reporting on other candidates. Although Cameroon's media is expanding to include private media, the different media outlets do not have the logistical manpower or the internal training of staff to provide nationwide coverage of campaigns.

After the 2011 presidential election, the Commonwealth election watchdog recommended that media outlets should examine the use of technology so as to leverage their resources with other outlets in Cameroon (Commonwealth Expert Team 2011). The use of new technology in the media can increase outreach to provide voters with the information to enhance their participation in the electoral process. The media does not only need to be independent, it should also adopt nontraditional innovations, such as web-based communication tools, that enable society to engage actively in the election process. The use of independent media outlets, and outlets such mobile phones, Facebook, SMS, and even Twitter services, is critical for communication during the elections, as this helps in gathering and transmitting information among voters. These media outlets can significantly increase voter turnout and mobilizes them to watch and protect the votes earned by various political parties and candidates.

The media, as we have discussed, is a valuable tool in the election process, but can also play a negative role during an election if it is used in an inflammatory way. It can incite violence during an election, which has been the case in Cameroon during previous elections where irresponsible statements by journalists incited violence rather than peace. There should be a mechanism to sanction any media outlet that incites violence and hate before and after elections. The civil society should also be able to monitor the media to make sure that it does not spread false information and propaganda.

CONCLUSION AND RECOMMENDATIONS

The increasing use of technology in elections across Africa has yielded positive outcomes in some countries. In these countries, elections have strengthened democratic institutions, fostered national unity, and have provided opportunities for economic growth and prosperity. Successful elections have also paved the way for national reconciliation and the return to democratically elected civilian governments, especially after an armed conflict. In some countries, including Cameroon, flawed elections have heightened tension, violence, and have eroded public confidence in elected officials and institutions. Corruption at all levels of the government, and with the political process, is pervasive to the extent that the country has often been ranked among the most corrupt countries in the world. Quite often economic vulnerabilities can force people to use voting as a means to access resources. Despite the relative calm that reigns in Cameroon after a series of flawed elections, Cameroonians are less certain about election outcomes more than ever before. This scenario has resulted in voter apathy and the distrust of elected officials and institutions. To ensure that future elections are credible, such elections should be transparent and inclusive. Political parties, the election management body, security services, the civil society, religious leaders, and the media should work hand in hand.

In the midst of the corrupt practices highlighted above, the use of technology—even if it is the best technology for reducing fraudulence in the election process—might not guarantee free and fair elections if the management of the electoral process is not independent. The use of technology is an effective tool in the Cameroon electoral process if it is well implemented to ensure that there is transparency and accountability.

REFERENCES

Abiosseh Davis. 2012. Voter Registration Goes High Tech in Cameroon. Counterpart International. http://www.counterpart.org/voter-registration-goes-high-tech-in-cameroon/

Ayogu Melvin. 2011. Cameroon's Presidential Election: Will the Votes Count? Retrieved on Thursday October 6, 2011 from https://www.brookings.edu/experts/melvin-ayogu/.

CCDR (Cameroon Center for Democracy and Human Rights). 2009. Cameroon Needs an Independent Electoral Commission: ELECAM not the Answer. CCDHR Policy Paper.

Commonwealth Expert Team .2011. Cameroon Presidential Election. Report of the Commonwealth Expert Team.

_____2013. Cameroon legislative and Municipal Elections 30 September 2013. Report of the Commonwealth Expert Team.

HRA (Human Rights Advocates). 2014. The Right to Vote: Interference by Voter Registration Laws. Human Rights Advocates, California USA.

Konings, Piet. 2004. Opposition and Social-Democratic Change in Africa: The Social Democratic Front in Cameroon. Commonwealth & Comparative Politics, Vol. 42, No. 3 pp. 1-23.

_____ 2006. Tyrants: The World's 20 Worst Living Dictators (2006) Quoted by the Huffingtonpost, http://www.huffington post.com/david-wallechinsky/the-worlds-worst-dictator_b_28679.html, accessed May 2011.https://www.brookings.edu/opinions/cameroons-presidential-election count/International Institute for Democracy and Electoral Assistance. 2016. Republic of Cameroon. http://www.idea.int/ elections /ict/country.cfm?id=46

Levine, V.T. 1964. Cameroon: From Mandate to Independence, Hoover Institutions Stanford, CA

Levine, V.T. 1986. "Leadership and Regime Changes in Perspectives" in Schatzberg, M.G. and Zartman , I. W. (eds), *The Political Economy of Cameroon*, Praeger: New York.

Mbaku, J.M. 1985. Measuring Economic Performance in Cameroon, 1972-1982. PhD Dissertation, University of Georgia, Atlanta, Georgia.

_____1993. *Regime change and the Growth of Governemnt in Africa: An Analysis of Political Sucession in Cameroon*, Economia delle Scelte Puybliche (Italy), Vol. 11, No. 1 pp. 29-39.

_____2004. Decolonization, Reunification, and Federation in Cameroon in Mbaku J.M. and Takougang J. (eds), *Leadership Challenge in Africa: Cameroon under Paul Biya*, African World Press, Inc., Trenton New Jersey.

Ndeh Martin Sango. 2011. Election Cacophony in Cameroon: Reading the Frustrations of an Oppressed Electorate 1990-2007. *CJDHR* Vol. 5 No. 1

National Democratic Institute, (NDI). 1992. Interim Report International Delegation to the Presidential Elections in Cameroon (1992).

Tah, Tembeng Hedley. 2014. Participation for Political Development in Cameroon. International Journal of Humanities and Social Science, Vol. 4, No. 7(1); May 2014.

ENDNOTES

1. The 1972 referendum, which ended the federal form of government, was orchestrated to give credibility to Ahidjo's decision to consolidate political power. Acha (2011) has given explicit evolution of the events in 1972 as well as the election that opponents viewed as misguided and manipulated.

2. Ahidjo's decision to resign in 1982 was not actually voluntary. His French physician revealed that he had a grave disease that made him incapable of exercising his duties as head of state.

3. International Institute for Democracy and Electoral Assistance (International IDEA) Strömsborg, SE-103 34 Stockholm, Sweden, www.idea.int

Chapter 17
Transformation of Elections in Great Maghreb: A Lesson Learned from Technology Integration

Loubna Dali — Bowie State University
Cosmas Uchenna Nwokeafor — Bowie State University

INTRODUCTION

Corruption can simply be defined as the process whereby a person of a particular function, public or private, accepts gift offers or promises to perform, delay or omit to do an act, directly or indirectly, as part of his/her duty. Today, corruption is a social evil that is spreading increasingly. It affects many regions of the world, such as Africa and the great Maghrebian countries. In general, the policy makers and public officials are always accused as the prime movers of this social evil. However, insightful analysis shows that politicians are far from being the primary culprits of corruption, and that the poor citizens themselves are guilty of this offense as well. Therefore, seeking to prescribe an antidote to the evil that is itself a component of the economic tyranny in society, we must first tackle poverty, which is considered a major cause of corruption, especially in the great Maghreb.

Before illustrating the factors that cause corruption and providing a solution, we will define the types of corruption. The criminal law distinguishes two kinds of corruption:

1. Passive bribery: Normally, when a person is holding a public occupation, and takes advantage of his position to solicit or accept gifts with promises or orders to perform an act of bribery, that person is named the corrupt.
2. Active bribery: When a person obtains or attempts to obtain, by means of gifts, promises or advantages, of a person exercising a public func-

tion, or to perform or delay or refrain from an act or delay its function, this person is named corrupter.

Both kinds of bribery are certainly complementary; however, they are separate and autonomous. They can be prosecuted and judged separately, and suppression of one is not subject to the sanction of the other. The corruption does not go unnoticed. Indeed, it generates effects which sometimes take on dangerous dimensions. This phenomenon also creates a breeding ground for favoritism, bias, and inequality. And as a result, citizens lose all faith in the public service. In addition to these negative aspects, corruption hinders economic development and negatively impacts its way to democracy and equal rights.

In short, corruption is an unhealthy act generated by selfishness and greed. It generates negative consequences. Sensitization and awareness are short-term solutions and the most obvious ones. Furthermore, we must also ensure the enforcement of laws and not keep them as ink on paper.

Many factors contribute to corruption in the Maghreb region. First, the low-salaried employees that seek dishonest gain find a way to satisfy their unbridled lust by committing acts of bribery. Second, the slow process of public services results in the people trying to bribe so that their services and goals are reached as soon as possible. Also, the laws against corruption are not strictly enforced. We can categorize the factors into three main categories, namely:

Individual Factors:
1. Human greed
2. Morals of the less powerful
3. Insufficient income
4. The urgent necessities of life
5. Consumptive lifestyle
6. Lazy or unwilling to work

Organizational Factors
1. Lack of exemplary leadership stance
2. Absence of a true culture of the organization
3. Lack of adequate and proper systems of accountability in government agencies
4. Weaknesses of management control systems
5. Management tends to cover up corruption in the organization

Social Factors
1. The values in the society are conducive to corruption
2. Corruption can be caused by the culture of society
3. The public is less aware of the main victims of corruption
4. The individual is less aware when he/she is involved in corruption

5. The public is less aware that corruption will be prevented and eradicated if people push for active application of legislation

Whatever the factor is, corruption remains a barrier that holds up the proper functioning of society. It causes the degradation of public service. Unfortunately, this may become a habit that prevents employees from performing their duties unless they are bribed. This will create serious, harmful effects that will deprive citizens of necessary public services because of their marginalization. Also, this practice corrosively affects the economic development of the great Maghreb countries.

Corruption, being the misuse of public and private office for personal gain, can take different forms, such as diverting funds, manipulating elections, accepting bribes, and inappropriate gifts. However, one of the most malicious types of corruption is political or electoral corruption. The latter is considered a deadly poison of democracy where the elected politicians use their ample opportunity to abuse their political powers at the expense of voters. Moreover, the measure indicates that the act of corruption varies among countries, depending on their economic and social characteristics.

Basically, elections serve two functions in representative democracies. First, they select political participants who enact public policies in light of constituents' preferences. Second, they permit citizens to hold their representatives accountable, and to punish them if they enrich themselves in corrupt or self-serving ways. In other words, elections provide both incentives for politicians to endorse certain kinds of policies, and constraints on politicians' misbehavior.

However, the electoral process, which is the key to all democratic systems, is increasingly impugned in Great Maghreb, thereby jeopardizing the democratic process in many countries. Electoral corruption is an unlawful manipulation of elections, personal interests, and institutions. The first participants of electoral corruption are politicians, and some activists generally seek to win at all costs. After their election, the corrupt politicians create a system based on corruption, nominating their family and friends to the highest positions. In addition, they lobby to amend the laws, text, or electoral code to their benefit. They also modify the institutions, which are involved in maintaining the rules and laws, and are responsible for overseeing the conduct of electoral operations.

On the other hand, the election goes through many phases, and the corruption can occur in any of them:

Registration fraud:
- Register in multiple jurisdictions
- Graveyard voting
- "Cleanse" the voter list
- Districting and re-districting

Voter fraud:
- Vote multiple times (ballot-box stuffing)
- Multiple voting
- Impersonation
- Vote buying, chain voting

Insider fraud:
- Throw ballot boxes into the bay
- Stuff ballot box after polls close
- Sleight of hand
- Voter intimidation
- Run out of ballots
- Ballot marking

Tallying attacks:
- Malicious talliers might calculate wrong results
- Give tallies bogus tools
- Inaccurate counts
- Ballot marking
- Manipulation of challenge procedure

Because of the severity of these impacts, whose extent is becoming heavier, ending corruption becomes a necessity that requires a severe sanction applied on different members of society involved in the practice. Several solutions aim to substantially reduce electoral fraud and corruption in our great Maghreb through seminars and events. Also, there are some control methods that will contribute to the reduction of this phenomenon. One of these methods is raising awareness by creating institutions that supervise and control the process of elections. To enhance the election performance, we can add some mechanisms such as:

- Control of public funding
- Control of political parties' expenses
- Involvement of civil society
- Dialogue and space that will unite all the participants

Yet, all the solutions stated above can be executed by the government. And, as civilians with IT backgrounds, we can contribute to our society and propose a new way to avoid the electoral corruption by introducing information and communications technologies (ICTs) into the electoral process. This will use the most recent technologies to improve the electoral process and reduce the corruption. We are proposing Internet voting as a way to facilitate voting and to raise the level of participation in elections; and also to ensure the credibility and the reliability of the process of elections. The inclusion of IT into elections will definitely open up new doors and will offer new possibilities for voting operations. However, there might be hidden vulnerabilities involved that we have to take into consideration while implementing our scenario, such as selling votes or cheating in auditing results. This might have the potential to compromise transparency or sustainability of the electoral process.

Our approach is based on secure systems using the most recent and powerful technology, the Trusted Platform Module (TPM) and the biometric authentication. As a result, our work will have a huge sense of flexibility, mobility, and cost-effective solutions. We propose the use of Cloud-based database programs supplied with automation software, which an electoral authority can use to:

- Enter, store, and use electoral roll data
- Automate the election process at its different stages, such as issuing and receiving the electronic votes
- Analyze election results data
- Record candidate details and facilitate the printing of ballot papers and the reporting of election donations and spending

CLOUD COMPUTING

Definition of Cloud Computing

Cloud computing is a network like the Internet that consists of a multitude of systems providing services. Cloud computing is a set of services and consumable data provided to users. For most users, the Cloud is a new computing model with a potential for savings. It easily accommodates development needs and allows the separation of IT management problems. Indeed, users called "Cloud Service Users" (CSUs) do not generally own IT infrastructure, but they have the ability to access or allocate computing Cloud services. These services are provided by the suppliers of services in the Cloud, and are called "Cloud Service Providers"(CSPs). However, in the industry and in the academic sector, there are many definitions for "Cloud." We chose the definition provided by the National Institute of Standards and Technology (NIST) covering all the essential aspects of the Cloud: "Cloud computing is a computing model to establish easy access and on-demand through the network to a shared pool of configurable computing resources (network, servers, storage spaces, applications and services) that can be rapidly provisioned and released with minimal management effort or interaction with the service provider."

Characteristics

The Cloud has many interesting features that make it attractive to CSU and the CSP. Vaquero et al., Buyya et al., and Gong et al. give a complete analysis of the characteristics of the Cloud. We present in this section the most significant characteristics of Cloud:

1. Easy access: Services hosted in the Cloud are generally based on the web. Therefore, they are easily accessible through a variety of Internet-connected devices. Furthermore, in order to achieve an elevated performance in terms of accessibility, many Clouds are composed of data centers (DCs) in several locations worldwide.

2. Low initial investment and advantageous pricing: Cloud uses a type of payment model called "pay for what you use" (see Figure 17.1). The CSU is charged based on usage rather than a flat rate, allowing considerable savings. Moreover, a CSP does not need a tremendous investment in infrastructure to deliver these services and start making profits. One simply rents the Cloud resources based on user needs.

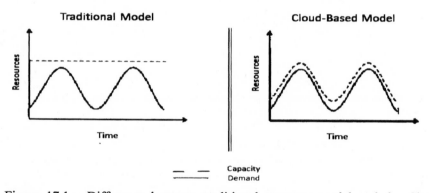

Figure 17.1 - Difference between traditional payment model and the Cloud model.

3. Grouping of shared resources and dynamic allocation and demand: The CSP has a group of IT resources that can be dynamically assigned to the resource consumers (CSU). This dynamic allocation of resource capacity allows great flexibility for CSP to manage their own resource use and operating costs.

4. Self-organizing and scaling: Resources in a Cloud environment can be quickly allocated and released according to the demand. In some cases, they must be done automatically. For CSU, services must be available and assigned at any time and in any amount. A CSP can easily expand its large-scale service to manage the rapidly increasing demand for services.

5. Service measured: The Cloud automatically controls and optimizes the use of resources through measurement capability with a level of abstraction appropriate to the type of service (e.g., storage, processing, bandwidth, accounts active users, etc.). The use of resources can be quantified according to the appropriate measures (the hours for CPU, bandwidth, etc.), monitored, controlled, and reported, providing transparency to the CSP and the CSU.

6. Virtualized Resources: Virtualization is a technology that creates an abstraction of the physical hardware and provides virtualized resources for high-level applications. A virtualized server is commonly called a virtual machine (VM) and we can implement more VMs on the same physical server. Virtualization is the main component of Cloud computing because it provides the ability to pool IT resources to server groups and dynamically allocate virtual resources on-demand to applications. We can virtualize many resources, such as computing resources, software, hardware, operating systems, and storage space systems. In addition, we can manage the virtualized resources without actually dealing with the physical infrastructure.

SERVICES MODELS

The main purpose of the Cloud is to offer services to users responding to all different levels and needs. We present in this section the main service models of the Cloud:

1. Software as a Service (Saas): SaaS stands for "Software as a Service." It essentially refers to software that is hosted on servers and is provided as a service. Some initial uses for SaaS include customer relationship management offerings, content management systems, video conferencing, and e-mail communication systems. SaaS applications are provided over the web, which means they can be accessed from any computer without any special software installed. In fact, many applications are designed to run through a standard web browser. When updates to a SaaS application need to be installed, they are simply installed on the server, which immediately ensures that all users are running the latest version. Unlike traditional software applications that require an upfront purchase, SaaS applications typically offer subscription-based pricing and are usually licensed on a per-user basis.

Like other forms of Cloud Computing, it is important to ensure that solutions sold as SaaS in fact comply with generally accepted definitions of Cloud computing. Some defining characteristics of SaaS include:

- Web access to commercial software
- Software is managed from a central location
- Software is delivered in a "one-to-many" model
- Users are not required to manage software upgrades and patches

- Application Programming Interfaces (APIs) allow for integration between different pieces of software

Many of the early adopters of SaaS were small businesses, primarily due to the low upfront costs and simplistic integration. Larger enterprises, however, have taken a somewhat more cautious approach to implementing SaaS solutions within their organizations, particularly for mission-critical applications.

2. Platform as a Service (PAAS): Platform as a Service (PaaS) brings the benefits that SaaS brought for applications, but over to the software development world. PaaS can be defined as a computing platform that allows the creation of web applications quickly and easily and without the complexity of buying and maintaining the software and infrastructure underneath it. PaaS is analogous to SaaS except that, rather than being software delivered over the web, it is a platform for the creation of software, delivered over the web. There are a number of different takes on what constitutes PaaS but some basic characteristics include:

- Services to develop, test, deploy, host and maintain applications in the same integrated development environment. All the varying services needed to fulfill the application development process.
- Web-based user interface creation tools help to create, modify, test and deploy different UI scenarios.
- Multi-tenant architecture where multiple concurrent users utilize the same development application.
- Built-in scalability of deployed software including load balancing and failover.
- Integration with web services and databases via common standards.
- Support for development team collaboration. Some PaaS solutions include project planning and communication tools.
- Tools to handle billing and subscription management.

PaaS, which is similar in many ways to Infrastructure as a Service, which will be discussed below, is differentiated from IaaS by the addition of value-added services and comes in two distinct ways:
- A collaborative platform for software development, focused on workflow management regardless of the data source being used for the application.
- A platform that allows for the creation of software utilizing proprietary data from an application. This sort of PaaS can be seen as a method to create applications with a common data form or type.

3. Infrastructure as a Service (Iaas): Infrastructure as a Service (IaaS) is a way of delivering Cloud computing infrastructure servers, storage, networks, and operating systems as an on-demand service. Rather than purchasing servers, soft-

ware, datacenter space, or network equipment, clients instead buy those resources as a fully outsourced service on-demand. In IaaS, there are some subcategories that are worth noting. Generally, IaaS can be obtained as public or private infrastructure or a combination of the two. "Public Cloud" is considered infrastructure that consists of shared resources, deployed on a self-service basis over the Internet. By contrast, "Private Cloud" is infrastructure that emulates some Cloud computing features, like virtualization, but does so on a private network. Additionally, some hosting providers are beginning to offer a combination of traditional dedicated hosting alongside Public and/or Private Cloud networks. This combination approach is generally called "Hybrid Cloud." As with the two previous sections, SaaS and PaaS, IaaS is a rapidly developing field. That said, there are some core characteristics that describe what IaaS is. IaaS is generally accepted to comply with the following:

- Resources are distributed as a service
- Allows for dynamic scaling
- Has a variable cost, utility pricing model
- Generally includes multiple users on a single piece of hardware

DEPLOYMENT MODELS

Private Cloud:
The Cloud infrastructure is provisioned for exclusive use by a single organization comprising multiple consumers (e.g., business units). It may be owned, managed, and operated by the organization, a third party, or some combination of them, and it may exist on or off premises.

Public Cloud:
The cloud infrastructure is provisioned for open use by the general public. It may be owned, managed, and operated by a business, academic, or government organization, or some combination of them. It exists on the premises of the Cloud provider.

Table 17.1: Cloud Deployment Models

Characteristic	Public cloud	Private cloud
Scalability	Very high	Limited
Elasticity	rapid and greater	rapid , but limited by the capacity of on-premise equipment
Self-On-demand	Very good	Very good
Cost	Very good, pay-as-you-go model and no need for on-premise infrastructure, pay-as-you go	greater installation, upgrade and maintenance cost
Security	The loss of control over protected or sensitive data by organizations	high level of privacy and security of the data and related applications
Reliability	Medium; depend on Internet connectivity and provider service availability	High, as all equipment is on premise
Equipment quality	The most sophisticated networking equipment on the market	Risk of obsolescence

Community Cloud:

The Cloud infrastructure is provisioned for exclusive use by a specific community of consumers from organizations that have shared concerns (e.g., mission, security requirements, policy, and compliance considerations). It may be owned, managed, and operated by one or more of the organizations in the community, a third party, or some combination of them, and it may exist on or off premises.

Hybrid Cloud:

The Cloud infrastructure is a composition of two or more distinct Cloud infrastructures (private, community, or public) that remain unique entities, but are bound together by standardized or proprietary technology that enables data and application portability (e.g., Cloud bursting for load balancing between Clouds).

Trusted Platform Module:

The TPM proposal will provide a different level of security namely:

1. Data Access Security
The election data is sensitive information that is private or privileged and must be kept secure. Thanks to the trusted hardware TPM, our system will be safeguarded and ensure that election processes run fairly and that elec-

tion results are not compromised by accidentally altered or deliberately sabotaged programs.

2. Password Protection

The authority and government employees who are responsible for counting and supervising the election process will have access to the database through their account and passwords. The data access needs to be protected. Several layers of password protection can be imposed. Particular software programs can be password protected also, so that even if an intruder can gain access to the network, they cannot run the vote counter programs.

3. Software Security

Computer software programs are made up of complex code. Computer programs that perform sensitive operations related to running an election must run correctly, or the success and legitimacy of an election could be jeopardized. For example, should an intruder breach security and get access to software's code, changes could be made that alter the computer-reported results of an election in a way that would be very difficult to detect. Software security, therefore, is another line of defense in the battle to ensure that electoral technology is kept secure. External auditors can scrutinize the code used in electoral computer systems and verify that it performs appropriately. Computer code that has been externally audited can then be "escrowed," or kept in secure offsite storage in an independent authority's control. This allows for the escrowed version to be compared to the "live" version of the code used for an electoral event. In this way, it becomes possible not only to verify that computer software is free of any hidden flaws or deliberate attempts at manipulation, but also to verify after the software has been used that its code has not been changed or tampered with since it was audited. This level of security may not be necessary for all software used by election management, however it is highly useful for crucial systems such as electronic voting and electronic vote counting systems.

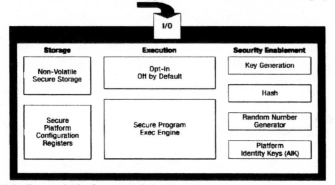

Figure 17.2: Trusted Platform Module Component

Biometric Authentication:

Biometrics are the automated recognition of individuals based on their behavioral and biological characteristics, for example, fingerprints, retina scans, palm print, DNA, voice, signature, gait, typing patterns, etc. These characteristics are denoted as biometric modalities. Since the biometric traits are intrinsically bound to the person, they can be used to establish his or her identity with a high degree of confidence.

The biometric system has two distinct phases: enrollment and recognition/comparison. During enrollment, biometric information (such as fingerprint image or voice data) is captured using specific sensors. This information is processed using specifically designed algorithms to obtain pertinent features. These features are used to create a reference biometric template for the user. The latter is required at the time of verification for comparison purposes, hence the biometric templates for all such registered users are stored in a central template (Cloud-based in our case) database for further comparison.

At the time of recognition/comparison, a fresh sample of the biometric measurement is captured under similar process and conditions, to obtain the features that will be compared with the stored templates. Typically, biometric systems can operate in two distinctive modes: (a) identification mode; and (b) verification mode.

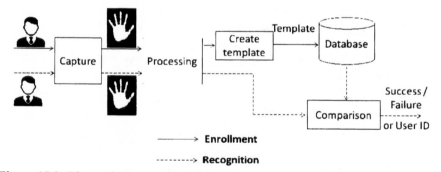

Figure 17.3: Biometric Recognition Process

Figure 17.3 illustrates a basic idea of a biometric-based person recognition system. In verification mode, the result of the comparison is either success or failure. In identification mode, the result of comparison is the User ID.

During identification, the information extracted from the fresh biometric data is compared with all the stored templates and the identity of the person to which the biometric data belongs is determined. In verification, the person who wants to get verified provides his identity along with his biometric data. A one-to-one comparison is carried out between the information extracted from the

fresh biometric data and the stored template corresponding to the provided identity, and the result of this comparison is either accepted or rejected. A central
template database is required for an identification system because all the templates are needed during comparison.

In our case, we chose the palm print for biometric authentication. The palm
is the inner surface of the hand between the wrist and the fingers. The palm print
is a rich source of information that is useful for personal authentication. The
most important features are the three principal lines (the heart line, the head line,
and the life line), wrinkles, and ridges. For this reason, and because of its uni-
queness and permanence, palm print has been used for a long time as a trusted
form of identification. They are highly unique, and are time invariant as they do
not change regularly as a person ages. The palm print is categorized into four
parts: Upper Palm, Thenar, Lower Palm, Hypothenar.

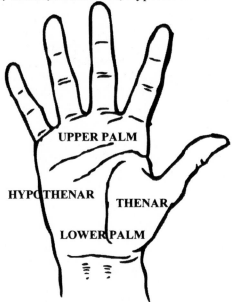

Figure 17.4: Palm print structure

The following steps show the basic workflow of the palm print system.

1. Extraction of palm print images: For extraction of palm print images,
    the whole hand's images are employed. Palm print images are taken
    from the center of a rectangle (tablet or Smartphone) that can enclose
    the whole area of interest in the palm.
2. Preprocessing techniques: For palm print images we used center re-
    gion of hand geometry images of a specific size. These images are
    also colored images. Firstly, they are converted into grayscale im-

ages. Then a specific threshold value is set for images for further processing.

3.   Feature Extraction: For palm prints, features are extracted such as corner points in grayscale images using features algorithms to find feature points. Then from these corner points we extract the strongest point descriptors. These corner points are common for both images in the form of Index Pairs with values of the total number of Index Pairs in images. The descriptors are extracted feature vectors and their corresponding locations, from a binary or intensity image. The function derives the descriptors from pixels surrounding an interest point. These pixels represent and match features specified by a single-point location. Each single point specifies the center location of a neighborhood.

The main objective of this combination (TPM and Biometric Authentication) is to secure the voting process that allows voters to exercise their right to express their choices regarding specific issues, pieces of legislation, citizen initiatives, constitutional amendments, recalls, and/or to choose their government and political representatives. Technology is being used more and more as a tool to assist voters to cast their votes. To allow the exercise of this right, the voting systems have these following steps:

- voter identification and authentication
- voting and recording of votes cast
- vote counting
- publication of election results

Our concept will invite all the citizens to vote. To do so, they will need:

- Smart Phone for biometric confirmation
- Internet connection for access to the voting website
- Identity number in the form of a unique number, so the voters will vote using their SSN instead of using their names

And, our proposed voting process will be as follows:

Voter identification:
This phase is required during two phases of the electoral process; first for voter registration in order to establish the right to vote, and afterwards, at voting time, to allow citizens to exercise their right to vote by verifying whether the person satisfies all the requirements needed to vote (authentication).

1.   The voter accesses a voting website and registers using his/her SSN.

2. Once registered, the server checks his/her eligibility and his/her voting status, in case he/she has already voted.
3. The server sends the ballot with different elected nominees to the voter.
4. The voter chooses the candidate that he prefers or agrees with, and submits his vote.
5. The voter confirms his vote with his/her palm print.
6. The server receives the vote, then validates the ballot (which includes symmetric encryption, hashing, camouflage, and signature of the voter) and adds it to its database.

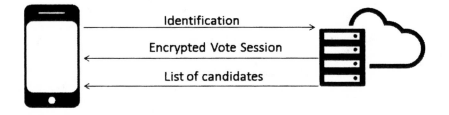

Figure 17.5: Identification Phase

Vote counting:
This is the phase of the voting process where the votes are counted and the voter is marked as noneligible for another vote.

1. The appropriate candidate number is increased.
2. The server updates the status of the voter in its database, so that the voter will no longer be eligible to vote.

CONCLUSION

This proposal of secure Internet voting is convenient for the voter. Regardless of how well polling places are designed and distributed, there could be no more convenient place to vote than from the comfort of one's home. By making electoral participation as easy as logging in to a website, checking a few boxes on a form, and clicking the "Vote" button, and confirming the vote via palm printing, it is likely that voter turnout, and hence the overall legitimacy of the results, may be improved significantly. It could also allow significant cost savings in the deployment and operation of physical polling stations, if the adoption rate of Internet voting is at a sufficient level. The counting and tabulating of electronic ballots is potentially much faster and easier than counting traditional, paper-based, or even optical-scan or punch-card ballots, which may represent significant cost savings as well.

There are three different forms of Internet voting:

1. Polling Site Internet Voting, in which voters cast their ballots via the Internet from client machines physically situated in official polling places, in which both the hardware and software of the client is controlled by election officials, and the authentication of the voters may take place by traditional means.
2. Kiosk Internet Voting, in which voters cast their ballots via client machines, in which the hardware and software are controlled by election officials, but distributed in public places (shopping malls, etc.) in which the physical environment and voter authentication are not directly under official control.
3. Remote Internet Voting, in which neither the client machines nor the physical environment are under the control of election officials. Whereas the first two methods are potentially much more secure, they also present few advantages over more traditional voting methods. The allure of Internet voting is only fully encapsulated in systems in which users are able to authenticate themselves and cast their ballots at their convenience, via home, workplace, or public Internet terminals.

REFERENCES

Abouelmehdi, K.,Dali,L.(2015). "Classification of Attacks Over Cloud Environment," World Academy of Science, *Engineering and Technology* vol: 9 no:5.

Abouelmehdi, K., Dali, L., El-Sayed, H., and Fatiha Eladnani, F. (2015). "Comparison Study of intrusion detection systems," *The International Journal of Information Security* (IJIS) Volume 4, October 30.

Attoh, A., Daniel, E. Gyimah-Boadi, D. E., and Annie Barbara Chikwanha, A. B. (2007). "Corruption and Institutional Trust In Africa: Implications For Democratic Development."

Bouzida Y., Cuppens F., Gombault S., (2006), "Detecting and Reacting against Distributed Denial of Service Attacks," IEEE International Conference on Communication, Volume 5.

Banerjee, P., Friedrich, R., Bash, C., Goldsack, P., Huberman, B.,Manley, J., Patel, C., Ranganathan, P.,Veitch, A.: Everything as a service: powering the new information economy. *Computer* 44(3),36–43 (2011). doi:10.1109/MC.2011.67.

Boampong, P.A., Wahsheh, L.A. (2012). Different facets of security in the cloud. In: Proceedings of the 15th Communications and Networking Simulation Symposium, pp. 5:1–5:7. Society for Computer Simulation International, San Diego, CA, USA.

Bentajer, A. Abouelmehdi, K., Dali, L. (2015). "An Assessing Approach based on FMECA methodology to evaluate security of a third party cloud provider", Journal of Theoretical and Applied Information Technology 30 April 2015 | Vol.74 No.3.

Callen, M. and Long, J. D. (2012). "Institutional Corruption and Election Fraud: Evidence from a Field Experiment in Afghanistan," Working Paper UCSD, September.

Chen, S., Wang, R., Wang, X; Chen, K. Z. (2010). Side-Channel Leaks In Web Application: A Reality Today A Challenge Tomorrow. Security and Privacy, IEEE Symposium - P. 191-208.

Dali, L., El-Sayed, H., Abouelmehdi, K., and Fatiha Eladnani, F. (2015). "A Survey of Intrusion Detection System," the 2nd World Symposium on Web Applications and Networking (WSWAN'2015) IEEE Xplore, Tunisia, March.

_____ "The Benefits of The Duo IPv6 and TPM to Enhance the Cloud Security," The 2nd World Symposium on Computer Networks and Information Security 2015, WSCNIS'2015, IEEE Xplore, Tunisia, Sept. 2015.

Gong, C., Liu, J., Zhang, Q., Chen, H., Gong, Z. (2010). The characteristics of cloud computing. In: 39th International Conference on Parallel Processing Workshop, pp. 275–279. IEEE Computer Society.

Gray, A. (2013). Conflict Of Laws and The Cloud Computer Law & Security Review Volume 29, Issue 1, February. P. 58–65 Washington, DC, USA. doi:10.1109/ICPPW.2010.45.

Hinden, R., and Deering, S. (2006). IP version 6 Addressing Arcitechture, RFC 4291, IETF,2006,P.25.

Hoffman, B. and J. D. Long, J. D. (2012). "Party Attributes, Performance, and Voting in Africa," *Comparative Politics*.

Höglund, K., (2006). Electoral violence in war-ravaged societies: The case of Sri Lanka. Paper prepared for the Workshop on Power-Sharing and Democratic Governance in Divided Societies, Centre for the Study of Civil Wars, PRIO, 21–22 August.

Ijim-Agbo, U., (2007). The Independent National Electoral Commission as an (im) partial umpire in the conduct of the 2007 elections. *Journal of African Elections*, 6 (2), pp. 79–94.

Lenk, A., Klems, M., Nimis, J., Tai, S., Sandholm, T (2009). What's inside the cloud? An architectural map of the cloud landscape. In: Proceedings of the ICSE Workshop on Software Engineering Challenges of Cloud Computing, pp. 23–31. IEEE Computer Society, Washington, DC, USA. doi:10.1109/CLOUD. 2009.5071529.

Lizhe W. and Gregor V. L.,(2008), "Cloud Computing: A Perspective Study," *New Generation Computing* Volume 28, Number 2, 137-146, DOI: 10.1007/s00354-008-0081-5.

Mohamed, E., Abdelkader, H., and El-Etriby, S. (2012). Enhanced data security model for cloud computing. In: 8th International Conference on Informatics and Systems, pp. CC-12–CC-17. IEEE.

Pasman, H. J. Jung, S., Prem, K., Rogers, W. J. and Yang, X. (2009). Is Risk Analysis A Useful Tool For Improving Process Safety? *Journal Of Loss Prevention In The Process Industries* 22 P. 769–777

Patidar, S., Rane, D., Jain, P.: A survey paper on cloud computing. In: 2nd International Conference on Advanced Computing Communication Technologies, pp. 394–398. IEEE (2012). doi:10. 1109/ACCT.2012.15 [9].

Sadashiv, N., Kumar, S.: Cluster, grid and cloud computing: a detailed comparison. In: 6th International Conference on Computer Science Education, pp. 477–482. IEEE (2011). doi:10.1109/ICCSE.2011.6028683

CHAPTER 18
Electronic Voting Operations and Capabilities in sub-Saharan Africa: A Cost-Benefit Analysis

Ephraim Okoro
Howard University

INTRODUCTION

This chapter discusses and evaluates critical issues facing democratization, the voting process, election outcomes, and the quality of governance in sub-Saharan Africa since independence. It further explores the future prospects of democracy and political development in the context of 21st century global political conditions and realities. The chapter specifically provides a cost-benefit analysis of technology/electronic voting operations and capabilities in conducting elections in the countries of sub-Saharan Africa. Finally, the chapter presents strategies for achieving political development, leadership accountability, responsible governance, and sustainable democracies in Africa.

Over the past several decades, there have been recurrent political issues and problems of enormous proportions in the attempt to establish democratic governance in many countries in Africa, especially in the sub-Saharan region, with varying degrees of leadership corruption and abuse. Research conducted by scholars across academic disciplines has investigated the persistent issue of government instability, poor electoral process, and lack of transparency in voting operations. Citizens, stakeholders, and the global community have expressed dismay about the failure of democratic practice in Africa as well as the poor quality of elections. Discussing Africa and the challenges of democracy and good governance in the 21st century, Adejumobi (2000) noted that democracy in Africa requires efficient and honest governance in financial management, and in the animation of civil society and its democratic values, readjustment in economic policy, and political agenda. The author further noted that many years of political instability, lack of governmental accountability and transparency, and the presence of military dictators left a good number of African countries "politically demobilized and economically decapacitated," placing the countries in global economic and political competitive disadvantage.

Over the past four decades, the World Bank, along with other democratic-oriented institutions, has maintained that government's ability to enhance participation in the democratic process is central to the success of elections both in Africa and in other parts of the world. A crucial challenge facing nascent democracies in Africa is to ensure effective participation and engagement by a majority of the citizens in the democratization process. As Coates and Pitroda stated in Adesina (2001), information communication technologies (ICTs) are the most potent democratizing tool ever used for electoral success and in ensuring democratic accountability. Additionally, the unimpeded access of citizens to information technology is the strongest support for political equality that the world has ever seen since the beginning of the Industrial Era. The author further stressed that the fundamental feature of well-functioning and responsible countries the world over, including Africa, is democracy, which is largely instrumental to healthy civil engagement and political development.

More than two decades ago, The World Bank (1994) identified Africa's political development problems as fundamentally a problem driven by unaccountability and disingenuous leadership, which essentially is the inability to use political power to manage a nation's political and economic affairs. As emphasized in Adejumobi (2000), the struggle for democratization, political accountability, and credible leadership is critical not only in liberalizing and achieving political liberties, but also in ensuring political commitment and stability for African citizens. A number of studies (Gymah-Boadi, 2004; Diamond, 2004; Okoro, 2010; Nwokeafor, 2013) agreed that there was a connection among poor political governance, political instability, and underdevelopment in sub-Saharan Africa. Furthermore, the World Bank (1989, p. 60) cited in Adejumobi (2000) explained that because countervailing power was lacking in African states, governmental officials in the countries were selfish, disingenuous, and consistently serving their own interests without fear of reprimand or punishment. Regrettably, political leaders and elected officials have built up private and personal networks of influence, rather than make state governments accountable for their systemic failure.

Political corruption expanded in African states to alarming proportions, with politics becoming personalized, and patronage has become essential to maintaining political power and influence. Leadership in most countries in sub-Saharan Africa exercises broad and untold discretionary authority, thereby compromising legitimacy and integrity of the political system.

POLITICAL MISGOVERNANCE AND DEMOCRATIC SHORTCOMINGS

Studies of recent years have characterized Africa's political development as replete with administrative failures, shortsightedness, and myopic leadership patterns. Acknowledging Ki-Zerbo (1996), Chabal (1992), Amin (1990), and Rodney (1972), Adejumobi (2000) emphasized that corrupt governance is predominant and endemic in sub-Saharan Africa ranging from parliamentary, military dictatorships, to a one-party style of political administration. The author identified two specific elements that were instrumental to Africa's misgovernment: first, that African nations inherited misrule and corruption from their colonial administrators; and second, that political arrangements, social orientation, and economic values practiced and promoted in the colonial era were not appropriate and conducive for adoption in Africa's post-colonial development phase.

Although Africa's early objectives focused on national integration, tribal and ethnic unity, and democratic development, the dominant practice demonstrated "dictatorship of development rather than democracy of development." Adejumobi and other political researchers determined that civil and political development would remain far-fetched and constrained in sub-Saharan Africa. Independently, these researchers determined that to establish and promote a credible and transparent government in Africa would entail four complementary factors: 1) Expanding and strengthening civil and political entities and engaging or utilizing democratic potentials; 2) demilitarization and demobilization; 3) reorientation of economic policy; and 4) re-evaluating and redefining the international context of democracy in Africa through reformation of the global economic and political order. Indeed, the failure of several democratic experiments in Africa, particularly in the sub-Saharan region, has consistently occurred as a result of political apathy, misfeasance, misgiving, and a lack of commitment by citizens.

The demand for political interest and involvement of citizens in the choice of their leaders, and their decision-making process, which constitutes the critical focus of political democracy (Sorensen, 1993), is a required prerequisite for sustainable democratization to be achieved in Africa (Adejumobi, 2000). Further, the World Bank (1994) contends that the strategy of structural or economic adjustment cannot reclaim Africa from her poverty-stricken environment. African leaders should complement institutional and capacity-building with credible governance, because the primary factors underscoring Africa's development constraints is the crisis of irresponsible and discreditable government.

TECHNOLOGY INTEGRATION IN ELECTIONS: PROMOTING ACCOUNTABLE GOVERNANCE

The capacity to elect credible leaders in Africa will certainly be the beginning to achieving sustainable democratic development. Understandably, the current election processes and democratic standards in Africa have attracted a range of negative analysis and criticisms. The attempt to democratize many countries in Africa has been unsuccessful because of the methods in which people were elected and the manner in which elections were conducted. A review of political elections in Africa in the past two decades leaves much to be desired, because many citizens have lost confidence in the nature of democratic rule, and a good number of citizens have not been participating because voting operations were risky and they lacked transparency. The quality of progress in Africa's political system has been exceedingly poor and utterly deplorable as a result of numerous challenges facing political governance in many countries. The World Bank's Sustainable Development Report on Africa (2008 p. 14) noted that democratic process in the continent is extremely fragile and untenable, and it emphasized that "the emerging structures of governance, political parties, elected institutions of the legislature and the executive, remain weak and not adequately institutionalized." The report further noted that in many African states, the lack of independence from the executive branch of government has grossly minimized or even compromised the effectiveness of watchdogs and advocacy roles in conducting the functions, duties, and responsibilities associated with democratic governance.

In order to realistically engender and institutionalize democracy, political development, and responsible governance in sub-Saharan Africa, these four major independent factors should be considered and consistently emphasized: 1) the strengthening of civil society and unleashing and actualizing its democratic potentials; 2) demilitarization and demobilization; 3) the reorientation of economic and political policy; and 4) reconstructing and transforming the international context of democracy in Africa by modifying the economic and political systems (The World Bank, 1994; Adejumobi, 1996).

POLITICAL DEVELOPMENT AND DEMOCRATIC REFORM IN SUB-SAHARAN AFRICA

Recent studies clearly indicate that auspicious institutional renewal and the need for democratization have preoccupied much of the development agenda in countries of sub-Saharan Africa. Diamond (2004) described the democratic struggles on the continent as a surge in despair over political and economic prospects toward the end of the 20th century, and at the beginning of the 21st century, which strongly called into question the quality of political reforms and development initiatives. While national commitment and the desire for democratic politics have remained a priority in African countries for decades, the outcome of political elections has been totally controversial, inefficient, dysfunctional, questionable, and grossly unacceptable. For this and other practical reasons, an important aspect of democratic reform in Africa should be the ability to organize and conduct a respectable voting process, which will allow the election of responsible and credible national political leaders with a high sense of integrity and credibility. Unfortunately, several attempts at enforcing effective and efficient measures of oversight for political governance have been in vain because of deep-seated corruption, which appears seemingly inherent in Africa's political system. Independent political experts and analysts have recommended technology integration in elections in Africa to sustain human efforts at democratization.

Expert opinions and political studies indicate that an important first step in fostering and strengthening democratic reforms is transforming the voting process in the countries of Africa in order to ensure inclusiveness, transparency, accountability, and integrity. Evidently, the obsolete methods of casting votes and electing political leaders in Africa over the years have contributed largely and significantly to the disturbing levels of that corruption, intimidation, and violence, which have besieged Africa's political systems.

As Gymimoah-Boadi (2004) explained in a brilliant assessment of democratic reform and political development in Africa, democratization and political progress on the continent encountered stiff and discouraging shortcomings, setbacks, and unprecedented deficiencies as a result of deep-rooted corruption, administrative selfishness, and political mismanagement. The inherent self-serving motives of elected officials can only be curbed if a sophisticated election process is introduced and institutionalized in order for credible leaders to be duly elected to run the affairs of African countries. Essentially, the establishment and sustainment of democracy must begin with fair and free elections in which citizens would be interested in participating, and would subsequently vote for credible candidates based on their track records. Political reforms must ensure that the process of electing people is credible and that the election result is acceptable without coercion, intimidation, or threats. Studies indicate that an election process with integrity would allow citizens to participate fully. Indeed, the continuing disenchantment of African citizens with the deplorable democratic patterns in African countries is the result of poor elections, apathy, and questionable election results.

Political scholars and authors contend that democratization and political development are two sides of the same coin. Therefore, it is almost impossible to achieve a credible democratic system, let alone a sustainable democratic government, without an election process in which a majority of the citizens can actively participate in campaigns and voting. As discussed in ACE project (1998-2015), several countries have evaluated the advantages and disadvantages of Internet voting capability as an avenue to enhance voter interest and participation. Of great importance to African citizens and voters is the assurance of integrity in the voting/election process, and reliability in order to make election outcomes acceptable. It stands to reason that the current method of electing political leaders in African countries using ballot and voting papers must be replaced with electronic voting technology, which has the capacity and methodology to enhance the quality of elections, elect candidates based on merit, and provide acceptable election outcomes.

More than two decades ago, an international conference was held in Ota, Nigeria, which was focused on "democracy and governance in Africa." It was unanimously recommended that political leaders in Africa recognize the significance and value of change for the common interests and benefit of African countries and their citizens, so that a lasting, positive impact could be established for leadership change, as well as the improvement of economic and human conditions. The former Nigerian Head of State Obasanjo and his associates (1991) stressed that political change should include the acceptance of the "redefinition of the concept of development providing for the full integration of the economic and human dimensions" for the betterment of the global society. Globalization calls for consistency and uniformity in governance, living standards, and conditions, as well as in political systems. For various important reasons, democratization in Africa is a necessary condition for acceptable political development and global recognition.

THE ADVENT OF ELECTRONIC VOTING TECHNOLOGY

The introduction of the electronic voting system is a significant process essential for the improvement of the outcome of elections, as well as for the reduction of fraud and corruption associated with ballot boxes and ballot papers. Another important factor in elections is gaining public confidence, which electronic voting is designed to establish. Research has shown that over decades, African citizens have questioned the outcome of election results because of dishonesty in the process—dishonesty that was often engendered by skillful manipulation of ballot boxes and ballot papers to favor specific candidates. Specifically, studies by Diamond (2004) and Gyimah-Boadei (2004) indicate that many countries around the world have embarked on technological development for adopting electronic voting technologies to improve election outcomes. Garson (2006) added that the term "electronic democracy" (e-democracy) is a collective concept involving democratic activities ranging from campaigns and elections, to election results. Electronic voting technology was designed and expected to enhance the efficiency, effectiveness, and applicability of the democratic process of electing qualified candidates to serve their countries.

The electronic capability improves democratic engagement by creating an effective platform for informing and engaging citizens in the political process. Macintosh (2006) explains that a valid election is one in which citizens participated freely and fairly to vote and select their representatives. The electronic voting system provides the much-needed freedom, convenience, and confidence to vote without fear of harassment and intimidation, which were associated with updated manual voting systems.

The introduction and supervision of electronic technologies is not a simple replacement of the updated ballot boxes and ballot papers with electronic equipment. The entire management and oversight of elections using the electronic voting system is fundamentally different from elections using traditional ballot papers. The new process requires total restructuring and reorganizing of the electoral sequence and its aspects to ensure adequate accountability. Furthermore, decisions to establish the electronic voting mechanism should be carefully and thoughtfully evaluated, with an expanded involvement and commitment of major national stakeholders, in light of a number of critical factors that will ensure success of the new system. The decision to introduce the electronic voting must be fully explained to the citizenry in order to respect the rights and interests of voters, citizens, and political candidates (Organization for Security and Cooperation, Europe Office for Democratic Institutions and Human Rights, 2003).

Researchers Achieng and Ruhode (2013) noted the widespread use of electronic voting in many parts of the world with commendable results. In their analysis of the adoption and implementation of electronic voting technologies, they noted that electronic voting and counting processes were successfully utilized in India, Brazil, Belgium, South Africa, and the Philippines. They added that the adoption of electronic voting was introduced in the Philippines because of widespread election fraud that characterized the country's national elections. In the sub-Saharan region, electronic voting technology was suggested and implemented in Nigeria and Ghana because of similar election fraud and mishandling. Democratic elections were conducted in Nigeria in recent years, and the results were challenged and questioned across the country because the process was discredited and unacceptable. According to Ahmad and his associates (2015), the elections in Nigeria caused a lot of discomfort to citizens as a result of complaints and problems, such as missing names of some registered voters, intimidation and disfranchisement of voters, multiple and underaged voting, snatching or destruction of ballot boxes, miscomputation, and falsification of results.

Alemika (2015) emphasized that the manual electoral system (ballot boxes and voting papers) created national disaster in the form of violence, conflict, and disruption, which diminished public trust and confidence in political governance in the country, causing intense division and disgruntlement. According to Nwagu (2011), Ogbuadu (2012), and LeVan and Uka (2013), several dishonest and greedy African politicians exploited the weaknesses and vulnerabilities of the obsolete traditional voting system (the paper-ballot method) to perpetuate huge electoral fraud in their countries, the killing of innocent citizens, and burning of voting locations to conceal election evidence. These incidents necessitated the exploration of electronic voting capability to ensure transparency, accountability, and safety during elections.

Additionally, the sophistication of the electronic voting technologies in African elections is expected to restore electoral dignity, voter confidence, and encourage more voter participation. For example, in the wake of numerous complaints, concerns, and discouragement in election results, the government of Nigeria established the Independent National Electoral Commission (INEC) and charged it with the responsibility of introducing and implementing the transition to electronic voting in the country. In support of electronic voting capability, Jega and Hillier (2012) noted that both developed and developing nations of the world are adopting and using electronic technology for credible and accountable election results.

ELECTRONIC VOTING TECHNOLOGY AND DEMOCRATIZATION

Independent of each other, political scientists and communication scholars Diamond (2004), Gyimah-Boadi (2004), Okoro (2010), and Nwokeafor (2013) emphasized the value of information and communication networks in campaigns, the voting process, and election outcomes. Specifically, Nwokeafor

(1992) and Okoro (1993), in their numerous studies on agenda-setting paradigms, explained the significance of raising the awareness of citizens and providing relevant information for the benefit of making informed and conscious decisions and choices in political elections. Political communication is equally crucial in elections and it is instrumental in creating the knowledge base of the voting public.

Voting and elections are two critical processes in democratization and political communication, and citizens deserve a fair opportunity to express their opinions and choices by casting votes without intimidation, harassment, or coercion. Indeed, to ensure voter confidence and participation, security, ease of use, process efficiency, and accountability, technology should be an integral part of voting and election methods. For instance, Ananda and colleagues (2012) cited the 2000 national election in the United States involving the famous "butterfly ballot" episode in Palm Beach, Florida, which caused a national controversy about ballot design, inconsistency of election rules, voter error, and allegations of fraud. The authors stressed this particular election malpractice, mishandling, and fraud because the incident engendered "a dramatic wave for new laws to be implemented in the United States." The incident also called for a review and evaluation of manual and electronic systems of voting in the country. It was well noted by international organizations involved in elections that technology is advancing and playing a crucial role in a variety of settings, including voting and elections. Therefore, they encouraged the introduction and use of electronic voting systems (International Peace Institute, 2011; Freedom in World 2010).

Several studies conducted after many election failures around the world validated the seemingly indispensable function of information and communication technology in both developed and undeveloped countries. As societies are changing, and growing more sophisticated in their institutional processes and methods, information technology is gaining more recognition and continues to play a central role in system improvement to cope with the challenges of globalization and modernization. Given the global nature of the world, the political environment of countries in Africa should improve their voting process in order to contribute to world economic development. As Tita and Gyimah (2010 p. 5) concluded in their analysis of electronic voting in sub-Saharan Africa, "A stable political atmosphere would imply a rapid and high economic growth, while an unstable political atmosphere would imply a low and slow economic growth." Therefore, there is a strong correlation between political stability of a country and its economic growth; in other words, a politically stable country will attract global investments.

Tadayoshi (2003, cited in Ayo & Ekong, 2008) explained the importance elections with regard to democratic movement because citizens will have the opportunity to make a significant decision regarding their choice of leadership. For this reason, political elections should be conducted in an atmosphere that guarantees a fair and free process, as well as ensures efficiency, credibility, and cost-effectiveness to the citizens and nations, which ultimately makes election outcomes acceptable and credible.

Since gaining independence in the decades of the fifties and sixties, many countries in sub-Saharan Africa conducted their national and local elections manually, using paper and ballot boxes, which were susceptible to manipulation and abuse by disingenuous electoral officers. Some of them received monetary compensation for falsifying election records and results. According to the African Elections Database (2007), manually conducted and supervised elections in many sub-Saharan African countries produced questionable and unacceptable results because of the inefficiency and weakness of the voting system. As a result, this chapter is intended to explore the usefulness of the electronic voting trend, provide a cost-benefit analysis of the methodology, and identify recommendations for its future use to minimize or avoid citizens' disgruntlement and disillusionment with democratic elections.

Evidently, the outdated voting method has created disappointing experiences in many countries with the sad result that voters no longer believe election results, and extremist voters who were impacted negatively by election outcomes have discontinued voting entirely. Because of negative and discouraging criticism of the outdated voting methods, some countries have transformed their electoral process, upgrading it with the electronic voting technology, and the subsequent outcome of their recent election results was satisfactory to a good number of voters. As noted in ACE Electoral Knowledge Network (2010), both developed and developing nations (India, France, Australia, the United States, Canada, Switzerland, Brazil, Japan, etc.) have successfully established and utilized electronic voting technology.

Recent elections in countries in sub-Saharan Africa (Nigeria, Kenya, Ghana, and South Africa, etc.) have reconsidered their voting methods and are now embarking on using the sophisticated electronic technology to ensure credible election outcomes. The E-voting Database (2010) indicates that electronic voting operation makes the counting of votes much easier, provides faster and convenient election participation, and attracts more voter engagement. Interestingly, the system is considerably cost-effective to use as well as increasingly reliable. The obsolete traditional method of voting in Africa involved casting votes into sealed or covered boxes, which were subsequently counted and reported by electoral officers. The African Elections Database (2007) found this method extremely cumbersome, unreliable, and replete with a surge of irregularities. This method of voting, according to election experts, was known to compromise democratic values, especially by falsifying results and intimidating voters at the polls. Furthermore, Indian Elections (2009) cited in Tita and Gyimah (2010) pointed out that the electronic voting machine (EVM) was introduced to save time and labor and to reduce problems and conflict associated with election outcomes in recent years—especially in the context of the developing world where many political candidates demonstrated extreme desperation and viciousness during campaigns and elections. A significant aspect of the electronic voting mechanism (Indian Elections, 2009) is its ability to maintain voting secrecy, and it has been described as "100 percent tamper-proof, with a touch of a button on the screen, the polling election results were made available." Additionally, voters were provided with simple and clear instructions, usually printed in bold characters, to guide the voting process and for faster decision making. For faster operations, the voting equipment is equipped with two interlinked units, with a ballot unit for voters and a control unit for the polling officers at the station, to function simultaneously.

The electronic voting system is operationally well-designed and equipped to be user-friendly, and an average voter spends a few minutes to cast his or her vote without any confusion or misinterpretation. Indian Elections (2009) explained that the ballot box and ballot unit in the electronic voting equipment provide a similar function for casting votes. This ballot unit is quite simple to perform and it displays the list of candidates in the elections. It has an inbuilt mechanism specifically designed to incorporate party identification and symbols. Within the voting time frame, voters are required to push just one button on the panel, which identifies desirable candidates and their affiliations. Similarly, the control unit/section on the electronic voting system provides control of the polling, which is exclusively used by electoral officers. This unit shows the total number of votes polled at any given time, indicates the time elections ended, and announces election results automatically. Election experts and the Indian Election Board (2009), described the electronic voting technology as highly sophisticated and functionally dependable, and noted that the system was remarkable for its independence, reliability, and validity. Moreover, the electronic voting technology is designed and built with "super-sensitive circuitry" that does not allow for invalid votes, irregularities, or vote duplication.

PATH TO DEMOCRACY AND DEVELOPMENT IN AFRICA

For nearly a century, voting and elections in Africa have encountered numerous unprecedented challenges, diminution, and degradation around the world. With the opportunities for self-governance following the decolonization of the African continent, this freedom engendered euphoria in a good number of countries. For many countries in the sub-Saharan region, their national independence appeared premature and underestimated because of the political instability, violence, and civil unrest that immediately preceded or accompanied their independence. As the International Peace Institute (2011 p. 1) noted, "Violence and coercion became a common means of changing power. Coups, countercoups, and aborted coups littered the political landscape on the African continent." However, there were a number of positive and exciting post-independence developments, democratic initiatives, and modifications with respect to democratization in Africa. Interestingly, the participatory political process developed in the decades of 1990 and 2010 noted, "the percentage of African countries holding democratic elections increased from 7 to 40 percent" (Freedom House, 2010). As the struggle for democratic governance gained momentum within the past three decades, there has been increasing need for accountability, transparency, and credibility of political leaders "whose domestic legitimacy is largely linked to the means through which they attain and maintain power" (International Peace Institute, 2011). Enlightened and educated African citizens consistently scrambled for democratic change and new political leaders to govern their countries, but little did they realize that the culture of their countries was not ready for change and self-rule.

In the wake of political independence, elections were held periodically that facilitated democratic governance in countries such as Ghana, Nigeria, Senegal, South Africa, and Mali, among others. Unfortunately, the elections were manipulated to establish self-serving, autocratic political leaders with established "dynastic successions on the continent" over the years. Similarly, some countries in sub-Saharan Africa (Zimbabwe, Kenya, Nigeria, Ghana, etc.) encountered a recurrence and resurgence of electoral violence and manipulation, which impeded democratization and political development over the years.

ELECTRONIC VOTING CAPABILITY: A COST-BENEFIT ANALYSIS

As a result of decades of electoral failures, confusion, and violence in Africa caused by using the traditional ballot papers and boxes as a voting method, election experts and international institutions recommended electronic voting as a viable and credible option for replacement. However, in order to ensure adequate utilization of this new technological device in Africa, this chapter provides a cost-benefit analysis to determine its effective and productive use, and to substantiate the rationale for introducing this device.

Expert opinions and empirical evidence strongly revealed that establishing electronic technologies for conducting elections is not a simple, basic replacement of the traditional ballot boxes and ballot papers. Evidently, conducting and supervising elections with electronic voting devices is fundamentally different from the process that was managed with paper ballots. The new electoral system requires a total restructuring and reorganizing of election and voting administration in significant ways, including establishing certification entities, vendors, voting/election administrators, and training in order to reap fully the benefit of the new voting operation. Research findings indicate that because of past election corruption and manipulation, building public confidence in electronic voting technology in Africa is critically important and can be established over a period of observation time.

COST OF USING ELECTRONIC VOTING TECHNOLOGIES

Because of the complicated nature of the electronic voting equipment, it was emphasized that electronic voting technology should be purchased ready-made and available for use, so that election authorities will not need to contract experts for extended training with regard to managing the system's specifications. In some cases, there may be different specifications appropriate for a country's election and voting needs. Additionally, the logistics for the deployment and placement of voting equipment involves more sensitivity than the distribution and deployment of ballot boxes at voting locations. As the National Democratic Institute, the International Foundation for Electoral Systems, and USAID (2002,

2007) explained, electronic voting technologies need sufficient infrastructure and a dependable power source to perform efficiently. There should be adequate polling stations and electoral officers for the equipment. Although some electronic voting equipment is built to operate with batteries, it is crucial to provide back-up batteries, as recharging may be needed from time to time.

Significantly, storage of the voting equipment needs specially designated locations with appropriately controlled climate and advanced security measures. Sufficient arrangements should be made for services, maintenance, and replacement of the voting system to ensure constant operational capability. Although the equipment does not break down often, it is advisable to set aside money for services, maintenance, and replacement, as the durability of the electronic equipment is not indefinite and may depend on the type of equipment in light of the rapid evolution of information technology in the 21st century. Moreover, certification processes for electronic voting equipment and software involve additional expense, because the operation should be performed by an independent organization and not by the vendor or election authority (USAID, 2007).

Electronic voting systems pose important and unique situations for election observers around the world. For example, how can staff/observers assess the workings of electronic systems? Why are the processes of vote counting and tabulation often invisible? What aspects of traditional observation remain relevant for electronic voting observation? What can and should be observed in the automated or electronic voting systems? What are the critical and essential access points in the electronic voting process that observers need in order to assess the integrity of the voting exercise? Does electronic voting present new dynamics or challenges for the interrelationship between relevant stakeholders, such as vendors, legislators, election officials, and others? Are there unique legal or legislative implications for e-voting systems? (The Carter Center, 2007).

The preceding questions and concerns are critical, and were assessed in this chapter in order to make a valid determination regarding the validity and reliability of the electronic voting capability in Africa, and to provide a broad cost-benefit analysis of the electronic voting device.

Voter education is another critical step in introducing and using electronic voting technology. Raising public/voter awareness, and providing widespread information, guidelines, and instructions would require a substantial amount of spending and oversight. Clear guidelines about the use of the equipment should be provided and distributed in many forms to voters in advance of election periods. According to the International Foundation for Electoral Systems, a critical factor to the success of the electronic voting equipment is the training of polling officials and availability of training manuals for staff and monitors to keep up with procedures and processes. Further, designated election supervisors should establish adequate and appropriate recruitment plans and staffing needs for daily voting operations.

In order to re-establish and sustain public confidence in democracy, maintaining accountability and credibility in elections is important and should be emphasized at all times to election staff, monitors, and supervisors. Although technology upgrades or transformation for credible elections are desirable, numerous studies and reports indicate that the process of acquiring electronic voting technology is quite a daunting experience that requires thoughtful planning and deliberation.

BENEFITS OF USING ELECTRONIC VOTING TECHNOLOGIES

Quite unlike the traditional voting system, there are many strengths and benefits associated with the electronic voting device that make it extremely unique and much more desirable, especially in developing nations with a high degree of election incidents. Several reports concur that the system allows for a faster vote count and tabulation of results. This makes manipulation of election results extremely difficult, as results are provided or announced in a timely fashion. In addition, election results are more accurate and valid as human error and other attendant issues are reduced to the barest minimum.

The International Institute for Democracy and Electoral Assistance (2011) concluded that electronic voting technology provides efficient management and reporting of complex and complicated electoral mechanisms that usually involve extensive and painstaking processes. Voter presence and participation have progressively increased around the world, especially with the availability of Internet voting systems. Additionally, electronic voting enhances and improves the presentation and analysis of complicated ballot papers and increases convenience for voters, which directly and indirectly encourages interest and participation.

The International Peace Institute (2011) stated that another critical advantage of electronic voting is fraud prevention at polling stations and locations, as well as during transmission, tabulation, and distribution of results, by eliminating human involvement. There is increased accessibility of ballot papers via radio for blind voters, with Internet voting as well as for household voters, and other voters overseas. Moreover, with the advent of the electronic voting system there is a significant reduction or total elimination of spoiled ballot papers, as the voting system has the capacity to warn about or detect invalid votes. Finally, there is a tremendous long-term cost savings in poll staff time and energy, and reduction in costs for the production, distribution, and management of ballot papers.

Over the past 20 years, research findings consistently and unanimously demonstrated the usefulness of electronic voting technologies, and citizens and electoral experts support the utilization of the new system as it clearly supersedes the paper-based system used in most developing nations. Countries with disappointing experiences resulting from the ballot paper method are gradually adopting the new technology, and voting has produced both exciting and encouraging outcomes to sustain democratic values. For example, the Philippines adopted an electronic counting solution to deal with problems and conflict associated with fraud during the counting, tabulation, and analysis of election results.

However, factors that affected the use of electronic voting technologies in specific countries were elements unique to those specific countries, such as logistical, cultural, political, and legal considerations. Overall, the advantages, benefits, or usefulness of electronic voting technology in democratic elections greatly outweighs the disadvantages.

CONCLUSION

Empirical research evidence and institutional report findings combine to substantiate that there is an undisputable connection between democracy and political development, especially in the developing countries of Africa. The World Bank (1998), Diamond (2004), and Agbaje (2004) among others strongly contend that Africa has lagged behind economically, and in sustaining democratic values and standards, because it has failed to uphold political government over the years. Unfortunately, standards of democracy have remained below the accepted threshold around the world. Efforts to promote sustainable democratic reform in Africa require collective commitment, and objective utilization of best practices, technological reforms, and recommended global strategies to guide development initiatives. Diamond (2004) summarized that elections are critically important to democracy, but sporadic elections in a country cannot account for sustainable political development. Time and patience are needed to establish effective, efficient, and credible electoral systems that can earn global recognition and commendation. Although recent political elections in some African countries were more competitive, responsible, and openly inclusive than those conducted under authoritarian or dictatorial African leaders, there is more work to be done to maintain democratic governments.

As Xenakis and Macintosh (2005) remarked, political development is the product of responsible democracy. Therefore, electronic voting should be designed to contribute significantly to enhance the election process in Africa, which ultimately would improve the low voter turnout. It should be noteworthy that among the many advantages of electronic voting technology, fraud prevention, trust in the innovation, and security of the equipment have increased acceptance and adoption of the system. The findings of this chapter, based on analysis of qualitative and quantitative studies and reports, adequately indicate that electronic voting technology has unquestionable benefits over the manual voting system. Indeed, the advantages associated with the electronic voting system can sustain voter confidence as it eliminates the corrupt practices inherent in the manual voting mechanism.

This chapter strongly recommends the continuing adoption of the electronic voting technology in Africa, especially in the sub-Saharan region. If African countries can leverage on the opportunities and benefits that electronic voting provides, elections should be more peaceful and acceptable, and political development will be within reach in the near future. The International Institute for Democracy and Electoral Assistance (2011) confirmed that electronic voting is a sophisticated tool for making the electoral process more efficient and effective, and for increasing trust in the management and supervision of elections globally. If appropriately introduced and adequately supervised, the electronic voting mechanism is capable of increasing the security of the ballot system, speeds up the processing of providing results, and can make voting and elections much easier. All in all, democratization will thrive in Africa if political leaders are democratically elected according to voting and election standards, if corruption and election fraud are curbed, and if disingenuous candidates eliminated. Then voters' confidence will be restored.

REFERENCES

Achieng, M. & Ruhode, E. (2013). The adoption and challenges of electronic voting technologies within the South African context. Cape Peninsula University of technology, Cape Town, South Africa.

Adesida O. (2001). "Governance in Africa: The role for information and communication Technologies." Economic Research Papers #65, African Development Bank Abidjan 01, Cote d'Ivoire

Adejumobi, S. (2000). Africa and the challenges of democracy and good governance in the 21st century. Addis Aba, Ethiopia.

Adejumobi, S. (2996). The structural adjustment programme and democratic transition in Africa. *Law and Politics in Africa, Asia, and Latin America.* No 4., 416-434, (1995), Adjustment eforms and its impact on the economy and society in Said Adejumobi and Abubaka Momoh (eds.). The political economy of Nigeria under military rule: 1984-1993, SAPES: Harare.

Agbaje, A. (2004). In Gyimah-Boadi, Democratic reform iin Africa: The quality of Progress. Lynne Reinner. Boulder: London

Center for Democracy and Governance (1999). "The role of media in democracy: A strategic approach. US Agency for International Development, Washington, DC

Democracy and Governance in Africa (1991). Conclusions and papers presented at a conference of the Africa leadership forum. Ota, Nigeria (November 29 – December 1991)

Diamond, L. (2004). Promoting real reform in Africa. In Gyimah-Boadi (2004) *Democratic Reform in Africa: The quality of progress.* Lynne Rienner Publishers. Boulder: London

Freedom House, "Electoral Democracies," in Freedom in the World 2010 available www.freedomhouse.org/uploads/fiw10/ElectoralDemocraciesFIW2010.

Garson, G. D. (2006). Public information technology and e-governance: Managing the virtual state, Sudbury, MA: Jones & Bartlett.

Geisler, G. (1993). Fair? What's fairness got to do with it? Vagaries of election observations and democratic standards. JournaGyimah-Boadil of Modern African Studies.

Gyimah-Boadi, E. (2004). *Democratic Rform in Africa: The Quality of Progress.* Lynner Rienner Publishers, Boulder: London

National Democratic Institute (2002). Implementing electronic voting in an election. International Foundation for Electoral Systems (2007). Electronic Counting in an Election.

Organization for Security & Cooperation, Europe Office for Democratic Institutions and HumanRights. http://www.osce.org/publications/odihr/2003/10/12345_en.pdf

Qadah, G. & Taha, R. (2007). Electronic voting systems: Requirements, design, and implementation. *Computer Standards Interfaces*, Vol. 29 No. 3 pp. 376-386.

Rodney, W. (1972). How Europe underdeveloped Africa: Bogle l'Overture.

Sorensen, G. (1993). *Democracy and Democratization*. Colorado: Boulder, Westview Press.

Svensson, J., & Skifteen, R. (2003). E-voting in Europe: Divergent democratic practice. *Information Polity*, Volume 8, Number 1, pp. 3-15.

The Carter Center Democracy Program (2007). "Developing a methodology for Observing electronic voting." Atlanta, GA. www.cartercenter,org.

Tita, B.A. & Gyimah, N.A. (2010. "Electronic voting: A possible solution for sub-Saharan Africa: A focus on the Ghanaian electoral system. Jonkoping International Business School.

The World Bank (1989). Sub-Saharan Africa: From crisis to sustainable growth, Washington, D.C.: The World Bank

Xenakis, A. & Macintosh, A. (2005). "Electoral administration: Organizational lessons learned from the deployment of e-voting in the UK," ACM International Conference Proceeding Series, Vol. 89, Atlanta, GA.

Zeydanli, T. (2015). "Elections and subjective well-being in sub-Saharan Africa." 4th LCSR International Workshop, Summer School, and NOVA Research Group. Moncialleri, Italy.

EPILOGUE

The content of this book, as demonstrated in the 18 chapters authored by worthy scholars of African extraction, has given elaborate answers to the question as to whether technology can revolutionize elections in Africa. Many African countries engaged in recent political elections that have used biometric voter registration, as well as the accreditation process before voting and the use of technological means to collate, record, and announce election results, seem to believe that the difference is clear. In Nigeria, Ghana, South Africa, Kenya, Uganda, Sierra Leone, Democratic Republic of Congo (DRC), Mozambique, Zambia, Malawi, Rwanda, Senegal, and Somaliland for instance, biometric technology was used to register voters—which, according to foreign election observers, addressed considerably the issue of election malpractice in these countries.

Bhalla (2012) argued that the greatest limitation of biometric voter registration is that it only counters the symptoms, not the causes, of electoral fraud and existing malpractice. In the entirety of Africa, there is no historical evidence of a deliberate strategy by any political party to rig elections through multiple registrations. All previous electoral registers have erroneously contained names of the deceased, the underaged, and foreign nationals. But the most significant type of electoral misdemeanor has been the physical stuffing of ballots and false recording of results by temporary election workers.

Most political parties in Africa, when elected into offices of power, have at times used their position to fund political campaigns and buy voters. This practice remains widespread in most African countries. Political parties continue to organize, and condone the intimidation of voters, often perpetrated by their youth. Biometric technology offers considerable scope and hope with which to tackle these transgressions.

Where electoral management is weak, the manipulation of polls persists, regardless of the accuracy of the voter register. Expectations about technology's role in elections must be realistic. Biometric voter registration is not a "magic pill" for eliminating fraud and electoral malpractice. Where institutions are weak, and perpetrators of electoral crimes are not prosecuted, politicians can find ways to achieve undemocratic ends. Elections are more than just a technical exercise that must be handled completely away from the persistent corruption and malpractice that have created serious and perennial challenges.

Africa should engage corruption and election malpractice head-on, and the fight should not be selective. The idea of pushing certain issues and vetting out the culprits in the war of corrupt practices during elections must be addressed across the board. Petitions against perpetrators of heinous election fraud and malpractice should know no boundaries, regardless of the offenders' party affiliations or respect to cronyism. The principle of nepotism, which has for years blanketed the culture of dealing with issues of corruption and rule of law, should be thoroughly investigated. The war against corruption is a very good one, and should be a welcome development in Africa—most importantly in the five sampled nations for this study—but it must be holistic and all-inclusive, and it must be within the ambit of both the existing laws in African countries, and fundamental human rights. There must be rule and order in the judicial system that addresses the common practice of trial before conviction. Africa should desist from the common practice where people are condemned even before trial by a court of law, which is questionable and amounts to arbitrariness and impunity, and is a corrupt practice in itself. There should be a limit to what corruption, fraudulent engagements, election malpractice, mischief, and deceit can accomplish. Therefore, leaders in African countries, including the political systems and their various teams, must brace up for leadership challenges and the absolute and strategic war against corruption and election malpractice. They must put a stop to their usual name calling and blame games associated with the shrewd politics they continue to play that have damaged democracy in the second largest continent in the world.

Index

H

I

J

CONTRIBUTORS

Augustin Ntembe is Assistant Professor of Economics at the College of Business, Bowie State University. Prior to coming to Bowie State University in 2008, he was Assistant Lecturer at the University of Buea, Cameroon. Dr. Ntembe currently teaches Principles of Economics courses, Business Statistics, Quantitative Methods for Business, and Intermediate Microeconomics. His primary research interests focus on economic growth, development economics, investment and capital markets, and poverty-related issues and the social sector.

Ayoade Olusola Bamidele joined Emmanuel Alayande College of Education, Oyo, in 1995, where he currently holds the rank of Senior Lecturer and Head of Computer Science Department. He received a B.Sc (Ed.) in Computer Science from Olabisi Onabanjo University, Ago-Iwoye, Ogun State and an M.Sc.in Computer Science from University of Lagos, Akoka, Lagos. His research interests include e-learning, ICT application, and database management.

Benjamin O. Arah is an Associate Professor of Government and Philosophy at Bowie State University. He received his education in Nigeria and the United States, and holds a Ph.D. in political science from Howard University. He has taught at several institutions, and currently teaches political science and philosophy at Bowie State University. His previously published works include *Africa in the 21st Century: The Media, Politics and Good Governance in Nigeria* (2014); *Socrates, Thoreau, Gandhi and the Philosopher/Social Activist-Dr. King: Politics of Civil Disobedience and the Ethics of Nonviolence Direct Action* (2012); and *The Competencies, Preparations and Challenging (New) Roles of Online Instructors* (2011), among others. Dr. Arah is currently working on two book projects on Logic and Critical Thinking, and Dr. Martin Luther King's lasting legacy (with Dr. Tamara L. Brown).

Cosmas Uchenna Nwokeafor, Ph.D., is a Professor of Mass Communication at Bowie State University, where he currently serves as the Dean of Graduate School. He has served as a Provost Fellow and Assistant Provost for Graduate Studies at Bowie State University. Prior to his current position, he served as the Assistant Dean and Dean of the College of Arts and Sciences respectively, as well as Chair of the Department of Communication. His professional experiences include leadership training at Harvard University, and the Oxford Roundtable workshop at Oxford University, London. He has conducted research on development communication, new communication technologies and development in Africa, the conundrum of autism, retention studies among students in historically black colleges and universities, and effective leadership in student retention. He serves as the president-elect of the Council of Historically Black Graduate Schools, and the program co-chair on the ICT for Africa Conference

Organization. Professor Nwokeafor was the past associate editor of the *Journal of Communication* (JAC), a scholarly journal currently housed at the department of English and Communications at California State University, Bakersfield, California. He has been involved in funded and unfunded grants, among which is the multimillion dollar project learning community Project LINC, National Science Foundation (NSF) proposal titled "Prince George's Partnership for Innovation," and a 4.5 million dollar National Science Foundation (NSF) grant titled "Training Institute for Practicing Mathematics and Sciences Teachers." He has published/co-published seven book chapters and is the author of numerous scholarly articles. Professor Nwokeafor reviewed John Merrill's book, *Global Communication,* and is the author of nine books.

Chike Patrick is a seasoned systems engineer and cybersecurity consultant with over 20 years of experience in information technology. He has directed security operations centers and cybersecurity programs at Duke University Hospital, Durham, North Carolina; and at IBM for the Ohio State Department of General Administration, Columbus, Ohio. As systems engineer, he had provisioned and implemented VMware, Novell, and Microsoft networks at various state and federal departments, leveraging technologies such as Novell Directory Services, GroupWise, Microsoft Active Directory, Microsoft Exchange, and VMware. Chike is an Adjunct Professor of Information Assurance at Bowie State University, Bowie, MD, and has completed a Doctor of Science degree in Cybersecurity at Capitol Technology University, Laurel. He enjoys writing and sports.

Chuka Onwumechili is a Professor of Communications in the Strategic, Legal and Management Communication (SLMC) Department. He joined Howard University full time in 2009 and served as Interim Dean of the School of Communications. Prior to his appointment at Howard, he served as Vice President of the Digital Bridge Institute (DBI) in Abuja, Nigeria; and Chair of the Department of Communications at Bowie State University, Bowie Maryland. Along with his role as Department Chair, Dr. Onwumechili is editor-in-chief of *The Howard Journal of Communications*, a position he assumed in September 2014. He has authored, co-authored, and co-edited 10 books and has also published peer-reviewed academic journals and numerous book chapters. Dr. Onwumechili' s research areas are varied, but currently focus on football (soccer) and communication, particularly as it intersects with the African continent.

Ephraim Okoro is an Associate Professor in the Department of Marketing, School of Business at Howard University. He teaches business communication, marketing communication, management communication, and principles of marketing. Formerly administrative dean, acting chair, and professor of management and marketing at Southeastern University in Washington, D.C., Dr. Ephraim Okoro has taught at the University of Maryland University College, Strayer University, and Bowie State University. His primary research interests focus on business/organizational communication, mass communication, intercultural communication, and global marketing/consumer behavior. Over the past 10 years, Dr. Okoro has authored and co-authored numerous book chapters, book reviews, and conference proceedings, and articles in peer-reviewed journals, including *Business and Professional Communication Quarterly, Journal of Innovative Marketing, China-USA Business Review, Journal of College Teaching and Learning, Journal of International Marketing and Exporting,* the *International Journal of Nigerian Studies and Development, and the Journal of Workforce Diversity.* He serves on editorial boards and presents papers across disciplines at regional, national, and international conferences. He is an active member of the Association for Business Communication, Eastern Communication Association, Association for Education in Journalism and Mass Communications, Political Science Association, Association for Supervision and Curriculum Development, African Studies Association, and the Organizational Development Institute. His contact information is: eaokoro@howard.edu; and drokoro93@gmail.com

Joseph Izang Azi is presently a lecturer with the Department of Industrial Design, Ahmadu Bello University, Zaria, Nigeria, where he studied Graphic Design and emerged with a First Class (Hons.) degree in 1989. He also carried out his Master's and Doctorial degrees in 1999 and 2007 at the same department. He was granted both the Fulbright and MacArthur Fellowships in 2005 and 2008 to visit the College of Imaging Arts and Sciences, Rochester Institute of Technology, Rochester, New York, for technical skill training in computer graphics and animation. He initiated the Interactive Child Learning Aid Project (i-CLAP) model design in 2002 as a Ph.D. research in industrial design and defended the dissertation in 2007. In contributing to the global research practice, Dr. Azi has presented his research results in several local and international conferences in Ghana, South Africa, and America. He has also published more than 20 articles in elite journals around the world. To further strengthen his mental capacity, he is currently running a Master's Degree program in Computer Graphic Design at RIT. He is keenly interested in the role of technology integration in education, hence his ambition to further develop the i-CLAP model to its logical completion for possible future implementation in Nigeria.

Kehbuma Langmia is a Fulbright Scholar/Professor and Chair in the Department of Strategic, Legal and Management Communication in School of Communications at Howard University. A graduate from the Mass Communication and Media Studies Program at Howard University in 2006, Dr. Langmia has extensive knowledge and expertise in information communication technology (ICT), intercultural/international communication, and social media. He has over 22 publications in the form of books, book chapters, and research articles in prominent national and international journals. He has given keynote speeches on information communication technology and social media at prominent national and international universities, including the Library of Congress, the National Intelligence University (Department of Defense, USA), Morgan State University, Bowie State University, Melbourne University (Australia), Bues University (Cameroon), Madras Institute of Technology (India), ICT University (Cameroon), Covenant University, and Temple University.

Kristie Roberts-Lewis is a native of Atlanta, Georgia, and received a Bachelor of Arts Degree in Criminal Justice from Fort Valley State University, a Master's of Public Administration Degree from Albany State University with a dual concentration in General and Human Resources Management, and earned a Ph.D. from Jackson State University in Public Policy and Administration. She is currently pursuing a Master's of Divinity from the Candler School of Theology at Emory University (May, 2013). Additionally, Dr. Roberts-Lewis is a 2010-2011 Leadership Fellow sponsored by the Black Women in Ministry Institute at the Interdenominational Theological Center. Dr. Roberts has also completed post-graduate studies at Beijing Union University in Beijing, China; Oxford University, Oxford England; a Fulbright Hays Fellowship in Ghana West Africa; and a post-doctoral fellowship at Syracuse University, Syracuse, New York. Presently, Dr. Roberts-Lewis works with Troy University in the Political Science Department, where she serves as a Professor/MPA Internship Director (Atlanta Site) and teaches courses such as Executive Leadership in the Nonprofit Sector, the Foundations of Nonprofit Management, Grant Management for Public and Nonprofit Organizations, Program Evaluation, and Public Policy, to name a few. Additionally, Dr. Roberts-Lewis serves on several committees: the MPA Admission Committee, Internship Committee, Student Association Adviser and the Course Expert committees for Public Policy, Non-profit Management, Program Evaluation, and Grant Writing for Public Managers. Finally, Dr. Roberts-Lewis has been inducted into "Who's Who among College Professors 2010"; "Who's Who of America in 2002"; and the National Association of Professional Women, 2013. Dr. Roberts-Lewis actively participates in the following organizations: Toastmasters International, the Conference of Minority Public Administrators, the American Society of Public Administrators, the National Forum for Black Public Administrators, Delta Sigma Theta Sorority, and currently serves on the board of Africa Inc., the Leaning Post, Inc., and H.O.W.W.

Loubna Dali is a Doctor of Science candidate in the department of computer science at Bowie State University, where she currently serves as a research graduate assistant in the department of computer science. She has published more than 10 referred journal articles in her field and is currently working on her dissertation. Loubna believes that education is a progressive discovery of oneself that affects eternity with endless influence. She received her Master's Degree with honors at the National School of Applied Sciences in Morocco. Eager to nourish her professional knowledge and explore the novelty of IT world through researches, she won the first prize among hundreds of students in the Research Expo 2015 organized by the National Science Foundation at Bowie State University. She was also honored to share her passion for research and mentor the undergraduate students in the First Annual "Summer Undergraduate

Research Institute" organized by the office of the provost at Bowie State University.

Matilda Yeboah-Fofie is a senior at Bowie State University pursuing her Master's in Public Administration and Management. She earned her Bachelor of Science in 2004 from Kwame Nkrumah University of Science and Technology, Ghana. She is the Vice President of Operations at G. Manu & Associates, Virginia, USA, responsible for the smooth and efficient daily operation of the firm's departments and a resource for meeting the firm's expectations. Her hobbies include traveling and cooking.

Michael E. Orok serves as the Dean of the School of Graduate Studies and Research at Virginia Union University. Orok previously served as the dean of the School of Graduate Studies and Research at Tennessee State University and also served as a Professor of Political Science and Public Administration/Chairman of the Department of History, Political Science and Public Administration at Albany State University in Georgia, and quite recently as the Professor of Political Science and Associate Provost for Academic Affairs and Graduate Studies at Alabama A &M University (AAMU) in Huntsville, Alabama. He is a past member of the Commission on Peer Review and Accreditation (COPRA) of the National Association of Schools of Public Affairs and Administration (NASPAA). He periodically serves as an accreditation off-site visit reviewer for the Southern Association of Colleges and Schools (SACS) in the area of graduate education, curriculum development, and student learning. He is the immediate former Vice President of the Council of Historically Black Graduate Schools (CHBGS), a 2005 graduate of the Millennium Leadership Institute of the American Association of State Colleges and Universities, founding President of the Southwest Georgia Chapter of the American Society for Public Administration, member of the executive committee of the Conference of Southern graduate Schools (SCGS), the 1st Vice President of the Conference of Minority Public Administrators (COMPA), and the treasurer of the Tennessee Council of Graduate Schools (TCGS). He was admitted into the Hall of Champions of the American Society for Public Administration, holds membership in the American Society for Public Administration and the American Political Science Association, and is the recipient of the Sweeney Award from ICMA. He is a Public Policy and Public Affairs consultant and a principal consultant with the Orok Consulting Group, LLC. He serves on the editorial board of the *Journal of Community Engagement and Scholarship* and is the founding editor of the *Journal of Public Affairs and Issues*. He has published book chapters and presented several papers on public management and student learning outcome assessment.

Otis Thomas is an Associate Professor of Mass Communication and the Chair of the Department of Communications at Bowie State University. Dr. Thomas brings a wealth of academic and professional experience to his leadership position at Bowie State, where he also serves as the Director of BSU-TV and WBSU

Radio. He has more than 30 years of professional experience, including reporter for CNN, NBC, CBS, and Cox television, and host of talk programs for Radio One Corporation, CBS Network, KMOX-AM/FM and XM Satellite Radio News in Washington, DC. He has conducted interviews with political and social dignitaries, including President Barack Obama; U.S. Senator for Maryland Benjamin L. Cardin; Maryland Governor Martin O'Malley; Maryland Lt. Governor Anthony Brown; Republican National Committee Chairman Michael Steele; former Maryland Governor Robert Ehrilch Jr.; former Maryland Lt. Governor Kathleen Kennedy Townsend; Journalist and Commentator Juan Williams. He is the distinguished voice behind Bowie State University television and radio advertisements, recruitment videos, and numerous other video and audio productions broadcast on WPGC, WKYS< WMMJ, Praise 104.1, and the Comcast and Verizon cable networks.

Oloruntola Sunday is a trained journalist, and a senior lecturer at the Department of Mass Communication, University of Lagos. He holds B.Sc and M.Sc degrees in Mass Communication from the University of Lagos, and a Ph.D. in Agricultural Communication from the Federal University of Agriculture, Abeokuta. He has published extensively in reputable local and foreign journals, including several chapter contributions in textbooks.

Siyanbola Afeez Babatunde is currently a doctoral student in the Department of Industrial Design (Graphic Design Section) Ahmadu Bello University, Zaria, Nigeria, researching the potential of advancing the patronage of Nigerian crafts on an e-commerce virtual gallery with special focus on aesthetics, ergonomics, and functionality. His first and second degrees were in Industrial Design (Graphic Design Section) at the Federal University of Technology Akure, Ondo State, Nigeria. He developed Graphics Design Visuals to brand Lay-by Bus Shelters in the Federal University of Technology, Akure, Ondo State. The project was designed to provide the blueprint for communicating the giant strides of Nigerian cities via branding using bus shelters as a medium of interface. Siyanbola has presented research papers at conferences and has publications in reputable journals in Nigeria. In enhancing his professional skills, he practices photography and consults for individuals and corporate organizations on branding and design requirements. He hails from Ilaro, Yewa South Local Government, Ogun State, Nigeria.

Sulayman Olubunmi Ganiyu: is presently a lecturer with the Department of Fine and Applied Arts, Adeyemi College of Education, Ondo, Nigeria. Ganiyu studied at the Department of Fine and Applied Arts, Obafemi Awolowo University, Ile-Ife, Nigeria, where he had both a BA (Hons.) in Fine Arts and an MFA in Ceramics in 1994 and 2000 respectively. Sulayman Olubunmi Ganiyu has presented research papers at local and international conferences. He has also published more than 10 articles in reputable journals around the world. He is currently doing his PhD research at the Department of Industrial Design, Ahmadu Bello University, Zaria, Nigeria, exploring the adaptation of traditional symbols and motifs in the production of white-ware ceramics. His keen interest is on the integration of local motifs and symbols into modern ceramics production with the aid of Computer Aided Design (CAD) and Computer Aided Manufacturing (CAM).

EDITOR

Cosmas U. Nwokeafor, Ph.D., is a Professor of Mass Communication at Bowie State University, where he currently serves as the Dean of Graduate School. He has served as a Provost Fellow and Assistant Provost for Graduate Studies at Bowie State University. Prior to his current position, he served as the Assistant Dean and Dean of the College of Arts and Sciences respectively, as well as the Chair of the Department of Communication. His professional experiences include leadership training at Harvard University. He has participated at the Oxford Roundtable workshop in Oxford, London, where his paper was among the top 10 papers published in the journal *Forum on Public Policy* online, Spring 2009 (http://forumonpublicpolicy.com). Dr. Nwokeafor also presented a paper at the 2013 Oxford Education Research Symposium in London. He was appointed by the United States Director General's Office of Performance Evaluation to serve on the United States Department 2014 Foreign Service Selection Board s-III that reviews the performance records of eligible classes FS-02 to FS-4 Specialist Diplomats for promotion to classes FS-01 to FS-03. He has conducted research in the areas of development communication, new communication technologies, and media role in development in Africa, the conundrum of autism, and retention studies. He once served as the secretary of the Council of Historically Black Graduate Schools/UMI ProQuest award committee chair of dissertation submission from (CHBGS) member institutions. He currently serves as the president-elect of the Council of Historically Black Graduate Schools. Dr. Nwokeafor was the past Associate Editor of the *Journal of African Communication* (JAC). He has been involved as a co-PI in some funded and unfunded grants, among which are the multi-million-dollar Project Learning Community (Project LINC), National Science Foundation (NSF) proposal titled "Prince George's Partnership for Innovation," and a 4.5-million-dollar National Science Foundation (NSF) grant titled "Training Institute for Practicing Mathematics and Science Teachers." Dr. Nwokeafor has received numerous awards, such as being a 6th-time awardee of "Who's Who Among America's Teachers"; "Who's Who in the Media and Mass Communications"; "Who's Who in American Education "; "Who's Who in America"; "Who's Who in the East"; and Who's Who in the World." He received an award as a Member of the International Authors, Writers, and Citizen Ambassador Program. Dr. Nwokeafor is a Pointer Institute for Media Fellow and American Press Institute and Capital/ABC Fellow. He has published nine books, seven book chapters, and is the author of numerous scholarly peer-reviewed journal articles. Dr. Nwokeafor reviewed John Merrill's book, *Global Communication.* Dr. Nwokeafor received a National Certificate in Education (Pedagogy) at the prestigious Alvan Ikoku College of Education, Owerri, Nigeria; a Bachelor's Degree in Journalism from Howard University in 1986; A Master's in Mass Communication in 1990; and a Doctorate in Mass Communication from Howard University in 1992.